MANCHURIA

WITHDRAWN

JILIN

LIAONING

Sea of
Japan

NORTH
KOREA

Chengde

SOUTH
KOREA

Beijing ★
Datong

HEBEI

Jinan

Yellow
Sea

SHANXI

SHANDONG

NEI MONGGOL

GXIA

River

Yellow

JIANGSU

JAPAN

Xian

HENAN

ANHUI

SHAANXI

Hefei

Nanjing

Shanghai
Huangpu River

ing

HUBEI
Wuhan

ling River

ZHEJIANG

East
China
Sea

Yangtse River

JIANGXI

FUJIAN

GUANGXI

Taipei

GUANGDONG
Guangzhou
(Canton)
Shenzhen

TAIWAN

Nanning

Hong Kong

NAM

Hainan
Island

South
China
Sea

PHILIPPINES

*Chaos Under Heaven*

## Also by Gordon Thomas

DESCENT INTO DANGER
BED OF NAILS
PHYSICIAN EXTRAORDINARY
HEROES OF THE RAF
THEY GOT BACK
MIRACLE OF SURGERY
THE NATIONAL HEALTH SERVICE AND YOU
THAMES NUMBER ONE
MIDNIGHT TRADERS
THE PARENT'S HOME DOCTOR (with Ian D. Hudson, Vincent Pippet)
TURN BY THE WINDOW (with Ronald Hutchinson)
THE CAMP ON BLOOD ISLAND
TORPEDO RUN
ISSELS: THE BIOGRAPHY OF A DOCTOR
THE DAY THE WORLD ENDED (with Max Morgan-Witts)
EARTHQUAKE (with Max Morgan-Witts)
SHIPWRECK (with Max Morgan-Witts)
VOYAGE OF THE DAMNED (with Max Morgan-Witts)
THE DAY GUERNICA DIED (with Max Morgan-Witts)
RUIN FROM THE AIR (with Max Morgan-Witts)
THE DAY THE BUBBLE BURST (with Max Morgan-Witts)
TRAUMA (with Max Morgan-Witts)
PONTIFF (with Max Morgan-Witts)
THE OPERATION
THE YEAR OF ARMAGEDDON (with Max Morgan-Witts)
DESIRE AND DENIAL
THE TRIAL: *The Life and Inevitable Crucifixion of Jesus*
JOURNEY INTO MADNESS
ENSLAVED
DEADLY PERFUME
THE GODLESS ICON

# Chaos Under Heaven

## The Shocking Story of China's Search for Democracy

## GORDON THOMAS

A Birch Lane Press Book
Published by Carol Publishing Group

A Birch Lane Press Book
Published by Carol Publishing Group
Birch Lane Press is a registered trademark of Carol Communications, Inc.

Editorial Offices: 600 Madison Avenue, New York, N.Y. 10022
Sales & Distribution Offices: 120 Enterprise Avenue, Secaucus, N.J. 07094
In Canada: Musson Book Company, a division of General Publishing Company, Ltd., Don Mills, Ontario M3B 2T6

Queries regarding rights and permissions should be addressed to Carol Publishing Group, 600 Madison Avenue, New York, N.Y. 10022

Carol Publishing Group books are available at special discounts for bulk purchases, for sales promotions, fund raising, or educational purposes. Special editions can be created to specifications. For details contact: Special Sales Department, Carol Publishing Group, 120 Enterprise Ave., Secaucus, N.J. 07094

Manufactured in the United States of America
10  9  8  7  6  5  4  3  2  1

**Library of Congress Cataloging-in-Publication Data**

Thomas, Gordan.
  Chaos under heaven : the shocking story behind China's search for democracy / by Gordon Thomas.
    p.  cm.
  "A Birch Lane Press book."
  ISBN 1–55972–059–X
  1. China—History—Tiananmen Square Incident, 1989.  I. Title.
DS779.32.T53  1989
951.05′8—dc20                                           91–20246
                                                            CIP

# Contents

# Author's Note

While this book is necessarily a compression of experiences, it is totally based upon the truth of honest recall. The identity of a number of people has been protected, usually by a change of name or the omission of a detailed biography. They are still living in China or have relatives there. With good reason they fear for their lives.

Most of the interviews were with eyewitnesses never before questioned. As well as personal testimony, they provided a wealth of official records, memoranda, and private material: diaries, letters, faxes, and telexes. In the end it resembled a small college library.

The ranks of all members of the Chinese government and its officials, as well as the People's Liberation Army, are those they held at the time of this story.

## A NOTE ON PRONUNCIATION

The pinyin system has been used for transcribing Chinese names. Thus Peking becomes Beijing. Introduced by the Communist party in the 1950s, the system needs a few pronunciation reminders. *Zh* is pronounced like the *j* in *J*ohn; *q* like the *ch* in *ch*ild; *c* like the *ts* in pa*ts*; *x* is always delivered with the same emphasis as the *s* in *s*he. However, for the sake of clarity, Hong Kong, Xiang Gang in pinyin, remains. The name may change in 1997 when the colony reverts to China.

# *Chaos Under Heaven*

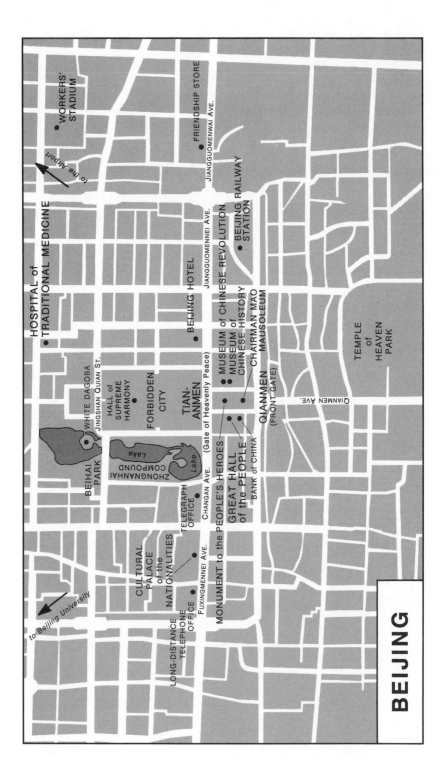

BEIJING

WORKERS'
STADIUM

FRIENDSHIP STORE

JIANGGUOMENWAI AVE.

to the Airport

HOSPITAL of
TRADITIONAL MEDICINE

JIANGGUOMENNEI AVE.

BEIJING RAILWAY
STATION

BEIJING HOTEL

WHITE DAGOBA

JINGSHAN QUIAN ST.

HALL of
SUPREME
HARMONY

FORBIDDEN
CITY

TIAN-
ANMEN

(Gate of Heavenly Peace)

MUSEUM of CHINESE REVOLUTION

MUSEUM of
CHINESE HISTORY

CHAIRMAN MAO
MAUSOLEUM

QIANMEN
(FRONT GATE)

TEMPLE
of
HEAVEN
PARK

QIANMEN AVE.

BEIHAI
PARK

ZHONGNANHAI
COMPOUND

Lake

Lake

CHANGAN AVE.

TELEGRAPH
OFFICE

GREAT HALL
of the PEOPLE

BANK of CHINA

MONUMENT to the PEOPLE'S HEROES

CULTURAL
PALACE
of the
NATIONALITIES

FUXINGMENNEI AVE.

LONG-DISTANCE
TELEPHONE
OFFICE

to Beijing University

# 1

# *The Tiananmen Trump*

JANUARY 1991
*Washington, D.C.*

In those first two weeks of 1991, despite the frenetic pace of events, time itself appeared to pass in slow motion as the entire world waited to see if there would be war with Iraq. In Washington hopes rose and fell as predictably as the flags on government buildings.

In one, the State Department, the last acts of diplomacy were being played out. Secretary of State James Baker and his staff detailed for those diplomats still able to reach Saddam Hussein—Arabs mostly, with a sprinkling of Europeans—the horrors awaiting Iraq if hopes died. It was a portrait of high-tech warfare the likes of which had never been seen: "smart bombs" with their own video cameras to show the very moment prior to impact, and guided missiles that could cruise down the streets of Baghdad looking for a particular building to destroy. It was the world of Buck Rogers finally come true. Nothing, and no one, those diplomats were told, could resist such a show of force.

But Saddam remained unimpressed. He saw himself as the avenger of the Arab people, chosen by Allah to redress the slights visited on Arabs for generations.

As the hours ticked by to the deadline for war set by the United Nations for Tuesday, January 15—and interpreted by Washington as expiring at noon Eastern Standard Time on that day—it became increasingly clear that Washington was conducting a dialogue with the deaf. Yet, anxious to show it was doing everything to avert what Saddam was predicting would be "the mother of all wars," the Bush administration was, for the most part, conducting its efforts as publicly as possible.

3

The exception was its dealings with the hardline Communist regime in Beijing. There, extraordinary secrecy prevailed. Only a handful in the administration outside President George Bush and Secretary Baker were aware of the precise ebb and flow of the discussions. These were first intended to persuade China to refrain from vetoing the United Nations resolution to use sanctions against Iraq shortly after it had invaded Kuwait and then, when the trade embargo failed, to persuade China to support a second resolution authorizing force to be used to expel Iraq from Kuwait.

The reasons for the secret dealings with China were rooted in the administration's embarrassment at having to depend on Beijing for support, coupled with a sense of pragmatism, which had come to permeate the Bush presidency more than any of its recent predecessors. To grasp that reality it is important to understand that both UN resolutions had been proposed in the high-minded guise of "restoring" Kuwait's democratic right to exist as a sovereign nation. Those Americans who squinted into the desert sun and spoke of being ready to fight "a just war"—one that would be swift and decisive, short and sweet, a Panama perhaps, but never another Vietnam—rarely paused to consider that democracy, as they understood it, had never existed in Kuwait. At best the Gulf kingdom was a family-run dictatorship that employed foreign labor under often harsh conditions: workers' passports were confiscated to stop them leaving until their contracts expired; abuses of basic human rights were commonplace. In some ways Kuwait was as repressive as the People's Republic of China.

Yet China, as a permanent member of the UN Security Council, had the power to effectively wreck Bush's determination to go to war unless Iraq obeyed the January 15 deadline.

For the President, Saddam had become a personal nemesis and a casus belli. At times the rhetoric from the White House was as fierce as that coming from Baghdad.

Bush had also learned much from his most recent experience of war. On December 20, 1989, he had ordered U.S. forces into Panama to arrest its de facto head of state, General Manuel Noriega. The UN General Assembly had denounced the invasion as a "flagrant violation of international law." But for the administration, and indeed many Americans, the lofty ends justified the means: The invasion of Panama would stop the drug traffic into the United States; it would restore "stability" in the region. And, of course, it would "restore democracy" to Panama.

By the time the Persian Gulf crisis was engaging President Bush, the reality of his intervention in Panama was all too plain. Federal agencies were reporting that the drug traffic there was running at preinvasion levels. Stability was as far away as ever in the region, and the prospect of a truly democratic Panama even further. And America itself continued to be branded as a bully and aggressor because of the invasion.

Bush knew he could not once more risk being accused of dangerous arrogance in assuming the role of the world's policeman by confronting Saddam. Consequently, since the very beginning of the Gulf crisis, he had worked hard to put together a coalition of Arab and non-Arab states to deal with Iraq. While he had made it clear that America would provide the bulk of the firepower, and in military terms would call the shots, it would do so with the blessing of the world. To that end it became critically important for Bush to be able to count on China.

The irony of the situation was most certainly not lost on the President.

Bush knew from the very beginning that the sheer speed and success of the Iraqi war machine depended, in significant measure, on China. In the past five years, the People's Republic had equipped it with 1,500 T-65 tanks, 9,000 Red Army antitank weapons, 150 F-7 jet aircraft, 12 million artillery shells and mines, and over 4 billion rounds of small-arms ammunition.

More sinister, China had sold to Iraq large quantities of lithium 6 hydride, a key component in the manufacture of a hydrogen bomb. Throughout 1990, the China National Non-Ferrous Metals Import-Export Corporation had shipped several dozen sealed plastic bottles of the grayish-white granular substance to Baghdad. Each bottle held 250 grams of lithium 6 hydride. The bottles were packed in lead and encased in metal barrels, each weighing 200 pounds. Each barrel had a label stating the substance was for use in the Iraqi medical industry.

On arrival in Baghdad, the barrels were distributed to Iraq's three nuclear facilities.

By the time Saddam invaded Kuwait, China had provided him with the means to produce a dozen hydrogen bombs. Each had an estimated destructive capacity of approximately fifty times that of the device released over Hiroshima.

With the lithium 6 hydride, several score Chinese scientists and technicians had traveled to Iraq. A number had helped China successfully build its own hydrogen bomb in 1967. Their presence, like the export of the lithium 6 hydride, was a breach of the UN Nuclear Non-Proliferation Treaty. But China had never signed that agreement.

Despite knowing all this, the President was still determined to parley with China. With Saddam firmly in his gunsight, Bush was ready, according to his aides, to "deal with just about anyone if it meant putting an end to the Baghdad bully."

The President, long castigated as a wimp, was preparing himself for a massive act of expediency, one that would reveal the kind of ruthlessness most doubted he possessed. Only those who had served under the President when he was director of the Central Intelligence Agency (CIA) knew that Bush had the steel to balance the fate of a few against what he saw as the greater good for America.

In this case the few were students: young Chinese who had tried in their homeland less than two years before to stage a revolution Bush had been reluctant to support, despite the fact that its genesis was the one word now being increasingly used in Washington to justify intervention in the Persian Gulf—democracy.

In those first weeks following Saddam's occupation of Kuwait the unmistakable whiff of a nation preparing for war was added to the atmospheric pollution of Washington. It was part gung-ho, part fear, and part resignation and even resentment that it should have come at such a time.

The Persian Gulf crisis came in the wake of the collapse of communism in Eastern Europe, and while the bone-picking continued over America's intervention in Panama. Yet the Iraqi action that burst upon the capital, catching unawares the powerful and the pretenders alike, had the potential to be more widespread than the quicksand of Vietnam.

The consensus in Washington was that deep in his fortified command bunker in Baghdad, Saddam had put into operation the first stage of a plan to reshape the Middle East in his image and create mayhem for the world's economic and political processes. Immediately at stake were Western oil supplies and the survival of Israel. Over both loomed the prospect of an even deeper worldwide recession, accompanied by the prospect of jihad, holy war, with Saddam leading hordes of fanatical fundamentalists in a struggle to the death against all Arab moderates and infidels in the region.

Saddam was no mere desert tribesman with grandiose dreams. He commanded the fourth most powerful military force on earth: a million men under arms, six thousand battle tanks in addition to those the Chinese had provided. With it came not only a potential nuclear capacity but also one of the world's largest stockpiles of chemical and biological weapons. There, too, China had played a key role, providing some of the ingredients and expertise.

In intelligence-gathering terms there was no great secret about any of this information. But the French and British security services, like the CIA, saw no real threat. Most agreed Saddam was "protecting himself"—the words are from a leaked report of the Service of External Documentation and Counterespionage [SDECE], the French security service, in July 1990—against Iran. Only Israel continued to warn about Saddam's probable intentions. But, not for the first time, Tel Aviv was out of favor in Western capitals. Its warnings were seen as self-serving.

The very day before Saddam invaded Kuwait, the CIA sent Bush a briefing paper on the region. It categorically stated that Iraq posed "no immediate military threat." Barely able to control his anger at such a grave intelligence miscalculation, the President had ordered, days after the invasion, a line drawn in the sands of Arabia across which Saddam would move at his peril.

The drift to war accelerated as through Washington's prism Saddam increasingly became the unacceptable face of Arab nationalism. For Bush it was soon all too clear that Iraq's leader was imbued with the Nietzschean principle that power is a good in itself. But the President determined America would disabuse Saddam of that idea, with the support of the rest of the world.

To maintain the moral high ground, Bush and Baker and their aides worked the phones out of Washington to cajole, remind, and reason or plead with nations to support the United States in a tough stand against Iraq.

Australia was quickly followed by Holland, Pakistan by Japan, Morocco by Egypt. The nations of NATO joined what remained of the Warsaw Pact. Mother Russia herself said she would support UN-approved action to drive Saddam out of Kuwait.

Finally only China still vacillated over the use of force in the two weeks before the UN deadline expired. While expressing its concern over Saddam's action against Kuwait, the Beijing regime continued to combine such talk with veiled criticism of an American-driven military action to remove Iraqi forces.

The longer China hesitated, the stronger grew the article of faith in Washington that the success of what was being planned—all-out war—depended on persuading the aged leadership in Beijing to support such action. No one in the administration undervalued the necessity of achieving this.

For a decade China had depended on arms sales to the Middle East and loaning out its technical expertise as yet another way to try and balance its embattled economy. In 1990, it had sold over $300 million worth of military hardware to Iraq, Iran, and Syria. That had also strengthened its political position as what Premier Li Peng had called "the new true friend of the Arabs."

With the collapse of Marxism-Leninism in half a dozen countries in eastern Europe, the People's Republic saw itself as the one surviving bastion against democracy. By definition, it had long held true in Beijing that anything bad for the United States was good for China.

Yet in its very role as communism's great survivor, China had given the United States a hold over it. Within the upper echelons of the Bush administration this advantage had come to be known as the Tiananmen Trump. The card had been slipped into the State Department's diplomatic deck following the massacre of students in Beijing's historic Tiananmen Square on June 3, 1989.

For the preceding fifty-five days those students, encouraged by a million, and more, of their fellow citizens, had called for basic human rights in a unique and most dramatic way. They had peacefully called for democracy in the face of one of the world's currently most intransigent regimes. Young men and women with names often difficult to pronounce and, at best, an imperfect grasp of English had held the entire world in thrall.

There was Wuerkaixi, then a twenty-one-year-old bantam cock, whose dark good looks and all-knowing smile went with the California-style denims he wore. The anchormen of the network evening news shows—Rather, Jennings, and Brokaw—hung on his every word. He did not disappoint them. His swashbuckling manner and confrontational style epitomized what was happening on Tiananmen Square. Within a week of first appearing there, Wuerkaixi received the ultimate accolade: His face appeared on T-shirts around the world.

Wang Dan achieved similar instant fame. At the time barely twenty years old, his wan face and physical frailty fitted the popular image of the fearless intellectual. His sweatshirts, baggy pants, and hand-me-down black cotton shoes became a style imitated on campuses around the world. His words were endlessly quoted. He had become the latest folk hero for a voracious media.

So had Chai Ling, an elfin-faced twenty-three-year-old. Her matchstick figure strode across the television screens of mesmerized nations. It somehow did not matter that what she said had to be translated. In any language it was a recognizable clarion cry, one that reflected her boundless energy and good humor. She was the revolution's La Pasionaria—and hauntingly pretty, too.

There was Liu Gang, tall, slim, and almost handsome, with a liking for Western-style casual clothes that could have come off the rack at Sears. He was the pensive-faced twenty-eight-year-old in the TV group shots of the student leaders—the brilliant, if at times quixotic, thinker, who knew which emotional button to push.

In those same group shots there sometimes appeared a young couple: Yang Li and his girlfriend, who like many of the student activists preferred to be known by one name, in her case her forename, Meili. Yang Li had the unfathomable face of a thousand generations of peasants, a physical reminder he was, indeed, the first of his farming family to have reached higher education. Meili had the pale skin of a city girl and the manner and mores of the middle class. They made a striking couple.

There was Yan Daobao. His tall and languid appearance masked a sharp political mind. To revolution he brought the broadening experience of a spell in California. With it came a preference for being known by his forename, Daobao.

Among them they had dominated the world's airwaves, showing themselves the natural masters of the news bite, the telling quote, and the dramatic decision timed to gain their cause the widest possible exposure. They had seemed unstoppable. The seeds of fire burning in their souls had appeared strong enough to sweep away their aged rulers and the deeply repressive system they had created fifty years before to control the world's most populous nation.

For those fifty-five days in Beijing, and elsewhere in China, it had appeared the students were going to succeed in overthrowing their recent past in the full glare of the media army drawn to witness what was happening.

No one—not the reporters on the spot, their editors at their desks—stopped to ask if this could really be allowed to happen, not just by China's rulers, but by all the other Western leaders, who each had a vested interest in ensuring that the status quo remained.

There was Britain with its vast trading ties to China. Her Majesty's then-prime minister, Margaret Thatcher, had made it plain that she wanted nothing—and no one—to threaten those trade links. Her attitude found its echo in Paris, Bonn, and all those European capitals where governments approved massive business deals with China, on any given day worth billions of dollars.

This attitude found its ready supporters in Washington, in all the corridors and offices where profit ruled supreme, where the view of China was primarily that of a vast untapped market. Its people—already more numerous than the combined populations of the United States, the Soviet Union, and all of Europe—represented a nation ready for Western investment and know-how. Every year twelve million more Chinese were born, each one adding to the attraction of the marketplace.

The students had threatened all this by using a word they insisted would shake off that cruel jibe of Karl Marx: that their country was "a carefully preserved mummy in a hermetically sealed coffin."

The word was democracy.

To emphasize the importance of their demand, the students had chosen as their rallying point the ninety-eight acres of Tiananmen Square. Larger than St. Peter's Square in Rome or Red Square in Moscow, larger than any square on earth, Tiananmen is still widely held among the superstitious people of China to be the very core of their world; they believe those who hold this "square of heavenly peace" will also control China's destiny.

For those fifty-five days, the square became the setting for unprecedented confrontation. On the one side were the students, who drew their strength from the truism that history for the Chinese is not an objective account of the past, but an endless morality tale, in which the characters must be explicit heroes and villians. Opposing them were those who believed it was their historical duty to ensure that China remained a world unto itself.

Among much else, at stake was China's place in tomorrow's world—whether it would become the next Pacific superpower in the twenty-first century, and what role the United States would have in guiding it there.

Weeks before the first student marched, in the small colony of embassies in China's capital, expectations had reached fever pitch. The diplomats knew from what people were saying, and sensed from the attitude of Chinese officials, that momentous events were taking place, that the founding fathers of the communist regime were increasingly locked in a deadly power struggle. Yet China, as they also knew, remained what it was at the time of the emperors: a country where mystery is a cult, secrecy a religion.

Ambassadors asked each other how they could penetrate the bamboo walls when their embassies were like so many fortresses permanently under siege by the agents of Public Security, the *Gonganbu*, who followed their every move, listened shamelessly to their telephone conversations, vetted their telexes, opened their mail, and interrogated their domestic staff daily.

American diplomats worked, albeit often uneasily, alongside their Soviet counterparts. The envoys of Britain and France found them-selves in the same *hutongs*, the alleys of Beijing, as their colleagues from Poland and Romania. Australia's diplomats dogged the paths of the Japanese. The envoys of Iran and Iraq hurried after each other. It was, remembers one European diplomat, "rather like something out of *Alice in Wonderland.*"

Yet at first it often seemed to the diplomats that their governments were not heeding what was being reported. In London, Washington, and elsewhere, China watchers in foreign ministries disagreed about what the portents meant; politicians tried to fit the pieces into their constantly changing global jigsaws.

But many weeks before the first public call for democracy rose over Tiananmen Square, a number of governments knew what was about to happen and, like the United States, had decided their responses would be dictated by wider considerations. For America, among much else, there was the need to maintain its CIA listening posts on the Sino-Soviet border and build upon its ever-expanding trading links with China. For the Soviet Union, there was the question of what effect the students would have on Mikhail Gorbachev's historic state visit to China. For Australia and other countries around the Pacific Rim, there were equally pressing economic and political questions to be considered.

In every capital city with ties to China, preparations on how to react gathered momentum with what was happening on the university campuses in Beijing. There, student factions were increasingly penetrated by the intelligence services of the superpowers, and their every change of plan became quickly known in Washington and Moscow. It was, said one intelligence officer there, the most penetrated student movement since the sixties. Those reports all helped leaders such as George Bush come to a decision.

While the world watched the unfolding drama in Tiananmen Square, President Bush was secretly balancing pressures from the CIA and his military and economic advisers on the one hand to do nothing to endanger the administration's links to the Beijing regime, and from the American people on the other to support the students.

In the end, political pragmatism prevailed. In Washington, London, and other capitals, decisions were taken that however harshly the Chinese leadership chose to deal with the students, those leaders would not be ostracized for long. There would be official condemnation, of course, if only to deffuse public anger over their actions. But it must not go beyond that: Political, military, and economic relationships with China were too important to be seriously disrupted.

In all the places where they could reasonably have expected a firm commitment of support—Bush's Oval Office, Thatcher's Downing

Street, and the offices of other leaders who fell into line—the students had become for all practical purposes expendable by those fateful days in June 1989.

They were crushed with a savagery that, for sheer ferocity equaled that displayed by Genghis Khan when he brought China into the Mogul Empire in 1263. Some seven hundred years later the descendants of Khan's warriors, serving in the People's Liberation Army, mangled the living beneath their tank treads and machine-gunned civilians in numerous cities and towns far from Beijing. People were burned alive or drowned. Afterward, the dead were cremated in great pyres whose stench lasted for weeks.

After watching them die on primetime television, President Bush issued carefully worded protests. He sounded genuinely anguished. But the economic sanctions he finally imposed on China were even more ineffective than those in force against Iraq in those opening weeks of 1991.

In 1989, China's leaders, weaned on a lifetime of violent retribution, were no doubt surprised and relieved at how light their punishment proved to be for crushing the principle over which now, eighteen months later, the United States was pledged to wage war against Iraq.

In January 1991 the Beijing leadership knew that the last vestiges of China's ostracism after the Tiananmen Square massacre were effectively at an end. Already, China was trading vigorously not only with the Middle East, but also with many other countries that had condemned its murderous actions in June 1989. Only the United States had continued to show a certain reluctance to forgive, if not quite forget. But the old men in Beijing could afford to wait.

Experience told them their moment was surely coming. China's humiliations by Western imperialism during the nineteenth century, its subjection to invasion and pillage by a succession of foreign warlords, and, more recently, attempts to remove the rigid communism they had imposed on the Middle Kingdom—all this was about to be avenged. America, the old men told each other, needed China more than China needed the United States. But Bush would have to pay a price, because China, too, had a Tiananmen Trump in its deck.

In those crucial two weeks before the UN deadline for war with Iraq arrived, both sides began to play their trumps for all they were worth.

The Chinese understood Bush. He had lived among them. His mind-set was closer to theirs than most other Western leaders'. He would understand their complexity, what they would want in return for their support. Besides, their demand would be no great surprise to the President, just as he could not have been astonished at how they had finally dealt with the students in June 1989. The Chinese leaders knew at that time that the President had a very clear understanding of what they would do. The CIA and other intelligence agencies had warned him. That he had chosen to act as he had, issuing little more than the mandatory protest, was an encouragement to play their Tiananmen Trump as calculatingly as any riverboat gambler.

In Washington the anonymous men of the State Department China Desk met their counterparts from the People's Republic's embassy a few blocks from the White House.

They made their separate ways along one-way Jackson Place to climb the six steps that lead up to the door of number 716, a government-owned brick town house with a long history of hosting clandestine meetings. The 113-year-old building, whose four stories seem out of proportion to its narrow frontage, had been the base for Vice-President Nelson A. Rockefeller's investigation into the CIA's notorious domestic activities in the sixties. It had been here, too, that a former CIA director, Admiral Stansfield Turner, had briefed Bush's predecessor, Ronald Reagan, about the close intelligence links between China and the United States when it came to spying on Russia in the days when Moscow was still the perceived enemy.

The precise cut and thrust of the negotiations—who first said what, who first went back for fresh instructions, who first bluffed and counterbluffed—is a matter of conjecture. One China Desk hand who was privy to some of the discussions likened it to "playing poker blindfolded."

Yet it was no winner-take-all game. Both sides knew they could walk away as victors.

On the conference table was a very simple premise. In return for Beijing's support at the United Nations, the United States would make no public objection to China's "final solution" for all their student leaders who had been imprisoned without trial after the Tiananmen Square massacre. Beijing had now decided they were to stand trial the day after the deadline against Iraq expired. If the cynicism of the move stuck in American throats around the table, none showed it. This, after all, was what real politics was all about.

Besides, those matchstick-like figures on Tiananmen Square who had less than two years before dominated the news were, perhaps thankfully, largely forgotten. Almost certainly there would be no public clamor over their fate. A fearful world had something bigger now to occupy its attention: the ever-advancing countdown to conflict in the Persian Gulf, the imminent possibility of the first full-scale war since Vietnam. So Secretary Baker's men and the diplomats of China told each other as they examined the advantages of cooperation.

Finally it was done. The Chinese could have their show trials without protest from Washington. Bush would have Beijing's support for a war like no other.

When it emerged that the President, in return for China's support, intended to say or do nothing to condemn such a flagrant mockery of what he held dear—democracy—one of China's foremost dissidents, Liu Binyan, scholar-in-residence at the Woodrow Wilson International Center for Scholars in Washington, wrote an impassioned plea. He asked Bush to remember there was no real difference "between the butchers of Beijing and the bully of Baghdad."

Liu documented in the *New York Times* how, since the onset of the Persian Gulf crisis, China had skillfully manipulated the event to its advantage "and rescued itself from being the pariah of the world. The U.S., Japan and the European (business) community, as well as the World Bank and the Asia Development Bank, are lifting sanctions and restrictions on access to China without any substantial improvement in human rights."

He listed a number of leaders in China's prodemocracy movement who had disappeared into the country's pernicious prison system. Liu pleaded with Bush to remember "these men are pleading for freedom for all of us. Please don't forget them so easily."

There was no response from the White House or from anyone else in the administration.

A decision had been taken. The Tiananmen Trump had been played by both sides.

This is the untold story of how the card was created from that noblest of motives, a desire for democracy, and the basest of motives, its suppression.

# 2

# *Seeds of Fire*

SUNDAY, NOVEMBER 6, 1988
*National Photographic Interpretation Center*
*Washington, D.C.*

The six-story structure on the corner of M and First streets in the southeast quadrant of the city is known as Federal Building 213. It resembles a warehouse and appears no different from all the others around the old Washington Navy Yard on the bank of the Anacostia River. It is, however, enclosed by a fence strengthened to resist a Beirut-style car bomber, and its gates are guarded by armed men.

There are further indications that this nondescript building houses some of the most important elements in America's strategic defense network. The first is the blue-and-white sign above the main entrance: NATIONAL PHOTOGRAPHIC INTERPRETATION CENTER. The second is the massive air-conditioning plant bolted to one side of 213. Seventy-five feet long and rising through floor after floor of bricked-in windows, the system cools the computers inside the building. Some are the size of a room, others of a house. The real monsters run the length of an entire floor. Day and night they sift and scan millions of pieces of information, slotting them into place among billions of items already stored in the database.

The computers are sophisticated enough to correct distortion coming from the imaging sensors aboard the satellites the United States has positioned in space, eliminate atmospheric effects, sharpen out-of-focus images, turn them into three-dimensional objects, enhance the contrast between objects and their backgrounds, and, if need be, remove them totally from their surroundings for

15

closer inspection. The computers also eliminate sun glare, take away shadows, and image objects totally obscured by cloud by using infrared radar. They can even use their radar "lenses" to penetrate the earth and locate a thermonuclear rocket secure in its silo, or missiles hidden in a tunnel.

The processors and photo interpreters make sense of what the computers uncover. They draw fact out of darkness by applying the art of informed conjecture. Among them on an average day the technicians study a million prints. In this building the truth was first established about the Chernobyl meltdown, Libya's poison gas factory, Iraq's use of chemical weapons in its war with Iran, and Pakistan's nuclear weapons. Those who work here kid each other they will be the first to see Doomsday.

On the third floor are the China watchers. As well as monitoring its military installations—missile silos, air bases, weapons factories, nuclear reprocessing plants—they keep track of China's agricultural and industrial development, its oil and gas production. They look for anything that can provide further insights into the country's present situation.

They study images varying from landscapes of twisted pines and misty waterfalls—the Shangri-la of ancient scrolls—to the arid steppes of the Gobi. The majestic topography does not interest them. They are looking for such clues as a new railroad spur, unfamiliar vehicle tracks around a factory, freshly dug earth near an air base. From past experience the technicians know such signs can speak volumes.

Now, eighteen months before the events in Tiananmen Square would become ingrained in the memory of untold millions of people, one of the photo interpreters assigned to keep watch over Beijing processed a sequence of satellite photographs taken from high over the city. They showed an area several miles to the west of the great square, which was as usual filled with milling crowds of sightseers.

The balding American with a degree in computer sciences knew that to those Chinese visible on his photographs, the square was the core of their world. At its very center, a little blob on the sat-photo, was the gate called Tiananmen. From it, a mere pinhead, was suspended the photo of Mao Zedong. It was a reminder that after nineteen centuries of European rule, fifty years of Communism continued to exercise its iron control over the people.

Today, what was happening on Tiananmen did not concern the technician. His interest lay in what was occurring in the city's western district. First he used an infrared scanner, rather like a microscope, to search every microdot of each print for details. He constantly checked against previous photos of the vicinity and he observed a change since he had last "tasked," or searched, the area.

On the keyboard of his video display unit, he tapped in instructions that gave him access to the computer in which all of China is reduced to digital imagery.

Moments later, on the screen appeared a high-definition three-dimensional image of a military barracks in a corner of the district. Its parade square was filled with hundreds of soldiers. The technician pressed a tab to produce a hard copy from the laser printer beside the screen. A 24″ × 24″ photo appeared in seconds. He keyed the next image onto the screen. In all he made fifteen prints. He arranged them on a viewing frame on the wall and peered intently at them, rather like a surgeon studying X rays.

Next he fed further instructions to the computer. Onto the screen came a succession of close-up images of some of the soldiers. Their heavy winter clothing was clearly visible. Again he made hard copies, and the clipped them beneath the others on the viewing screen. He typed in a further command. Onto the screen came a star bedded in cloth. It was an enlargement of a shoulder-tab of an officer's uniform.

The technician took a print and compared it against a number of others, trying to match the blow-up with epaulets on the photos. He began to select photographs, laying them out on a long table beside the printer. After a while he started to make notations on the prints, using a marker pen to draw circles, arrows, and boxes around various objects. Finally he asssembled the prints into a set. Then he began to type on the keyboard.

"Nineteen photographs processed. They cover various resolutions. No cloud cover or atmospheric distortion. Photo sequence (1–8) shows the People's Liberation Army Barracks Number Four in Wangshow District, West Beijing. Photo sequence (9–13) shows it is currently HQ of the 27th Army. Photo sequence (14–19) indicates elements of the Army are leaving. They are probably being sent to Tibet...."

His report completed, the technician electronically transmitted it. Simultaneously it would appear in the Central Intelligence Agency's Office of Imagery Analysis at Langley and in the Analysis Center at Bolling Air Force Base operated by the Defense Intelligence Agency.

From there it would make its way up through the intelligence community—the generic term for all U.S. intelligence agencies and departments of which the director of Central Intelligence is the most senior officer—until finally, if deemed important enough, it would form part of the President's Daily Brief, a summary of the most sensitive and exclusive of gleaned intelligence.

The last time the technician's work had appeared on the brief had been when he had processed details about the previous year's student unrest in Beijing. Then, the satellite cameras had clearly caught the reaction of the Beijing authorities, a massive crackdown with widespread street arrests. Since then there had been no noticeable sign of student activity.

The technician began to study the latest images from the Zhongnanhai compound in Beijing.

The satellite cameras had again photographed a group of old men shuffling along the towpath beside their private lake. The interpreter's task was to identify who was present and who was missing from the Chinese leadership. The intelligence analysts at Langley, the State Department, and other federal agencies had learned to tell a great deal from a man's presence or absence on the towpath, from who he walked beside or avoided. When a man was not there, was he sick? Or out of favor? Or even dead?

The technician knew this report would have an eager reader in Vice-President George Bush, soon, barring an unforeseen disaster, to become the forty-first President of the United States. When he was director of Central Intelligence, Bush had insisted he be shown every intelligence item about China, however inconsequential. The old men of Zhongnanhai had long been a Bush fixation. He had been known to call at the oddest hours for more details about their latest sightings. He was like a birdwatcher. No matter how many times he saw them shuffling along, George Bush wanted to know more.


MONDAY, NOVEMBER 7, 1988
*Zhongnanhai Compound*
*Beijing*

Some of those old men walked with the help of tubular steel frames. Others used sticks fashioned from the hardwoods of the rain forests bordering Burma and Vietnam. Their movements were measured, like those of automatons, as metal and wood supports clunked over the ground. Several needed the assistance of a nurse; each woman was young and physically strong. Following at a distance, male attendants propelled electrically driven wheelchairs equipped with oxygen cylinders should any of the aged leaders require resuscitation. Behind came the ambulances. Over fifty people were required as backup for this evening stroll by men who looked like ghosts in faded photographs.

They were the survivors of that most epic of feats, one almost unequaled in the annals of war: the Long March of 1934. They had made an unforgettable two-year journey of six thousand miles—across mountain ranges and provinces larger than most European states. Theirs was at once a strategic military retreat, an escape from the terrible reality of brother killing brother, and a major and significant Communist migration, leading to eventual nationhood. When it began on October 16, 1934, 86,829 soldiers, each one solemnly counted and promised a special role in his country's future, headed out across China. Few, even their leaders, knew their destination. Many would die before it could be reached.

One of the first decisions of the surviving cadres after Mao Zedong proclaimed a new China on October 1, 1949, was to create their compound in the lee of the Forbidden City, from which the Emperors had ruled for seven hundred years.

The 250 acres of Zhongnanhai had been turned into one of the most fortified enclaves on earth.

Today there are guardposts in the most unexpected of places: cut into the trunks of trees, each niche just large enough for a man to wedge himself in position; in the wooden pavilions dotting the parkland; concealed in shrubbery. There are sensors, tripwires, and remote cameras. No aircraft is permitted to overfly. Only helicopters ferrying the old men to and from their summer palaces in the hills to the west of the city disturb their peace in the middle of one of the world's most congested cities.

Their homes are scattered along the eastern shore of the lake. Many are the size of palaces, with often thirty and more bedrooms, swimming pools, and Jacuzzis. They are furnished with artifacts removed from the Forbidden City. Each mansion has its retinue of servants and guards, who live on the northern side of the lake in several barracks-like buildings screened by trees.

There are over a hundred varieties of trees and shrubs planted in the grounds, each a reminder of the vegetation the old men saw on the Long March.

The leaders' workplaces overlook the western lakeshore. Mao had ordered the lake stocked with carp. Initially, a hundred thousand were dumped there; over the years the number of protected fish increased to several million. The water is dark with their feces, and on a summer's day an unpleasant smell rises from the lake.

The few foreigners admitted to this sanctum, diplomats, visiting dignitaries, are generally brought to the prime minister's compound.

The uniform style of its buildings and the careful alignment of their shrouding roofs creates a feeling of unassailable authority.

The architecture, say his enemies, and they are many, had been carefully ordered by the country's first minister, Li Peng. At sixty-one years of age, the dominant parts of his character had intensified, creating in him a near megalomania, a preoccupation with his astrological calendar, and a fascination with fungi: the most potent mushrooms prepared in a broth, which he drank slowly to regenerate his essential *Qi,* which all Chinese believe to be the driving force of life.

He also had two obsessions. One was flying his kite. He had the most elaborate silk kite in all Zhongnanhai. In the summer months, when the air was thick and moist and warm, he would spend hours sending it spinning, the tails flowing in perfect concentrics, creating the swirling circles of the master calligrapher he was.

The other obsession, one guaranteed to darken his face, was the students of China. In his mind their education, instead of inspiring gratitude, had made them question the authority he represented. He had crushed them before; he would do so again. Yet he also secretly feared them, and he had prepared accordingly.

Beneath the compound's rolling lawns and paved walkways, one finds a place still more secret and inaccessible. It can be reached only from inside the homes and offices of the old men. Should the day come and the high walls of Zhongnanhai be breached, this would be their escape route, through steel doors in the basement of each building to elevators descending to a railway platform. The old men, their families, and others chosen to go with them would board a train that would haul them fifteen miles underground to an airfield in the Western Hills. From there they would be flown to one of several other protected enclaves to continue to rule China.

The train is permanently manned and ready to move at short notice.

Until recently, the old men had every reason to believe they would never have to use it. They had created a dictatorship like no other. It was the most perfect of all control systems: the people watching the people. Those who reported any deviation from the Party line—and the Party had one for everything, from sex to marriage, from birth to the actual form of approved funeral—were given extra food and privileges. Generations of children had been encouraged to inform on their parents and teachers, on anyone who stepped outside the defined limits of what is permissible. The system had always been at the core of what is still the world's most profound revolution.

It had begun with Mao's promise of "socialistic transformation" of the economy. His stated goal was to equal, and then surpass, the industrial capacity of Great Britain, the country that had been China's only peer in industrial production at the turn of the century and had inflicted some of the worst humiliations on China.

Initially Mao's vision had enjoyed widespread popular support. China was ready to make a dramatic leap into the modern age.

Then came the plan to merge the country's agricultural cooperatives into the so-called People's Communes. The new system led to massive population dislocation, violence, and famine. Economic blight swept the land. Some twenty-seven million people died.

Mao, his paranoia more acute than ever, launched the Cultural Revolution. He mobilized the youth of China to do his bidding. Millions of teenagers wielded power far beyong their understanding. Deng Xiaoping and other leaders were exiled.

The lesson of how to use the nation's young was not lost on Deng when he regained power in the wake of Mao's death. Deng too wanted to see China a world economic power. To achieve this goal, he courted China's much-maligned intellectuals. He also set about winning over the country's younger generation, that half of the nation's population born after the founding of the People's Republic. They now numbered some 650 million articulate and ambitious men and women under thirty. Encouraged by Deng, they increasingly gave voice to demands for higher education, good jobs, decent housing, and protection against arbitrary exercises of authority. Above all they demanded the right to at least a modicum of expression. They asked for some form of democracy.

For a while it seemed as if Communism and the right of choice would coexist. Foreign investment flowed into the country. Private enterprise thrived, especially in the consumer sector. China's brightest and best were encouraged to study abroad. Harvard University reported Beijing University was among the top ten feeder schools in the world for America's graduate programs. But the sheer pace of the changes and the problem of a state and private sector operating in tandem created tensions.

Nowhere were these tensions more keenly felt than among the old men in Zhongnanhai. Some said the freedoms created a loss of ideological control, that the very authority of the Party was in danger of being swept away. Others argued the loosening of restrictions was the unavoidable consequence of reform. The debate became fiercer, the battle lines more clearly drawn.

Once more the students became a focal point for the divided leadership. They were increasingly at the forefront in challenging the monopoly of the Party to make policy. The students wanted greater economic reforms, faster. They demanded political pluralism, now. They insisted on full human rights, not merely a relaxing of restrictions, and at once. They wanted democracy, immediately.

Some of the old men cautiously supported them. Others, like Li Peng, ferociously argued that even a tinge of democracy would eventually destroy the China they had created. They pointed to what was happening in Russia. The first sign of democracy was threatening to topple the Kremlin itself.

These evening walks along the lakeside, once a chance to relax at the end of a day, had become often tense occasions.

Among those leaning on the arm of a nurse was Yao Yilin, seventy-two years old. His clothes hung on him. With his head of gray cobwebs and crumpled cheeks, he looked like a scarecrow. Only his eyes remained sharp; they watched from their corners, giving his face a shifty look. When he was happy, he whistled through his teeth, though no one had ever seen him laugh. When he was angry, his skin, already taut, drew tighter around his eyes and mouth.

Yao was a hardliner, who said the greatest danger China faced would be for its people to forget their recent past. For Yao, there could be no compromise with the uncompromising discipline that had made China the great alternative to Soviet Marxism. His voice was even more querulous on those occasions when Hu Yaobang joined the group on the towpath.

In 1982, Deng had confirmed Hu as his successor, appointing him Party secretary. Hu stunned everyone, inside and beyond Zhongnanhai, by placing himself at the forefront of not only economic reforms but also political changes. He began to attack official ideology, the hitherto sacred totem. He defined Marxism without the usual Leninist imperatives. He set about shaking the Party to its core.

Within four years he had swept the country toward a new society that few could have dreamed possible. The students hung on his every word. Young voices gave throat to one demand: democracy. There were near riots as hundreds of thousands challenged the Party's authority. Deng was forced to send in battalions of police. The leading demonstrators were either shot or sent to labor camps. Many were children of senior cadres. The elders of Zhongnanhai personally petitioned Deng to sack Hu. Reluctantly he did. But he insisted there would be no further punishment.

Hu had continued to promote Western ideas, encouraging China's youth to imitate the life-style of America's and Europe's young. Hu himself had visited Western fashion shows and gone to premieres of foreign films.

As usual the former Party secretary general walked unaided. Hu's

Western-style clothes somehow increased his resemblance to an ornamental garden gnome. He had a pointy chin and solemn dark eyes that darted everywhere, from the carp in the lake to the guards trailing behind the old men. Hu had once joked to President Carter's foreign affairs adviser, Zbigniew Brzezinski, who was now a member of President Bush's Foreign Intelligence Advisory Board, that inside Zhongnanhai some people didn't feel safe.

As the daylight began to fade, one man continued to move briskly among the others. The gossip, hearsay, speculation, and complaints flowed around him like water around a rock. No one asked what he thought. People had learned not to do that.

Qiao Shi was unusually tall for a Chinese, almost six feet. But he stooped, rumor had it, as a result of too many hours as a child spent studying the written Chinese language. Through native intelligence and sheer will, he had found his key to the world of radicals, strokes, phonetics, and recensions. The discipline of learning and remembering was a good training for his present position. As director of the Chinese Secret Intelligence Service, CSIS, he had been China's spymaster for the past fourteen years. He was on this day close to his sixty-fifth birthday, still with a taste for French cognac and Cuban cigars. But his laughter never quite reached his eyes. They had a way of making people's heads turn. It was more than a curious magnetism. It was an ability to suggest he could see what they were thinking.

He ran intelligence networks that extended across the Pacific into the United States and Europe and back again through the Middle East into China. He was a chief with hundreds of spies in place and a budget for bribery and blackmail rivaled only by those of the CIA and KGB. He answered only to Deng Xiaoping. The labor camps of central China were filled with those who had dared to challenge Qiao.

Because of who he was, even the most senior of the cadres treated him with respect. No one would have dared to point out that for a man in his position, he was a poor dresser; often his chain-store socks did not match. He usually looked as if he had gone to a shop in one of the city's alleys and reached for the first garments at hand. People assumed there was a purpose to this style, other than eccentricity.

They reminded themselves Qiao had always been a sly one. His entire career consisted of adroit, low-key moves; he had moved from one ministry to another with the minimum of notice. One day he had been a diplomat, the next entrenched as head of state security.

The essential certainty concerning Qiao was that he knew all the secrets, the peccadilloes and personal shortcomings within the leadership. He knew who was already corrupted, who could be corrupted. He knew the exact state of Deng Xiaoping's health and how long he was likely to remain in office. Qiao had his spies everywhere.

Now his agents were reporting that the students once more showed signs of unrest. Qiao had urged that their leaders should be arrested. Deng Xiaoping had refused. He had made it clear he would do nothing until the outcome of the struggle between two of the other old men.

One was Li Peng.

The other was Zhao Ziyang, the new Party secretary. Recently Zhao had taken to wearing tinted glasses in his thick frame spectacles. His enemies—like the prime minister's, they too were many and multiplying—said this was a further sign of his affection for Western standards. Tinted glasses went with Zhao's wardrobe of silk suits, his fondness for Kentucky bourbon and reading Bismarck. At seventy, Zhao remained perfectly cast in the traditional role of the wise adviser who did not flinch from telling Deng hard truths. For years he and Li Peng appeared politically twinned. They sat side by side in the Politburo and on the review stand for the great parades on Tiananmen Square; they shared the toasts at important state banquets. Li Peng's remoteness seemed the ideal foil for Zhao's ebullience.

Their friendship was now dead. Some said it was over on that summer's day in 1987 when Deng decided Zhao would have Hu Yaobang's post. Like everyone else, the prime minister recognized it was Deng's way of anointing Zhao as his new successor.

Zhao had surrounded himself with some of the ablest of China's young scholars and technocrats. Many had studied abroad. Others came straight from China's universities into the think tanks he established around Beijing. They had produced a raft of proposals for further economic and political changes. These included freeing prices and disposing of state-owned companies into private ownership.

Zhao skillfully removed from office many conservatives who protested these ideas were as reformist as Hu's. He did so at the time Deng announced he was retiring from the day-to-day political scene to concentrate on managing the affairs of the Central Military Commission. No one doubted the commission's importance in the country's affairs, but everyone also knew the commission could run perfectly well without Deng constantly at the helm.

Deng Xiaoping, the great architect of change, had cleared the stage for an epic struggle, one as titanic as any Mao had engineered. Recognizing that the Marxist-Leninist praxis, the unity of theory and action, no longer commanded universal respect as the only way to social reconstruction, the country's supreme leader had deliberately decided on a monumental gamble: to risk China returning to political instability while a murderous struggle continued around him as to whose policies would lead the nation into the next century, Zhao's or Li Peng's.

In appointing Zhao as Party chief, Deng plainly indicated his own preference. Yet in allowing Li Peng to apply the brake, Deng was also showing he was not prepared to allow unrestricted political dissent to outpace economic reform.

The grain deficit, the pork shortage, and every kind of bureaucratic malfeasance had become an issue. So had the rising expectations of the people. Li Peng argued these were far beyong the state's capacity. He had recently said "ideological flexibility" had reached "maximum tolerance"; China was already in an inflationary spiral that was in danger of going out of control.

Zhao had continued to urge that China should allow free enterprise to flourish. He called for more foreign investment and for China to "embrace the world." That was, he said, the only way to curb inflation and unleash economic dynamism, create a true market economy, ensure growth, and satisfy the ever-louder demand for democracy.

For the young intellectuals, especially the country's students, his had been a vision for China's Camelot. At first it seemed that Zhao would sweep all before him. But a year after he had proclaimed his ideals, inflation and corruption continued to increase. Finally the students had started to criticize Zhao for not doing more to curb both.

Li Peng had increasingly attacked what he branded "revisionist innovations" and condemned Zhao for leading the nation's youth dangerously astray.

Zhao needed the students' support to convince his opponents in Zhongnanhai that the monolithic world they had all created was doomed and that social rebirth was only possible by recognizing "we are not in the situation envisaged by the founders of Marxism." The Party secretary had begun a recent speech to the Politburo by saying: "We cannot blindly follow what the books say. China's only way forward is for a prolonged period of nonsocialist economic growth."

Li Peng condemned such ideas as "an ideological formula largely devoid of ideological content" and Zhao's approach as "an open threat to the Party."

Deng had listened impassively.

Clearly, all three saw that the country's students were both pawns and trumps in the developing crisis.

# 3

# *Illusions*

Some of those students pedaled down the avenue toward the massive gateway of Beijing University. It was late afternoon, the light already fading. With them was Cassy Jones, an American. She was a contract teacher, one of a number from overseas on campus who taught mostly languages. They were known as foreign experts.

Cassy was a couple of inches taller than most of the other cyclists and, at thirty, almost a generation older. Yet her freckles and lithe figure made her look like a student, even if no one on campus had her flaming red hair. As usual, it was braided into a ponytail. It gave her face a leaner and more determined look.

For as long as she could remember, China had held a fascination for Cassy. As a teenager she had been drawn to its exotic etiquette. At the end of high school she went on to study its language at college, majoring in Cantonese. Postgraduate studies improved her Mandarin. Several universities offered her positions. In the next six years she taught at several.

Cassy had voted Democrat until George Bush. She had supported his bid to be President because she knew he had spent time in China. She had cheerfully told some of the students she would have voted for any American politician who wanted to know more about their country.

Her attitude made Cassy one of the most popular foreigners on campus among the students. As usual, several vied to cycle close to her, to practice their English by asking more questions about life in America.

26

Among them was Li Yang, the first member of his peasant family to have made it to university. The twenty-year-old cycled effortlessly, his calf muscles hardened from a childhood spent toiling in his parents' rice field on the banks of the Yangzte River. Li had a brother, Bing, who was a soldier in the People's Liberation Army.

Next to Li rode his girlfriend, Meili, a petite twenty-year-old who liked wearing colorful scarves. Cassy was struck by how well the girl fitted the old Imperial image of beauty, the perfect oval face inset with almond-shaped eyes and rosebud lips. Meili's skin was pale. Cassy supposed her indoor pallor was a further attraction for the son of laborers.

Beside them the slight figure of Wang Dan pedaled steadily. In his padded jacket, baggy pants, and black cotton shoes, he looked the archetypical student. As usual the twenty-year-old was engaged in serious debate with those around him, his eyes glinting with passion behind the heavy frames of his glasses.

Yan Daobao rode alongside Cassy. His tall, muscular appearance contrasted with his soft way of speaking. But Cassy now knew that Daobao's languid ways masked a sharp political mind and determination. Like the others around her, he passionately believed China must embrace democracy if it was to take its rightful place in the world. As usual he cycled with one hand resting lightly on her shoulders, despite the rule that forbade any physical contact between foreigners and students.

There was so much Cassy was still coming to terms with about Daobao. The intensity of his feelings. The way he spoke to her, looked at her, touched her. She remembered only too vividly how they had met the day after she had arrived on campus and gone to the English Department.

The department appeared deserted, its bare corridors and stairs echoing like those of some abandoned monastery. The library was well stocked, with books in a dozen languages rising from floor to ceiling.

Cassy became aware a young Chinese had entered the library. He stood inside the door, watching her, arms folded. She smiled quickly and turned back to the shelves.

He told her where she could find Shakespeare and Dickens.

He had a gentle voice for someone so big and strong. She was also surprised by the American accent. Cassy asked if he was another foreign expert.

He shook his head and introduced himself, family name first, Chinese-style: Yan Daobao. He had spent the summer visiting a cousin at Berkeley. She remembered she had read there were over twenty thousand Chinese students in the United States. Daobao reached up and pulled down a book.

"Thomas Wolfe." He smiled his shy smile. "They never let us read about our own decadence."

Cassy let it pass, not wanting to be drawn into criticizing her host country. She asked if the library stocked Norman Mailer. He nodded. After a pause he asked her name and why she was there. In fluent Mandarin she told him.

His smile broadened. "A foreign expert who speaks our language. Very good."

As simply as that, their friendship had begun.

For the next hour Daobao led Cassy from one section to another, pulling out volumes, commenting and smiling. She was happy to let him.

At the poetry section she selected Schopenhauer's *World as Will and Idea* and said the book should be filed under philosophy.

Daobao took it from her and began to riffle through the pages.

Cassy looked into his face and said Schopenhauer argued that chance meetings often produced the most powerful sexual impulses.

Daobao said that was a very important observation.

The library door flew open. A short man in Mao jacket and baggy trousers stood on the threshold, his glasses glinting in the hard neon lighting. He rushed toward them, speaking Mandarin with such speed she barely understood him. All she clearly caught was his name and position: Pang Yi, political officer.

Daobao calmly stepped between her and Pang Yi, who continued to scold. They had no right to be here! The library was closed until term opened! Why were they here? A foreign woman and a student? That was not permitted!

Daobao abruptly thrust the book into Pang's hands, nodded to Cassy, and walked out of the library. She followed, leaving Pang speechless.

At the end of her first day of teaching, Daobao waited in the corridor outside the classroom. He asked if she would like to come to an art exhibition. He was frank.

"It will be very boring. Party-approved art. I have to go. It is Comrade Pang's little punishment. He knows I hate art. Especially state-approved art. But if you come, it will be more bearable."

Laughing, she accepted.

At the entrance to the exhibition they found a scroll containing another of Mao's edicts. "Art, for art's sake, art which transcends class or Party, art which stands as a bystander to, or independent of, politics, does not in actual fact exist." The paintings reflected this sterile canon: portraits of healthy, smiling, pink-faced workers; landscapes filled with tractors; and the centerpiece, a huge oil painting of a hydroelectric plant with high-tension power lines draped across the countryside. There was not an abstract or nude to be seen.

As they left Cassy said, "Schopenhauer would have hated the paintings."

Daobao admitted he had returned to the library and borrowed the book. He had sat up most of the night reading it. He had wanted to know more about sexual impulses.

His directness continued to captivate her. Two nights later he took her to dinner in a restaurant behind the Friendship Hotel. They stayed until closing time. He cycled back with her to the hotel. After they dismounted, without a smile, with no word, but with great seriousness, he took her hands and gently removed them from her bicycle handlebars. She gave him no encouragement. He looked steadily at her. She thought he was like someone about to leap from a precipice, hoping she would catch him, not knowing if she would. He leaned down and gently kissed her on the mouth.

It seemed the most natural thing when she kissed him back.

In the evenings and on weekends they went for walks in the city's parks. They took the cable lift up Fragrant Hills, hoisted through the air in twin chairs to the summit, serenaded by loudspeakers playing "The Blue Danube" and other Strauss waltzes, and they strolled through the parkland at the peak. There were never any awkward silences between them.

She only fell silent when he expounded his views on China. Daobao said it was a country never designed for the social engineering of Communism. The promises to end poverty and backwardness had led to a system in which corruption was endemic. Fraud and open profiteering were an increasing problem. Only the other day a senior official in the oil distributing ministry was discovered receiving kickbacks of $1 million to divert fuel to the black market. How many more like him were hiding in the bureaucratic woodwork? Only full democracy, Daobao said, could flush out those profiteers.

Cassy thought Daobao could be very naive at times.

Beyond the Beijing University campus gate more cyclists merged with the group. Cassy thought again how in his California-style denims Wuerkaixi looked like another foreign expert. She still found it hard to believe he was a leading activist. The son of an important Party official in remote Turkestan, Wuerkaixi had been raised and protected in the shadow of the Party. Yet when he entered Beijing Normal University the year before, he had quickly established himself as a radical.

He had spoken about the "intellectual failure" of Communism. How it had underestimated the importance of ethnicity and nationalism. How its policies were derived from a fatal misunderstanding of human nature. How it had failed to understand the basic craving for the right to self-expression and, above all, to enjoy political choice. How the Party failed to understand the connection between mass economic prosperity and the individual desire for personal freedom. How Communism had turned out to be a tragedy. Born out of impatient idealism, it promised a better and more caring society. Instead it had created oppression.

An hour after leaving the university, the cyclists reached Changan Avenue, the city's main thoroughfare. They slowly passed a long strip of billboards advertising sewing machines, vacuum cleaners, refrigerators, ovens, washing powders, and, always, family planning.

Daobao explained the signs concealed the site of Democracy Wall.

In 1978 a worker had displayed a handwritten poster offering the first public criticism of Mao. Others followed. Soon every city had its Democracy Wall. One of the most popular posters was a translation of the American Declaration of Independence: "We hold these Truths to be self-evident, that all Men are created equal, that they are endowed by their Creator with certain unalienable rights, that among these are Life, Liberty, and the Pursuit of Happiness." Democracy Wall had become the focus of a spontaneous, grass-roots movement for human rights in China.

Daobao continued speaking, his voice low and somber. He described how after four months the army had been sent to tear down the posters. The tension deepened his voice, driving him on. The past, she sensed, had left a deep scar on his psyche.

His parents, he explained, never understood about democracy. The family had a roof over their heads and sufficient food. They had not expected any more. His uncle, his mother's youngest brother, a teacher and a bachelor, seemed different. Every day after class he went to Democracy Wall to join in the protests. His school *danwei* or unit, expelled him. Short of imprisonment, there could be no greater punishment.

Cassy knew everyone in China must belong to a *danwei*, the place where they study or work. Even the youngest child in nursery school had to belong. Without a *danwei* affiliation a person was not allowed the basics of life. Instead, he or she literally became a nonperson, with no entitlements and no future within the state's all-embracing, all-constricting frame.

His uncle would have starved had Daobao's mother not taken a portion from her own family's bowls to feed him. An informer reported this kindness to the street *danwei* committee, who warned Daobao's mother that her family's food allowance would be reduced unless she stopped. His mother had hidden his uncle's bowl, feeding him secretly late at night. But the *danwei* was still after revenge. His uncle was a scholar, while its members were mostly uneducated. They deepened his public humiliation by making him stand before them to confess his crimes.

After six months, his uncle's school *danwei* said he could have a job at the school—cleaning toilets. Children he had taught were encouraged to spit on him. They were still doing so when he committed suicide. No one was allowed to go to the cremation except the family, because the *danwei* decided anyone who had advocated democracy should receive the minimum of mourning.

Daobao looked at her and said all that must be very hard to understand. She nodded. It was.

They reached the staff entrance of one of the city's hospitals. A porter led them to a door at the end of a short corridor and pressed a bell-push. There was a faint hum, and the door slid open. Cold air rose from the darkness. Cassy found herself in a concrete chamber. In the far wall was a steel door, opened by pressing another button. Beyond was a tunnel.

Daobao explained they were in the city's nuclear defense system. Mao had ordered it built in 1969 when he thought the Russians were going to attack. Every major city in China had its network of shelters.

The group moved through one tunnel after another, each isolated by its steel doors, each section lit by the same low-wattage lights. At regular intervals were intersections with cross tunnels disappearing into the darkness. There was a distant humming sound. Daobao said it was the air conditioning.

They finally reached a large chamber with rows of benches, sufficient seating for hundreds. In one corner stood a podium. Daobao explained the place was originally intended for cadres to lecture the people on the virtues of Communism while they sheltered from a Soviet atomic holocaust.

Cassy shook her head, bewildered. The others settled themselves on the hard seats. She joined them.

Daobao walked to the podium, his head almost touching the curved roof. He stood for a moment, running a finger around the collar of his shirt, as if he wanted to free something inside. When he spoke, it was with a sudden certainty.

He reminded them they wanted so very little, and not for themselves, but for all those they spoke for. Applause swept the chamber. He silenced it with a wave of a hand. He said the time was fast approaching when they would again take to the streets. They must be ready to lay down their lives. That was a small price to pay for democracy.

For the first time Cassy felt uneasy.

His voice filling with passion, Daobao added they could be sure that the Western democracies would support them, and none more so than the next incumbent of the White House, George Bush. Daobao said he was certain the future President would understand how important it was to support the students in their aspiration to see China shake off the shackles of fifty years of stultifying Communism.

Once more Cassy thought how naive Daobao could be.


SAME DAY, SAME TIME
*Hospital of Traditional Medicine*
*Beijing*

Five floors above the chamber, in a small and hopelessly cluttered office, worked Professor Jia Guangzu, sixty-three, director of the hospital's "traditional medicine" department for the past nine years. He and his staff dispensed treatment that was far removed from modern Western concepts. A short man with a high domed forehead, the professor appeared a powerful advertisement for the figurine of the Longevity Goddess on the desk. Her ageless marble face rose above the mound of paperwork and medical products.

Jars were filled with slivers of deer antler for treating flatulence and scales of lizard skins for curing apoplexy. Vials contained the powder of pearls he prescribed as a tranquilizer. Tiny containers of snake oil for blood pressure, and bottles of antiasthma pills made from the intestines of water rats, stood alongside sachets of crushed caterpillar, given for night sweats. There were pretty little boxes of powdered tiger bone for hypertension, tubes of ginseng jelly for baldness, extract of oxen penis to improve bone marrow, and frog essence to treat constipation.

Tongue diagnosis was Professor Guangzu's speciality. He could tell at a glance whether a stomach was not behaving properly, whether the fissure in a tongue indicated cancer or chronic hepatitis. Nowadays, people didn't always show proper respect for this ancient and, to

Professor Guangzu, totally reliable method. If they did they wouldn't write the kind of curt and time-wasting letters he had to answer.

The State Insurance Office was challenging the cost of procedures. Could he explain an increase of a yuan, less than a dime, for burning the powdered root of the artemisia plant on the skin of a psoriasis sufferer? Or an extra yuan for every anesthetic performed by acupuncture?

The penny-pinching of the bureaucrats at times made Professor Guangzu wish he had taken up the offer to train the "barefoot doctors," the physicians who tramped the countryside, going from one commune to another, treating villagers. He envied them their freedom.

Jenny, his daughter, had written that whenever she mentioned the scheme, her American colleagues were genuinely amazed to hear that young doctors were prepared to dedicate their lives to working in primitive conditions and live among illiterate peasants.

Sometimes he thought Jenny had become too Americanized. She had been in Los Angeles for over two years and was halfway through her postgraduate surgical studies. Her letters were increasingly filled with descriptions of what she called "the good life" in California: its supermarkets with their abundance of cheap food; low-cost fuel and cars. Their apartment was four times the size of what she and Zhong, her husband, could hope to rent in Beijing. It even had two separate bathrooms and a gas-fired barbecue on which she grilled steaks, each larger than a month's meat allowance for either of them in China.

Too much protein, he had gently reminded her, was bad for the blood. Zhong would confirm that. His son-in-law was a researcher, working on a cure for cancer.

The professor was glad they had gone to study abroad; he would be pleased when they returned. Jenny and Zhong had important roles to play in using what they had learned to benefit China. He also wanted his grandson, Peter, born in America, to grow up Chinese, not someone exposed to the life-style of southern California.

And, though he would never admit it to them, he would be glad to have them home because he was lonely. Since his wife had died ten years ago and Jenny, his only child, had gone to the States, there had been no one person he could really talk to except Hu Yaobang. But his evenings with his old friend were infrequent. Despite his loss of office, Hu was still involved in Politburo affairs.

Professor Guangzu would have liked to have discussed with Hu the newspaper clippings Jenny had enclosed with her last letter. There was a story about how an immigration judge in San Francisco had granted political asylum to a Chinese couple who asserted they had fled Beijing after the man's wife had been forced to have an abortion under the Chinese government's policy that each family should have no more than one child. The issue had triggered a fierce debate in the United States. The professor suspected Hu would growl and ask what all the fuss was about—and how resisting Chinese family policies could amount to "political dissent."

Professor Guangzu felt that of more interest to the former Party chief would be the newspaper report that to supply the vast Chinese appetite for new airplanes, the Boeing Company and the McDonnell Douglas Corporation had launched a campaign to sell China four hundred planes in the next decade. Hu had always said China was one of the last great frontiers of air travel as a people used to crowding on trains discovered the convenience of planes.

Professor Guangzu had no doubt that the next President of the United States would want to do nothing to rock such a massive deal. Jenny had kept him informed on Bush's campaign for the White House. What had struck the professor was the way Bush wasted no opportunity to say how "fundamentally important" China was to the United States. Time and again the words appeared in the pile of newsclips from Jenny on his desk. On some she had scribbled next to Bush's references to China: "Can we really believe him?"

Jenny, her father thought, had become for him that most baffling creature, a *radicalized* American, ready to tilt at all kinds of authority. She was like those students who met in the nuclear bunkers: full of heady talk and dreams of changing their world. He was not altogether against that. But a country like China could not be changed overnight.

Professor Guangzu began to deal with his correspondence. It included a large envelope that bore the seal of the Office of the Party Secretary for Beijing. Professor Guangzu had met him once, at a reception for a visiting delegation of Soviet doctors. The secretary had struck him as short on grace, humor, and temper. Hu had growled that the secretary was Deng's lapdog.

Professor Guangzu had wondered if such outspokenness had contributed to Hu's downfall. Nor had Hu learned to control his outbursts of volcanic temper. In a man of his years that was medically dangerous. It could precipitate a stroke or heart attack. But Hu refused to take the extract of pig's liver the professor had prescribed.

Professor Guangzu opened the envelope. It contained a revised disaster plan for Beijing, a blueprint for coping with any foreseeable calamity. His hospital had been designated to deal with victims from Tiananmen Square.

# 4

## *Secrets*

A t this hour, 6:30 A.M., only the tip of the Washington Monument is touched by the morning sun. Across the river the headstones remain in shadowy rows on Arlington's cemetery hill. The three men in the black government car each knew someone laid to rest beneath the stone markers.

The Oldsmobile had bulletproof windows, an armor-plated body, and antimine flooring. Only the official car of the President of the United States has similar protection. The Oldsmobile came with the job of director of Central Intelligence (DCI).

William Hedgecock Webster had held the post since March 3, 1987. Occupying a corner of the back seat, reading, in repose he remained genuinely intimidating. Perhaps it was because of his aura of total formality: his formal blue suit, his formal way of initialing each page before he read.

Under Webster, the CIA remained the nation's leading intelligence analyst, the unseen arm of U.S. foreign policy, frequently dealing with people the State Department found it diplomatically inappropriate to converse with.

But the presidency of Ronald Reagan was about to end, and after twenty months in office Webster had certainly read the newspaper speculation as to whether he would remain as the nation's chief intelligence officer in the forthcoming administration of President George Bush.

The best the press and media had ever said about Webster was that he was "safe"; under him there would be no more of the madcap missions that had enlivened and clouded the tenure of his predecessor, William Casey. Reporters described Webster as having "brought to the CIA an abiding concern for efficient administration," turning the agency from "being democracy's not very secret policemen into an annex of the Library of Congress."

Bush had once run the CIA. Would he want to have the agency continue to operate on Webster's guidelines, or would he want to rekindle old fires and once more make the CIA more aggressive? The director knew that the answer, and his future, would become clearer after his first meeting of the day. It was another briefing to the transition team that was looking at the CIA for the new administration. This morning the subject was China.

Before the car entered the George Washington Parkway, Webster had read the NID, the National Intelligence Daily, an agency-produced summary of the main overnight intelligence developments, and the PDB, the President's Daily Brief, which contained the most sensitive and exclusive items from all U.S. intelligence agencies.

Among them was a report on the Chinese government's deal with Britain's Cable and Wireless Company to purchase fiberoptic communication equipment, sophisticated enough to ensure it was virtually secure against electronic bugging. The system was to be used to completely rewire the Zhongnanhai compound.

When China first tried to buy the equipment three years earlier, President Reagan personally convinced Prime Minister Margaret Thatcher that the sale would seriously hamper the CIA's intelligence gathering. The agency often shared with Britain information it obtained in the People's Republic. Mrs. Thatcher canceled the contract.

In a DCI EYES ONLY memo Webster had inherited from a predecessor, Admiral Stansfield Turner, the agency's policy of spying on its allies was clearly encouraged. Turner wrote that "no one could surprise like a friend." Mrs. Thatcher's approval of the deal once more showed that.

Webster had learned that Mrs. Thatcher had recently reminded her cabinet of China's continued readiness to allow two U.S. monitor stations to operate on Chinese territory a mere three-hundred miles southeast of Semipalatinsk, long the main test center for Russia's nuclear weapons. The facilities gave technical intelligence gatherers in Washington an invaluable "window" on the Soviet Union. Mrs. Thatcher also noted the overall increase in America's trade with the

People's Republic. The message was clear: She was not going to allow Britain to miss an opportunity like the Cable and Wireless deal.

The CIA had long ensured Zhongnanhai was liberally sprinkled with electronic bugs. Lives had been risked to plant the listening devices in the compound's buildings and trees and along the paths surrounding its lake. CIA officers regularly left the U.S. embassy in the city's legation quarter to drive past Zhongnanhai. Their cars carried diplomatic number plates and were fitted with gadgetry to "vacuum" conversations gathered by the bugs. Though the Chinese Secret Intelligence Service electronically swept Zhongnanhai with regularity, Webster took pride in knowing that for every device located, another soon took its place.

Bush had laid great store on information obtained from bugging the Chinese leadership compound when he was head of the U.S. Liaison Office in Beijing in 1975 and, a year later, director of the CIA. He had spent many hours of his twelve-month stint in his suite on the seventh floor at Langley reading the intercepts of the old men who run China.

Webster was determined to convince Bush the Cable and Wireless deal was not a mortal blow, like those that had decimated U.S. intelligence gathering in Iran and Lebanon. As well as Zhongnanhai's ground bugs, ultrasophisticated hardware in space made him privy to military and political secrets being discussed by China's leaders.

Their words were sometimes snatched out of the air by aircraft hurtling through the earth's outer atmosphere at twice the speed of sound. What they missed, other equipment silently garnered.

A hundred miles out in space, satellites routinely observed the tidal wave of China's two hundred million city dwellers surging to work. The satellite sensors were so sensitive they could distinguish between the beeping and honking of the three-wheelers and the jingle of bicycle bells or separate the everyday sounds of China's villages, home for two-thirds of all the world's farmers. Their cameras were so powerful they could, if required, have identified the type of fur on Li Peng's hat or the tint in Zhao Ziyang's glasses.

Between 1,000 and 10,000 miles further out in space were more satellites, endlessly monitoring China's radar, measuring its ranges, frequencies, and power levels. At 23,300 miles—the geosynchronous orbit, where objects in space remain stationary in relation to the ground—were yet more continually listening to, among much else, the microwave-link telephone conversations between members of China's widely scattered People's Liberation Army. At 60,000 miles, a quarter of the way to the moon, a solitary satellite waited, ready to capture the first double-flash of a thermonuclear device being activated in one of China's launch sites.

Webster had been told by the National Security Agency, like every DCI at his first briefing: If a farmer slaughtered a pig in China's remotest province, within minutes NSA could provide a playback of the animal's screams.

Primarily, though, the system was to support politics at its highest level. The result of its eavesdropping helped to create U.S. foreign policy, shape a suitable diplomatic response, exploit differences.

For some months now Webster had been using it to help him decide how to take advantage of the increasing dissension within Zhongnanhai. A key question was whether Deng Xiaoping was still sufficiently skilled to play off the warring factions and ensure that the political structure of China did not crumble.

Webster had asked the agency's China analysts to predict how far Deng would allow matters to go. The great upheavals of the past had led to huge loss of life; there had been at least a million executions in the campaigns of the early 1950s, an estimated 28 million deaths in the Great Leap Forward, 100 million uprooted or killed in the Cultural Revolution. Would Deng allow Zhao Ziyang's policy conflict with Li Peng to provoke another slaughter?

Most crucial of all, what would be the role of the People's Liberation Army in dealing with such a conflict? Would the PLA side with Zhao or Li Peng? Or would the army remain aloof until the power plays within Zhongnanhai were clearly resolved? So far, despite overtures from both Zhao and Li Peng, the commanders of the seven military regions had given no indication what they would do.

However, General Yang, commander of the 27th Army, the largest of the PLA's forces, had now spoken out about the need to control the students should they take to the streets. The electronic net cast over China had enabled Webster to learn that the general had begun to canvas for support among his fellow commanders. He had told them that if there were trouble, the 27th was ready to deal with the situation "by whatever force is necessary."

The CIA's analysts saw the students as responsible for much of the erosion of Party authority. Licensed and encouraged by Mao, at first they were the vigorous voice of proletarian power. Then they began to act autonomously, and eventually mindlessly. Finally, on April 5, 1976, they had rampaged through Tiananmen Square, with Mao himself the target of their fury. Deng Xiaoping became a hero, calling their action "a popular uprising." He had stamped his imprimatur on the legitimacy of mass protest in the heart of the capital. He had done so again when the Democracy Wall movement briefly flowered. It had helped consolidate his political position.

Agency analysts still disagreed whether Deng had cynically exploited the students or had been forced to suppress them by the conservatives of Zhongnanhai as the price for their support.

Now, a decade later, a new generation of students had emerged determined to transform their motherland.

CIA files contained details about their leaders. Wuerkaixi was described as "a super activist. Image conscious and prepared to lead from the front. Not all students like his confrontational style." Wang Dan was "working to create an independent student union movement." Yang Li was "one of the leading student strategists," Yan Daobao "a militant." Liu Gang, a twenty-eight-year-old physics major at Beijing University, was characterized as "brilliant, if at times a quixotic thinker." Chai Ling, a twenty-three-year-old graduate student at Beijing Teacher's University seemed "a born revolutionary— more committed than most of her male compatriots."

The student leaders were credited with being "well spoken" and "choosing their targets shrewdly. They draw moral strength from nationalism, the hard facts to support their arguments from the *Wall Street Journal*. They cite the Pope on the strategic struggle against social evil and know how to exploit Gorbachev's *perestroika* for their own ends."

The files repeatedly stated that the student leaders knew how to take an issue, human rights, and show that the basic denial of choice was what ultimately separated Communism from democracy and would, in the end, doom it.

An analyst had noted that in China "the State monopoly on mass communications, the lack of a multiparty system, the absence of a genuine market economy, allowed student leaders to constantly reiterate that a nation which shaped so many of the laws of civilization should now be allowed to live within their framework."

It was a heady philosophy. But was it strong enough to change the course of China's political life? And, most crucial for Webster, should be recommend to the new administration that the United States begin to support the students in their aims? Should Bush encourage them to push for greater reform, freedom of speech, assembly, and association? Or should the incoming President be told to curb his support for their democratic aims so as not to weaken the growing commercial and other ties linking the two countries?

The United States had played an important part over the past decade in helping China's to become the fastest growing economy in the world. American corporations had made huge profits from doubling or even quadrupling the incomes of millions of Chinese and giving them a better standard of life. Yet with the GNP of the People's Republic still only averaging $350 a year per capita, more huge profits were to be made from business joint ventures. Americans were digging mines and operating luxury hotels in China. The lure of the market was often its sheer size: A manufacturer had only to sell one can of cola in a year to each of those billion Chinese to become very rich. In addition there was the bonus of paying low wages; the average Chinese industrial wage was about $60 a month, less than a day's salary in the United States. There was also the attraction for U.S. investors of training cheap labor with American technology, making China still more dependent on the United States.

All these were important considerations in Webster's mind as he tried to decide what advice to give the President's team.

Shortly after 7:00 A.M. the Oldsmobile passed beneath a bold green-and-white overhead sign on the freeway:

CENTRAL INTELLIGENCE AGENCY
INTELLIGENCE COMMUNITY STAFF
NEXT RIGHT

The CIA was the most conspicuous of the world's secret intelligence services, spreading itself over 219 acres of pleasant and partially wooded countryside along the banks of the Potomac. Its location, nine miles to the northwest of the White House, made it a landmark for pilots landing at Washington's National Airport.

Webster placed his files in a leather briefcase before the Oldsmobile passed the guardpost at the entrance to Langley. Beyond, the headquarters building showed its age. The complex had been built in the late fifties, an era when concrete, not glass, was in architectural favor. Landscaping only emphasized the building's squared, bunker-like appearance. The $46 million extension added in 1982 appeared to be tacked on.

The agency itself had become a vast bureaucracy, with its own fiefdoms, each engaged in a constant struggle for office space and additional money. Webster regularly spent time trying to settle internal rivalry that mocked the verse from the Gospel of St. John inscribed on a marble wall in the lobby: AND YE SHALL KNOW THE TRUTH, AND THE TRUTH SHALL MAKE YOU FREE.

Beyond the plaque are five color-coded elevators, each programed to stop only at certain floors. On the first six floors the corridor walls are white and bare. On the seventh floor the walls are paneled to match the light oak doors, and paintings hang the length of the corridor leading to the director's suite. No one can reach it without a computer-checked pass allowing use of the blue elevator.

Shortly before 7:30 A.M., Webster entered the conference room beside his office. Waiting there was his deputy, Robert Gates, a cautious professional who had risen through the ranks. Standing beside Gates was a gaunt, monklike man, Brent Scowcroft. He was going to be Bush's national security adviser. With him were four other members of the transition team.

When they were seated, each with a copy of his position paper before him on the table, Webster told them: "I am going to switch things around a bit. I want to start with the student situation. I want to show you why they are probably going to be the key to what we can expect."

From this moment onward George Bush would be fully apprised of exactly what the students of China were planning. At each step they took he would be given a choice of options, which ultimately came down to two: to support or not support them. That was the bottom line, an updated version of President Truman's famous saying that the buck stops here.

It was an awesome responsibility, and as he began his briefing, Webster had no real idea how the next President would shoulder it. For his part the CIA director would be evenhanded, merely presenting the facts and being careful not to shade them with opinion. That could come later, if he were confirmed in his post.

WEDNESDAY, NOVEMBER 16, 1988
*Embassy of the United States of America*
*Beijing*

The American Embassy compound is the largest in the legation quarter. It occupies most of one side of Xiu Bei Jie, a tree-lined avenue. Tall iron railings separate the ill-kept roadway, which is China's responsibility, from the pathways and lawns that are America's and as carefully tended as those outside any federal building in Washington.

During the hours of daylight, Chinese stop and peer through the railings. Perhaps they are envious so much ground should be landscaped when they could put it to good use rearing ducks or raising crops; perhaps they dream of going to a country that can afford to squander so much land.

The onlookers are quickly told to move on by the militia who patrol the avenue. The rifle-toting young men in olive uniforms and forage caps wear rubber-soled boots that enable them to move quietly. They are most numerous around the compound's entrance; there are always half a dozen watching everyone who comes or goes.

The real surveillance takes place in the car parked opposite. The vehicle contains Chinese intelligence service agents. Day and night they keep watch and are in radio contact with other CSIS cars positioned around the foreign legation quarter.

The CIA agents who make their sweeps around Zhongnanhai have long learned to accept being followed.

They work from a building in the compound known as Spook City, which has the appearance of a mansion in upstate New York. It has white walls and a solid-looking front door. Its windows have antibugging alarms, primed to go off if any listening device is trained on the glass. Hidden detectors warn of parabolic microphones directed against the building. The roof has a number of aerials.

The chancery is the most imposing building in the compound. Its exterior would grace an affluent American suburb. The ground-floor reception rooms are imposing. But behind the fire doors in the hall lies a warren of offices. Here, many of the embassy's 110 diplomats work in often crowded conditions. For them China is another hardship posting in the service of their country.

One of them, James Laracco, the counselor for economic affairs, saw the usual huddle of young Chinese standing outside the main gate of the compound. Since early morning they had been waiting to be interviewed by one of the consular officers, who would decide who should be given visas to travel to the United States. Muffled in scarves and padded overcoats and jiggling on their heels against the cold of a bright winter's day, they practiced their English on the bored marine in the guard house.

Laracco was a neat and meticulous man who brought to his work a formidable intellect, able to reduce the most complex issues to concise sentences. For most of this day he had been working on a report explaining some of the problems China would have to address during the first term of the Bush administration. The report was part of a briefing package for the President-elect.

Laracco wished Bush could be standing here with him, watching the young Chinese around the guardpost. He would tell the next President they were part of the problem confronting China. There were millions more like them, educated and disenchanted. And out there in the vast hinterland were a far greater number, uneducated but equally disenchanted. They presented China's leaders with a growing threat.

The problem facing Laracco was how to convey that opinion without sounding alarmist.

His legal pad was already covered with his analysis of why ten years of economic reforms had failed. As usual, he had jotted down headings, the framework in which he would fashion and contain his arguments.

"Population: no motivation to work harder. Inflation: remains on the increase. Government has failed to curb corruption," Laracco had written. He began to expand his argument. "The result is that the rising standard of living, and expectations, parallel the rising complaints. Past legacies continue to burden the country."

He penned a judgment. "The economy remains trapped in a no-man's land. On the one hand the reformers, led by Zhao Ziyang, are unable to move closer to a genuine market-oriented economy, while the conservatives under Li Peng are trying to return to total centralized control. It is a recipe for disaster."

He believed the disaster could be triggered by China's greatest and most pressing problem: how to cope with its population growth.

It had needed almost 4,000 years for China to produce a population of five-hundred million. Yet in three decades, the 1950s to the 1980s, the figure had doubled. Mao had encouraged the soaring birth rate, arguing that the larger the population, the greater would be China's work force. It was a piece of Marxist dogma that did not take into account the basic problem of too many mouths and not enough food.

Mao had also introduced a public health program that had pushed the average life expectancy from thirty-two years in 1948 to sixty-four in 1988.

To counter the problem of longevity coupled with a population explosion, Deng Xiaoping had introduced the most stringent family planning in history. Each city and province received quotas for the number of babies allowed to be born each year, and local committees decided which families should bear children. Every woman had to formally report her menstrual cycle; anyone who missed her period and was not on the approved list for having a baby was automatically sent to an abortion clinic.

These measures were intended to reduce China's rate of population increase to zero by the year 2000. But it continued to increase by twelve million a year, requiring a further seven million tons of rice to feed the extra mouths.

Laracco knew that a large number of Chinese now lived in semistarvation with a daily calorie intake almost half that of the United States. The average Chinese male adult ate only fourteen pounds of meat a year, thirteen of fruit, twelve of fish. Women averaged half that quantity. The authorities insisted that was sufficient for them to live on.

Increasingly, the birth-control policy had run into opposition from the peasants, who made up 80 percent of the country. They claimed they had always been able to feed the large families they need to work the land.

Once there had been sufficient work for unskilled hands. Now, slowly but surely, mechanization was making inroads. A tractor could do the work of fifty men; only one drove it, the others went on the employment scrapheap. But they still had to be fed. The economist feared the disaster could be triggered in rural China.

There, the number of adults unemployed now totaled nearly two-hundred million. By the end of the century it would be over three-hundred million, based on the present birth rate. Yet the government options were limited. To introduce unskilled labor into the economy would slow down expansion and create greater inflation. To do nothing for a growing untrained labor force would create further unrest. Yet China could not afford the costs of an ever-expanding welfare state. To feed and house so many unemployed would prove a tremendous challenge for any government. For China's it would be insuperable.

Laracco began to formulate his next point. He too saw the students as having a key role in China's future. They had learned from the mistakes of the past. He had little doubt that in any new protest movement they would be better organized and more persuasive and appealing. The inarticulate unemployed could well be swept along by the student's passionate entreaties. A brute force of such magnitude would be almost impossible to subdue. Then China itself would be engulfed by ferment. Foreign investment in the country would be destroyed.

Over the past decade $11.5 billion had been invested by the United States, Japan, and Europe in China.

Currently Portman Cos, the Atlanta-based developer, was engaged on a $175 million building project in Shanghai. The Dow Chemical Company had a $56 million contract to erect a processing plant near the seaport. The Texas-based Helen of Troy Corporation had contracts worth $68 million for hairdryers produced in China. The American Telephone and Telegraph Company was engaged in a multimillion-dollar joint venture with the Chinese to manufacture joint transmission systems in Shanghai. The General Foods Corporation had a similar deal to produce tapioca and instant coffee and other beverage mixes. American toy makers, garment makers, and distributors of cheap telephones, calculators, and radios from China had all helped to swell an investment program that was part of China's sensational ten-year romance with the West in general, and the United States in particular, that had begun when President Jimmy Carter normalized relations with China in 1979.

Despite his pessimism over what had happened in the past decade, Laracco still believed that the only way forward for China was for the United States to continue to draw the country into "a web of economic, technological and military ties which would prevent the Middle Kingdom from plunging back into internal struggle."

He would recommend that the new administration should do nothing to encourage the students.

# 5

# The Watch Keepers

Yang Bing found the cold most penetrating while standing guard on the roof of the Great Hall of the People in the center of Beijing. Bing was the twenty-four-year-old elder brother of one of Cassy Jones's students, the muscular Li. Bing shared the pride of their peasant parents that Li had been the first in the family to enter the portals of Beijing University. But nowadays Bing had little else in common with Li. Bing suspected part of the reason was because he was a member of the People's Liberation Army. Li could not understand the pride Bing felt being in its ranks.

Of the 3 million Chinese who were annually eligible for callup, only 750,000 were accepted. Each conscript served three years. Those with an aptitude for soldiering were invited to stay and maintain the army's strength of 3.5 million. The remainder were discharged to the reserve. This force currently numbered 18 million highly trained men and women who could be swiftly mobilized to defend the motherland.

In a year Bing had moved from conscript to fighter. The promotion carried an increase of three yuan, making his pay the equivalent of $8.50 a month. He hoped to transfer to the officer corps; that would double his income.

Physically Bing was like his brother: short and stocky with powerful shoulders and legs and dark skin. Nevertheless, Bing found it painful to realize how different they had become. Li quoted what the Party called Bad Elements, banned writers and poets, and read copies of proscribed books. He attacked the government and even

46

berated Deng Xiaoping. Bing had told Li such heresy would surely bring tears to their parents' eyes.

Bing knew Li's new friends were responsible. From the outset, he had felt uncomfortable with them. Wuerkaixi, in his American clothes and that all-knowing smile on his lips. Liu Gang, who also dressed like an American and drank out of a can. Chai Ling, who had looked disdainfully at his soldier's uniform. Yan Daobao, with his superior ways, and the American woman, Cassy, who asked her careful questions. The more she tried to make him talk, the more uneasy he had become. His political officer said foreigners were at their most dangerous when they are pleasant and smiling. Wang Dan didn't even smile. He just sat there, staring, only once in a while stirring himself to challenge some statement. And Meili, Li's girlfriend. Bing had never seen a Chinese girl so forward. She smoked and drank alcohol and wore makeup. Thankfully, in a few hours' time they would all be gone from his life.

This evening he would board the military train for the long journey across China to Tibet, to meet up with the rest of the 27th Army. Matters there were serious, his platoon leader had said.

Now, as dawn lit the curved roofs of the Forbidden City, Bing knew four more hours of duty remained. The rest of his platoon kept the same silent watch from the roof of one of the most massive buildings in the world. Bing had learned a million volunteers had needed only ten months to erect the Great Hall. The political officer had allowed a momentary smile to cross his face as he described this achievement as "the power of the collective family to achieve anything the State wants."

Li had called the Great Hall an architectural monstrosity, outdated and numbed in its own enormousness. That was a week ago, when his brother once more challenged what they had both been taught to believe. They had met in one of the cafes near the Beijing University campus, and Li had asked Bing if he knew that only 4 percent of the population were Party members.

In between mouthfuls of food Li had continued. "We have sixteen million unemployed in our cities. Mostly young people with no faith in the Party. No faith in the leadership. No faith in anything. You know why? They are being robbed. There is one law for those in the Party, another for the rest. That's why the Party likes to keep its numbers so small. So that its members have more to share among themselves from their robbing."

Bing had looked at Li, wondering what was happening to his brother. He asked Li what he was trying to do. Ruin his future? Betray their parents? Bing's sudden anger surprised himself.

Bing continued to scan the expanse of Tiananmen Square's ninety-eight acres of paving stones, each painted with a numeral for easy regimentation during official demonstrations. The square could hold over a million people. His political officer said there was no other like it on earth.

Li had seen it as the place where the Red Guards first pledged themselves to Mao in a delirium of flags. His brother had assumed the role of teacher. No one, he explained, had been spared from their violence. Scientists, lawyers, doctors, teachers, and, of course, intellectuals, all became victims. Reputations were ruined, lives laid waste. All that was good and innocent was destroyed. Ornamental trees and flower beds were dug up. Household pets were destroyed; there had been mounds of rotting cats and dogs in the streets of Beijing and other cities. Whatever Mao ordered had been carried out blindly, without a moment's thought. One day he decreed keeping goldfish was criminal, and the Guards had gone on the rampage, smashing fishbowls across the country. On another, Mao pronounced playing chess to be immoral. Millions of boards and pieces were burned. When Mao outlawed stamp collecting, many of the country's priceless collections had been destroyed.

How, Bing had asked, did Li know all this?

His brother gripped him by the shoulders. "One of my teachers. He was there. He saw it all. He told us."

He asked Li why he believed his teacher.

No one could lie about such things, Li said. Not about half a million people casually murdered and tens of millions starved to death. No one could lie about that.

In the strengthening light, Bing could make out the red banners and yellow stars draped across the pediments of the Museum of Chinese History and Revolution. He scanned the Forbidden City, studying its bridges, walkways, and gateways. Nothing disturbed its peace.

Soon the light was sufficiently bright for him to pick out individual faces in the first shoal of cyclists emerging from the *hutongs*, the lanes which lead into Changan Avenue, Beijing's version of Fifth Avenue. They kept a steady and near-uniform pace, ignoring the traffic policemen endlessly gesticulating from their little islands in the middle of the boulevard that ran for ten miles through the center of the city.

Bing focused on an area northeast of the Forbidden City. As usual, a pair of sentries stood at either end of a bridge over a lake, ready to repel anyone foolish enough to approach Zhongnanhai. On the near side of the bridge, a line of stakes rose like dragon's teeth from the water, encased in barbed wire, their points sharpened as a further determent. Having carefully scanned the water and the surrounding banks, Bing peered into the leadership compound.

A figure stood on the towpath. Bing made out the sharp and foxy face of Yang Shangkun, the country's president. For a man in his eighty-first year he still performed his *taijiquan,* the traditional morning martial arts exercise, with grace.

He was joined by another warmly clad figure. Bing did not need his binoculars to recognize Wu Yi, the vice-mayor of Beijing and Yang's mistress. She wore the bright blue tracksuit the president was rumored to have specially ordered for her from America.

Unaware they were being observed, the couple began to move around one another in graceful shadow play. Several hundred miles in space a satellite camera captured the moment and transmitted it, as part of the early morning sweep of the city, to the National Photographic Interpretation Center in Washington. The technicians responsible for monitoring China now had fresh orders.

They were to keep track of any signs of "untoward student activity." The order had come from CIA Director Webster and formed part of a general brief to the agency's operatives in China itself. President-elect Bush had specifically asked Webster to keep him personally updated on events in China with, according to one operative, "particular emphasis on what those students might be thinking of doing."

In ordering that, the incoming President was signaling that China's students were very much a matter of concern for him, though Webster still had no clear idea exactly how Bush intended to reflect that interest. The CIA knew that to second-guess the President-elect on the matter was as tricky as predicting events in China. The country's aged leadership had an uncanny knack of confounding outsiders. At the moment, Webster had been told, "they are bumping over only small potholes on the road to reform."

But those students could change everything.

SAME DAY, LATER
*Foreign Legation Quarter*
*Beijing*

The first meetings of the day, some over breakfast, were being held in various embassies as diplomats and professional intelligence officers resumed the endless task of trying to discover what the Chinese leadership was planning.

In the Canadian chancery on San Li Tun Lu, Ambassador Earl S. Drake was closeted with senior staff. The Secret Intelligence Service officer assigned to the embassy began by briefing them on the latest visit to Beijing by a Canadian-born rocket scientist, Dr. Gerald Bull.

A brilliant but fatally flawed personality, Bull, a sixty-year-old rocket weapons specialist, had fallen out with his own government, and subsequently his CIA paymasters. Bitter and angry, Bull had hired himself out to first the South Africans and then Iraq. He had promised Saddam Hussein to build a series of superguns, each with the capacity to fire a shell several hundred miles. Months ago Bull had come to China to discuss with the state armaments corporation, Norinco, how it could be part of that deal.

The intelligence officer reported on the outcome of the latest meeting between Bull and Norinco executives at the Beijing Hotel. In return for unlimited funding, Bull would design a gun capable of shooting small satellites into space for about 5 percent of the cost of a conventional rocket launch. The Chinese thought the gun had a huge military potential for themselves and one they could profitably market to clients in the Middle East, apart from Iraq.

China's arms sales were a substantial part of its annual $80 billion exports. These were made possible by massive loan packages from the World Bank and the Manila-based Asian Development Bank. German banks had advanced $2.1 billion of export credits, and Japanese finance houses had loaned Chinese industrial directors almost $6 billion to keep exports flowing.

Not only could China be plunged into recession if the students created serious unrest, but foreign confidence in China's ability to honor its commitments would fade.

The Canadian intelligence officer suggested that if the students once more took to the streets, there could be a significant difference in their tactics this time. They might appeal to the West to openly support their demands. Canada could well find itself in the forefront of such an appeal. In the officer's view, "that could rock more boats than a stiff breeze does on the St. Lawrence Seaway."

It was agreed that monitoring the student activity should become an important part of Canada's intelligence presence in Beijing.

A similar decision had already been taken at the French embassy a few compounds further along the street. There Ambassador Charles Malo and his minister-counselor, Gerard Chesnee, had sat over breakfast with Nicholas Chapuis, the cultural counselor. With them was the embassy's senior intelligence officer, who operated under the cover of being one of the French attachés.

Chapuis, a likable, glad-handing diplomat, had spent the previous day talking to students and their foreign expert teachers at one of the university campuses. He had learned of the meeting held in the nuclear shelter. In Chapuis's view, the students were "muscle flexing."

Ambassador Malo warned that nothing must be done "in the name of France" to encourage them. To do so would place at risk the thousands of contracts between French and Chinese companies amounting to $4 billion, much of it in low-wage light industry.

Similar sentiments were being expressed in missions as far apart on the political spectrum as the Soviet Union's and Australia's. In a score of embassies throughout the legation quarter, diplomats were beginning to focus their attention on the country's student population. In the words of Lindsay J. Watt, New Zealand's ambassador, "these young folk had the potential to raise a whole storm—and when the dust settled there'd be no telling what had been blown away."

SAME DAY, STILL LATER
*Zhongnanhai*

Next to the prime minister's compound stands a smaller one, dominated by a squarely-built building, surrounded by a paved area containing a helicopter landing pad and parking space for fifty cars. The building's roof is festooned with aerials similar to those visible on the American embassy's Spook City. It also has an inner courtyard with an ornamental pond and a landscaped miniature garden.

Qiao Shi ran China's Secret Intelligence Service from the only office with direct access to the courtyard.

Several other CSIS buildings are scattered throughout the city. Counterintelligence is on West Qiananmen Street. Foreign intelligence operates from a modern building near the city's main railway station. But the spying activities of several thousand men and women are coordinated from the office with its pleasing views of shrubs and bushes in the secluded courtyard.

Adjoining Qiao Shi's office is the computer room. Its many millions of details stored on tape include information about every Chinese student studying abroad and the country's 14,489 accredited diplomats posted around the world, along with the names of all foreign contacts they had in their communities.

Also on tape were the identities of all Chinese convicted of, or suspected of being involved with, drug trafficking, and records of the CSIS role in their discovery, especially in the United States. There CSIS had worked closely with the Drug Enforcement Agency and the Federal Bureau of Investigation.

It was a striking example of the hidden links and interdependencies between intelligence services. All were sworn to deny these bonds existed.

Cooperation with the United States resulted from a meeting between William Casey, then director of the Central Intelligence Agency, and Qiao Shi in December 1984. Casey was the first American intelligence chief to recognize the mistake of looking at China as merely a massive regional threat. With its nuclear weapons, long-range submarines, orbiting satellites, and intercontinental ballistic missiles, China had become a world power.

Casey had flown secretly to Beijing to meet Qiao. Among much else discussed had been how the power of China's drug dealers now matched that of the Mafia in the United States and the drug barons in Colombia. Chinese cartels controlled over 60 percent of New York's heroin market. Every major North American city had its Chinese godfather, mandarins infinitely richer and more powerful than any dynasty emperor. An increasing amount of the cocaine from Colombia and the Golden Triangle in southeast Asia was actually marketed by men whose lineage went back to the big-city opium dens in the 1800s.

None of this could have surprised Qiao Shi. Under his direction the CSIS had manipulated the drug traffickers of Asia to hook U.S. servicemen in Vietnam. But inevitably, with drug-taking respecting no barriers, China had found itself with a growing addiction problem, especially among its students. According to Casey, Qiao had proposed "a joint intelligence venture" to combat the traffickers.

A top-secret meeting was held at the Mandarin Hotel in Hong Kong between senior CSIS officers and a team from the CIA, FBI, and DEA in January 1985. As a result the U.S. agencies had continued to receive information from the CSIS about any drug-running operations targeted against the United States; in return the CSIS were provided with the names of all known Chinese traffickers.

CSIS help had produced some spectacular results, including the now celebrated Goldfish Aquarium case in San Francisco. A million pounds of heroin had been discovered wrapped in cellophane and condoms inside fish imported from Asia. American federal agents had taken the credit for the bust. Privately they admitted they could not have succeeded without the CSIS team that had trailed the consignment across the Pacific.

Qiao Shi had approved handing over valuable information CSIS possessed about the Triads. With an estimated million members scattered worldwide, the ancient Chinese secret societies were the largest drug traffickers on earth.

Nothing seemed too small or too much on the periphery of mainstream intelligence to escape Qiao Shi's notice.

Five years before, when unrest had first surfaced in Poland and Hungary, the intelligence chief had persuaded Deng Xiaoping to create a 400,000-man armed police force that would be directly under CSIS control.

Qiao Shi recognized that to operate effectively, the force must be trained and equipped like Western riot-control teams, with rubber bullets, tear gas, and water cannon. To defend themselves, his men must be dressed in the same kind of protective clothes used by specialist teams in America and Britain. He had spent hours studying videos of the British Army in Northern Ireland.

But Western firms continued to be discouraged by their governments from selling China the lightweight body armor, weapons, and training techniques needed to subdue rioting crowds. With the Cable and Wireless deal in place, China's diplomats in Washington had begun to suggest that the United States should be careful of losing more business to Britain.

The diplomats had been helped by an old and still powerful friend, former Secretary of State Henry Kissinger. More than any other American, he had been responsible for promoting U.S. investment in China, creating a specialist consultancy to do so. In the past five years billions of dollars had been channeled into the Chinese economy through Kissinger Associates.

To further encourage trade, Kissinger had created the prestigious American-China Society, with himself and former Secretary of State Cyrus Vance as cochairmen. Board members included ex-Presidents Gerald Ford, Jimmy Carter, and Richard Nixon, former National Security Advisers McGeorge Bundy, Robert McFarlane, and Zbigniew Brzezinski, and former Secretaries of State Dean Rusk, Edward Muskie, Alexander Haig, and William D. Rogers.

Kissinger Associates had persuaded clients to invest heavily in China. Chase Manhattan Bank had recently invested $270 million in the Daya Bay Nuclear Power Plant, which had an integral role in producing China's nuclear weapons. Another of the bank's multi-million-dollar investments underwrote leases for the purchase of aircraft by the Civil Aviation Administration of China.

Kissinger had arranged for American Express, a company of which he was a board member, to invest $138 million in a thirteen-year loan to build an office complex in Beijing. At the same time he had arranged for another company of which he was a board member, the American International Group, to establish a joint venture with the People's Insurance Company of China to handle insurance and reinsurance on mainland China. The business was currently worth $25 million annually. Atlantic Richfield, another client of Kissinger Associates, had invested $170 million to develop the South China Sea natural gas field.

On the military front, Kissinger had continued to play what was called by Qiao Shi his "China card," allowing the United States to help China to upgrade its satellites and purchase advanced missile guidance systems. One of these systems had been sold to the People's Liberation Army by the Israelis in 1987, with full U.S. approval. Currently Grumman Aviation had a contract to provide advanced avionics for the Chinese Air Force's entire fleet of F8-2 interception jets, while Garret Aerospace was providing the engines for the C-8 fighters, the air force's short-range interceptors.

Against these genuinely massive investments, Qiao Shi knew that the question of his riot-control gear was a trifling matter. But Henry Kissinger was not a man to miss a deal. He had told China's spymaster not only that he would receive the gear, but that U.S. investment would increase even further once George Bush was in the Oval Office.

Qiao Shi believed the ability of Kissinger Associates to lobby even more effectively within the Bush administration would be enhanced by the presence of two top officials who had been members of the multimillion-dollar consulting company that bore Kissinger's name.

They were Lawrence Eagleburger, who would take over the number two slot at the State Department and become one of President Bush's most trusted troubleshooters, and Brent Scowcroft, who had been director of the Washington office of Kissinger Associates. He would be Bush's national security adviser. Together with James Baker, the two former employees of Kissinger Associates would form the policy-shaping "troika" around Bush.

Qiao Shi could reasonably have expected such close friends of China to allow nothing to upset the cordial business relationships between the two countries. Most certainly they would not permit a group of almost penniless students with radical views to disturb America's huge financial investment in China.

# 6

## *States of Mind*

THURSDAY, NOVEMBER 24, 1988
*Washington, D.C.*

Outside the unprepossessing brick town house at 716 Jackson
Place across from the White House, government cars came and
went, depositing members of the Bush transition team. The dozen
men strode briskly up the six steps into the building, glad to be out of
the raw early morning air. After coffee, the men who would set the
course for the next presidency settled themselves around the dining
room table to listen to another briefing from Webster.

They had greeted the CIA director warmly, taking their cue from
the President-elect. A few days ago Bush had asked Webster to stay
on. There was now a new zest about the director. He no longer looked
like a man who had been given bad news by his doctor, but someone
with a new sense of life.

Webster extended a personal welcome to each team member. To
John Tower, the designate secretary of defense, the director seemed
like a host greeting a bunch of cronies, rather than the country's
intelligence chief about to "spill some more of other people's secrets."

The presence of John Sununu, the former governor of New
Hampshire, showed the President-elect could continue to surprise;
Bush had just appointed him to be his White House chief of staff.
Webster knew that Sununu was strong-willed, often tactless, and
inclined to charge full tilt. The director was ready to fend off any
ideas Sununu might have of using the CIA on some Mission Impossible. There were problems enough as it was. The intelligence summary he had prepared contained an update on every major global
sphere of trouble. It provided an overview of what was likely to

happen between now and when Bush formally entered office in late
January next year.

Next to the former governor sat James Baker. Bush had already
made it clear that as well as being secretary of state, Baker would be
his de facto deputy. Though Baker had little foreign policy experience, he was on a fast learning curve. Webster had told senior aides
that Baker had "a real grasp of the realities." The director planned to
use the secretary as a sounding board for proposals he wanted Bush
to endorse when he was in office.

The director had also made his own careful assessment of each
member of the team, their strengths and weaknesses, who was a team
player, who an out-and-out loner. It would help him decide who
should be on the list for BIGOT, the slim buff folder with a double
blue stripe on the cover that was hand-carried by a CIA officer to a
small group of people in the highest echelons of government. The
folder contained either reports from a key field agent or details
about some forthcoming ultrasensitive intelligence operation.

So far only Baker had been approved for access to the list. Almost
certainly Bush would want Brent Scowcroft, the man seated opposite
Baker, to have access, too.

Scowcroft was the transition team's hardliner, with a penny-
pinching manner that went all the way back to his days as a child in
Ogden, Utah. Now, half a century later, his Mormon faith continued
to sustain him in a lifetime spent behind Washington's closed doors.
He liked to say he knew where all the bodies were buried. Since 1987
he had run the Washington office of Kissinger Associates. It had
given him an insight into the financial interplay between the United
States and China better than any other man's in the room.

Next to Scowcroft sat John Tower. Webster doubted if he would
ever make it to office. The FBI checks the President-elect had
insisted on for all his nominees had revealed Tower to be a wom-
anizer with a drinking problem. Defense was no place for a man who
could be blackmailed. But for the moment Tower was privy to what
Webster was unfolding.

He took them on a world tour, moving from Latin and Central
America to Asia and South Africa. The next stop was Russia.

Webster said the country was in trouble. He added emphatically:
big trouble. As well as having many economic problems, Moscow was
finding it increasingly difficult to maintain homogeneity; there were
too many ethnic groups and autonomous republics seeking independence. Webster added, Gorbachev could be presiding over the
collapse of Soviet Communism.

Tower shifted in his chair. "He'd never allow that," Tower said.

"He'd have to go back to the old ways. Terror and mass deportation. Break the people before they get a chance to break the system."

Webster hesitated. How far should he go? Should he tell them that only a week ago he had once more flown to London to interview a top-ranking KGB defector who had been brought out of Russia into Finland by MI6? That for the past two years the man had been providing invaluable insights into Gorbachev's thinking? That the defector had told him that not only Russia, but the whole of Communist Europe, was on the brink? One wrong move and it could go either way: collapse, or end in bloody civil war.

This kind of intelligence, Webster decided, he didn't want to share with the transition team. This was still BIGOT-list, or President-elect's ears-only, information.

Webster turned his attention to China. Despite its huge army, nuclear weapons, and intercontinental ballistic missiles, it still had little ability to influence international events.

For the next half hour he gave them an incisive picture of China's attempts to improve its nuclear arsenal. Its most advanced missile, the CSS-4, now had a range of 10,000 miles and carried a 5-megaton warhead. By the early 1990s it would be able to carry multiple warheads. China's two other "showcase weapons," the CSS-3 and CSS-2, had, respectively, a 5,000-mile range and a 3-megaton warhead, and a 2,000-mile range and 2-megaton warhead.

"Any of these weapons on offer to their clients in the Middle East?" asked Tower.

Webster shook his head. Representatives of Israel, the only country with a worthwhile intelligence service still operating in Iraq and Iran, had assured him of that.

The director focused their attention on China's internal situation.

Ideological disagreement was deepening within the leadership. The outcome depended on whether the economy could remain on its ambitious course without inflation getting totally out of control. Yet if the economy remained on track, it would only increase the pressure for fuller democracy. That pressure was now beginning to come from outside the country.

Many of the forty million Chinese living overseas had been both wealthy and had kept their emotional links with their motherland. They had welcomed its reconstruction by pouring in money. In the past year alone $15 billion had been invested by Taiwan. In all, Chinese overseas investment totaled $70 billion. With it had come a call for greater democracy and the often thinly disguised threat to withdraw funding unless the demand was met.

The country's students were mobilizing. As usual, they were being led by those on Beijing's campuses, where a total of 180,000 students were in residence. There was still no clear indication of what they would do to push for democracy.

Webster said there was one question that would have to be faced and answered. Should the United States support the demands for democratization and encourage its allies to do so, or should it sit back and watch how political dissent would develop?

There was silence in the room. Then Baker said there was no need for him to remind everyone that as little as possible must be done to disturb America's economic, political, and intelligence links with China. The secretary of state—designate then demonstrated how well he had absorbed the briefing paper Webster had circulated.

"China faces two clear problems. One: Who will take over from Deng? None of the Politburo members has the power to prevail over others in a factionalized environment. Two: The Chinese government is not strong enough to regulate the economy even if it can be tough with political unrest. That unrest could increase as the benefits from reform reach their peak and the sources of economic growth become harder to predict."

Baker than summarized the report prepared by James Laracco, the counselor for economic affairs at the United States embassy in Beijing. Baker painted a portrait of a China in the grip of low efficiency and growing inflation, currently at 30 percent, with some food items at over 100 percent. Corruption was endemic, the credibility of the Party slipping, and the threat from student-led demonstrations growing more serious.

Bush turned to Baker. "As soon as an opening arises, I want to go to Beijing." He made a chopping hand motion. "I want to sit down with Deng Xiaoping. I want to see where he's going." Another chop. "I want to see how far we can go with him."

Webster nodded. He told the room that the aged Emperor Hirohito of Japan was finally at death's door; he could only survive, at most, a few more weeks.

Bush was smiling. "Perfect. I go to the funeral, and on the way home I call in to see Deng."

He once more chopped air.


WEDNESDAY, DECEMBER 7, 1988
*Beijing*

In a tiny apartment in the north of the city, the morning routine of Kao Jyan and his mother absorbed them both. While he shaved, she pressed his olive-green uniform and burnished the stars on the collar and shoulder tabs until they gleamed as brightly as the jacket buttons. As he dressed, she prepared breakfast. While they ate, she reminded him again that no one else in the apartment block had a son in the People's Liberation Army.

Though a year had passed since it had happened, she still enjoyed telling people that he had been promoted to captain instructor at the National Defense University, and that General Zhang Zhen, its president, had personally chosen him to be one of the academy's tutors. One day, she would add, her son would be a general, as famous as old General Zhang. He was a survivor of the Long March, like her husband.

Jyan hated when people said he looked like his father, the same bony frame, eyes set deep in a long face. He preferred to think he had acquired his mother's gentle voice and caring ways. When he thought of his father nowadays, Jyan could only clearly remember his hands: calloused, broad-fingered, and practical. They had been able to mend anything. But they had been violent hands, suddenly lashing out, sending his mother and himself reeling. His father's rages had been swift and terrible right up to the day he had been killed in a road accident.

His mother recounted the respect a new neighbor had shown when she had told her about Jyan. He smiled, indulging his mother, knowing his position gave her an extra cachet on the local street committee. As long as she seemed happy, so was he. Theirs was the close relationship that often develops between a widowed mother and an only son with no girlfriend.

At twenty-seven Jyan had become the youngest instructor at the military academy Deng Xiaoping had opened in 1986. Deng had promised the campus would turn out a new kind of military professional. Its graduates would still have to understand the subtleties of Marxist-Leninist doctrine, but they must also be versed in computer sciences and information technology. Jyan lectured on military tactics in urban situations.

To celebrate his appointment, he had given his mother a Japanese radio. This morning, as usual, her twiddling with the knobs had awakened him. He had also bought the refrigerator in the corner of the living room, purchasing it from Number One Department Store in Wangfujing Street, where PLA officers receive a special discount. Another perk was his secondhand Nissan. The right to a car came with his post. The car could only be used for official business, and every week Jyan was allowed enough gasoline for the fifty-minute drive to and from the campus in the Western Hills.

Despite these signs of affluence and position, the life-style of Jyan and his mother had altered following his father's death. They had been moved to this high-rise near Coal Hill, a two-hundred-foot high man-made mound that is the highest point in Beijing. Their neighbors were factory workers, often crude and noisy, not at all like the office staff they had lived among when his father was chief assistant to Undersecretary Wang at the ministry.

The Wangs had lived a few doors from them, and in the year Shao-Yen's father arranged for her to go to film school, he had signed the papers for Jyan to enter the army. His mother had said this was the undersecretary's first move to groom him to be a husband for Shao-Yen. Until the day she left for America, his mother had hoped they would marry.

His mother was full of such romantic notions, which he found strange, because she could be so tough when sitting as a member of the street committee. She would not hesitate to order a pregnant wife to an abortion clinic or forbid a worker to transfer from one shop floor to another. But when it came to his marrying she could be quite blind, not stopping to think that the Party would never allow him to wed someone like Shao-Yen. The social gap between the families was now too wide. Her father was firmly entrenched in the upper echelons; he and his mother had slipped to within a few rungs from the bottom. Perhaps that was why Shao-Yen had not written from America. She too was now in a very different world. He accepted that. But he hoped they would always be friends. He'd wondered if his mother really understood when he said he'd be quite happy with that.

She still regarded Shao-Yen's decision to leave China as beyond her understanding. How could anyone want to give up a secure and comfortable life to live among foreigners on the other side of the world? In many ways, he knew, she found Shao-Yen as bewildering as his cousin, Sue Tung. She had also gone to California, giving up a teaching career while leaving her husband behind.

He had always found Sue a pleasant and lively woman, and he had been surprised at the man she had married, who was cold and domineering. Jyan had assumed Sue's decision to go to America was her way of ending the relationship. Usually, though, it was a husband who left his wife at home.

Sue had written regularly. Her campus life seemed as pleasant as his. He'd read her letters to his mother. Recently Sue had mentioned an American, a man she called "my Rod."

His mother said she had no business getting involved with a foreign man. The Party strongly discouraged such relationships, even for Chinese abroad, she reminded him.

Now, as she cleared the breakfast table, she announced Sue was going to get divorced. His mother often kept important news until just before he left the apartment. Satisfied she once more had surprised him, she explained her sister had telephoned with the news.

Jyan sighed. As an officer he was allowed a telephone. But it, like the car, was only to be used on official business.

His mother looked around the room, her face still unlined in a body thickened by age.

"Young people think marrying is a game. They marry carelessly and divorce lightly. Your cousin should think of what's good for the country. A strong family is a strong country."

She looked at the mantel clock by which his father had regulated his life. The morning homily was over.

Sharply at seven, Jyan left the apartment and made his way to the forecourt. Early though it was, the first of the bamboo-framed strollers, each holding a swaddled baby, were already out, parked among the pedicabs and bicycles. His was the only car.

He drove west through the morning rush hour. In another thirty minutes it would almost be impossible to move any faster than the continuous flow of massed cyclists. Passing the heavily guarded gates of Zhongnanhai, he turned onto Changan Avenue. On his left was the Great Hall of the People.

This morning Jyan would lecture junior officers on how to clear Tiananmen Square in an emergency: an earthquake, a plane crash, or a major fire in the Great Hall or one of the other buildings in the area.

Jyan had helped devise a plan for troops to be quickly moved into the square by helicopter or through the network of tunnels that led to the nuclear shelters.

He would use time flowcharts to show how an efficient military operation must be able to clear the vast square in a matter of minutes, even in rush hour. Soldiers would block off all side streets, stopping all traffic except emergency vehicles. Other troops would divide the civilians in the square into manageable groups and shepherd them to safety. It would call for close coordination and good communications. Orders would have to be obeyed without fail. Given the panic that any disaster brings, many decisions would have to be made on the spot.

Jyan had tried to think of everything, including what should happen if Tiananmen Square once more became the focus for civil unrest. He would repeat to the class the standing instruction. The army would remain uninvolved unless the disturbance became sufficiently serious to threaten the safety of the nation. Then the army would move as it would against any enemy.

SUNDAY, DECEMBER 18, 1988
*Beijing*

Cassy reminded Daobao that in a week's time it would be Christmas. As they walked among the stalls in the web of streets behind the windswept expanse of Jianquomen Avenue, he towered over her, his strong, hard-muscled body she had come to love wrapped in a topcoat he had bought in America. In his best student's voice, he recited that the 1978 constitution guaranteed people the freedom to believe or not believe in religion, but only atheism could be propagated.

She laughed, her hand brushing quickly against his, the only intimacy they dared risk in such a crowded place in broad daylight. The street committees were always active in this district; its members had the authority to arrest them for any infringement of the Party's moral code. Public affection was regarded as bourgeois even for a married couple. Between a Chinese and a foreigner such open intimacy was a sign of decadence.

The law made relationships like theirs even more difficult. No foreigner could marry a Chinese who served in the army or the political departments of the Party or who worked "with State secrets." Diplomats, interpreters, and even tourist guides were also forbidden to marry non-Chinese. All others had to get permission from their local political officer.

Daobao pointed to one of the stalls. Plastic Father Christmases could be found among the bric-a-brac imported from Hong Kong.

She said she was surprised there was a market for such trinkets. He reminded her how fervently the United States had tried to convert China to Christianity in the last century. A few million "rice-bowl Christians," people who converted for a guaranteed bowl of church food, were still scattered around China. As long as they did not proselytize, they were left alone.

They turned into a side street selling aromatic spices and roots. The air was pungent and heavy.

Daobao pointed to a sack of bark, explaining it was officially sold to strengthen vitality. But men used it to improve their sex drive, even though to do so had been forbidden since Mao had said "too much physical sex saps the revolutionary will."

They came to the butchers. There were scores of stalls, each displaying its specialty. One was festooned with necklaces of frogs, pierced through still pulsating gullets and suspended by fore and rear legs. Another displayed trays of dessicated snakes and dried seahorses. Daobao said that when they were ground together, the powder was supposed to prevent women giving birth to baby girls.

Cassy knew that for the Chinese birth is not the beginning of life, nor death its conclusion. Every new child formed another link in the endless chain of human perpetuity that stretches back further than anyone can recall and, it is fervently accepted, will continue until the end of time itself. To ensure the human chain's preservation, it was important to show respect for the dead. Traditionally, a son had always been thought better able to do so as well as ensuring the continuity of the family line.

As they walked away from the stall, Daobao said that no matter how hard the Party tried, it was impossible to shake off the prejudice against girl babies, especially in rural China. When Cassy asked what happened to them, Daobao looked uncomfortable. Finally he said many were killed at birth; those allowed to live were sold by their parents, usually when they reached puberty. The money was used for another pig or a piece of farm equipment, anything to make life easier.

She asked what happened to a girl when she was sold. Daobao breathed out slowly and said what had always happened: The child became a wife for an old man or ended up in a brothel. Cassy asked why the Party allowed this to happen. He pursed his lips and said many of the traffickers were cadres. Cassy asked how extensive the traffic was. Daobao gave another slow expulsion of breath; she had come to recognize this as a sign of his anger. The numbers ran into thousands, he said. Thousands in a year? she asked. In a month, perhaps even in a week, he replied.

"My God," she murmured, not knowing what else to say.

They walked past turtles and tortoises being carefully selected from boxes, quickly weighed, and casually dismembered. There was a stall with cages crammed with cats and kittens, mewing and scratching at the wire. Customers used sticks to poke them, trying to estimate how much meat lay beneath the fur. The stallholder expertly fished out the doomed animals and wrung their necks.

She reminded herself that what went on in the slaughterhouses of Chicago was really no different, and she tried to believe that the dogs on an adjoining stall, skinned from the neck down, their entrails in bags hanging from their necks, were no less off-putting than the sheep or pigs she had seen displayed by European butchers.

Several stalls were devoted to thrushes. Thirty or more were crammed in a cage. Further along ducks formed the display. There were hundreds of them, squashed head to tail in their cages, totally unable to move.

Beyond was a trader who had over fifty monkeys of all sizes. Despite herself, she stopped. The stallholder looked at her curiously. Daobao told her the creatures were killed for their brains. She turned away. "There are times when I wonder if I'll ever understand your people."

Daobao smiled. "There are times when I wonder if we'll ever understand ourselves."

Beyond, at the mouth of the street, a large group had gathered around a man selling footwear. Among them were Wuerkaixi and several other students.

Despite the cold, Wuerkaixi was wearing his California-style denims. He gave an all-knowing smile that at times seemed almost supercilious to Cassy. The cold had caused Wang Dan's spectacles to mist over and made him wrap his hands inside the sleeves of his padded jacket. As usual he was in debate with, among others, Liu Gang, who wore a scarf with his Western-style jacket and cords and sipped a soft drink as he listened. They all greeted Cassy politely.

She knew that all over the city little groups were meeting like this every day, and she had detected a growing confidence among them. Daobao had said the students were now too important, too well organized, for the Party to crush.

She wished she had his confidence.


MONDAY, DECEMBER 19, 1988
*Central Intelligence Agency*

Late in the afternoon, half a dozen men were in the conference room adjoining Webster's office. Each was an agency specialist on China who had come to the seventh floor to present his view on how Bush should respond when he went to Beijing.

The trip was at the top of his foreign travel agenda when he became President. From Zhongnanhai had come an indication Bush would be welcomed as an old friend. The visit would depend on the timing of the state funeral of Japan's Emperor Hirohito. Against all expectations, he was clinging to life.

A technician from the Political and Psychological Division had brought psycho profiles of China's leaders. It had been President Reagan's idea to have such evaluations videotaped, because he found film "easier to digest than the written word."

The tape of Hu Yaobang described his "emotional disappointment" and "sense of isolation" now that he was out of office.

Li Peng's video identified his supporters. Skilled editing had isolated one old face from another.

"Chen Yun. Aged eighty-four, so frail he has not appeared in public for ten months. He is moved everywhere by wheelchair," intoned the narrator as a series of computer-enhanced photographs showed a figure being wheeled beside the lake in Zhongnanhai.

Another ancient face filled the frame. "Wang Zhen. Eighty-one years old and the former deputy chief of staff of the People's Liberation Army. Today he still exercises great influence on the PLA."

The screen was filled with the face of an old woman. "Deng Yingchao, widow of Chou En-Lai, who had been Mao's prime minister. She is the adoptive mother of Li Peng."

The narration began to explore Prime Minister Li Peng's personality: "For him power and the past are synonymous. The protege of the old, they look to him to protect all they hold to be true."

Zhao Ziyang's video began with pictures of him at a podium, addressing a large audience. The narration explained, "He argues that change will be painful in the short term, but less painful than the agony China will face if there is no change."

A montage followed of crowded street scenes, window shoppers, empty factory floors, and banks with closed doors. It ended with peasants walking wearily from fields. The commentary gave meaning to the images.

"There is panic buying. Inferior goods are being bought simply as a hedge against rising prices. There have been runs on the banks in Beijing, Shanghai, and elsewhere. Factory workers have downed tools. Peasants are being paid for their crops with promissory notes that do not fall due for a year or longer."

Finally a succession of photographs showed Deng Xiaoping over the years. The commentary acknowledged him as one of the most adroit politicians on the world stage. "A manipulator, perhaps his greatest skill is being able to have others carry out his wishes. He has always been able to distance himself from the unpleasant."

Deng was shown entering the Great Hall of the People, addressing the Politburo, waving to the crowds at a rally in Tiananmen Square, saluting at a military parade, clapping at massed ranks of children passing in review. Deng always appeared pensive. The commentary suggested a reason: "He is haunted by the past. That one day, some one will try and destroy all he holds to be sacred—the Party he has fashioned in *his* image, the State he has created after *his* fashion, the China that reflects *his* image."

The screen went to black.

Webster immediately took up where the narration ended. He said that barely a year ago Deng had announced China could not survive without dictatorship, that it was essential to the country's future. Yet the freedoms Deng had allowed were now encouraging writers, artists, academics, and, above all, the country's students, to increasingly and openly debate China's future. But where did that leave Deng's commitment to dictatorship? And, if he were to exercise it, what should be Bush's response as President?

MONDAY, DECEMBER 26, 1988
*United States Embassy*
*Beijing*

In Spook City it was business as usual for the handful of CIA officers who comprised the agency's Beijing station. Most of them had spent their Christmas Day making the rounds of other missions, listening and picking up the latest information. Their travels had yielded very little, except a few hangovers.

The exception was the man the others called Tom. He had spent his Christmas on a train returning from Nanjing. Ostensibly he had gone there to address the local business community in his guise as a member of the embassy's economic staff. In reality he had visited an asset, or informer, a student at Nanjing University.

Tom deemed what he had learned sufficiently important to encrypt and transmit to Langley: The students' union at Nanjing University, until recently moribund, was once again highly active. At a recent meeting attended by several hundred students, their leaders had said the economic situation was in a mess because of mismanagement by the central government.

"In our discussions, a [Tom's asset] said that the overwhelming reaction of the meeting was there must be change and that the students must lead the way," Tom reported to Langley.

# 7

# *The Roof of the World*

FRIDAY, DECEMBER 30, 1988
*Lhasa, Tibet*

High in the mountains Bing Yang flattened himself against the frozen scree, the fur lappets on his cap secure over his ears. The cap somehow gave his peasant's face a still more determined look, making him appear rather like his brother, Li, one of the student activists at Beijing University. And, just as much as Li was a radical, so Bing had become still more of a Party idealist. The short time he had spent in Tibet had convinced him of the danger China faced from political activism of any kind.

An automatic rifle was cradled in Bing's arms. The rest of the platoon was spread across either side of the track rising from the Kyi Chu River, which marks the southern boundary of Lhasa, Tibet's capital.

At this hour, seven in the morning, the sun was still a diffuse pink behind the brooding Tangla hills. Daylight comes to Lhasa two hours later than in Beijing, four-thousand miles to the east. But in Tibet, as all over China, Beijing time prevails, a reminder that the meridians, and even the sun itself, remain obedient to the dictates of the rulers in Zhongnanhai.

Far down in the valley the bells on the yak herds tinkled. In the rarefied, crystal-clear air, sound, vision, and smell are all enhanced. With daybreak the moaning wind increased, sending spumes of snow swirling. Bing had never known such cold.

It had taken some of the soldiers days to become acclimatized. A few with persistent altitude sickness had been sent back to lower levels. But apart from a blistering headache on the first day, Bing had suffered nothing. He credited his good health to sipping green tea and breathing slowly.

They had all been told not to wash: water at this altitude irritates the skin and removes its natural oils, an essential protection against the ultraviolet rays.

The sky was so blue it appeared almost black. Across the valley the unwalled city seemed like a village, so overpowering was the massive structure towering over it. Whatever the time of day—pick dawn, blinding noon, or amethyst evening—it remained awesome and forbidding, a castle set upon a fortress set upon a mountain. Six hundred feet of sheer white walls ended in the glittering golden roofs of the Potala, once the home of the pontiff-ruler of Tibet, the Dalai Lama.

Wherever he turned, Bing's eyes were drawn back to its monstrous beauty, its thousand windows like air vents keeping it afloat. It was the most intimidating building Bing had ever seen.

He focused for the moment upon one of the mounds of enormous cabbages on the opposite riverbank. On previous mornings Tibetan women, wrapped in dark gowns, had come to take some of the vegetables, and the sound of their voices had carried clearly. Now there was only silence.

Trucks approaching the city had been halted at roadblocks in the next valley. Those attempting to leave Lhasa would be stopped by more checkpoints within the city. Lhasa was as isolated as Tibet itself, a secret, hermetic land, had been for centuries.

Everyone knew why. Everyone was waiting for the sound to return.

It came again with a suddenness that brought low "aahs" from Bing and the men around him. The roar rushed across the windswept mountains, over forested slopes, and into the deepest of the gorges. It passed over the buildings China had erected as evidence of its determination to stay: a sports stadium, a revolutionary museum, a hospital, ugly apartment blocks. The sound surged over the old city, the Parkor, where many of the buildings were fifteen hundred years old, their exterior walls and windows protected from the sun by great drapes of black yak wool. The noise seemed to fill every corner of the sky. It was the sound of jet engines at full pitch.

A mile away, over the city, the three J-5s made another sortie. Swooping in over the Pala marshes to the east, they passed just above the tops of the temples before banking and climbing over the gilded roofs of the Potala. Even at this distance the sound of the turbojets was shattering.

Bing could well imagine the panic the MIGs were causing in the narrow streets. The shock waves from their engines would be powerful enough to shake the flowerpots and set ritual bells tingling in all those deep-set window frames, each lacquered the same shiny black. He had been told the black was to ward off evil spirits. It was beyond him how people could possibly be reeducated when they believed such nonsense.

The aerial maneuvers were timed to coincide with the end of morning prayers, when thousands of red-robed monks would be emerging. The intention was to panic counterrevolutionaries into fleeing before the 27th's main sweep.

The bulk of the army was deployed along Tibet's frontier with India. From its bases there, it was conducting operations against Tibetan guerrillas. As part of this drive, units of the 27th had been sent to Lhasa, which had long been the main center of resistance.

At a signal, tanks and troops would simultaneously move from the West Gate below the Potala, down the road from the Sera monastery in the north, and out through the network of canals in the east. Street by street they would drive forward, the soldiers checking every building.

Bing and the other soldiers spreadeagled on the mountainside were positioned to block any escape to the mountains by this one route deliberately left open. Any person fleeing would be a counter-revolutionary. Anyone who resisted was to be shot. But prisoners were needed as examples to the population that resistance was futile.

The planes reformed for another run. They swooped below the jagged white mountain peaks, the rising sun behind them, so that in the town no one could see the fighters coming. They once more burst over Lhasa. In a tight roll over the river, the MIGs banked and hurtled toward the Potala. The planes' afterburners seemed to blend with the sun's rays, sending golden-red shards bouncing off the gleaming roofs.

Bing watched them vanish behind the mountains. The wind carried the sounds of panic from the town. People were running, men, women, and children, in their thick, dirty *chubas*, gownlike garments fastened at the waist with thick woolen belts. A few of the men wore Western-style jackets, the women invariably plaid head-scarves. Faces were begrimed with years of smoke from the yak-chip fires that swirled from thousands of chimneys. They were running back into the squat, white-walled buildings where they lived or worked, running just as the briefing officer had said they would. Bing continued to watch, the cold now forgotten with the prospect of action finally here.

On the train journey from Beijing, the political commissar had lectured them over the loudspeaker in every carriage about what was happening in Tibet.

He said that ever since the People's Liberation Army "liberated" Tibet in 1950, to make it "free from imperialist oppression and to consolidate the defenses of China's western borders," reactionaries had tried "to arouse the people." Many were students, who resisted all attempts to pacify them. They refused to speak Chinese and insisted upon worshiping at their shrines and temples, prostrating themselves before gods officially discredited since the country's liberation.

The center of all this religious madness was their obsessive desire to see the return of their living god, the *Kundum*, the Dalai Lama. He had fled when China occupied the country.

His supporters were well armed and dangerous. Their weapons had been discovered under cairns, only allowed to be erected in honor of local deities, and in *chortens*, burial mounds, supposed only to contain holy relics. Explosives had been found in prayer wheels and even concealed inside the felicity scarves Tibetans were still allowed to carry and exchange as symbols of reverence and respect. They were killing those Tibetans who wanted to attend the self-criticism public meetings the Party had introduced. They were murdering members of the PLA. In the past month fifty officers and men had been killed in separate incidents.

The commissar read out each name and described the manner of each death: a catalogue of shootings in the back, garrotings, knives slipped under rib cages, and bombs exploding under vehicles. The counterrevolutionaries had even entered a barracks and slit the throats of sleeping soldiers. Bing was properly horrified.

An hour after they had crossed the Yangtze into Tibet, he saw his first Tibetans. The train stopped to refuel at the foot of a valley. Halfway up its side a monastery clung to the cliffs, its white walls framed with conifers. Vultures were perched in the trees. The commissar described how Tibet's dead are left out in the open to be consumed by the huge predators.

The Tibetans struck Bing as undernourished and servile, shuffling out of his path as they murmured incantations and continuously turned the little prayer wheels in their hands. Curious, he stopped a man and asked to inspect one. The Tibetan silently handed it over. Bing saw it was a slim metal cylinder on an upright axle; a weight attached to the cylinder by a thin chain created a flywheel and made it easy to keep the wheel in motion with a movement of the hand. Inside the cylinder was a tiny scroll covered with characters. Bing handed back the wheel; the man bowed his head and walked away, rubbing the wheel to remove any trace of Bing's fingerprints.

At the monastery Bing watched pilgrims placing coins on stones and among the wool tufts on the pine trees. He felt uneasy at such piety and was nauseated by the sour smell of coagulated yak butter, used to form thousands of lamp wicks. There were statues sculpted from yet more yak butter, saints set in nests of gilded wood, and everywhere myriad-headed figures of carved godlings. Over them all rose the endless repetition of mantras and the twirling of prayer wheels.

Stuffed apes, bisons, and bears were propped against the monastery's colonnades. How, Bing asked himself, could people accept that these mangy figures had divine power? Or the living creatures many Tibetans carried, the puppies, kittens, and chattering monkeys? Animals should be eaten, not worshiped. How was it possible that the warm, brown Yangtze he had grown up alongside had its source in this strange and forbidding land?

All night the train climbed and climbed. In the darkness he stood in the corridor with Lee Gang, the brother of Liu Yang, the student at Beijing University. Lee Gang's tank was on one of the flatcars behind the carriages. It was strange, Bing mused, how siblings could be so different. Yang, with his penchant for Western-style clothes and drinking out of a can, was as unlike Lee as Bing now was from his own brother.

In the shared companionship of traveling, Bing told Lee Gang about the letter he had written to his brother before leaving Beijing, expressing concern over his growing radicalism. The young tank commander admitted he too was concerned over how university life had affected his own brother. He added that all the Party could do was try and make students see their errors. But if all else failed, they must be taught the hard lesson the 27th was being sent to administer to the reactionaries of Tibet.

Bing stared out at the icy void beyond the window. After a while he said it would be one thing to kill traitors, quite another their own flesh and blood.

Lee Gang considered. When he spoke his voice was certain. Revolutionaries could not be regarded as flesh and blood.

Bing felt an admiration for him, for his honesty, for his courage in being ready to choose between personal ties and the greater need of the national family.

They stood in silence listening to the bleating of the engine whistles, one up front, one at the rear, pulling and pushing them through the mountains, through the night, Bing hoping he would never have to discover if he had Lee Gang certainty.

Late the next day, the train stopped once more. Bing and several hundred other soldiers disembarked. Their role in the operation was explained to them by their company commander, Tan Yaobang. He had stood before them, his lean, strong face weatherbeaten, his close-cropped gray hair hidden by his fur hat. He had to shout to make himself heard above the wind. In the minutes before Tan led them into the mountains, Bing sought out Lee Gang and asked him to mail the letter to Li, counting out the money for the postage. He was increasingly anxious for Li to change his way as soon as possible. He hoped the letter, with its reminder of all the "good things" the state provided, would convince Li to give up his radical ways and those dangerous student friends.

Tan set a brisk pace, making it hard to believe he was a man in his mid-fifties. They marched through the bitter night; at dawn they found what shelter they could. When they reached their destination Tan showed them how to burrow into the ground and make sure their equipment did not catch the sun as it rose and set. He permitted no fires, and they ate only cold rations. At night Tan had moved among them quietly retelling his own experience in Korea, when he had survived for days on a bowl of rice eaten each morning in similar subzero temperatures.

Now, huddling against the scree, watching the jet fighters disappear, Bing envied Liu Lee the warmth of his T-69. Its commander had said the tank was not only equipped with the latest armaments, including a laser range-finder, but also possessed a heating system to keep out even Tibet's harsh winter.

As the MIGs returned to make a further pass, Bing focused on the opposite river bank. Several men had appeared. Some headed along a path downriver, others in the opposite direction toward the ferry crossing. There would be no escape either way. Tan had placed soldiers to intercept both tracks.

The remaining pair carried an oblong-shaped boat made of yak hide. They shoved it into the water and clambered on board. They began to row furiously, heading for directly below where Bing waited.

He released the safety catch on his gun, settling himself into a firing position. The wind sent flurries of snow whistling over the slope, momentarily obscuring his view of the river. On either side he heard the clicks of weapons being primed. From behind a rocky spur

Tan called out they should not fire unless absolutely forced to do so. They must take prisoners.

The swirling snow eased, and Bing could once more see the boat battling against the current. Over his shoulder he glimpsed Tan crawling over the ground to the next group.

From the roof of the PLA headquarters compound in the center of the city, a signal rocket soared into the sky. It burst close to the vapor trail of the jets disappearing to the north.

Bing quickly focused on the West Gate. Lee Gang's T-69 rumbled into sight. More tanks were coming from the north. Platoons of soldiers were beginning their house searches. He swung back to look at the river.

The oarsmen were halfway across, rowing steadily, expertly picking their way through the eddies and swirls. The wind clearly carried their shouts of encouragement to each other.

Downriver, an armored personnel carrier appeared. Its machine gun started to fire at the Tibetans on the path. They fell in strange, lifeless heaps. From somewhere behind, Bing heard Tan's short, furious curse. The machine gun fell silent, its traversing barrel looking for new targets.

Bing could see the oarsmen plainly now, no longer shouting, saving their energy, concentrating on rowing.

The boat was lost to view as it came beneath an overhang. The wind momentarily eased as the sun rose above the mountains.

Vultures appeared above the dead Tibetans. They wheeled in a tight circle, their cries clear above the rush of water and the sound of vehicles moving deeper into the city. The machine gun fired another short burst, and several birds plummeted into the river. The others rose ponderously into the sky, flapping back across the water to settle in the rocks around Bing. Though the nearest vulture was some distance away, its fetid smell made his nose wrinkle.

Below him was the sound of sure feet hurrying over the treacherous ground. A little distance apart, the two oarsmen were moving crabwise across the scree, expertly going from one piece of cover to another.

One of the platoon rose, pointing his rifle, shouting for the men to stop. Without breaking his stride, the first Tibetan lunged forward, the impetus of his movement driving home his dagger.

Bing saw the look of surprise on the soldier's face. Then the rifle fell from his nerveless hands, sliding down the icy slope. Even as the soldier began to buckle, the Tibetan reached to free his knife. As he did so, half a dozen guns cut him down. He dropped where he stood, his face, an arm, and a leg shattered.

Soldiers rushed to tend their wounded comrade. Bing stumbled down the scree to take the second man prisoner. He was surprised to see how young he was; he could have been no more than sixteen. His chuba was torn and his hide boots split at the seams. Bing searched him, removing a crude dagger.

Tan came sliding down the scree in a torrent of furious words. He had wanted prisoners, not corpses, he roared. A dead Tibetan was worth nothing. He hurled the corpse down the scree, where it lodged in a gnarled tree a little way above the river.

There was a sudden rush of wings as the vultures swooped on to the tree. They fought with each other over the pickings, using their wings to keep their balance. Beaks and claws dug deep into the flesh, and the constantly flapping feathers sent sprays of blood into the air.

Tan ordered Bing and two other soldiers to take the prisoner to headquarters in the town. He detailed more men to form a stretcher party. The wounded man was no longer conscious. Blood seeped through the field dressing.

The prisoner began to sob, covering his face with his hands as the birds rose into the air, carrying away their spoil.

One of the soldiers prodded the youth with his gun, motioning him to walk in front. Behind Bing came the stretcher-bearers.

Tan used his field radio to summon a jeep to meet the ferry that would take them across the river.

By the time they reached the boat the soldier was coughing gobs of blood. The bearers laid him on the open deck and packed another dressing into his wound. It did not stop the blood running out of his mouth. When the blood began to freeze on his lips, giving them a grotesque, clown-like appearance, Bing realized the man was dead.

One of the escorts turned to the prisoner and punched him on the temple so violently that the youth collapsed against Bing. Bing hauled the Tibetan to his feet, carefully positioning himself between the youth and the others. He warned them not to touch his prisoner again. To reinforce the point, he placed a finger on the safety catch of his rifle.

The rest of the journey passed in uncomfortable silence, the others staring down at the dead man, Bing watching them.

On shore, the corpse was laid on the floor of the jeep. Bing motioned the youth to get in. The others followed, squashing into the back. Horn blowing, the jeep roared through the streets. Through the windshield and the yellow celluloid windows of the canvas sides, Bing could see the mounting panic. Soldiers were everywhere, driving the population before them.

The jeep roared across a bridge, past the guards at the entrance of the 27th Army headquarters, and onto the parade square.

Hours later, Bing continued to watch the square, known as the People's Ground, as it steadily filled with Tibetans. They had been assembling all morning under the watchful eyes of the soldiers. By noon, he calculated, there must have been over a thousand present.

Bing's prisoner stood on a loading platform in front of a large building with a beam and pulley used to haul grain and other supplies.

Bing stood with two other soldiers to one side of the platform. Pinned to its front was a bright red banner bearing the words JUSTICE IS THE PEOPLE'S RIGHT.

At a table on the platform sat PLA officers. Two Bing only knew by sight. The third was Lee Gang. Near him was the political commissar who had addressed the troops on the train journey. He continued to harangue the crowd as he pointed to the prisoner. This reactionary had tried to kill those who were there to protect them. He had betrayed the ideals in which they all believed.

The commissar walked over to stand beside the youth. With one hand he reached forward and twisted the boy's face toward the crowd. This was their enemy, he screamed. Bing saw the soldier operating the loudspeaker system frantically adjusting the amplifier as the commissar's voice rose. This was the enemy of the people! The commissar was drowned by a howl from the speakers.

He thrust the microphone toward the youth's face and demanded a confession. The boy kept his head bowed. No sound came from the crowd. Liu Lee leaned forward and, in a sharp and peremptory voice, ordered the prisoner to confess.

The youth admitted he was a counterrevolutionary who had obtained arms from the imperialists and was the enemy of the Tibetan and Chinese peoples. When he had delivered his admission he stood with head lowered.

The commissar turned back to the crowd. They had heard him. What did they have to say?

Bing saw the Tibetans looking uneasily at each other, bowing their heads, murmuring softly. The commissar pointed to a woman near the front. What did she have to say, he demanded. Bing had seen the commissar speaking to the woman earlier. In a trembling voice she said the youth had committed crimes against Tibet.

The commissar scanned the crowd, alighting on a man; Bing had seen the commissar address him earlier too. The man gave the same answer as the woman. Twice more the commissar picked out people in the crowd who responded similarly. The woman was speaking again. The youth must die for betraying Tibet.

The cry was taken up by others.

Bing watched the commissar marching back and forth across the platform, extending his microphone toward the crowd so that it could pick up the shouts.

Suddenly, like the water gushing through a dam Bing had seen burst on the Yangtze, everyone was shouting in a sudden and unstoppable rush. The prisoner must die for betraying Tibet! The commissar raised his hand. The crowd fell obediently silent. He turned and faced the trio at the table. One by one the judges gave their verdict.

The commissar signaled for Bing and the other soldiers to climb onto the platform. When they had done so, he went to the rear of the platform and fetched a coiled rope with a noose already fashioned at one end. He gave his instructions quickly.

One soldier balanced on the shoulders of another to secure the rope to the beam. The noose dangled several feet above the youth's head. With Bing supporting the youth's feet, the other soldier forced his head into the noose. Until this moment he had not struggled. Now he began to thrash, fighting to break free of the hands that were preventing him from dying.

The silent crowd watched the contortions. Then, as the exhausted youth grew still, the commissar stepped forward and tapped the soldiers with his microphone. One by one they stepped back. The body started to turn slowly in the wind.


SATURDAY, DECEMBER 31, 1988
*Beidaihe, China*

Shortly after dawn the helicopters lifted out of Zhongnanhai and into a sky the color of sturgeon. Each was filled with members of the Politburo. In loose formation the armada headed east into a sky made even grayer by the smoke from kilns and factories.

Soon the helicopters passed near the industrial coal-mining city of Tangshan. Thirteen years ago many of the leaders had flown there to inspect the damage after one of the worst earthquakes to strike China. Over two hundred thousand had been left dead, a million injured, and four million homeless. Now a new industrial colossus once more stood on the uncertain earth, the pollution from its thousand factories and coal-processing plants blotting out the horizon.

This morning the old men had other thoughts to preoccupy them. They had been summoned at short notice by Deng Xiaoping. For the past week China's supreme ruler had been resting at Beidaihe after another course of chemotherapy, an attempt to halt his slowly progressing cancer. Over the past year, Deng had recuperated between treatments at the coastal resort used only by the Party elite.

An hour after leaving Beijing, the helicopters descended over Beidaihe, passing over the imposing villas and wide streets lined with hibiscus and oleanders.

The resort had been built by the British for their diplomats at the turn of the century as an escape from the stifling heat of Beijing in July and August. Forty years of Communist occupation had not removed an atmosphere of empire. The landscape was dotted with mock Tudor residences and bungalows that looked as if they had been transported from the south coast of England. Beyond their guarded perimeters surged a sea as leaden as the English Channel in winter.

Deng's mansion stood on a headland to the north of the resort. The helicopters settled close to waiting limousines, and the Politburo members were driven to a conference hall.

When they were seated in heavy red-covered armchairs, replicas of those used for Politburo meetings in Zhongnanhai, Deng explained he had summoned them to hear the arguments for and against keeping China on its present economic course.

For the rest of the day, the room echoed to increasingly angry and divisive debate. Familiar positions were restated. Prime Minister Li Peng and his supporters insisted that "bourgeois liberalism" was undermining the very patriotism and socialist values on which the country depended for its future. Party Secretary Zhao Ziyang reiterated that with economic reforms must come new freedoms.

The arguments raged to and fro. Li Peng argued that the ability of the state to regulate the economy had been fundamentally weakened as a result of the decentralization of the "economic decision-making power." Zhao countered that the real problem was the failure to curb the corruption that continued to erode Party authority, something he too did not wish to happen.

Figures were bandied around the room. The population was increasing at an average of twelve million a year. Every twelve months the number of people China had to feed increased by more than the population of New York, Los Angeles, or London. Yet now there was already an "excess of unemployed," 180 million manual laborers alone. Li Peng conceded they represented an "explosive problem" to the central government that was getting worse as the number of unemployed in urban areas grew.

Zhao insisted the only way to solve the problem was to create a virtually new political-economic system, one that would open its doors to Western ideas.

Do that, rasped Li Peng, and China's "ideological purity will be contaminated." The time had come to curb the "liberal economic reform policy" and be ready to face the consequences. If that meant dealing firmly with unrest, so be it.

Late in the afternoon, Deng addressed the factions. In a long and rambling speech, he reviewed what had been said. He seemed to veer toward one point of view, then another. Finally he announced he wanted Zhao Ziyang to modify his policies; perhaps, after all, they had been too liberal, too early.

Li Peng had won a crucial victory.

# 8

# *Persuasion*

Sunday, January 1, 1989
*Beijing*

Cassy wore a thickly padded jacket against the biting cold. Similarly clad, Daobao and Yang Li cycled on either side, leading her unerringly through the alleys as they headed diagonally across the city on this New Year's Day morning.

The two students from time to time smiled reassurance at her. Daobao said again in his soft voice that there was nothing for her to worry about. She was just another foreign expert being shown around the back streets of Beijing by her students. Li nodded.

They emerged from a *hutong*, an alley, crossed an avenue broad enough to accommodate a passenger plane, and entered another lane of gray brick walls and doors made of tin or wood. Every *hutong* seemed to lead a self-contained existence; each had its small factories, shops, and restaurants. They maneuvered past handcarts stacked with produce. The already narrow and crowded alley was further constricted by tiny stalls set up in doorways. In the courtyards beyond, Cassy glimpsed pots and trays and window boxes: Anywhere seeds could be germinated, they were. Daobao explained that several families used one yard to grow produce or raise ducks. They shared a stall to sell their products and divided the profits.

Li had not spoken since breakfast, when he read them Bing's letter reciting the benefits the state provided and attacking student radicalism. When he finished, he folded the letter carefully and put it back in its envelope. Then he took a match and set fire to the paper, shielding the flames with his hands so the fire did not spread.

Cassy wanted to say that burning the letter would change nothing, that his pain would only go away when he could sit down with Bing and talk about their differences. But in the past weeks Li's whole attitude had changed. Even toward his girlfriend, Meili, he appeared distant, as if he wanted no one to get really close to him, nobody to know what he was really thinking.

Daobao said it was because Li was now one of the student movement's strategists. He had sounded so serious; Cassy had managed not to smile. True, the students were meeting in increasing numbers to air their grievances, but she still found little to suggest they were a cohesive movement. They seemed to be separate groups, most with no designated leader, although Wuerkaixi and Wang Dan often articulated the views of one group to another.

In these past weeks Cassy had walked with them through the streets and alleys, listening as they discussed the need for free speech and increased funding for education and teachers' salaries. None of these demands had struck her as representing a properly developed political theory, let alone a detailed blueprint for change. She had thought again they sounded so very young, so very trusting.

No one seemed to be thinking where all this was leading. Yet whenever she expressed a doubt, Daobao brushed aside her fears with the same certainty she had seen him show when boosting the confidence of others. At times it struck her that Daobao really believed he could shift the bureaucratic balance simply by repeating that one word often enough, *democracy*. It was as if the word had assumed magical proportions for Daobao, and he wanted everyone else to share that magic. He had told her he wanted to use democracy to "only destroy the bad and make even better all that is good in our society."

In pursuit of this vision, Daobao and Li had suggested she should make this long bicycle ride with them. Daobao said the diplomatic corps was bound to turn out in force to attend the New Year's Day concert in the Jianguo Hotel, and no one would be surprised at her presence, or when she introduced her companions. Foreign experts were always showing off their favorite students to other foreigners. Li had given her his half-smile. Sometimes it could be quite intimidating, she decided.

They pedaled through the street markets, tiny islands of capitalism, the air filled with the shrill of barter and the warble of birds carried in cages. She still had not grown used to the way an old man would hold a cage close to his face and trill to an imprisoned lark or finch. Girls with too much lipstick, and old women walking arm in arm, stared at her, not quite believing a foreigner was among them.

Cassy thought about the careful way Li watched the sudden moments of tension between Wuerkaixi and Wang Dan. Wuerkaixi was increasingly the swashbuckling go-getter, Dan the same reserved student she saw in class. He would not be rushed into anything. Li, she suspected, was trying to decide who would eventually win this battle of wills.

He maintained the same careful approach to Liu Gang. The physics student had thinning hair and rounded shoulders, giving him a scholarly appearance. She wondered if Gang's choice of Western-style sports clothes and drinking from a can was a conscious attempt to balance his seriousness.

Entering another *hutong*, Daobao said this was where the Cultural Revolution had actually started. The Red Guards had come straight from Tiananmen Square to destroy the eleven silk-weaving factories that had been in the alley for centuries.

She asked why they had done that.

He looked pained. Because they had been told to. Didn't she think that was the great national failing of the Chinese, that they always did what they were told?

She glanced at Li. He was staring resolutely ahead. There was no way of knowing what he was thinking.

Daobao pointed out men lounging outside the Exhibition Center. They were *Gonganbu*, the footsoldiers of the Ministry of Public Security, on the lookout for any suspicious contact between foreigners and Chinese inside the cavernous hall. It was one of the places, he said, where homosexuals risked breaking the law to meet. The *Gonganbu* received a special commendation for every one they caught.

She said she found the idea of rewards for arrests genuinely shocking.

Daobao shook his head. Homosexuality was still a serious crime. Last year Pang Yi, suspecting one of the teachers was homosexual, had arranged for the *Gonganbu* to send two men to pose as students. They came to class and slept in a dormitory for almost a whole semester, until they caught the teacher. He had been giving good grades to certain students in return for sex. Daobao said the man had been "put up on the board."

She had seen the public notice boards with photographs of offenders standing handcuffed between policemen. She asked what happened to the teacher.

Daobao took his time to answer. He said the man had been executed.

Cassy was too stunned to speak. Finally she asked what had happened to the students.

Daobao sighed and explained they were sent to a labor camp.

They pedaled in silence the length of a *hutong* before he returned to the subject, saying the Chinese were a very traditional people, especially about sex.

They entered another warren of alleys. Daobao pointed to a large, concrete-walled building ahead. The blinds on its ground-floor windows were drawn. A ramp sloped from the closed front door. Two cars were parked illegally on the sidewalk. Their blue-suited chauffeurs stood smoking and talking, ignoring passers-by. Daobao dismounted; the others followed.

Cassy asked what was in the building. Daobao told her to be patient. He and Li continued to watch the door.

It swung open. A man in a shapeless gray uniform emerged and called to the chauffeurs. Stamping out their cigarettes, they hurried into the building. They emerged with two trolleys stacked with chickens, sides of meat, boxes of fish, and crates of fresh vegetables and fruits. With them was a middle-aged woman, dressed incongruously in a bright blue tracksuit and fur jacket. Her feet were encased in expensive calf-length boots.

When the man in the gray suit reached the cars, he darted forward and opened the rear door of one. Without a glance or a word to anyone, the woman slid in. The flunky closed the door and rushed to help the chauffeurs load the second car. They drove off, and the man quickly wheeled the trolleys back into the building. The door closed behind him.

Daobao turned to Cassy. "You have just seen privilege at work. Politburo members come here and take away stuff by the carload. It's all subsidized. A whole pig costs about the same as a few ounces of pork in the shops. A crate of whiskey less than a bottle."

The familiar tension was back in his voice. He nodded toward the building.

"This place is filled with the very best from all over the world. You can even get prawns here every day."

The tension made Daobao's face stiffen. Cassy knew prawns were a luxury available to ordinary Chinese only on New Year. Li mounted and pedaled away. They followed him.

There were several similar stores, Daobao explained. One stocked the latest foreign videos, another current bestsellers from New York and London. Each book was marked *Nei-bu*, restricted, meaning it could only be read by the purchaser or his or her immediate family.

Some shops sold only the newest fashions from Paris, others, objets d'art from around the Pacific. One store stocked furniture from as far afield as Canada and Bavaria. Another offered the most up-to-date sports equipment.

It was privileges like these the students wished to change, Daobao said. Trotsky had been right when he said all revolutions started for the same reason: because some people had an unfair advantage.

Cassy reminded him Trotsky had also said those who started revolutions often had no clear aims or leadership. Daobao replied Trotsky had also written it was enough to have a common hostility against the existing regime. She saw the half-smile was back on Li's lips.

They crossed the broad expanse of Dongdan Street. Daobao pointed to an open doorway with strips of silver tinsel pinned to its lintel. Men and women were walking under the decoration into the building. "They've decided they want to get married. So they come to a place like this. The Party operates hundreds of marriage bureaus around the country," Daobao said.

Li broke his long silence. "The Party encourages marriages between people who have the correct political outlook and are prepared to work together for society." He gave *correct* and *together* a mocking obeisance.

"Until quite recently the Party had the total right to decide if a couple were suitable for each other. Now it just 'advises.' You'd be surprised how many take that advice because they don't want to make what the Party calls a 'mistake.'"

Passing the bureau's door, Cassy glimpsed a room filled with men and women sitting on hard-back chairs. A couple of middle-aged women emerged, giggling softly to each other, clutching forms in their hands.

Daobao called out to ask if they had found husbands. They looked at him, startled. Then they hurried away, their confusion plain. He grinned at Cassy.

"My cousin met her husband at one of these places. She was fat and fifty and no man in her village would look at her. She had teeth like this." Daobao bared his gums in imitation of a rabbit chewing. "The bureau matched her with somebody twenty years older. All they had in common was that he had the same kind of teeth!"

They separated outside the Friendship Store on the corner of Ritan Road. Li had insisted it was a risk for them to go together to the hotel; the *Gonganbu* were bound to be out in force there, looking for foreigners. They would meet her in the lobby. Cassy thought again that China hadn't changed since the time of the emperors: It remained a country where mystery is a cult and suspicion a religion.

As she parked her bicycle in the hotel forecourt, two agents gave her a quick look before turning back to note the numbers of cars with diplomatic plates. They did so openly. She wondered if this was another of those petty exercises of authority for its own sake.

After checking her coat, she went to the lobby. Its carpets were Indian, the furniture from half a dozen countries, and the staff recruited from the *hutongs* and sent through a hotel school. The Jianguo was intended to give its guests a feeling of familiarity, that this could be any hotel anywhere.

The lobby was set up for the regular Sunday morning concert. Tables were crowded together; those near the door were mostly occupied by Chinese managers and foreign technicians.

The managers sat primly straight, blinking about them, smiling politely at some booming remark delivered in the thick accent of central Europe. The technicians were dressed as if they had come straight from the factory floor, wearing tieless shirts and heavy jackets and trousers. Slavic-faced women were smothered in makeup and laughed a lot among themselves, matching their men beer for beer. The Chinese invariably sipped soft drinks.

The tables in the center were occupied by Western and Hong Kong businessmen dressed in sober suits like their Chinese guests'. Their women were smartly dressed and coiffeured and smiled at one another a great deal while the men sat with heads close together, concentrating on completing a deal or settling a contract. For them the lobby was another office.

Between potted palms at one end of the room, the orchestra tuned up. The half dozen rows of molded plastic chairs facing them were already full.

Cassy recognized familiar faces. The Greek ambassador was deep in conversation with the Italian ambassador. She had met them at a social evening at the French embassy. A few seats away, the Hungarian first secretary sat beside his counterpart from Sweden. The two diplomats had arrived in Beijing at the same time as she had. Cassy had told Daobao she knew probably a dozen envoys. That had given Li the idea to come here with her.

He and Daobao were standing near the bar. She waved at them and began to edge past the tables, heading into the room. They moved across the lobby toward her.

She recognized Raymond Burghardt, the counselor for political affairs, and his wife, Susan, the First Secretary Billy Huff and his

wife, Lorraine, at the American embassy table. Burghardt was
talking to a florid-faced man with heavy jowls at an adjoining table.
The others seated there were listening respectfully to the conversation. The man nodded in an oddly pedantic way.

"That's Troyanovsky, the Soviet ambassador. Last year he gave us a
talk on diplomacy," Daobao murmured behind her.

Cassy was close enough now to hear Burghardt asking about the
prospects for a Sino-Soviet summit. Troyanovsky was saying it was
too early to know, but he'd heard that Bush was planning to visit
Beijing soon after he was inaugurated. Burghardt smiled and said
advance men from Washington had flown in a few days earlier to
conduct a preliminary reconnaissance.

This time Li spoke. "The one with jug ears next to the ambassador.
That's Boris Kovik. Don't be fooled by his smile. He's KGB. Always
hanging around the campus."

Nearby a group with distinctly English accents were ordering
more drinks. Among them was Brian Davidson. The tall, fair-haired
young diplomat was the press attaché at the British embassy.

Burghardt was saying he'd heard that Deng Xiaoping's doctors
were starting a new course of chemotherapy. Troyanovsky said the
drug was Russian.

Cassy realized the lobby was a familiar place for them all, one for
exchanging information, for checking, verifying, or discounting
rumors.

Li looked at Cassy and then toward a table that still had several
vacant places. A couple of men sat toying with beers. One was
strongly built with a clear complexion and an honestly happy smile.
The other was solemn-faced with thick spectacles.

Cassy smiled at him, pointing at the vacant chairs and raising
three fingers.

The man nodded.

Cassy walked over to the table with Li and Daobao. She introduced
herself and then the students.

The bespectacled man said he was Brendan Ward, second secretary at the Irish embassy, and his companion was Ian McGuinness, a
plant manager with Siemens.

Ward ordered a waiter to bring drinks. Li sat next to the diplomat.
As if it were the most natural thing in the world to say, he told Ward
how very fortuitous it was he had met him, as he was planning a term
paper on Ulster. One of the many issues he wanted to deal with was
the Irish Republican Army's use of hunger strikers to make a political
point. How, asked Li, did the strikers prepare themselves for fasting
to death?

Ward looked at him quizzically. But before he could reply, the orchestra began its opening number.

As they settled to listen Cassy saw Li's half-smile again. She suspected it was there because she had maneuvered the introduction he had wanted.


MONDAY, JANUARY 2, 1989
*Central Intelligence Agency*

At the first 9:00 A.M. staff meeting of the new year, Webster and his senior aides considered the Politburo meeting at Beidaihe. The National Security Agency had put together a full account. NSA staff supplement the work of CIA officers operating undercover from U.S. embassies and carry out the majority of eavesdropping operations abroad, regularly providing verbatim transcripts from high-level foreign government meetings.

Part of the report had come from satellite surveillance and the agency's own ultrasecret and state-of-the-art collection technology. Some of the details had been confirmed by the National Reconnaissance Office, the low-profile agency with special responsibility for what its brief only called "other overhead intelligence gathering." This included the use of not only satellites but also spyplanes. The NRO reported primarily to the secretary of defense. In practice, Webster controlled their activities. A portion of the report had been marked SCI, for Sensitive Compartmented Information, indicating that its content was especially sensitive and would only be seen by those on the BIGOT list, still only a handful in the incoming Bush administration.

Many questions were being discussed at the staff meeting: Would Party Secretary Zhao Ziyang become increasingly isolated? Or would he try even harder to push through his reforms? And if he did, would he appeal for public support? Would he continue, for instance, to use newspapers such as the *World Economic Herald* to promote his ideas? Published in Shanghai, the paper now had an influence far beyond the city. It was read in all the capitals of the world and recognized as an advocate for reform.

Would Prime Minister Li Peng, secure in his new power, simply ignore Zhao? Or would he take the first real opportunity to attack him publicly at the next meeting of the National People's Congress, China's parliament? It would be dangerous for the prime minister to do this and then discover that an insufficient number of delegates supported him. That would seriously damage Li Peng's credibility. It could even make Deng think again about supporting his prime minister in a power play against Zhao.

Fang Lizhi, the most astute of China's intellectuals and a physicist hailed as the country's Sakharov, had once more put his huge authority behind the call for human rights. Fang's strategies had underpinned the 1986–87 student political protests. As a result he had been dismissed as vice-president of the University of Science and Technology at Hefei. But because of his worldwide reputation, no other action had been taken. Fang had continued to run a highly vocal campaign for change from his Beijing apartment. An old friend of Zhao's, he demanded much that echoed the Party secretary's beliefs. The day of the Beidaihe meeting Fang had written to Deng asking that he release all political prisoners. "Without the right to express democracy, there can be no development," he had concluded.

If Fang had made the appeal with Zhao's full approval, that undoubtedly placed the Party secretary openly in sympathy with student demands and must surely further encourage their militancy. With Fang behind them, and Zhao behind him, would the students want to translate their demands into action?

Webster's analysts said that if they did, the most likely day they would choose was the coming May 4, the seventieth anniversary of an important date in China's recent history.

On May 4, 1919, four-thousand students had marched into Tiananmen Square, protesting China's humiliation at the peace conference in Versailles. The victors of the First World War had decided that Japan, not China, should receive Germany's former territories on the Chinese coast. The students had chanted that China's humiliation was the result of a corrupt political system.

The May the Fourth Movement, the first recorded organized student protest in China, had swiftly grown to challenge the country's entire educational and social system. That summer too Beijing had echoed with the call for unprecedented political change, an end to China's feudal rule and the introduction of rule by law. The chant for "democratic reform" had been heard in Tiananmen Square for weeks.

The protest had eventually led to the birth of the Communist Party, and May 4 had remained a highly emotive celebration in the Party calendar. But recently Deng had tried to play down its importance. His focus was on the coming October, the fortieth anniversary of the founding of the Chinese state.

Yet Webster and his staff knew that May 4 would prove critical, given the current mood of China's students.

It fell on the eve of the forthcoming Sino-Soviet summit; Gorbachev could find himself in Beijing in the middle of student upheavals. Would he want to postpone his historic meeting with Deng until Beijing's house was in order? Or would he use the student protests for his own purposes, to push the idea that even in China, Communism must change?

It would be unthinkable for Deng to cancel the May 4 celebration. But could he control it? And would Zhao use the occasion to invite further reforms? Would the students echo his demands? Would the Party secretary be ready to set the youth on a path that could plunge China into chaos? Would Hu Yaobang emerge to support them? And how would the protest be stopped? What would the Army do? The commander of the 27th Army was still canvassing support from Tibet for his fellow commanders in China to take a strong line with any future unrest. Would he succeed?

Webster wanted as many answers as possible before Bush went calling on Deng.

He told his staff the key to China's future could once more be in the hands of young people who almost certainly did not understand the responsibilities they had. In every contact the agency had with them, the director stressed, absolutely nothing must be done to encourage them to believe the United States would do anything to support their aims.

# 9

## Camelot, Almost

FRIDAY, JANUARY 6, 1989
*Beijing*

Professor Guangzu waited outside the main hospital entrance for the car to collect him for dinner with Hu Yaobang. He wore a dark Mao jacket and a tieless white shirt closed to the top button. In an inside coat pocket was a slim case holding a set of acupuncture needles. He never went anywhere without them.

At the end of his last lecture of the day he had reminded his students to do the same. Several had smiled indulgently. Attitudes had changed since he was a student.

Over Tiananmen Square the fog was suspended like a false ceiling into which the colonnades of the Great Hall of the People, the Monument of the People's Heroes, and Mao's mausoleum abruptly disappeared. On the other side of Changan Avenue, he could just make out the huge portrait suspended from Tiananmen Gate, Mao's coal-black eyes staring with an intensity that seemed to send the mist swirling uneasily.

For centuries the gate had been the epicenter of authority. Beyond lay the old Imperial palaces, the Forbidden City, from which the emperors had ruled, convinced their moated domain was the very center of the universe and themselves divinely blessed to govern. They had rarely gone beyond the high palace walls, content to have their proclamations read from the balcony of the Gate of Heavenly Peace.

Almost forty years before, Professor Guangzu had stood with over a million other people before this imperial relic and listened to Mao promise a new China. Instead there had been brutality, waste, and terrible personal suffering.

Deng Xiaoping had finally said he would end all that. He had tried; no one would deny that. But he had failed; how could he not? The factional battles; the "struggle between two lines," as the battle between the hardliners and moderates had once been called; the arrest of Mao's widow, Jiang Qing, and her three leftist comrades, forever to be vilified as the Gang of Four; the endless turmoil within the Party and government; the removal of Hu from office: All this had created apathy, cynicism, and fear.

Hu's firing as Party secretary had been a particular blow to liberal political reforms. Despite his puny size and a penchant for coloring his hair black and sometimes wearing outmoded "Kipper-style" neckties, Hu had been respected by both the students and the uneducated masses. They saw him as a politician with only China's best interests at heart. Yet he had been sacrificed by Deng in a carefully calculated move for Deng to remain in office. Not for the first time had the ultimate ruler of China shown he could be both highly manipulative and malevolent. In removing Hu, Deng had added to his own reputation as the Great Survivor, the man who had himself survived three political purges and lived virtually on a diet of dog meat and sixty extra-strong Panda cigarettes a day, and to hell with what his doctors said about exacerbating his cancer.

Yet despite Deng's promise to modernize, the idealism, the energy, and the almost messianic fervor that had imbued the early years of Communism were no longer there. No matter how hard Deng tried to rekindle the enthusiasm of the people for a political system, it continued to lose what remained of its original appeal.

Professor Guangzu knew that part of the reason was the country's plodding bureaucracy, the system that allowed petty officials to demand full explanations for every yuan that was spent. That attitude stifled even the most energetic of the young and spread resentment.

Some of his own students were now politically active. He had heard them talking of the need to clear their minds of "outdated" Marxist dogma and saying that "complete Westernization" was the only way to modernize. They attacked the absence of human rights. Many spoke with a passion that surprised him; medical students had never been at the forefront of protest. It had made him wonder what the student engineers and economists, the traditional activists, must be saying.

At the heavily guarded western gate to Zhongnanhai one of the sentries checked Professor Guangzu's name against a master list.

Then the barrier was raised and the car drove slowly into a broad driveway close to the lake.

Hu's home was at the southern end, its roof low and sloped and finished with traditional tiles. Lanterns were suspended from the carport. A security man rose from his chair in a corner and came forward, nodding deferentially as Professor Guangzu alighted.

Hu opened the richly lacquered front door. He was dressed in a dark Western-style suit that hung on him incongruously, his wrists sticking several inches below the cuffs. His hair gleamed unnaturally black from a recent dyeing. Behind stood his wife, Li Zhao, a small trim woman with her long hair, still naturally black, coiled in a bun. She wore a full-length dress with a high mandarin collar. To Professor Guangzu, she always looked like a dowager empress.

They greeted him warmly and led him in to dinner, not to the large dining room on the left of the hallway reserved for more formal entertaining, but to a small room opposite where the family ate. Its walls were hung with photographs of Hu as Party secretary, with foreign leaders such as President Nixon and Prime Minister Thatcher. There was also a framed piece of Mao's calligraphy. Written on the Long March, it had been a wedding gift to Madame Hu.

The table was set with Chinese red-and-white porcelain. The family cook had prepared the food and stood ready to serve it.

Professor Guangzu was the only guest; the Hus rarely entertained nowadays.

The meal was simple but delicious: hot-sour soup followed by roast duck, grilled fish, and a dessert made from almond paste. Tea was served with each course.

While they ate, Hu delivered a discourse on various newspaper articles that had appeared in that day's *People's Daily*. He said it was not enough for Zhao Ziyang to predict that soon two-thirds of the country's economy would be outside state control. That still meant almost a third was in the hands of no fewer than 107 separate government departments. These were overstaffed and inept, Hu continued. What was needed, he added, was the "kind of housecleaning that regularly occurs in the West." There senior managers were fired when they failed; in China they were given more staff to create further chaos.

The more he spoke, the more excitable he became, half-rising from his chair, waving his hands to emphasize a point, his face purple, a vein throbbing in his temple. The sight alarmed Professor Guangzu.

Pausing only to drink tea, Hu switched direction.

That afternoon, he explained, he had attended a Politburo meeting where Qiao Shi, the country's intelligence chief, had again warned that the students were beginning to "mobilize seriously." Hu described how Qiao Shi had identified the student ringleaders including Wuerkaixi, Wang Dan, and Chai Ling.

Hu deftly sketched portraits of the leaders. Wuerkaixi, born in remote Turkestan, the son of a local Party official. The former Party secretary growled, Wuerkaixi had all the fervor of one of those born-again Christians Hu had seen on TV. And he didn't like the way Wuerkaixi aped American dress! The professor smiled. Tonight, Hu was dressed like a Wall Street broker.

Wang Dan was the steadying hand among the students, Hu went on. And he put up with no nonsense from the flamboyant Wuerkaixi. Chai Ling's elfin face masked a true revolutionary's mind; if she had been on the Long March, she would have commanded a woman's battalion. Hu remembered Liu Gang from the last student protests in 1986–87, which had finally led to Deng dismissing Hu for speaking up for the students.

Among them, the dozen or so key student leaders had the intellect and determination to effectively mobilize the campuses.

Professor Guangzu sensed Hu's enthusiasm for what the students were doing—creating an atmosphere of growing confrontation with the authorities.

Among the latest demands the student leaders were circulating around the campuses was that the incomes and assets of every member of the Politburo and their relatives be made public. Hu said he had not been surprised this demand had brought angry protests from many of his fellow Politburo members: A number of them had substantial deposits in Swiss bank accounts and, through their families, considerable investments in stock markets around the world.

Qiao Shi had told the Politburo that the students wanted the ban on street marches lifted and the right to have their demands fully reported in the press. This had produced even angrier murmurs, which had further increased when Hu had intervened.

Professor Guangzu asked what his host had said.

Hu smiled his impish, garden-gnome smile: He had told the Politburo that the student demands were reasonable. There had been an uproar. Cadres had shouted at him from all sides.

And Deng, asked Professor Guangzu, how had Deng responded?

Hu shook his head. Deng had just sat there following the debate, saying not a word.

And Zhao Ziyang?

Hu sounded almost resentful. Zhao had also sat there and said nothing, not even when Qiao Shi had stood up and insisted he should now be allowed to arrest the student leaders. The intelligence chief had remained on his feet staring fixedly at Deng.

Professor Guangzu asked about Deng's reaction.

Hu looked around the table, drawing on an imaginary cigarette in a passable imitation of Deng. After a while Deng had motioned Quio to be seated and then said that the students should be allowed to go on making their plans, Hu reported. That had produced further murmurs. Deng had waved for silence. Then he had said, "When we know who they all are and what they all want, we can deal with them."

Hu slumped further in his seat, once more imitating Deng smoking.

Professor Guangzu asked what Zhao had said to that.

Hu raised a finger to his lips: nothing. When it came to the students, he continued, there was something about Zhao he no longer trusted. If it suited him, his successor as Party secretary would sacrifice them just as ruthlessly as Deng had done for his own survival.

"Survival," Hu said in his high-pitched voice. "That is all they are concerned with."

Hu began to speak with passion. The students could continue to count on his total support; through him they could reach the very core of government, even Deng himself. Once more half out of his chair, his excitement plain, Hu said that despite Deng's decision to ease up on reforms, matters had progressed too far; expectations had been raised that could not be lowered.

Madame Hu rose to her feet and gently but firmly pushed her husband back into his seat, the way a mother might deal with an overexcitable child. Hu smiled sheepishly at her. Waiting until she had resumed her place, he continued more calmly. Deng had created a trap for himself: In ordering limited economic freedoms he had misjudged the mood of the people, who wanted full political freedom.

Hu once again began to rise from his chair. His wife turned toward him, shaking her head.

This time he ignored her. He said that if the people didn't get what they wanted, they would fight for it. Not just the students but all the people.

Hu sank back in his chair, staring in turn at each of them. His voice solemn, he promised he would lead the fight from within the Politburo.

SATURDAY, JANUARY 14, 1989
*Beijing University Campus*

Late in the afternoon, from a window in Daobao's dormitory block, Cassy watched the students converging on the barracks-like building. Behind her, close to a hundred already sat on beds and on the floor and leaned against the walls. The air was foggy from cigarette smoke.

Daobao, Cassy was glad to see, had managed to kick the smoking habit. She could observe him at the far end of the room, standing tall and still, only his eyes taking in the steady stream of newcomers.

The dark-skinned Yang Li and his pale girlfriend, Meili, were among the other student leaders. Standing with Daobao, Li had confided to Cassy a few days ago that when "this is all over" he hoped to marry Meili and take her back to his home on the banks of the Yangzte River. Cassy had privately wondered how the daughter of a middle-class family would blend into the hard village life.

Li's words, "when this is all over," reminded Cassy how far the students seemed determined to push for reform. This meeting was the latest in a number of gatherings in which the student leaders had promoted their demands.

Daobao had constructed a makeshift platform by resting planks on lockers laid on their sides. Wang Dan was gingerly testing his weight on the boards. He wore another of his seemingly unlimited supply of sweatshirts.

Outside the building, Cassy could see the students Wuerkaixi had ordered be posted to signal a warning in case Pang Yi or any other of the political officers should show up. In that event the student leaders would switch back to discussing the ostensible purpose of the meeting, science and art within the framework of the state.

When the dormitory was completely filled, students sat on each other's laps. Some of the girls perched on top of bedside lockers or curled up on window ledges.

Daobao had reserved a place for Cassy to one side of the platform. Satisfied it would hold his weight, Wang Dan raised his hand for silence.

He immediately launched a withering attack on the economic policies of the central government. He called it an economy where "everyone sells and buys but no one creates anything."

Other speakers followed, decrying "the dead hands" controlling policies that were designed "to improve only their own fortunes."

Finally, Wuerkaixi rose.

He flashed the all-knowing smile that had become as much his trademark as the California-made denims he wore like a uniform.

Cassy had to admit, when Wuerkaixi had the floor he was electrifying. Every gesture seemed perfectly timed; every flick of the eyes, pause, and inflection proclaimed him either a carefully rehearsed, or a born, orator.

He spoke fiercely about the leadership's luxurious life-style. His voice trembling with anger, Wuerkaixi began to describe how the leaders, "not satisfied with their own embezzlement, encourage their children to pillage our nation."

Wuerkaixi then cited how the Kang Hua Company, the largest in China, was "deeply engaged in officially approved speculation" under the stewardship of Deng Xiaoping's son, Deng Difang. All the sons of the top leaders were engaged "in one kind of racketeering or another," including the four sons of Party secretary Zhao Ziyang.

"We are told to work hard and practice frugality while our leaders cheat us and future generations!" Wuerkaixi cried. "That is why we have inflation! That is why our consumer goods are often of poor quality! That is why all of us here have a duty, to China itself, to go out and change the situation!"

He stepped off the platform to thunderous applause.

Watching Wuerkaixi make his way out of the dormitory followed by Daobao and the others, Cassy thought again how this country was awash with resentment and anger, coupled to an awareness of who was responsible. The combination was a potent mixture that, if ignited, could spread with the speed of a bush fire.

# 10

## *Presidential Pragmatism*

MONDAY, FEBRUARY 6, 1989
*Beijing*

Cycling to work, Cassy sensed that throughout the city on this chilly winter's morning, millions of Chinese continued to repeat one word, *Bush.*

In a few days the newly elected President of the United States would come to Beijing, giving China the honor of being the second nation he would visit after his inauguration. The President and the first lady would arrive from Tokyo after attending the funeral of Emperor Hirohito later in the month, but that would be largely a matter of protocol, not politics. Having the new leader of the Western world come for a state visit was being seen as a major political coup for China's leadership.

No one doubted that as well as the glittering pomp and ceremony, there would be some very tough bargaining that would have far-reaching implications for China's future. One of Cassy's friends, an American diplomat in Beijing, had reduced the Bush visit to two questions: "Can the President and his hosts ensure that China continues its economic openness while not losing its ideological purity? Can China's leaders ensure that domestic factors be made to interact with external factors?"

Other diplomats with whom Cassy was friendly, especially those from Europe, had predicted that Bush would go out of his way to convince his hosts that the last thing America wanted was to push Beijing backward, either to isolationism or into the arms of Moscow.

When she had told Daobao, he had been genuinely shocked. He

said all the student leaders had hoped President Bush would deliver a clear statement asking for an acceleration in human rights in return for continued U.S. economic support.

Once more she had thought how naive the students were. She was certain their aspirations were low in the calculations of America's foreign-policy makers. Her U.S. diplomat friend had told her there was simply too much at stake to risk upsetting Deng Xiaoping and the other old men of Zhongnanhai.

A number of her Chinese friends said that the Bush visit was further proof of China's standing in the world. This feeling had been reinforced by the news of the Sino-Soviet summit scheduled for May, which would officially mark the end of the long freeze in relations between the Communist superpowers.

Cycling through the campus Cassy once more experienced a warm glow of pride in simply being an American. Students called out to her asking what Bush was like.

Her attempts to get her students to follow the prescribed curriculum were good-naturedly brushed aside in a bombardment of similar questions. Had Bush kept up with the Chinese language, which he had shown signs of mastering when he had been posted here as the American ambassador? Would he be able to force the pace of democracy? Would he speak out on human rights? Would he use what the Chinese press was now constantly referring to as his "old friendship" with Deng Xiaoping not only to promote trade, but to develop the idea that China must become a more open society?

Cassy repeatedly said the President was sure to be sympathetic on all such matters. Privately she was less certain. She had attended another meeting of the student leaders. Wuerkaixi had said it would be "foolish and dangerous" to expect anything from Bush because U.S. trade with China was now running at $14 billion a year. The President would say or do nothing to disturb that situation, Wuerkaixi predicted.

Now Yang Li had returned to the subject in his usual oblique way. "Cassy," he began, "I would like to ask a question."

She had told everyone to call her Cassy. Li was one of the few students who did.

"Shoot," she said.

Several of the other students had turned to look at Li. Even before he spoke she realized that what he was going to say would be addressed to them. He had often done this before, using her as a conduit to make a point to the others. There were sides to Li she did not always like.

Li folded his arms before he spoke. "Do you think President Bush understands that China is to Gorbachev what Europe was to Peter the Great, a stage for him to try out his new political thinking?"

Cassy shook her head. "I've no idea what the President thinks." There was a deliberate sharpness in her voice. The idea that she was infallible on American foreign policy had begun to wear thin.

But Li continued to press. "Many Chinese feel the visit of the Soviet leader is not only a rapprochement with our people, but represents the first real challenge to the new administration in Washington. If that is so, then Bush will most certainly do nothing to upset our leaders. Therefore all our expectations will be based on a false premise. So should we not try and make our views known to the President?"

There are murmurs of agreement throughout the room. Conversations sprang up among several students as they debated what Li had said. From his desk in the back of the class Li gave her his half-smile.


SAME DAY, LATER
*The Great Hall of the People*

In a salon in the Great Hall of the People, the full Politburo had assembled at midmorning on this Monday to discuss the Bush visit. As usual Deng sat to one side wreathed in cigarette smoke, taking little direct part in the discussion but not missing a nuance.

Foreign Minister Qian Qichen began by saying that the United States could no longer regard its relationship with China as being based upon a common opposition to Soviet expansion in the region. Americans now realized that China was at "the takeoff stage." Every U.S. company doing business in the People's Republic was anxious to develop those links, especially at the expense of the Japanese.

Murmurs of satisfaction came from those seated around the foreign minister. Many of the old men still bore the scars, and memories, of the war they had fought against the Japanese fifty years before.

As usual the Politburo were seated in a semicircle of armchairs, each with its stand ashtray on one side and spittoon on the other. Behind each chair sat key advisers, taking notes. In addition, behind Hu Yaobang's chair stood an official informally known as "The Coat Tail Puller." His sole function was to restrain Hu when the passion of his argument forced him to his feet. Deng had ordered the official to be present after Hu had stood up and addressed the Politburo, his face so suffused that he had alarmed his colleagues.

Now, however, Hu sat slumped in his armchair, listening as Qian Qichen continued to argue that Bush would be anxious to present the United States "as an Asian power." Sensing the bafflement of some of his listeners, the foreign minister explained the phrase: America wished to be a major partner in China's plans to replace Japan as the next superpower to emerge from the Pacific. Bush had indicated this desire by nominating James Lilley as his next ambassador to China. The diplomat had served in the region before and was known to be "a friend of China's." Henry Kissinger had spoken for Lilley. In the foreign minister's view, there could be no higher recommendation.

Kissinger Associates had been helpful over the Bush visit, as always, providing supplementary briefing papers on U.S. expectations and what the new administration was prepared to offer in return. The United States wanted to increase its economic ties with China. In return it would view with understanding how China resolved its internal problems. Stripped of all the verbosity that characterizes so many Kissinger Associates documents, it came down to that simple tradeoff.

Hu Yaobang bestirred himself to ask a question: What would Bush say about the East Wind deal?

A few months ago China had sold Saudi Arabia a supply of East Wind missiles, each with a range of two thousand miles. The deal had stunned the Reagan administration, which had until then clung to the belief that neither Beijing nor Riyadh would alter the balance of power in the Middle East without at least checking with the United States. Reagan had dispatched his secretary of defense, Frank Carlucci, to seek assurances that such missiles would not be sold to what Reagan had defined as "the terrorist club," Libya, Iraq, Iran, and Syria.

In Beijing Carlucci found himself in a not unfamiliar position for a Western emissary: a victim of Chinese subtlety. The Chinese said, of course, they wished to do nothing to encourage the dangerous spread of missiles, overlooking the fact they had supplied Iraq and Iran with a vast quantity of Silkworm missiles capable of delivering poison gas warheads. But, Carlucci had been reminded, the Chinese take pride in being one of the world's masters of rocketry. And naturally they had a living to make, and such arrangements included selling their weaponry to North Korea, their friendly neighbor. What happened to such weaponry after that was really no concern of China's.

Every member of the Politburo knew what really happened. From the North Korean port of Nampo, the missiles and their support electronics were exported to the Middle East through CITIC, the Chinese trading-banking-industrial development corporation, many of whose key posts were filled by the sons of the old men in the salon.

Behind Hu's question was another; would President Bush put aside his personal determination to say or do nothing to offend his hosts and ask about those arms transactions?

Deng's answer was brief. If his "old friend" so far forgot himself as a "polite guest" to pose an embarrassing question, he would be firmly reminded how it could harm friendly relations between the two countries.

Deng paused and looked around the semicircle of attentive faces. He settled on Zhao Ziyang.

"I will leave it to you to convey to the President our thoughts on the matter," Deng said.

The Party chief nodded.

Prime Minister Li Peng then raised the question of possible student protests during the President's visit.

Deng's voice was harsh. "That must not happen."


SATURDAY, FEBRUARY 26, 1989
*Beijing*

Flanked by their advisers and aides, Deng Xiaoping and President Bush sat in the splendor of the Great Hall of the People. Around them hundreds of reporters and photographers waited to record the first exchange between the two leaders.

Deng began by expressing "a very hearty welcome." Then, as if he needed to remind himself, he added, "Furthermore, we have been good friends for a long time."

Bush then made one of his peculiar hand-chopping motions, as if he were practicing *taijiquan,* the martial arts exercise.

The small talk between the two leaders developed a surrealistic tone, with Deng saying Bush was "quite an athlete" and the President mumbling, "I keep tryin', keep ridin' my bicycle." Deng then said they had one thing in common, playing bridge, drawing from Bush the comment, "You're too good for me." That prompted Deng to remind the President they had never played together. Bush chopped more air: "I gave up bridge a long time ago. Too complicated. Too difficult. You're the expert."

Deng beamed his panda-smile. "No, it is even more difficult for you to find time to play bridge. It's a tough job being President of the

United States. You could be the champion of the world in terms of the business of state."

Bush's hand movements went into overdrive. "There is much change in the world, so many big things are happening. I've come here at an interesting time, both an opportunity and a challenge. I'm delighted that Mr. Gorbachev will come to China. It's a good thing."

Both men then turned to the press corps and shook hands several times. After a few minutes White House minders and officials from the Chinese Information Ministry ushered out the media.

The leaders were left alone with their aides. Bush's included Secretary of State Baker and National Security Adviser Brent Scowcroft; Deng was flanked by Prime Minister Li Peng and Party Secretary Zhao Ziyang. There was a lengthening silence.

It was broken by Zhao saying how much they were all looking forward to the Texas-style barbecue Bush had invited them to attend as a climax to his visit. To give the occasion an authentic atmosphere, a large supply of Lone Star beer had been flown in, along with prime U.S. steaks and Idaho potatoes.

Deng apologized for not being able to attend, blaming his doctors, who insisted he must go to bed early. It was the only clue he gave that he was not in good health. Deng added that the Chinese party would be led by Li Peng and State President Yang Shangkun.

Once more there was silence. Bush and his entourage knew why. China's most celebrated dissident, astrophysicist Fang Lizhi, had been included on the guest list in a belated move by Bush to appease what the President had called "the liberal element" in the United States.

Before leaving Washington, Bush had studied the CIA's profile of Fang, described in the document as "China's Andrei Sakharov." It was a typical piece of work from the CIA's Political/Psychological Division, as heavy on the small details as it was on more important issues. Fang's "good cheer and guilelessness" were noted. So was his whinny of a laugh. His penchant for permanent-press slacks was recorded, together with the tortoise-shell glasses that gave him a slightly owlish appearance. Fang's "political formlessness seems rooted in his personality." He had become "an icon" to China's students. The document ended with extracts from Fang's more celebrated speeches calling for reform in China.

Fang was to be the token dissident at the banquet. He would be there to dispel a growing impression that the new administration had established what Fang himself had recently called "a double standard on human rights," tough on the Soviet Union and soft on China.

Already Bush's spokesmen, confirming that Fang had been invited, had made it clear that Bush had no intention of actually meeting the dissident, any more than the President intended to raise the subject of human rights in his discussion with China's leadership.

It was Zhao Ziyang who raised the subject. He launched into what some State Department officials came to call "a tongue-lashing" on the danger for anyone who meddled in the internal affairs of China.

While Bush sat somber-faced, hands clasped in his lap, Zhao delivered Deng's message that those Chinese dissidents who advocated Western-style democracy could cause the nation's economic reforms to fail.

"That will neither contribute to the stability of China's political situation, nor will it be conducive to the friendship between our two countries," Zhao concluded.

The warning shot drew no response from Bush. During the rest of the meeting the discussion concentrated on how America could improve its trade links with China. Li Peng predicted that by the time China absorbed Hong Kong in 1997, U.S. trade with the People's Republic could be around $20 billion a year, not only securing America's position as China's main business partner, but giving the United States an even greater power base in the Pacific.

Hours later when Fang and his wife set out by car to attend the barbecue at the Great Wall Sheraton, they were stopped by police and told their invitation had been canceled, almost certainly on the orders of Deng Xiaoping. Next day, as he left China, Bush expressed his "regret" that Fang had not appeared at the festivities. "It has been quite a party, just like back home," he told his hosts before boarding Air Force One.

Even before the plane left Chinese air space, the first posters were being put up by the students around Beijing University. They demanded the right of "full intellectual and political freedom" and "the right to meet whom we wish in the name of democracy."

The students had finally delivered their first public proclamation.

Cycling to class, Cassy saw that Pang Yi and Beijing University's other political officers were already busy tearing down the posters. But no sooner had they removed one than another took its place.

MONDAY, MARCH 7, 1989
*The Prime Minister's Residence*
*Zhongnanhai*

Prime Minister Li Peng faced an unpalatable truth on this windswept morning. In the past week posters calling for democracy had appeared on campuses throughout the capital and in other university cities. Many of the posters called for support for the May Fourth Movement and its demand for "a new China."

Students and intellectuals were being asked to give voice to the demands at a rally in Tiananmen Square in two months' time, May 4. The rally would commemorate the seventieth anniversary of that celebrated occasion in 1919 when a ragtag procession of students had made their way to the square to protest a corrupt political system.

Security Chief Qiao Shi had once more suggested a roundup of the student leaders. But this time Li Peng had ordered nothing must be done. Coincidentally with the rash of posters, those who championed reform, led by Party Secretary Zhao, had suffered further setbacks in the Politburo. Their rallying cry, "a free economy frees everything," was no longer heard. And Zhao himself had become an object of suspicion in student and intellectual circles after Li Peng had arranged for his aides to leak to the Chinese and foreign media an account of the Party chief's "tongue-lashing" of Bush. Not only had the revelation rocked Zhao's credibility, but it had also, more importantly, restored the power of those Party elders, hardliners to the core, who until then had found themselves shunted aside as policymakers. Back with a vengeance, wheezing and spluttering, they issued a common cry about the dangers that came from granting "too many freedoms, too fast."

Rather than have the student leaders arrested and risk public demonstrations, Li Peng intended to weaken them by destroying their one champion, Zhao Ziyang.

The previous day the prime minister had begun to do so from the podium of the National People's Congress, China's parliament. Then he had delivered a cleverly couched attack on "the shortcomings and mistakes in our guidance." It had sounded like classic Chinese self-criticism. But everyone present knew that the words were aimed at Zhao.

Now, as the prime minister pressed for a further attack on his rival, events in Tibet were coming to his aid. That country was gripped by the most serious violence since the Chinese occupation. Li Peng had sent orders to the 27th Army that the "correct solution" was "a full show of force."

MONDAY, MARCH 13, 1989
*Lhasa, Tibet*

Yang Bing felt broken glass and slivers beneath his boots as he prodded open another dark, polished door with his rifle. The young soldier was deep inside the Jokka Kang, the most holy of all the temples in the Pankor, the old city. All around him was the sound of gunfire, sporadic now after twenty-four hours of street fighting with the thousands of Tibetan monks who had launched themselves, often with no more than primitive weapons, against well-equipped soldiers. The result had been a slaughter. Hundreds of monks had been shot down, thousands more wounded.

Bing's platoon was among those ordered to seek them out and kill them on the spot.

Many had sought sanctuary in the Jokka Kang, over thirteen hundred years old and housing the most famous of all the country's sacred statues.

The platoon had advanced through the rubble of the streets to reach the older walls of the temple. Its massive carmine-colored gate, covered with gold inscriptions in Tibetan, hung off its hinges; it had been struck by a round fired from one of the Chinese tanks that had swept through the city.

Beyond the gate a group of monks had pelted the arriving soldiers with stones from one of the brightly painted galleries. They had been quickly dispatched with machine gun fire.

The platoon had then sprinted into the building, their boots slipping on the stone-flagged floor, slick with the body oil of pilgrims who had prostrated themselves on the holy ground down the centuries.

Inside the temple the soldiers had split up to search the red-pillared galleries and the rooms leading from them.

Bing found himself advancing past butter lamps in every niche and chapels dank with yak-dung smoke. Everywhere there were paintings and carved statues of animals, birds, and flowers. Heavy steel curtains secured with large padlocks had blocked the way to the main chambers. The locks had been shot off and the curtains ripped aside. Beyond were many bodies.

An hour after entering the Jokka Kang, Bing had reached its upper gallery. Entering the room he saw that its windows had been blasted out, probably from aerial strafing. The bullets had dislodged replicas of dragon heads and bells made of copper-covered gold from their wall mountings.

The room itself appeared to be some kind of storeroom; it was filled with lacquered gold and vermilion furniture and the low square stools covered in satin that Tibetans like to sit on while drinking rancid-tasting buttered tea.

A monk was cowering in a corner of the room beside a broken dragon's head. He was young, probably no more than fifteen, and wore the robe of a novice Lama. Blood had congealed on his sleeve. The boy rose to his feet, his mouth working but no words coming.

Bing shook his head and motioned for the monk to sit down. Then Bing turned and left the room, closing the door behind him and marking it with a penciled red star to indicate it had been checked.

From another part of the temple came more bursts of gunfire.


SAME DAY
*Beijing*

Two thousand miles away in Beijing, Jeanne Moore, an American-born editorial assistant on the English language *China Daily*, proof-read next day's editorial on events in Tibet. It began uncompromisingly.

"The Lhasa riots show how we must value a stable environment. Haste and impatience for progress on the question of democracy will only increase the sources of instability."

A tall, intense idealist, Jeanne was married to a Chinese academic, Jiang. She worked on the paper to maintain a standard of life that was close to her own upbringing. Her position often gave her "a glimpse behind the scenes."

After reading the editorial she telephoned her husband and read it out to him. Jiang gave no immediate reply. But when he spoke his voice was somber.

"We are entering a new and dangerous phase. The Party is determined that no one, inside or out, will succeed in challenging those who now control our destiny."

# 11

# *Death in the Politburo*

FRIDAY, MARCH 8, 1989
*The Great Hall of the People*

Shortly after 9:00 A.M. a cavalcade of Red flags swept out of
Zhongnanhai, crossed Changan Avenue, and entered the inner
courtyard of the Great Hall of the People. Each limousine contained
a member of the Politburo. The more decrepit were accompanied by
a doctor and a nurse carrying an emergency medical kit. In the
courtyard itself were parked ambulances from several of the hospitals
in the immediate area, including the one where Professor Guangzu
worked. More doctors and nurses accompanied the ambulances.

This was the first full meeting of the Politburo since Prime
Minister Li Peng had attacked Zhao Ziyang before the country's
parliament. The one person who could have intervened, Deng
Xiaoping, had chosen not to be there to witness the ferocious verbal
assault on the Party secretary. Deng had later told the previous
holder of that office, Hu Yaobang, that he stayed away because he
"wanted to live longer."

Now China's supreme ruler and Hu walked unaided from their
limousines into the Great Hall. Deng wore a custom-made charcoal-
gray Mao suit. Hu had chosen to wear another of the Western-style
suits he had made in Hong Kong. As usual, the trousers were pulled
too high, revealing Hu's passion for bright red socks.

Although they chatted amicably, the atmosphere around them was
tense. The aftereffects of the violence in Tibet continued to reverberate through the leadership. Hardliners such as Vice-Premier Yao
Yilin and Li Xiaming, Party secretary of Beijing and political
commissar of the city garrison, a key post should anything like the

106

Lhasa uprising occur here, saw events in Tibet as impinging directly on what was happening in China, part of a deep-seated conspiracy against the Party.

Despite his uncompromising warning to President Bush, which he had been ordered to deliver by Deng, Zhao Ziyang still believed the students were no more than idealists, intending no harm to the country, and no real threat to the leadership. In this view he was supported by, among others, Yan Mingfu and Hu Yaobang.

Apart from his close friends Zhao and Hu, Mingfu was the only real moderate present. Like all converts, he was fervent in his belief, which he called "the advocacy of government by conciliation." A keep-fit enthusiast, the abstemious fifty-eight-year-old Mingfu shared with Zhao and Hu an interest in history and music, as well as in the need to propel China toward economic reforms. As usual, they ignored Vice-Premier Yao Yilin, an ultraconservative steeped in a lifetime of socialist central planning. He sat slumped in his chair, breathing noisily.

Beside the rough-tongued Yao sat another formidable figure, Li Xiaming. The squat, muscular sixty-three-year-old moved like the schoolboy boxer he had once been. His opponents called him "Deng's lapdog." In reality he was a powerful figure in his own right.

Prime Minister Li Peng, as usual, sat cold and aloof. But behind the deadpan gaze he had an eye for a pretty girl; legend had it that he personally chose all his female staff. Two of them stood close by, ready to bring any papers he might require.

Beside him sat Qiao Shi. The old spymaster once more looked as if he had slept in his clothes. Before coming into the room he had lit another of his eight-inch-long Cuban cigars.

Close to Deng sat Yang Shangkun, the state president, eighty-two. His trim figure was the envy of many of the others. They put it down to his long-running affair with Wu Yi, the vice-mayor of Beijing, who had a reputation for sexual athleticism.

As usual, the "Coat Tail Puller" was positioned behind Hu's chair. Seated along one wall of the salon were aides ready to take notes or produce documents for their masters.

The meeting began pleasantly enough. There were expressions of relief that the worst of the trouble in Tibet appeared to be at an end. State President Yang Shangkun was instructed to send congratulations for a job well done to his nephew, commander of the 27th Army.

Li Peng then addressed the Politburo. Reading from notes, usually extemporized on such occasions, the prime minister began to review what was happening on the campuses of Beijing and elsewhere. He painted a picture of students "corrupted" by "overexposure to

# CHINESE COMMUNIST PARTY NATIONAL CONGRESS 中国共产党中央委员会

**General Secretary:**
Zhao Ziyang
赵紫阳

### Central Committee Politburo
### 中央政治局

**Standing Committee:**

| | |
|---|---|
| Zhao Ziyang | 赵紫阳 |
| Li Peng | 李鹏 |
| Qiao Shi | 乔石 |
| Hu Qili | 胡启立 |
| Yao Yilin | 姚依林 |

**Additional Members:**

| | | | |
|---|---|---|---|
| Wan Li | 万里 | Yang Rudai | 杨汝岱 |
| Tian Jiyun | 田纪云 | Yang Shangkun | 杨尚昆 |
| Jiang Zemin | 江泽民 | Wu Xueqian | 吴学谦 |
| Li Tieying | 李铁映 | Song Ping | 宋平 |
| Li Ruihuan | 李瑞环 | Hu Yaobang | 胡耀邦 |
| Li Ximing | 李锡铭 | Qin Jiwei | 秦基伟 |

## Secretariat
## 中央书记处

**Members:**
Hu Qili
胡启立

Qiao Shi
乔石
Rui Xingwen
芮杏文
Yan Mingfu
阎明复

## Discipline Inspection Commission
## 纪律检查委员会

**Secretary:**
Qiao Shi
乔石

## Advisory Commission
## 顾问委员会

**Chairman:**
Chen Yun
陈云

---

# NATIONAL PEOPLE'S CONGRESS 全国人民代表大会

## Standing Committee
## 常务委员会

**Chairman:**
Wan Li
万里

**Vice-Chairmen:**

| | |
|---|---|
| Wang Zhen | 王震 |
| Xi Zhongxun | 习仲勋 |
| Ulanhu | 乌兰夫 |
| Peng Chong | 彭冲 |
| Wei Guoqing | 韦国清 |
| Zhu Xuefan | 朱学范 |
| Ngapoi Ngawang Jigme | 阿沛·阿旺晋美 |
| Bainqen Erdini Ooigyi Gyaincain | 班禅额尔德尼·确吉坚赞 |
| Seypidin Aze | 赛福鼎·艾则孜 |
| Zhou Gucheng | 周谷城 |

| | |
|---|---|
| Yan Jici | 严济慈 |
| Rong Yiren | 荣毅仁 |
| Ye Fei | 叶飞 |
| Liao Hansheng | 廖汉生 |
| Ni Zhifu | 倪志福 |
| Chen Muhua(F) | 陈慕华 |
| Fei Xiaotong | 费孝通 |
| Sun Qimeng | 孙起孟 |
| Lei Jieqiong (F) | 雷洁琼 |
| Wang Hanbin | 王汉斌 |

---

# STATE COUNCIL 国务院

**Premier:**
Li Peng
李鹏

**Vice-Premier:**
Yao Yilin
姚依林

**Councillor:**
Li Tieying
李铁映

**Councillor:**
Qin Jiwei
秦基伟

**Councillor:**
Wang Bingqian
王丙乾

**Councillor:**
Song Jian
宋健

# The Old Men of China

**Alternate Member:**
Ding Guangen
丁关根

**Military Commission**
军事委员会

**Chairman:**
Deng Xiaoping
邓小平

**President:**
Yang Shangkun
杨尚昆

**Vice-President:**
Wang Zhen
王震

**Secretary-General:**
Peng Chong
彭冲

**Central Military Commission**
中央军事委员会

**Chairman:**
Deng Xiaoping
邓小平

**First Vice-Chairman:**
Zhao Ziyang    赵紫阳
**Vice-chairman:**
Yang Shangkun 杨尚昆

**Vice-Premier:**
Tian Jiyun
田纪云

**Vice-Premier:**
Wu Xueqian
吴学谦

**Councillor and Secretary-General:**
Chen Junsheng
陈俊生

**Councillor:**
Wang Fang
王芳

**Councillor:**
Zou Jiahua
邹家华

**Councillor:**
Li Guixian
李贵鲜

**Councillor:**
Chen Xitong
陈希同

westernization" who were becoming "class enemies" of the people. Once more they were threatening to destroy the very fabric of their society and were being encouraged to do so by intellectuals such as Fang Lizhi.

Li Peng then mounted an increasingly angry attack on China's most renowned astrophysicist, calling him "arrogant," "destructive," and "a friend of bourgeois Western thinking." He reminded his audience that Fang had written to Deng Xiaoping in February demanding the release of "so-called political prisoners," and that finally the National People's Congress had decided "after the most careful study" there was "no need now" to free any prisoners.

The attack had gone on for some ten minutes, punctuated by murmurs of agreement from the hardliners, when Hu Yaobang first intervened.

He said it was wrong to lay the burden of blame on one man. China's problems were the result of the inability of some of those around him to recognize that with education had come an awakening that could not be stifled and must not be.

Half-rising from his seat, only to be gently but firmly tugged back down again by the watchful official, Hu asked rhetorically: Who would want to see a return to the time Mao had condemned all China's intellectuals as a "stinking category"?

Murmurs of support mixed with those of protest.

Li Peng continued criticizing Fang for his latest statement to an American newspaper, that the students "are counting the days to May 4." The prime minister said this comment was tantamount to "encitement" for the students to take over a celebration that belonged to the Party. The May 4 celebration was of "a patriotic event," which had paved the way for Communism. Any attempt to use it to promote "this nonsense" about democracy and other political ideas would be completely unacceptable.

There were cries of support from the hardliners.

Vice-Premier Yao Yilin's rasping voice said that "the problem" went all the way back to the schools. "Teachers have forgotten the reason why they teach, to instill proper patriotism and true socialist values."

Beijing Party Secretary Li Xiaming led the cries of support with a strong attack on those "who want to pamper our youth with foolish ideas instead of pressuring them to be our next line of defense against the spread of bourgeois liberalism."

To make absolutely clear who he meant, Li Xiaming turned and faced Hu.

Li Tieying, the Politburo member responsible for school education, had started to speak when again Hu intervened.

What Hu, the former Party secretary, had listened to was a recipe for "social disaster." This was the way back "to our dark ages of anti-intellectualism," when education had been run on the proverbial shoestring. Students had lived in abject squalor, and teachers had earned less than a road sweeper.

Suddenly Hu was on his feet, brushing aside the official tugging at his jacket. He had started to say something about "the only hope for China" when he stopped. For a moment longer he stood slack-mouthed. Then he collapsed halfway back into his chair before sliding onto the floor.

There was stunned silence, then near pandemonium. Some of the old men backed away as if they could not bear to be in the presence of mortal illness. Zhao Ziyang knelt beside Hu, helping Yan Mingfu to loosen Hu's collar.

Then the first doctors and nurses arrived. Hu was pronounced alive despite his major heart attack. He was placed on a stretcher and rushed from the salon to a waiting ambulance.

The Politburo meeting was abandoned. By then Deng Xiaoping had already left the salon. He had made no attempt to come near the stricken Hu.


SAME DAY, LATER
*Central Intelligence Agency*

On Webster's desk was a report marked CONFIDENTIAL, the lowest form of classification within the agency. It signified the material could "reasonably be expected to cause some form of damage to the national security."

The document was the combined efforts of the half-dozen Chinese-speaking agents who had accompanied Bush on his visit to China. On returning to Washington they had assembled in a fourth-floor conference room at CIA headquarters.

One of the agents was a veteran of the days when the CIA had shipped arms to the Afghan rebels via China. Another had in 1979 helped create the first intelligence ties with China. The high point had been China's agreement to the construction by the CIA Directorate of Science and Technology of two signal stations in western China, near the border with the Soviet Union. The stations were still keeping tabs on Russia's arms control agreements.

The report the agents had compiled was less dramatic than that. In their days in Beijing, in the guise of visiting newsmen, the CIA operatives had spoken to a number of students and their supporters.

Gullible and unsuspecting about who they were confiding in, several student leaders, including the voluble Wuerkaixi and the studious Wang Dan, had revealed enough to show that the students were only waiting for an excuse to demonstrate.

The report concluded that the students believed that by calling for democracy, they would automatically receive the endorsement of the Bush administration despite the President having gone out of his way in China to give them no such encouragement.

Having initialed the report and sent it on its way through the labyrinth of the Washington intelligence community, Webster ordered one his assistants to draft in his name an encoded instruction to Beijing Station—housed in that splendid colonial-style mansion known as Spook City—in the embassy compound, to intensify its surveillance and penetration of all student activities.

The CIA had invested more, and had more to lose, in China than any other foreign intelligence agency. What Webster had once called "a bunch of kids politically wet behind the ears" were most certainly not going to be allowed to threaten that investment or the billions of dollars American businesses had placed in China.

SAME DAY, LATER
*Hospital of Traditional Medicine*

Professor Guangzu continued to watch Hu Yaobang from the doorway of the intensive care room. Heartbeats moved across the monitor positioned near the bed. Hu's eyes, pupils slightly dilated from the drugs he had been given, watched the monitor, as if he realized his grasp on life had been reduced to the silent trace endlessly crossing the screen.

Hu had been brought to the hospital from the Great Hall of the People. Since his arrival, there had been the usual complete news blackout about his condition. Long ago Deng Xiaoping had ordered no bulletins would be issued if any of the leadership fell ill. If they died, he would decide when the announcement would be made.

Public Security agents had arrived soon after Hu, sealing off the second floor cardiac unit where he had been brought. Other patients had been moved out, and only essential medical staff were permitted on the floor.

Gathered round Hu's bed were the hospital's cardiac specialist and his team. Western-style medical equipment surrounded the bed. The continuous clicking and pinging of screen and control panels reassured the medical team that all was not lost. The specialist had recently spent a year in the United States and had outfitted his department with the latest monitoring equipment. However, other departments in the hospital offered a mixture of Western and traditional treatments.

Professor Guangzu suspected that in this starkly lit sterile room there was no room for *Qi, Yin and Yang*, the ancient beliefs he swore by, or for his understanding that successful treatment depended on accepting that humanity did not exist in a vacuum, but that life or death was only a minute part of the universe and could be influenced by everything else in the cosmos. Here, only state-of-the-art Western medicine prevailed.

Professor Guangzu saw that Hu had sensed his presence. But he waited while the team around the bed finished their business of checking instrument readings, drips, and the leads that ran to sensors attached to Hu's chest. Satisfied, the team withdrew, each in baggy white top and trousers, their plastic sandals flapping on the bare floor as they left the room. At the door the specialist spoke to Professor Guangzu.

"Please stay only a little time with him. He is very tired, and there is every chance of another heart attack. But we have done everything possible."

Professor Guangzu nodded. He well understood that behind the polite words was the unspoken order not to interfere in Hu's treatment. A request to have Hu transferred to his own department had been refused by the hospital administrator. The order from Zhongnanhai was that Hu must remain in the cardiology unit. The administrator had added, not bothering to hide the malice in his voice, that it was "fitting" that Hu, "such an admirer of the West," should be treated only by its methods.

Stepping over the cables on the floor, Professor Guangzu reached the bed. For a moment he looked down at Hu. Like so many others he had seen who had come close to death, the professor saw in Hu's face a determination not to be torn from life.

"Well, my friend, how are you?" asked Professor Guangzu.

"The better for seeing you," Hu whispered.

"You must be careful. The heart is the center of all emotional activity and thought processes," Professor Guangzu reminded Hu. "Tell me what happened before you collapsed."

Hu described the scene in the Politburo. Professor Guangzu nodded. It was an all too familiar clinical story. Every practitioner of traditional medicine knew that a person was made up of the five basic elements: earth, fire, metal, water, and wood. And the elements each had its corresponding sound, color, and weather conditions. Within that framework diagnosis was made easier by remembering that wood always destroyed earth, earth destroyed water, water destroyed fire, fire destroyed metal, and metal destroyed wood.

None of the machines around the bed could hope to understand that life-style and emotions are all too often the underlying causes of all ill health. Yet it was obvious to any exponent of traditional medicine.

In his anxiety to win over his fellow Politburo members, Hu had obviously generated so much inner anger that it had brought on a heart attack. The result had been a loss of positive vitality, Qi. The energy force had ceased to flow through the meridian that stimulated the heart. In turn, the deficiency had increased five of the Seven Moods—anger, anxiety, sorrow, fear, and horror—at the expense of the job that normally kept them in proper balance. The result had been the heart attack. Every textbook in traditional medicine would have confirmed these steps to diagnosis.

Professor Guangzu spoke to Hu. "This is a cold day. So wood was needed to produce fire. And fire corresponds to the heart in the body. Some fire is good. Too much is dangerous. This time the fire created an imbalance in your body. Here, show me your tongue."

Hu put out his tongue as far as he could. Professor Guangzu gave it a long, silent scrutiny. He placed three of his fingers on Hu's right wrist and touched Hu's left wrist with his forefinger to test the pulse there, then reversed the process. As he did so he closed his eyes, feeling, timing, and sensing, in all, twelve pulses in Hu's wrists.

"You certainly have an imbalance of Qi," said Professor Guangzu.

"Can you treat it?"

"Yes, of course. But you are not my patient."

Hu shook his head. "This is my body. I will decide who will treat it."

Professor Guangzu nodded. "Very well. I will see what can be done."

From his pocket he produced the case with his set of acupuncture needles. He quickly inserted them along the twelve body meridians that stimulate the heart. When the needles were in place, the professor twisted them in turn, setting them gently vibrating. After each movement he asked whether Hu had "felt the presence of Qi."

After a while Hu began to nod and say, "I feel Qi."

SAME DAY, SAME TIME
*Foreign Legation Quarter*

Despite the security procedures news of Hu's heart attack quickly reached the foreign embassy quarter.

Soviet Ambassador Troyanovsky was in the middle of a planning meeting for the forthcoming Gorbachev state visit when the news came. He immediately thought, "This is not going to create a potential problem for the visit. Hu had no real authority." Nevertheless, Russian attachés were instructed to probe their Chinese contacts to discover how ill Hu was and what had been under discussion in the Politburo when he had collapsed.

First Secretary Kauokin, a KGB official at the embassy, began his own inquiries by calling Qiao Shi's office. An aide said the security chief was not available.

The American embassy learned of Hu's illness through its press and cultural attaché, McKinney Russell. He had heard it from Jeanne Moore. The *China Daily* editorial assistant had picked up the news from a contact in the hospital.

U.S. diplomats at once began working the phones, calling other friendly missions and sources in government. In a surprisingly short time they had pieced together an accurate account of what had happened. A report was faxed to the State Department.

By then most embassies also had an idea of what had occurred in the Politburo. It was left to French Ambassador Charles Malo to articulate the view of many foreign diplomats. He felt that "Hu's illness was only significant in how the students would react."

SAME DAY, EVENING
*Beijing University*

In the campus coffeehouse there was not a seat to be had. Students lined the walls, listening to Li Yang describing what had happened to Hu.

Cassy saw that the student leader's deep-felt emotions were clear. As he had stood up to speak Meili squeezed his arm, her face whiter than usual at hearing the news.

Until then Cassy had not realized what a powerful public speaker Li was; he had a vibrant voice and a way of repeating key phrases. He constantly reminded his listeners that Hu had been struck down supporting them; therefore they had a duty to support him. The best way to do this was to ensure that the May 4 gathering in Tiananmen Square would be a resounding success.

Somebody pointed out that the occasion fell only two weeks before the Gorbachev visit and that the leadership would be particularly anxious to ensure there would be no embarrassing demonstrations before such a historic occasion.

Li Yang gave another of his half-smiles.

THURSDAY, APRIL 13, 1989
*Washington, D.C.*

DCI Webster's reading on the way to work this morning included a report prepared by the FBI on Chinese intelligence activities in the United States. The FBI believed that "countering spies from the PRC is a growing problem, one nearly as large as that posed by the Soviet Union and its allies." The report claimed that the Chinese could be about to intensify their spying activities through the nearly nineteen hundred diplomats accredited to its Washington embassy and various consulates throughout the country, especially the one in San Francisco. The consulate there was "ideally placed," the FBI report said, "for Chinese agents to steal or illegally purchase data on weapons and systems technology" from northern California's vast defenses industry.

A number of the Chinese spies could be among the more than twenty thousand Chinese students at American universities, possibly coerced into spying for their country by threats against their families back home. Webster fully approved of the FBI recommendation that surveillance be increased on all Chinese students.

The FBI report also warned that some students might try to organize protests in the United States in support of the growing calls for democracy emanating from Chinese campuses. That would cause considerable embarrassment to Washington and the U.S. business community.

Webster knew that the FBI was not alone in expressing concern about China's students. The CIA's Moscow station had reported the Kremlin viewed with "real concern" the prospect of the students trying to embarrass Gorbachev during his state visit. From London had come evidence of "anxiety" within the Foreign Office that the students would interfere with Britain's delicate negotiations over the future of Hong Kong, due to be returned to China in 1997.

CIA officers in Paris and Bonn reported that the French and German governments were under increasing pressure from their business communities to do nothing to encourage China's students in their search for democracy.

One report, which had intrigued Webster, had come from the U.S. embassy in Dublin. It revealed that student leaders had visited the Irish embassy in Beijing and spoken to a diplomat there about the precise techniques needed to run a successful hunger strike. The diplomat, after stressing that the Irish government did not support such methods of protest, had given the students details of how the IRA manipulated public sympathy by such methods.

Webster doubted if the Beijing authorities would allow matters to go that far.

SATURDAY, APRIL 15, 1989
*Hospital of Traditional Medicine*

Late in the morning Professor Guangzu made another visit to the former Party secretary, Hu Yaobang. He had come twice a day. They had been left alone by the medical team to talk. During each visit the professor had inserted his acupuncture needles. He was convinced his intervention was responsible for Hu's remarkable improvement.

Apart from the heartbeat monitor, all the other equipment had been removed from the bed. All that remained was the emergency bell-push.

Hu sat propped up by pillows, wearing an old-fashioned night-shirt, listening intently as Professor Guangzu explained how the day before Li Peng had been forced to break Deng Xiaoping's standing order about not discussing any illness of a Politburo member. The prime minister, cornered by the foreign press as he left Beijing for a visit to Japan, had admitted Hu was in hospital but recovering.

Then, Professor Guangzu said, had come a most extraordinary disclaimer. From his coat pocket he produced a clipping from the *People's Daily* and read aloud to Hu.

"Li Peng said he wished to emphasize that the illness of Comrade Hu had nothing directly to do with the Politburo meeting he had been attending when he was taken ill."

The professor handed the item to Hu. "You see, my friend, how worried your opponents are. They are frightened people will think they tried to kill you!"

"When I get out of here, they will have more cause to fear me!" Hu replied.

They spoke for a little while longer, mostly about the need to spread reform; then the professor left, saying he would return in midafternoon for a further chat.

At noon Hu had his usual lunch of soup, noodles, and tea. Afterwards he slept for a while. At 1:00 P.M. a nurse made another check on Hu. These examinations occurred every fifteen minutes now that he was no longer on the danger list.

Hu awoke at some point after she had recorded her visit on his chart hanging at the foot of the bed. The demand of nature upon a full stomach was probably the reason. Hu should have used the bell-push and asked for a bedpan. Instead, he decided to make his own way to the bathroom adjoining his room. He was halfway across the floor when he collapsed.

The nurse found him when she made her quarter-past-the-hour visit. By then Hu was already dead from a second massive heart attack.


SAME DAY, MIDAFTERNOON
*Beijing University*

Cassy was describing the intricacies of English grammar when the classroom door burst open. Daobao stood there, a portable radio in his hand.

"Have you heard?" he burst out. "Hu Yaobang is dead! The radio has just said so!"

There was a scramble as students rushed to surround Daobao. Moments later Radio Beijing repeated the announcement it had first broadcast at 3:02 that afternoon. "The death is announced of Hu Yaobang, the true Communist fighter and great proletarian revolutionary, a great Marxist whose life is forever to be glorious for his contribution to economic structural reform...."

The announcement concluded with the assurance Hu "was given all possible medical attention but to no avail. To our great sorrow he died at 0753 today."

One small unresolved mystery concerned the reason why the authorities had altered the actual time of Hu's death. A possible explanation suggested that they moved back his passing by several hours so as not to give the impression of unseemly haste in announcing his death.

In a rush the students left the classroom, followed by Cassy. She saw that on the campus the first hastily scrawled messages of condolence were being stuck up, along with white flowers fashioned from tissue paper and bits of wire. The flowers were the first symbols of mourning for Hu.

As she followed Daobao across the campus, Cassy saw that hundreds of students were converging on the coffeehouse.

"What's going to happen?" Cassy asked as they reached the building.

"The time has come for action," Daobao replied.

She saw that the door of the coffeehouse was already smothered with messages.

"We have lost a true man," a student had scrawled in black ink on an old newspaper. "Our champion has gone," read another. "We have lost our great hope," said a third.

But even as she watched, the tone of the tributes was changing. Li Yang stuck up a message that read "False men are still living. The wrong man has died."

Meili affixed a scroll: "Xiaoping is still alive at the age of 84. Hu Yaobang, only 73, has died first. Those who should die still live. Those who should live have died.

Murmurs of agreement greeted this blunt statement.

Another student stuck a poster with an even simpler message beside the scroll: "Hu's death shows Deng Xiaoping no longer has a mandate to rule."

Cheers rose from the large crowd gathered before the door.

Suddenly there was a commotion at the back of the crowd as Pang Yi appeared with several political officers. They began to thrust their way toward the door, on which someone was pinning a paper banner bearing the words OUR DEMOCRACY DOOR.

"Take those down!" shouted Pang Yi.

"No!" Daobao said. "They stay!"

He forced his way to stand before Pang Yi. Behind Daobao the students formed a solid mass to protect the door.

For long tense moments Pang Yi and the other political officers stood their ground. Then, abruptly, they turned and walked away. There were muted cheers from the students, which Li Yang and Daobao quickly silenced.

By now Cassy estimated there were close to a thousand students milling outside the coffeehouse. Many were sticking more white paper flowers on tree trunks or weaving wreaths. Those closest to Democracy Door were asking each other what they should do next. Cassy sensed a feeling of uncertainty.

Suddenly Daobao's voice rose above the conversations.

"We march! Let us go to Tiananmen Square! There we can express our feelings to those who are responsible for Hu's death!"


SAME DAY, SAME TIME
*The Great Hall of the People*

News of Hu's death had been telephoned to the Politburo, which had resumed the session interrupted by Hu's collapse. This time Deng Xiaoping was not present. Li Peng was still in Japan. The discussion on education under the chairmanship of Zhao Ziyang was once more abandoned to discuss Hu's death.

Everyone present knew that the death of a leader provided the opportunity for public protest in the guise of mourning. It had not needed Vice-Premier Yao Yilin to remind those present in the salon of what had happened when Chou En-Lai, China's prime minister for a record twenty-seven years, had died of cancer in 1976. His death had come when Mao himself was on his deathbed. Radicals in the Party had tried to suppress any public mourning for Chou En-Lai on the grounds it was "untimely." Chou En-Lai had died in January. But by April, when the Chinese traditionally honored their dead during the Qing Ming Festival, there was no holding back the crowds. They had poured into Tiananmen Square in their tens of thousands, carrying wreaths and reciting poems of mourning for a popular and respected leader. At the same time they had expressed their opposition to Mao's hated wife, Jiang Qing, and the other radicals. What had begun as mourning swiftly gave way to angry political protest. Finally Qiao Shi had sent in his public security forces and armed police to clear the square. There had been considerable bloodshed and hundreds of arrests.

Now, anxious to avert mourning for Hu being used as an excuse to voice protest, the Politburo acted swiftly.

Li Xiaming and Yang Shangkun began to draft the official obituary to be broadcast by Radio Beijing. Qiao Shi's mastery of the language was called upon to convey the all-important right tone. Fulsome praise was the order of the day. Hu's "loyalty" to the Party was repeatedly praised. He was "a great statesman" who had "conferred lasting benefits on the Party and the people." He was a "true revolutionary" not only China, but the world, would mourn.

Care was taken to make no mention that he had been ejected from office as Party secretary two years before for supporting previous student demands. He was simply described as having "continued to serve the Politburo to the very end of his noble life."

The state president read the final draft to the Politburo. There was general agreement that it affirmed that Hu had remained true to Party ideology and in no way implied he had supported those who were "liberal" in the Western sense of the word. The eulogy was sent off to the studio of Radio Beijing.

The Politburo had been about to return to the education issue when the sound of chanting could be heard in Tiananmen Square.

Zhao Ziyang was among the first to reach one of the huge windows in the Great Hall.

Moving across the vast expanse of the all but deserted square were columns of students. Many were dressed completely in white, the symbol of deep mourning. Others wore white headbands. All carried white flowers or wreaths. The column leaders held aloft banners and huge photographs of Hu.

From the window the stunned Politburo could read the words on the banners.

Students leave Beijing University to go to Tiananmen Square a few days before the massacre. (PHOTO: *Courtesy Cassy Jones*)

In this dormitory building on the campus of Beijing University, student leaders met in secret from April 1989 onward to plot their moves. Other students maintained guard by posing as soccer players.

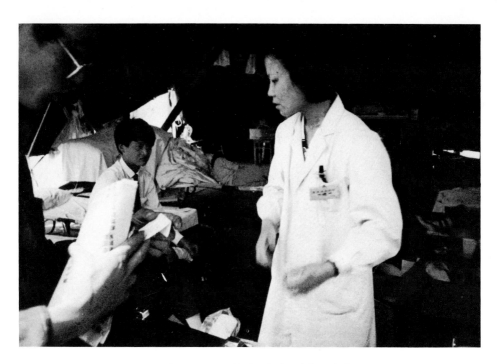

Dr. Jenny Guangzu in the field hospital she helped her father set up in
Tiananmen Square. It was crushed by tanks in the massacre.

Another view of the field hospital set up by Professor Guangzu and his
doctor daughter, Jenny, in Tiananmen Square.

PLA soldier Yang Bing (in second row, right) is photographed with his platoon in the suburbs of Beijing, two days before they went into action in Tiananmen Square. One of the soldiers is carrying a practice target.

The entrance to the Forbidden City.

PLA junior officers at the National Defense University, near Beijing, photographed in late May 1989, at target practice. They would use their skills to deadly effect against the students.

Shao-Yen Wang, the actress daughter of a powerful member of the Chinese hierarchy who had come to America to develop her career in Hollywood, found herself caught up in a real-life drama. (PHOTO: *Courtesy Shao-Yen Wang*)   At right: Shao-Yen Wang today. She is a budding model in California. (PHOTO: *Courtesy Hao Bing*)

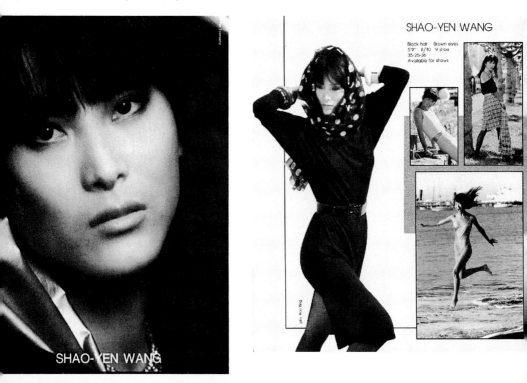

SHAO-YEN WANG

Black hair   Brown eyes
5'9"   8/10   9 shoe
35-25-36
Available for shows

SHAO-YEN WANG

Dr. Jenny Guangzu and two student helpers are pictured on the morning of Saturday, June 3, 1989, in their field hospital in Tiananmen Square. The atmosphere is relaxed. No one suspected that 12 hours later they would be engulfed with casualties before tanks crushed the hospital.

Another view of the square on the Saturday before the massacre. There are no soldiers visible, but in the Great Hall of the People thousands of troops were assembling.

Students camp out in Tiananmen Square. Many have with them their worldly belongings; many have also made wills bequeathing their possessions to relatives.

This was the student's Democracy Wall. The posters carried messages of support. But from where the students needed it most, world leaders, there was no encouragement. The West's rulers had other matters to consider, and the students were low down on the totem pole of pragmatic politics.

Newsmen wait. Many of the hundreds of reporters and TV crews in Tiananmen Square on Saturday, June 3, 1989, felt it was going to be a slow news day.

It is Saturday afternoon, June 3, 1989, and another student rally is in progress. It would be one of the last.

The cleared area is a place where student leaders could meet outside the crush in the square. In the background are the roofs of the Forbidden City.

HU MUST BE REHABILITATED read one. THERE MUST BE AN END TO SPIRITUAL POLLUTION urged another. But the most common repeated time and again the same demand: CHINA IS ENTITLED TO DEMOCRACY."

Qiao Shi reportedly was the first to react. He went to a telephone to call the public security forces. Before he could do so, Zhao Ziyang intervened. The Party chief reminded everyone what Deng Xiaoping had said. There must be no rush to action.

"Let us see what they will do," concluded Zhao. "Then we can decide what action to take."

Like the others he turned back to the window to watch the students draping a twenty-foot-long white banner around the Monument to the People's Heroes. It was emblazoned with the words "SOUL OF CHINA."

It was the first formal tribute to Hu. For a moment the banner fluttered alone on the pediment. Then Daobao and Li Yang hung their banner on the monument, proclaiming China was entitled to democracy.

In that gesture Hu's death became irrevocably linked to the students' demands.


SAME DAY, SAME TIME
*Tiananmen Square*

As dusk settled over Tiananmen Square, Daobao climbed on to the pediment of the Monument to the People's Heroes. Despite the chill of the evening, he wore only white cotton trousers, a white shirt, and a matching bandanna.

Cassy saw his face was flushed, a sign of the anger he felt.

Below, Daobao could see several hundred students looking up at him, with Cassy in their midst. The last of the visitors to the Mao Mausoleum paused to watch, then hurried on. Beyond, Daobao caught a glimpse of the brightly lit windows of the Great Hall and the tiny figures in them. Army sentries were standing around the square, uncertain what to do.

For a moment longer he surveyed the scene. He felt this was "a supreme moment, when anything was possible."

When he spoke his voice was calm and certain.

"Long live Hu Yaobang! Long live democracy! Long live freedom! Down with corruption! Down with bureaucracy!"

The first slogans had been articulated for the greatest challenge China's Communist rulers had ever faced. Behind the words were a decade of tension between economic reform and political stagnation.

They expressed a powerful idealism and a yearning for that most basic of freedoms, the right to live outside the limits set by Mao Zedong. Forty years before, he had defined democracy as no more than the right of "anyone to speak out, as long as he is not a hostile element."

Now, his voice growing in power, Daobao signaled the need to break free from that constricting bond. He continued to repeat the slogans. Those grouped around the great obelisk began to echo them, their voices blending in unison, giving the words a deeply moving and haunting effect.

Cassy felt at that moment she was "part of history and privileged to be the only foreigner to be here to witness it."

She was wrong. Watching discreetly nearby was the CIA officer, Tom. From now on either he or one of his colleagues would maintain a permanent watch on the activities in the square. Other intelligence operatives would closely monitor developments on the city's campuses. Their reports would enable the analysts, linguists, psychologists, and behaviorists at Langley to piece together what was happening. To help them to anticipate new events, still more agents would continue to "vacuum" up the mumbled words of China's leaders in their compound in Zhongnanhai, capturing their fears and growing fury over what had begun to unfold beyond the high walls of their compound. The technology of the most sophisticated intelligence-gathering agency in the world was being brought fully to bear on the last great secret society on earth.

# 12

## *Overtures*

**D**aobao called the brief appearance in Tiananmen Square by the students "a testing. We wanted to see how the authorities would respond to a deliberate illegal action."

The Chinese constitution recognized the right to demonstrate. But after the massive student protests of 1986–87, Li Xiaming, Party secretary of the city, had introduced a by-law forbidding all public demonstrations that did not have the written consent of the Public Security Office. In practice it only issued permits for state-approved demonstrations.

On the seven-mile journey back to the campus on Saturday evening the students had been ebullient: There had been no move by the authorities to intervene.

Later Daobao promised a packed meeting in the coffeehouse, "They will do nothing because we will insist we are only showing respect for Hu."

Throughout Sunday the Beijing University campus students had divided their time between turning the campus into a sea of white paper flowers and wreaths while the best calligraphers prepared banners, and consulting student leaders on other campuses in Beijing.

Late on Sunday evening the student leaders came together in a lecture hall at the University of Politics and Law in the city's western suburbs.

Eyes blinking owlishly behind thick-framed glasses, Wang Dan read out a message from Fang Lizhi, who was an authentic hero to the students. "The death of Hu is an opportunity for you to show the government you are unhappy with the present situation." Hours before, Fang had issued a similar statement to foreign journalists who knocked on his door seeking comment on Hu's death. Fang's support was greeted with jubilation by the student leaders; they had long seen him as someone who could look beyond the immediacy of the situation and judge its long-term effects.

As if in anticipation of victory, Wuerkaixi wore a new denim jacket, a gift from one of the foreign expert teachers on campus. His smile was even more all-knowing. In contrast, Yang Li had become still more withdrawn, as if the demands of being one of the movement's planners weighed heavily. Daobao remained his calm, gentle self, though admitting to withdrawal symptoms from having given up smoking.

Another student had given Wang Dan a stronger pair of shoes, but the near-sighted student leader steadfastly refused to abandon his sweatshirt and black baggy pants. He said proudly that his clothes were as distinctive a uniform as Wuerkaixi's. Chai Ling, as usual, had no time for such nonsense. Her slim legs were encased in a pair of old jeans, her face devoid of makeup.

At meetings, the student leaders also revealed the first hint of discord among them. Wuerkaixi, Daobao, and Yang Li were among those who called for all-out militancy: abandoning the classroom to demonstrate throughout the city's campuses, and then marching in force on Tiananmen Square. But even they had no clear idea what they would do there or how long they should stay.

At this Sunday night gathering Wang Dan and Liu Gang continued to lead the call for caution. Nothing must be done that would allow the authorities to say theirs was not an act of genuine mourning but only of protest. Dan urged they must move slowly and carefully, all the time trying to anticipate responses from the public and the leadership; they must constantly keep the memory of Hu to the forefront. Posters must call for Hu's remains to be placed in a coffin alongside Mao's in the mausoleum on Tiananmen Square. Other posters should tell Deng Xiaoping to admit he had made a mistake in dismissing Hu. But the content of the calligraphy "must be dignified and appear nonthreatening to the leadership. This will then place us in a position where the leadership will still feel unhappy with us, but will have to accept our motives for demonstrating."

There would be time enough, Wang Dan added, to decide what to do after this opening maneuver. The important thing was to make "a dignified statement" to the memory of Hu Yaobang.

But now, on this Monday morning, a plethora of new slogans and posters had sprouted on campuses not only throughout the city, but across the country. While some paid respect to Hu, many strongly condemned the Party and its leaders. There were blunt attacks on the crisis in education and in the economy, the rampant corruption and the lack of morality among Party officials, the resistance of the leaders to genuine political reform, and the suppression of freedom in the media. Most startling of all, thousands of posters launched a personal attack on Deng Xiaoping.

Daobao and another student had been jointly responsible for organizing what they called "our poster war."

The militant students continued to plan. Wang Dan and the others who had urged caution were swept along by the determination and enthusiasm of Wuerkaixi.

The death of Hu Yaobang and the student protest in Tiananmen Square had produced a flurry of activity among foreign diplomats. Throughout Sunday they had composed appraisals and sent them to their foreign ministers.

Some of the judgments were based on reports from intelligence operatives. Agents from the CIA, the KGB, and European intelligence services had tapped their contacts on campuses—students and tutors, some of them "foreign experts"—to try and assess how the student leadership would respond to the former Party secretary's death. Dogging their footsteps were Qiao Shi's agents on a similar mission. One European intelligence officer would recall that "not since the good old days of Berlin at the height of the Cold War could I remember so many of us out on the hoof."

Britain's ambassador, Sir Alan Donald, had dispatched to London a lengthy telegram clearly warning that Hu's death would be apotheosized by the students into a symbol for democratic reforms but was "unlikely to change the balance of power among the leadership."

Donald, a tough pragmatist behind his easygoing smile, had been in Beijing for less than a year. But his reputation as one of Britain's most astute diplomats in the Far East had been established from his time as political adviser in Hong Kong. The Chinese regarded the fifty-five-year-old Donald, who was fluent in Mandarin, as someone with whom they could do business. He had shown that by boosting Britain's bilateral trade to a new record £1.5 billion a year. With it had come an increase in joint ventures, especially in technology and manufacturing. Donald had also played a key role in encouraging the Chinese to believe Britain would do nothing to jeopardize the handing over of Hong Kong. Underscoring his telegram was a reassurance that Hu's death would not change Britain's deepening relationships with the Middle Kingdom.

The same sanguine view was being expressed to their governments by other senior diplomats in Beijing. The student march on Saturday night was seen by Raymond Burghardt, the counselor for political affairs at the American embassy, as no more than "letting off a little steam."

However, by this Monday morning a rather different view was beginning to prevail in the embassy.

CIA officers had got wind of the meeting at the University of Politics and Law and learned of the rash of posters that had appeared overnight attacking Deng Xiaoping and the leadership. The intelligence officer known as Tom had returned to the embassy with photographic evidence showing the extent of the protest posters. He told colleagues that Beijing University campus "is awash with banners calling for just about anything."

Diplomats and intelligence officers making the rounds of the city's other campuses found the mood tense and expectant.

This feeling was confirmed by Jeanne Moore, the young American journalist employed on the staff of the Party's English language newspaper, *China Daily*. When Jeanne had come to work on Sunday, she had been given a copy of the Politburo eulogy for Hu Yaobang to translate into English. It had struck her "as a fairly typical piece of leadership-speak."

The mood in the newspaper's offices on Jintai Xilu was as tense as on the campuses.

Jeanne was sure that "the editors knew, from their own conversations with Zhongnanhai, that Hu's death had caused great public speculation. In any other country this would be the major political story of the day, but this was China. Nothing could appear, would appear, without official sanction. And no one was going to give us that. The tension we all felt was caused by frustration at being forced to accept the situation. But we also sensed that the students could be up to something serious. It was the same feeling just before the 1986–87 rising, the same edginess and expectancy."

She had called the paper's bureaus in Shanghai, Guangzhou, and Hang Zhou. They reported that Hu's death had led to posters critical of the party and leadership appearing at local college and university campuses.

Leaving the office on Sunday night, Jeanne saw the staff bulletin board contained several expressions of sympathy over Hu's death.

Impulsively, she had organized a collection among the staff to buy a wreath for Hu.

This Monday morning she had gone to a florist near the *China Daily* compound and purchased one fashioned from spring flowers. Walking from the shop, holding the large wreath in both hands, she had felt slightly foolish. She had no idea where she should place the tribute.

When she returned home her husband, Jiang, a distinguished academic, told her what the students next planned to do. Jeanne realized she had found the solution to what to do with the wreath. She told Jiang she had also decided to keep a diary "to record all those things that were beginning to happen but would never find their way into print."

Barr Seitz, a tall, ruggedly handsome Yale graduate and another of the foreign experts teaching English at Beijing University, knew on this Monday morning "that the action was just around the corner, and I sure wanted to be part of it." He confided that to the diary he had started since arriving in China.

Seitz, whose father, Raymond, was a senior State Department official in Washington, had come to Beijing the previous September after majoring in Chinese political science. Like most other foreign experts he received a monthly salary of $120 for teaching one class a week. He used his ample spare time to improve his written Chinese.

The first months of his diary mostly contained the standard impressions of any visitor to China: its living customs and cultural roots; how its astronomy and irrigation techniques are the envy of the world.

But gradually Barr's observations sharpened. He had brought something of his father's eye to the paradoxes of China. His diary was filled with questions about them: How can China answer to no one in agriculture, yet has to import grain? Why does its musicians, who have one of the best of all musical traditions, create some of the worst modern music?

Setting out to answer his own questions, Barr had developed a keen and sensitive ear for what was happening around him. What he had heard and seen in those weeks past convinced him the students "are ready to blow."

During the weekend a student had brought Barr home to meet his family. The youth and his parents had spent all their waking time talking about the portents of Hu's death.

Barr had once been struck how "desperately the Chinese asked for change. My hosts were simple people with no great aspirations, except to have more of what any American would regard as the basics of life. A TV, fridge, maybe even a car. They tried to fit Hu's death into that framework. Would his departure be used by the hardliners to cut back on such things or would it be used as a chance to push forward? I couldn't imagine that kind of debate taking place anywhere else. It was a forcible reminder just how different were the value systems here from back home."

On the way back to the campus, the student had told Barr: "You know those movies where the cavalry ride in and drive out the bad guys? Well, we are the cavalry. You want to ride with us?"

Barr had smiled and said he would think about it.

By this Monday morning he had decided what he would do. He would try to get a part-time job with one of the U.S. TV network bureaus which would be reinforcing their local staff to prepare news stories for the forthcoming Gorbachev visit. With his knowledge of the language "and how this town works," the twenty-two-year-old figured he could hold his own "with any of those media stars when it came to getting things done, Chinese-style." Working with a network would also give him a chance to get an overview of where the "student cavalry" were heading.

Cassy Jones had spent most of Sunday walking around the campus, "just sensing the mood."

After Daobao had addressed the coffeehouse meeting, he had taken her aside.

"Cassy," he had said, his voice strangely formal, "we must put on ice our feelings. There will be no time for personal relations for a little while. All my energy will be needed for what is to come."

He had shaken her hand quickly and left. She realized then that she still "had a lot to learn about Daobao's priorities." Cassy did not yet know if she felt "sad or a little angry at the way he had decided things."

By Sunday afternoon the criticisms on the posters were more pointed, she noticed. Returning to the coffeeshop, she listened while Meili had read aloud a lengthy poem listing Hu's accomplishments and criticizing the attitude of many of her fellow students. The poem reminded Meili's listeners that Hu had been removed from office because he had defended the students against the leadership. And yet, Meili intoned, why hadn't all the students supported him at the time? Now he was dead. And now was the time to honor all Hu had stood for.

Meili received sustained applause for her reading. Cassy was puzzled. In class Meili had not shown any great literary aspirations. Yet the poem had considerable artistic merit. When Cassy questioned her, Meili laughed.

"The poem was written by the best poet in Nanjing," she explained.

"But how did you get hold of it so quickly?" Cassy asked.

Meili laughed again. "Easy. We have fax machines. Also computers and telephones. Wuerkaixi arranged it all."

She looked fiercely at Cassy. "You know what Mao said about war being the highest form of struggle for resolving contradictions? Well, we are getting ready for war."

Now, on this Monday morning, Cassy could "smell the whiff of action in the air."

She had arrived to find her classroom empty. Daobao soon appeared and told her there would be no lessons for the foreseeable future. He too chose the metaphor of war to explain to her what the students were going to do.

"This is our first full day of action to bring about what we most want, your kind of democracy. You have fought many wars to obtain it. We are willing to do the same, but not with weapons, only words. We think they are more powerful than any gun. People will listen to our words, and make this a peaceful war."

Once more he was gone before she could respond. For a while Cassy remained in the classroom alone. Then she walked out into the campus, where thousands of students were assembling with their banners and posters and photographs of Hu.


SAME DAY, SAME TIME
*The Foreign Office*
*London*

Susan Morton, a coltish twenty-eight-year-old with chestnut hair that framed and softened her jaw and cheekbones, was a research analyst at the Foreign Office. China was her brief. She spent her day often reading secret messages about developments there and writing reports that helped influence how Britain should respond.

On her desk were copies of the latest newspapers from China and Hong Kong. Nothing caught her eye. There was also a small pile of diplomatic telegrams.

Ambassador Donald's was on top. Like all those reports the office receives from its 350 outposts, the one from Beijing was addressed to

"Prodrome." The classical Greek for "forerunner" had been the office's telegraphic address for over a hundred years.

The telegram had been typed by Communications on a machine devoid of lowercase letters. Susan could have read the opening words from several feet away. "THERE IS AN ECHO OF THE RECENT PAST BEGINNING TO REVERBERATE IN THE UNIVERSITIES...."

Susan riffled through the other telegrams. There was nothing that could not wait. She turned back to Donald's message, reading it slowly with total concentration. It described the beginnings of a new student movement. The highly experienced diplomat believed that it could grow sufficiently powerful to confront the leadership in a way no previous movement had.

The students were calling for the separation of Party and state, the decentralization of power, the streamlining of bureaucracy, and the introduction of "full legal standards." They wanted "a channel for their demands and the voice of the masses to constantly reach the higher levels." They wanted "social consultation and conversation" with the leadership. If their demands were not met, they would take to the streets in increasing numbers. The death of Hu Yaobang had provided them with the perfect excuse.

In her analysis, Susan developed Ambassador Donald's prediction that Hu's death would be apotheosized into a symbol of democratic reforms. In her judgment, any protest would most probably be rooted in previous unsuccessful demands: the call in 1983 for an end to "spiritual pollution"; the demand in 1986–87 for an end to "bourgeois liberalization." Likely to be added to these would be demands for the rehabilitation of the victims of those previous campaigns, including Fang Lizhi's January request for the freeing of all political prisoners; demands for the disclosure of the private bank accounts of the top leaders and their families; demands for full freedom of speech and freedom of the press; and, of course, Hu's last demand for increased expenditure on education and better treatment of intellectuals.

Susan neatly encapsulated the probable effect of Hu's death on the leadership. In many ways he had never been a strong Party leader; he had only had a limited role in the actual shaping of the reform policies that had so dramatically altered the face of post-Mao China. Much of the credit for reform must go to Zhao Ziyang.

Susan reread her submission. Then she began to add to, rewrite, excise, and shape it, so that it fitted the office style, which has hardly changed over a century.

SAME DAY, LATER
*The Great Hall of the People*

Once more the Politburo had assembled to try and agree upon a policy document on education. Party Secretary Zhao Ziyang had summoned the leaders of China's eight supposedly democratic parties to join in the discussion. The parties were no more than symbols of the political system that had existed in China before Mao had taken over. Their leaders remained at the edge of the absolute power of the Party. But Zhao needed them there, to rubber-stamp his own liberal plan for the future education of China's youth.

Zhao had been speaking for some time in his reedy, somewhat high-pitched voice, when once more there was an intervention from Tiananmen Square. The first of thousands of students were approaching the square. They began to sit in an ever-expanding circle around the Monument to the People's Heroes as, one by one, their leaders draped banners and photographs of Hu over the pediment. The first of hundreds of wreaths were propped around the obelisk.

In the salon the Politburo watched what was happening with mounting anger. State President Yang Shangkun spoke for many when he said in his distinctive bullfrog voice that this must stop, *now.*

Once more Zhao used his authority. He pointed out the TV crews and photographers who were accompanying the marchers.

"The world is watching," Zhao was later quoted as saying. "Let us do nothing that will allow them to criticize us."

Then faintly but with mounting fervor came the sound of thousands of voices singing the first verse of China's national anthem, followed by the first two verses of the "Internationale."

SAME DAY, LATER
*Tiananmen Square*

Jeanne Moore had quickly persuaded her editors of the need to have a firsthand account of what was happening, even if they could not publish it. Several hours before, she had learned that students all over the city were planning to march to Tiananmen Square. Her editors had agreed, with the proviso she must do nothing to embarrass *China Daily.* They approved of her laying a wreath.

She went to her apartment in building 23 of the newspaper's compound, dressed in warm clothes against the subzero air, and took bus 9 to Tiananmen Square, arriving shortly after the first columns

of marchers. She laid the newspaper's wreath at the foot of the
obelisk, placing it among the other floral tributes.

Jeanne then began to write down her impressions. They would be
among the first detailed accounts of the birth pangs of an extraordinary moment in China's history.

"A full moon is rising over the monument to revolutionary heroes.
Tightly packed on the top platform, north side, students giving
speeches, but very hard to hear, no loudspeaker. Students going
hoarse trying to make themselves heard. The crowd, though incredibly pressed, was surprisingly civil and made an effort to be quiet to
hear. The demands were for freedom of press and speech, for
political pressure (to be free), for human rights, for multiparty
system."

On the pediment of the monument, Yang Li continued to articulate these demands. Extending his hands dramatically toward the
Great Hall of the People, he shouted.

"We demand you open the bank accounts of the leaders! Tell us
how much you earn! Tell us how big are your bank accounts in Hong
Kong, San Francisco, and Zurich!"

The first sustained burst of cheering came from the students.

"We demand you tell us about the bank accounts of your sons and
daughters!" Li Yang continued to shout, his voice raw.

The cheering grew louder.

"And we demand you tell us about the bank accounts of your
mistresses!"

A great wave of giggling and laughter rippled through the crowd.

To Jeanne the mood was "part carnival, part political."

Moving through the crowd, she noted that it was often impossible
to hear what the students on the pediment were saying. "On the grass
at the edge of the square quite a few are playing cards. Some young
women. But only three foreigners besides myself were in sight, three
men, correspondents, who walked around together getting quotes.
Every time they stopped to interview someone, a crowd formed. At
one point they were joined by two policemen who pressed into the
crowd and took notes. Over all this the full moon rose slowly against a
slate blue sky."

The foreign TV crews and photographers had by now departed. It
didn't seem to be much of a story, largely because the authorities were
doing nothing to stop the catalogue of criticism and demands coming
from the pediment.

Reaching the east side of the square, Jeanne saw a score of buses
and jeeps filled with armed police parked in front of the Museum of
the Revolution. The police, like many of the students, were playing

cards. The park benches were completely filled with lovers oblivious of their presence.

Jeanne wrote in her notebook: "Young men lie with their heads in the laps of their girls, who often read them poetry. Just like any other night."

It was not.

SAME DAY, LATER
*Zhongnanhai*

In the compound the lights burned late into the night. Prime Minister Li Peng had returned from Japan and had gone into a closed session with, among others, Beijing Party Secretary Li Xiaming, the rasp-voiced Vice-Premier Yao Yilin, and Qiao Shi, the country's intelligence chief.

Western intelligence sources, piecing together what was discussed, concurred that the meeting accepted Li Xiaming's urging to alert the commander of the 38th Army, currently responsible for the city's garrison duty, to place his troops at a state of readiness. At the same time the central military commissar should be asked to review troop displacements throughout the country. Particular attention should be paid to the possibility of withdrawing at least part of the 27th Army from Tibet should trouble develop in Beijing. The 27th had proven itself in urban warfare in Lhasa.

# 13

## *Surges*

Shortly after 4:00 A.M., alarm bells sounded throughout the compound. Moments later lights came on in the villas along the lake. The doors leading to the underground railway were opened in preparation for the evacuation of the country's octogenarian rulers. The train was made ready to take them under the earth to the airfield in the western suburbs. The unprecedented activity at this hour was recorded by a U.S. satellite and transmitted to Washington.

Four days had now passed since the first student demonstrations. In that time, as the electronic spying from outer space continued, U.S. intelligence operatives had worked their way in among the students. Often they posed as journalists, joining the genuine reporters who had begun to arrive in Beijing to write advance stories about the forthcoming Gorbachev state visit and were on hand at this early hour to witness events at Zhongnanhai.

Scores of Public Security agents took up positions inside the compound walls. They were equipped with the Western-style riot gear Qiao Shi had requested, which had just arrived, speeded on its way with the help of Henry Kissinger. Other guards began to assemble behind the lattice-work screen placed across the red-lacquered entrance gateway to conform with the traditional belief it would ward off any evil spirits attempting to enter the compound under cover of darkness.

It was not spirits who were massing at the gateway, but over five thousand students. Their ranks stretched all the way back to Tianan-men Square, where another estimated fifty thousand had assembled

134

throughout the night. They represented every university in the city. Until an hour ago they had been good-natured, singing songs and reciting poems to each other.

The previous day, Jeanne Moore had watched Yang Li walking around the pediment shouting into his megaphone. Like Cassy Jones, the American journalist was impressed by the student leader's skill at working an audience.

"Ask yourselves this! Why is it so hard to achieve democracy in China? Because the people in power have been nothing more than one form of dictatorship after another!"

A huge roar swept the square: "Down with the Communist party! Long live democracy!"

Late in the evening, the mood had changed. As the chimes from the Telegraph Building on Changan Avenue began to ring the hour, with the opening bars of the Maoist anthem, "The East Is Red," student leaders began to urge the crowd to sing the "Internationale" again.

All at once, Li, quickly followed by Daobao and Wang Dan, had left the pediment to move through the throng.

"Let's tell the leadership what we think! Let's tell them what we want!" they repeatedly cried out.

The chant was taken up around them. In a great surge the students had moved out on to Changan Avenue. Swept along, Jeanne continued to fill her notebook with impressions.

"Taxis and buses screeched to a halt. Cars began to pile up as the students blocked the entire width of the avenue. They were shouting all the time: 'Long live democracy!' 'Long live Hu Yaobang!' Bus passengers hung out of windows, bewildered and more than a little frightened by what was happening. A traffic policeman stranded on his platform appeared stunned. Then he reached for his two-way radio and began to speak."

The students surged past him, holding aloft red banners proclaiming DEMOCRACY.

As they surged along Changan Avenue, they started to sing patriotic songs. It was "like something out of an epic movie" to Cassy.

For the past two days she had hardly left Tiananmen Square. What little sleep she managed had been snatched on the steps of the monument. Students had shared their food with her. The previous day she had gone with their leaders across the square to present a formal petition of demands to the Politburo.

An officer emerged from the Great Hall of the People and told them they were breaking the law. She watched with pride as Daobao replied it was still permissible, as it had been under the emperors, to present a petition seeking redress for any legitimate case of discontent. The functionary had ordered them off the steps and stomped back into the building.

At that moment Wang Dan stepped forward. Raising a scrawny arm toward the building, the history student, now one of the mainsprings of the student movement, once more displayed a fine sense of occasion. He delivered a short, sharp warning to the back of the retreating flunky.

"Please tell your masters we can wait for days for an answer to our demands. After all, China has waited for centuries for democracy."

A great whoop greeted the words. Dan then organized the first sit-in of the demonstration. Hundreds of students had squatted on the steps, oblivious to orders from the PLA sentries to move on. The soldiers had finally given up.

To Cassy "this was the first student victory. They had shown that a combination of determination, strict discipline, and sheer gutsiness could work."

A second victory had swiftly followed. Late the previous evening three members of the National People's Congress had emerged from the Great Hall to reluctantly receive the petition. One of them promised to pass it to "superior government departments."

Watching a door of the Great Hall close behind them, Wang Dan reminded the students: "The only way to achieve all we want is to stay here in the square. No matter what they threaten to do, we must not leave!"

As word spread of the demonstration in Tiananmen Square, similar protests were under way in other cities. In Shanghai and all along the Yangzte Delta, students were on the march. From the port city of Tianjin, students had faxed support to their Beijing colleagues. From Nanjing had come another faxed message, calling for concerted action to remove "the jackals and wolves who now hold sway. There is no time to wait! Now is the time to act!"

As Jeanne Moore stood in the Wednesday morning darkness, the young reporter could see that among the students outside the gate of Zhongnanhai, the rallying call was being translated into action.

In the crowd she saw Wuerkaixi, Wang Dan, Daobao, and Yang Li leading the endlessly repeated chant.

"Li Peng! Come out! Li Peng! Come out!"

The last vestige of mourning for Hu Yaobang was lost in the deep, throaty cry of thousands of young voices demanding the appearance of the prime minister.

Through the lattice-work screen, Jeanne could see lights turning on all over the compound and shadowy figures running and shouting. Then scores of Public Security agents ran out of the gate and began to push the students back, advancing slowly shoulder to shoulder, forming a perimeter around the gateway.

For the moment there was silence. It was broken with Daobao's shout.

"Don't be frightened! Long live democracy!"

He turned and yelled at the police lines.

"Send for Li Peng! We have no quarrel with you! We only wish to speak to him personally!"

The police continued to move forward. But now the students were also on the move, their ranks shoving against the guards'. Locked together, the two masses surged back and forth.

Suddenly from the compound came the amplified voice of Security Chief Qiao Shi. "Students! You have one minute to withdraw and return to your universities! If you do not, you will be arrested. The majority of you are the victims of a small number of people who are spreading rumors and poisoning your minds. Do not let them! Leave now! Go back to your campuses!"

An uneasy silence once more fell over the students. Those around Cassy were murmuring to each other that they must not take protest too far. Many began to turn and walk away. She saw the defeated look on the faces of Daobao, Wang Dan, and the other leaders. Then, as they too turned and left, Cassy saw Wuerkaixi. He was moving quickly through the students, speaking quietly and urgently.

"Go back to the square. I shall address you there."

With those words the twenty-one-year-old education student had made his bid to establish his total authority over the students where the others had failed.

SAME DAY, LATER
*National Photographic Interpretation Center*

On the third floor of Federal Building 213, technicians continued to process the flow of information from satellites over Beijing and other sites in China. The images included not only the scenes in Tiananmen Square and in and around Zhongnanhai, but also what was happening in the various garrisons in the capital. Troops were being placed on standby, but so far none had been sent to the scenes of disturbance.

Elsewhere in Washington, the eavesdroppers of the National Security Agency were beginning to collate data coming from their sophisticated collection technology on the ground and in space over

China. Among much else, they had picked up radio traffic out of Zhongnanhai to Tibet ordering units of the 27th Army to be ready to return to Beijing at short notice.

The reports from the National Photographic Intelligence Center, together with those of the NSA, made their way upward through the multiple levels of the intelligence community, pausing to be read and initialed at places such as the National Reconnaissance Office—a highly secret, low-profile agency jointly managed by the Department of Defense and the CIA—the Bureau of Intelligence and Research, the State Department, the Defense Intelligence Agency, and the National Foreign Intelligence Board, on which all the heads of U.S. intelligence agencies sit. Finally the reports would make their way into the White House office in which the President's Daily Brief is composed.

The reports would give him a clear idea of what the students were doing and the options the Chinese leadership was beginning to formulate to deal with them. The President would be told that a military response was on the list of probable actions.

SAME DAY
*Tiananmen Square*

Daylight broke over Tiananmen Square to reveal an extraordinary sight. There were now close to a hundred thousand students spread over the slabbed ground. Some had set up tents to keep out the cold; others lay curled in sleeping bags or wrapped in blankets. Thousands of banners hung limp in the early morning mist.

Cassy thought the scene resembled "a medieval pageant." She had spent what remained of the night snuggling beside Daobao at the base of the Monument to the People's Heroes. He had hardly spoken to her; she had sensed his dejection over how quickly the students had turned and left Zhongnanhai. At dawn he had kissed her quickly on the cheek and gone off to join the other leaders at the pediment.

She could see them now, huddled around Wuerkaixi, nodding at what he was saying.

Wuerkaixi was telling them that "our only hope is to use Article 35 to legitimize what we are doing." This article of the Chinese constitution is a bill of rights giving every citizen the right to speak, publish, and, most important, organize "a lawful assembly to demonstrate and to petition."

Wuerkaixi then suggested a parameter for future demonstrations. "We must remember to always acknowledge the right of the Party to lead and the impossibility of creating an American-style democracy in our society. What we want is change within the existing framework."

While one of the students hurried away to get the exact wording of Article 35 and select key passages from it for more poster displays, Wuerkaixi addressed the gathering in the square for the first time.

It was a masterly performance. Wuerkaixi took control of the crowd at once by first addressing the hundreds of police and Public Security agents in their paramilitary uniforms who were lining the edges of the square.

"Do nothing, because we are doing no wrong! This is a lawful assembly under the constitution," Wuerkaixi shouted through one of the microphones that had begun to sprout all over the monument's pediment.

Several of the police smiled and waved good-naturedly.

Then he turned to the tens of thousands of students, many squatting on the group eating breakfast. With the skill of a street-corner orator, Wuerkaixi seized upon something his audience could all readily see, the thousands of banners and posters.

Pointing to one cluster away to his left near the Mao Mausoleum, whose messages were an attack on the Four Basic Principles of the State, Wuerkaixi began a careful and measured attack.

First he ridiculed blind adherence to Mao's kind of Marxism. Mao had said that only one kind of political thinking was correct. Wuerkaixi insisted this was a "direct violation of the freedom to think." Next he challenged the "blind adherence" the leadership demanded to all it said or did. That was "a dangerous autocracy." Then Wuerkaixi delivered a rousing dismissal of the "dictatorship of the proletariat," which gave the party the right to suppress the people at any time with any kind of force it chose. Next he challenged the very concept of socialism as practiced in China. He described it as "the greatest threat to market reform, which is the only hope for the future of our country."

The first sustained cheer of the day greeted this salvo.

Wuerkaixi then opened a freewheeling discussion, inviting his audience to step up to the pediment and address the crowd. Many did, speaking haltingly at first, then with increasing euphoria. Others, more cautious, wrote out their comments or criticism for Wuerkaixi to read aloud. He conducted the forum to which he brought a theatricality, strutting and flourishing his hands. Pausing briefly, he turned to Wang Dan and said: "You see, all they needed is to be organized. Everything is going beautifully."

So it seemed.

*The Hospital of Traditional Medicine*

Professor Guangzu looked at the young doctors and students who stood respectfully silent in his office. They had approached him as he ended his early morning visits to patients, requesting they be allowed to send a delegation to Tiananmen Square with a wreath for Hu Yaobang.

"I have no objection to that," he told them. "But I cannot allow you to stay there. Your place is here. If there is trouble and there are casualties, your work will be needed."

One of the students, a thick-set man called Chen, had then made the suggestion that led to this lengthening silence. He proposed the hospital should set up and run a first-aid post in the square for any students who might need medical help.

Professor Guangzu knew this was easier to suggest than to do. It would need approval from the hospital administration, which would almost certainly refer the matter to higher authority, which most definitely would refuse to do anything to help the students. Yet the more he considered it, the suggestion seemed a sensible one, given the hospital's designated role in the latest disaster plan. To have a first-aid post would certainly help should there be the kind of trouble Madame Hu had predicted.

The professor had visited her late the previous evening, not in Zhongnanhai, but at 25 Kuaijisi Alley, a *hutong* behind the Forbidden City, where she and her husband had recently obtained a more modest dwelling for their retirement. The house had previously belonged to Madame Hu's family.

After her husband's death his widow had moved there, where it would be easier to receive the thousands of visitors who wished to express their condolences. Floral tributes had overflowed, filling houses along the length of the *hutong*.

During Professor Guangzu's time with her, Madame Hu had expressed her fears that the students would "do something that will go beyond mourning." She was anxious to avoid any demonstration that would diminish public respect for her husband.

Returning to the hospital late the previous night, the professor had walked through Tiananmen Square and felt that what was happening was summed up by a banner raised before Tiananmen Gate. It read: WE HAVE WOKEN UP.

Going about his morning ward rounds, he had seen through the windows that hundreds more students were walking or cycling toward the square. Mingling with them were older people, workers and the unemployed. They too carried banners proclaiming their status and demanding better conditions.

Professor Guangzu came to a decision. As part of their training under the city's disaster plan, the medical staff regularly took part in field exercises, going to Tiananmen Square or some other public place and setting up a field post. He had the authority to call a rehearsal any time.

Professor Guangzu ordered Chen and a number of other doctors and students to go to Tiananmen Square and prepare a medical facility post. They should remain there until he recalled them. If challenged, they should say they were on a training exercise.

SAME DAY, SAME TIME
THE NATIONAL DEFENSE UNIVERSITY
*Beijing*

Driving past the checkpoint, Captain Instructor Kao Jyan entered the pleasant surroundings of the military campus, driving past well-tended lawns and a succession of white stone buildings. Waiting for him on the steps of the main building was an aide. He said Colonel Fan Zhichi, who was in charge of all instructors, had called an immediate meeting in the main lecture hall.

Jyan did not have to be told why. Passing Zhongnanhai, he had seen the street cleaners pulling down the last of the posters and banners the demonstrators had stuck to the walls of the compound. A patrolling policeman had told him what had happened. Turning on to Changan Avenue, Jyan heard the cheers coming from Tiananmen Square.

In the lecture hall Colonel Zhichi gave a full account of events overnight in Beijing and elsewhere.

"Lawless elements" were calling for the overthrow of the Party and had thrown bricks and bottles at the police. There had been disturbances in three military regions several hundred miles from Beijing. Army units there had gone to full readiness. The 38th Army was ready to move into Beijing. Units of the 27th Army would come from Tibet in a few days and would be based fifty miles from the capital.

But the order from Zhongnanhai made clear no military intervention would occur for the time being. When and if it came, the university's instructors would play their part in implementing the plan they had devised to bring in troops either by helicopter or through the network of tunnels beneath Beijing. Speed and determination would be the key to success.

SAME DAY, LATER
*Tiananmen Square*

Brian Davidson, the press attaché at the British embassy, and Brendan Ward, second secretary at the Irish embassy, disagreed over the size of the crowd in the square.

Ward, a solemn-faced twenty-seven-year-old blessed with an acerbic wit, estimated the number would comfortably fit into Lansdowne Road, the rugby stadium in his beloved Dublin. That made it around sixty-five thousand. Davidson, a tall, fair-haired twenty-five-year-old preppy, who had been born in Jamaica and raised in Northern Ireland, put the number "as likely to overflow Wembley Stadium on Cup Final day," close to a hundred thousand.

The two diplomats had been firm friends from their first meeting, drawn to each other in part by a common understanding of the problems Britain faced in Ulster and an abhorrence of what the IRA represented.

Their embassies had sent them here, in Davidson's words, "to do a little sussing," to find out what was happening. Behind his carefully nurtured mannerisms, snappy dress, and hard-won street savvy was a cool head. Fluent in Mandarin and with a good grasp of the nuances of Chinese politics, Davidson was a rising star in the British embassy compound. Ambassador Donald shared a view common among senior staff: Davidson could one day be British ambassador to China.

In Ireland's small and widely spread diplomatic service, Ward was also considered a comer. Unlike Davidson, he had "no real love affair with China." Lacking the language, he found the Chinese remained almost as great a mystery as they had been the day he arrived in Beijing.

But this morning one mystery had become a little clearer to the Irish diplomat, the purpose of the inquiries Daobao and Liu Yang had made about IRA hunger strike methods some weeks ago. Seeing the extent of the protest, for Ward "the penny dropped. These people would go all the way, and that could include hunger strikes. There was a determination about them to succeed that was both inspiring and a little scary."

He and Davidson continued to move slowly through the crowd, listening and noting down what was being said. Davidson reminded Ward that Mao had said violent protest was the logical continuation of politics.

Ward said the scene didn't look so much a potential battlefield, more like an outside version of a gathering of the gypsies in his own country. There was that same good-tempered watchfulness.

Other foreigners were also making judgments.

The Russian embassy had sent over a dozen diplomats, including Minister-Counselor Vladimir Kudinov and Counselor Anatoly Bykov. The Russians were moving determinedly across the square, pausing from time to time to compare notes. Kudinov found the situation "a little hard to understand. For many it seemed to be an excuse for a day out."

Boris Klimonko, the embassy's first secretary and a fluent Mandarin speaker, busily copied out the details of the floral tributes to Hu around the Monument of the People's Heroes. While the majority came from campuses, he found a surprising number from within the Party itself. Some of those had messages that could be construed as support for the students. The one from the *People's Daily,* the mass-circulation organ of the Party Central Committee, bore a thinly veiled reminder that Hu had said protest could be beneficial. A similar sentiment accompanied the massive wreath from the Communist Youth League, with which Hu had been so closely associated.

As Klimonko continued his basic intelligence gathering, students from the Central Institute of Fine Art arrived with a giant black-and-white framed photograph of Hu. They hoisted it on the monument's pediment, pointing it so that Hu's gnome-like face stared resolutely out over the heads of the crowd toward the portrait of Mao on Tiananmen Gate.

Raymond Burghardt, the U.S. embassy's counselor for political affairs, one of several American diplomats monitoring events, was suddenly struck by the "vision that Beijing now had two very separate and rival sources of authority: Hu and his students, Mao and those in his mold."

Others too were coming to the conclusion that two different versions of Communism were confronting each other. Among them were the growing number of foreign intelligence officers who had slipped out of the legation quarter to take stock for themselves.

Some, like the middle-aged and jovial Boris Kavik of the KGB, were easy to spot; moving through the throng, he shook hands and proffered cigarettes. Like the other Russians, Kavik was primarily concerned with discovering how long the students intended to stay in that square. Several told him they would remain until the planned May 4 rally. That would leave an eleven-day gap before Mikhail Gorbachev's state visit, due to begin on May 15.

Intelligence officers from the CIA and European intelligence agencies were trying to discover whether the Russians themselves were encouraging the demonstrations, either as part of the "wind of change" currently sweeping through the Soviet bloc and fanned by calls for democracy there, or to create what one intelligence officer called "a little mischief, to wrong-foot the Chinese leadership before Gorbachev came."

The CIA's Tom would report no evidence had so far emerged indicating either to be the case. The demonstrations appeared to be totally inspired and controlled by students.

Nevertheless, on this Wednesday in the vast, crowded expanse of Tiananmen Square, the local foreign intelligence community continued to watch the students and each other. Posing as newspeople or supportive onlookers, the agents continued to work their way into the trust of the students. They made no attempt to directly infiltrate its leadership on the monument's pediment, concentrating instead on those camped around it. No doubt flattered to be the object of such attention, the students spoke freely about their hopes and plans.

By midday the intelligence officers could confirm what diplomats such as Brian Davidson and Brendan Ward were reporting to their superiors: The demonstrations were going to continue and intensify.


SAME DAY, SAME TIME
*San Francisco*

Shao-Yan Wang, the daughter of a high-ranking official in Beijing, watched the television pictures of the scenes in Tiananmen Square with mounting excitement. Time and again she thought she saw familiar faces as the camera panned over the crowd. The reporter kept saying this was a peaceful demonstration to mark the week of mourning for Hu Yaobang.

Shao-Yen realized the reporter clearly had little understanding of the Chinese language, or he would have understood the snatches of Mandarin she heard students shout at the camera.

"Hu Yaobang didn't have a foreign bank account!" cried one. Another said: "Help us overthrow dictatorship." A third, in a husky Beijing accent, appealed: "People of the world, listen to us!"

As the camera focused on the Mao obelisk, Shao-Yen saw a poster that would probably have meant nothing to foreigners but was full of portent for her. It read: TZU-HSI MUST NOW RETIRE. Empress Tzu-Hsi had continued to rule at the end of the nineteenth century long after she had promised to give up power. The poster was clearly a pointed reference to Deng Xiaoping's insistence on remaining in office.

All too soon the TV report was over. Shao-Yen telephoned her father in Beijing. She could hear the concern in his voice as he told her about the march on Zhongnanhai.

"That has never happened before," he said.

"What will happen now?" she asked.

"No one knows," he replied. "But I fear there will be much more trouble. It is good you are not here."

Something in his voice stopped Shao-Yen from telling him of her efforts so far to interest Americans in China's desire for democracy. One of Qiao Shi's agents could be listening. She had heard they monitored all calls to and from China.

After speaking to her father, Shao-Yen telephoned Chinese friends in the Bay area to report what she had seen on TV and what her father had said, including his prediction of further trouble.

"We must all try and see what we can do to help," she concluded each time.

But no clear plan emerged. In many ways she and her friends seemed like all those students she had seen milling around Tiananmen Square, Shao-Yen thought.


SAME DAY, NIGHTFALL
*Tiananmen Square*

Professor Guangzu picked his way through the sprawling students. He could remember nothing quite like this. During the Cultural Revolution the square had been filled with the Red Guards, many of them as young as the students now occupying Tiananmen, and their violent slogans. More recently, in the 1986–87 demonstrations that had led to Hu's purging for supporting the students, the prevailing mood had also been of aggression.

But now "a great peace" hung over the square. To Professor Guangzu it seemed "sufficient that the students were there. They kept on repeating the same chant, though none I spoke to could explain what the words actually represented. Beyond this call for democracy, there was no tangible thought-through political philosophy."

Yet he recognized that the very vagueness of what the students were calling for was a strength. They could incorporate into their chants almost any demand that might help to bring about a change in the country's cultural system.

In the crowd of several hundred thousand, the professor noticed a considerable number of workers were also present. More were arriving. They repeatedly told the students that they had come to lend more support. Yet he could see little that would reinforce the concern Madame Hu had expressed, that the gathering would exploit her husband's death. The students' posters were no more than he had expected.

Reaching the first-aid tent, he learned his staff had not yet had to treat a single injury. He sat for a while and chatted with them. Shortly before 10:00 P.M. he left. There had still been no call for his staff to deal with any injuries. The crowd was one of the most well behaved he could recall.

Professor Guangzu had almost reached Changan Avenue when he saw thousands of students parading from the west side of the square, repeatedly chanting "Bring us Li Peng!" Recovering from the suddenness of what was happening, he joined the people running down Changan, the Avenue of Eternal Peace. Professor Guangzu sensed then that "the time of tranquility was over."

Among those leading the second charge to Zhongnanhai were Li and Daobao. The decision to carry the protest to the leadership compound again was spontaneous, they would insist. In Daobao's words, "We had been sitting around all day waiting for a response to our demands. It made people excitable and frustrated." Those emotions were joined by anger as the crowd ran along the street.

Once again the indefatigable Jeanne Moore was among them. As she was swept into the approach road to Zhongnanhai, she saw that at least a thousand police had formed lines further down the street. The crowd charged them at full tilt. The first line gave. Fifty feet further on, the second line held, then collapsed. Only one row of police stood between the mob and the gateway to Zhongnanhai.

Sensing victory was theirs, they paused. It was a mistake. Within moments the two broken police lines had reformed, cutting off the people still approaching from Changan Avenue. At the same time hundreds of police emerged from the compound, brandishing leather belts. Behind them were rows of armed militia.

Trapped between the two forces, the students lost their resolve. They turned and ran back through the reformed police ranks. Reaching Changan Avenue, they squatted across the wide thoroughfare, completely disrupting traffic.

It struck Professor Guangzu as a pointless display.


SAME TIME, SAME DAY
*Los Angeles*

Professor Guangzu's daughter, Jenny, and her husband, Zhong, were engaged in another of their arguments.

Dr. Jenny Guangzu had the same nut-brown eyes as her father, but her hair was thick and black, like her mother's. People often found it hard to believe she was thirty and had been a qualified surgeon for the past four years. She looked like a premed student, and she was not bossy or arrogant as many expected a doctor to be.

Americans have such a funny way of speaking, she had told Zhong. Her husband said this was because they are often so badly educated; there was nothing worse than listening to adults talking like children, he had added.

Nowadays, Jenny realized, he complained about most things, especially on those days when the hospital where they both worked was half-shrouded in smog. No matter how often she told him the weather had been far worse in Beijing, he continued to find fault. When it wasn't the smog, it was the cholesterol in the food or the way the hospital was run and the profits it made.

Though her father had never said so, Jenny knew he was disappointed she had married Zhong. Her husband was too dogmatic for her father. Jenny had hoped America would liberate Zhong. Instead he had become increasingly more assertive that China offered a far more worthwhile life-style than America. Once more it had led to an argument.

This one had been triggered by one of the TV reports from Beijing. After watching it, Jenny had said that China could be on the verge of the great breakthrough to democracy. Significantly, the authorities appeared to be making no attempt to end the protest, which could indicate that the moderates within the leadership had managed to convince Deng Xiaoping to further extend reforms. They might return home to a country dramatically changed for the better.

"For the worse!" Zhong had stormed. If democracy meant the kind of capitalist world they lived in now, he wanted no part of it for China.

Jenny looked around the living room of their apartment in West Hollywood. It contained a TV, stereo, a VCR, and good quality furniture. In the kitchen were a dishwasher, microwave, washing machine, and refrigerator. She didn't know one home in Beijing that was similarly equipped. Here there were no street committees snooping and prying. She could say and do what she liked.

The argument had followed a familiar path, with Jenny extolling the freedoms of America and Zhong becoming increasingly critical. They still had not resolved their differences when they fell asleep.

# 14

## A Time of Decision

FRIDAY NIGHT–SATURDAY MORNING, APRIL 21–22, 1989
*Beijing*

Standing below the pediment of the Monument to the People's Heroes late on Friday evening, Cassy felt that the entire city appeared on the move under cover of darkness. The demonstrations were in their sixth day.

Changan Avenue was lined with people, as it would be for any big parade. They were mourners for Hu Yaobang's funeral, which would take place late next morning in the Great Hall of the People. She estimated there could be over a million people waiting patiently to pay their respects. More were emerging from the alleys on either side of the broad avenue.

As midnight approached, a great stirring came from the crowd. In the distance Cassy and the others on the pediment heard the sound of singing growing louder.

Students from all the city's campuses had begun to march toward Tiananmen Square, chanting and singing, in columns of fifty to several hundred people each. Traffic police stood numb and helpless on their podiums at intersections. Public Security agents worked frantically to film and photograph faces in the advancing columns, then gave up, defeated by sheer numbers.

As they arrived on Changan Avenue, the student marshals with each column gave a brisk order. Picking up stride, the marchers burst into the Chinese national anthem: "Rise up, you who refuse to be slaves."

Her eyes brimming with tears of pride, Cassy turned to Daobao. "You did it!" she said. "You all really did it."

148

"Everybody helped," Daobao grinned, watching the columns taking up their predetermined positions in the square. Nothing had been left to chance.

The planning had begun the night before, following the students' third failure to gain entry to Zhongnanhai. Over fifteen thousand students had tried to storm the compound. This time the police had sprung a well-prepared trap. They had emerged from the alleys around Zhongnanhai, waving the leather thongs they used for crowd control. At the same time, loudspeakers from inside the compound had unleashed a continuous denunciation, repeatedly calling the students "reactionaries," a condemnation second in gravity only to "counterrevolutionary" in official-speak.

Half-deafened by the loudspeakers and stunned at the way the police suddenly attacked them, the students turned and fled. This time they were not allowed to go unmolested. They were chased and often severely beaten.

Professor Guangzu's first-aid post was soon filled with casualties. Several required hospitalization.

Hours later the rain had begun, washing away the blood on Changan Avenue. The downpour had also driven most of the students on Tiananmen Square back to their campus dormitories. They had left their posters and banners behind. Standing guard over the emblems was a token force of no more than five hundred students. Sodden and hungry, they had appeared to be no threat, and the police had ignored them.

"The protest movement had looked all but washed out," Jeanne Moore had recorded in her notebook. She had gone home to sleep. A few hours later, she received a telephone call from a contact at Beijing University. The rain had stopped, and fresh posters had gone up, demanding revenge and renewed action.

The messages on the posters had been composed by Meili, whose meticulous calligraphy had already become a hallmark of the demonstrations. Her latest messages were as uncompromising as always. "The blood of our classmates must not have been given for nothing"; "Since the time of the First Emperor, we have lived under a dictatorship. This must end."

By dawn on Friday the posters were being tacked up on every door, tree, and pole in the campus.

That morning Wang Dan and Wuerkaixi had addressed student leaders in the university's coffeehouse. Hundreds of students gathered outside to stop any attempt by the campus political officers to halt the meeting.

Wuerkaixi's denims looked as if he had slept in them. His voice was hoarse from hours of public speaking. Wang Dan's eyes were red-rimmed behind his spectacles. Though both of the student leaders looked exhausted, they had lost none of their verve.

Wuerkaixi reminded his listeners that the protest of 1986 had been led by provincial campuses such as Hefei and Changhai.

"That must not happen now," he insisted. "It is our duty here in the capital to show leadership! We must control matters from here. In that way we will have a movement that will be coordinated and not diffuse as before."

Wuerkaixi had then proposed they form a Beijing Students Solidarity Preparation Committee drawn from all the city's campuses.

Nine members were quickly elected: Wuerkaixi; Wang Dan; Chai Ling; her husband, Feng Conde; Liu Gang; Xiong Yan, a law student, whose job it would be to provide the legal arguments needed to justify protest; Yang Tao, a history student; Yan Daobao; and Yang Li. Among them they represented the entire spectrum of the students' points-of-view.

Wuerkaixi, Chai Ling, and her aggressive-voiced husband, Feng Conde, were the recognized militants. They could count on the support of Daobao and Li. Daobao found that giving up smoking had made him increasingly short-tempered, while Li now almost never showed that half-smile which had annoyed his brother Bing.

Wang Dan represented the articulate voice of moderation. While he was not against continued public demonstration, he wanted to operate strictly within legal constraints. To that end he was supported by Xiong Yan, who could recall the dry words of Chinese jurisprudence with no apparent effort. Yang Tao was another moderate, bringing a calming authority to discussions.

The first collective decision of the committee was to produce a manifesto. It bore all the "marks of too many hands turning out too many characters," in the verdict of Barr Seitz, the young American foreign expert who taught English at Beijing University. To him the style of the manifesto "was more like a Party document, but given the contents it was also a time bomb with the fuse lit."

A big-character poster, called an "Open Letter to Beijing College," listed the tactics. This Friday night, every student in the city would march to Tiananmen Square. There they would remain until further notice. They would be fed and watered in rotation. There would be a call for volunteers to go on hunger strike.

After she read a copy of the poster, reporter Jeanne Moore sensed "it was part of a new and very different game plan. The manifesto bore the signs of learning from past mistakes, of understanding the need to stiffen resolve now that the authorities had struck back. In many ways it was a declaration of war."

Her judgment was affirmed by the intelligence operatives and foreign diplomats monitoring student activities. In the legation quarter three miles to the east of Tiananmen Square, reports were compiled and forwarded to Washington and elsewhere.

In the Beijing office of Kissinger Associates, staff sent an update on the demonstrations to the consultancy's office in Washington, with a copy to the American-China Society, housed in the same building in the capital. The report would be distributed by Henry Kissinger to his fellow board members, former Presidents Jimmy Carter, Richard Nixon, and Gerald Ford, as well as executive members Alexander Haig, Robert McFarlane, and Zbigniew Brzezinski. Some of the most powerful men in the United States had "had their alarm bells rung," a Kissinger Associates employee would say.

President Bush's brother had also been alerted. Prescott Bush was a consultant to Asset Management, International Financing and Settlement Ltd. Its Chinese interests included financing the building of an $18 million country club in Shanghai, a wood-processing plant in rural China, and a satellite-linked computer database network based in Beijing. He was among the first of a growing number of U.S. businessmen who feared that the students' decision to take up permanent residence in Tiananmen Square until their demands for democracy were met could wreck all their carefully nutured plans.

Throughout Friday, Daobao had played his part in ensuring that from now on, matters would go exactly as the committee ordained. While other members made telephone calls and sent faxes to provincial campuses asking them to send delegations to Tiananmen Square, Daobao and Yang Li had busied themselves with preparations for what was intended to be the largest demonstration since the Cultural Revolution.

An action committee had selected student marshals to supervise the marchers and songs for the columns to sing. As they passed close to the walls of Zhongnanhai, they would sing the "Internationale," then, coming onto Changan Avenue, the opening verse of the national anthem with its call to rise and be free. Each student would bring sufficient food for several days and a bedroll.

Now, as Friday night passed into the first hour of Saturday morning, the totally disciplined columns continued to arrive in Tiananmen Square. The night was mild, the atmosphere tense. As the last of the columns arrived, the first of several thousand police were being bused onto Changan Avenue.

At 5:00 A.M., the voice of Chen Xitong, the mayor of Beijing, roared over the square's loudspeakers announcing that the area and the surrounding streets would be sealed in three hours for the funeral of Hu Yaobang.

From the pediment that had now become the source for all student pronouncements, Wuerkaixi calmly announced that the students were not going to leave but intended to hold their own funeral for Hu.

A great gasp swept the square and the crowd on Changan Avenue.

"All around me people are saying no one has ever dared upstage an official ceremony," Jeanne Moore scrawled in her notebook. "Plans for the whole funeral have been carefully stage-managed to make it a Party-only occasion. No public viewing of the body to allow the focus to be Hu. No foreign delegations. Every one of the several thousand guests a Party member."

With breathtaking bravado, Wuerkaixi had calmly announced the students intended to disrupt the single most important event in the Party calendar so far this year.

Minutes later Chen Xitong's voice once more spoke from the loudspeaker: The students must now leave.

At Wuerkaixi's order, everyone sat down in a concerted move. Around the monument, the student marshals locked arms. The student leaders waited on the pediment.

Police began to cordon off the square. Jeanne Moore, one of the few foreign reporters inside, continued to write furiously.

"The police are not armed, but some have removed their belts and are slapping them against their hands inches from the students' faces. In other places, the confrontations are more good-natured. When the police and students push against each other, the students embrace the police and chant 'People's cops should love the people! People's cops should join the people!' A group of spectators on a restaurant roof are urging the crowd to break through the police lines, singing for encouragement the Chinese national anthem. When they reach the words 'The Chinese people have reached a critical point, Let's march forward under the enemy bombardment', the students and police, who have been on the point of violence, break out in laughter."

At 5:20 A.M., first light, Wang Dan and Wuerkaixi walked up the steps of the Great Hall of the People and knocked loudly on its center door. Three officers in dark Mao jackets appeared and said they were from the Funeral Organization Office. The senior officer started to express concern that all the Party's efforts to give Hu Yaobang a fitting funeral were now in jeopardy.

The Goddess of Liberty—the very symbol of student aspirations—rises proud and defiant over Tiananmen Square on the night of Saturday, June 3, 1989.

In the "consult area" a group of student leaders including Li Yang (far right in spectacles) discuss their next move late on Saturday afternoon. But already the die had been cast by the aged rulers of China.

The first confrontation. Troops arrive in a western suburb late on Saturday afternoon, June 3, 1989, and form a line across the street. Anyone attempting to cross will be shot.

Li Yang (foreground) leads a procession of students past the Great Hall of the People on Saturday, June 3, 1989.

Daobao and Li Yang's girlfriend, Meili, photographed in Tiananmen Square on the evening of June 3, 1989. Hours later they would be fleeing the might of the PLA soldiers—including Li's brother, Bing.

The Goddess of Liberty rises above the tens of thousands in the square on the Saturday afternoon of June 3, 1989.

Students assemble around the foot of the Mao monument in Tiananmen Square as they await the arrival of the army.

The troops arrive in Tiananmen Square. There is a confrontation.

PLA tanks rumble into Tiananmen Square as the students try to stop them by sitting in their path. Later, many would be crushed for such bravery.

The bodies lay everywhere in and around Tiananmen Square.

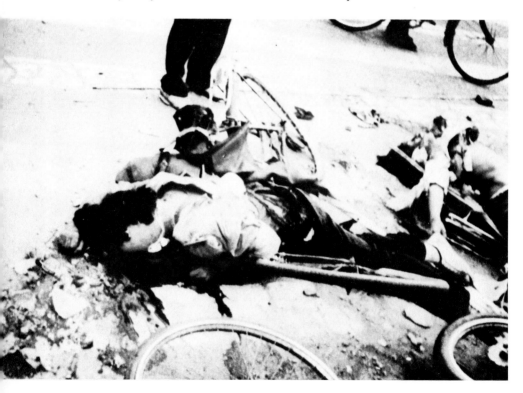

TOP: The Beijing Government put up this poster to "commemorate" the "bravery" of the PLA in suppressing student "counterrevolutionaries." CENTER: Students at Beijing University read the official version of events. BOTTOM: Gordon Thomas (left, back to camera) outside Deng Xiaoping's compound in Beijing. The visit enabled him to further research the events there prior to the massacre.

PLA Company Commander Tan Yaobang with author Gordon Thomas in Tiananmen Square. In the background is the Great Hall of the People. This, like other meetings with PLA officers, was arranged by the military commissar.

Melinda Liu, a *Newsweek* correspondent whose reporting was one of the highlights of media coverage.

Author Gordon Thomas talking to one of the 100 eyewitnesses to China's Night of Infamy that he interviewed.

(PHOTO: *Cassy Jones*)

With one of his hand flourishes, Wuerkaixi said the students did not intend to disrupt the rites. But they had three demands. First, they wanted a firm guarantee there would be no police violence against anyone in the square. Second, they wanted a delegation to be admitted to view Hu's body to pay respects on behalf of all the students. Third, they wanted a complete explanation "from the proper authorities" for the police violence on Thursday night.

The official blinked furiously in the gathering light, then turned on his heels and walked back into the hall. He left the door ajar.

Wang Dan and Wuerkaixi sat on the stone steps, staring out at the endless rows of squatting students who had swung round to face the Great Hall.

Forty minutes later the senior official returned. The two students rose to their feet. In a strangled voice the functionary said the only demand that would be accepted was a guarantee for the students' safety.

"Then I must inform you," Wang Dan said in his most formal voice, "that we will continue to stay here until further notice."

Without waiting for a reply, he and Wuerkaixi walked back down the steps.

SATURDAY, APRIL 22, 1989
*Zhongnanhai*

At 9:00 A.M., Deng Xiaoping arrived from his compound half a mile to the north of Zhongnanhai. He made the journey underground, brought from beneath his mansion on board a red carriage.

At Zhongnanhai's underground station the carriage was coupled to others and pulled by a small but powerful electric engine the short distance to the cavernous bowels of the Great Hall. Elevators bore the supreme leader and his colleagues up to the salon where the funeral rites would be held.

Lesser guests had been escorted through a ten-deep cordon of police and soldiers outside in Tiananmen Square.

Realizing that Deng and Prime Minister Li Peng had, like the emperors of old, refused to show their faces to their subjects, the students were singing and chanting poems of praise for Hu mingled with cries of contempt for the Party leaders.

They had only broken off to fall into respectful silence when Madame Hu appeared with her family. With them walked Professor Guangzu. He felt the anger of the students "was like a flame close to a box of dynamite. One mistake by the authorities and anything could have happened."

Inside the Great Hall Madame Hu led the mourners in a slow file past her husband's coffin. Zhao Ziyang then delivered his eulogy, while Deng Xiaoping stood watching impassively. When the Party secretary completed his carefully scripted remarks, Deng turned to Madame Hu, arms extended as if to offer condolence.

She waved him away. For a moment Deng stood, more ashen-faced than usual. Then he walked out of the salon, his face a mask. Li Peng and Zhao Ziyang quickly followed him.

As other mourners emerged into Tiananmen Square, many visibly flinched at the sea of flags and banners. The first thunderous chorus broke over them:

"We want dialogue! Down with dictatorship!"

The voices drowned out the funeral dirge coming through the loudspeakers. Then from the pediment Wuerkaixi called for silence. It came at once.

Cassy watched Wuerkaixi, Wang Dan, and Daobao walk slowly and purposefully across the square, the ranks of students parting before them. It reminded her of "the showdown in *High Noon*."

Wuerkaixi carried a rolled scroll in his hand. Reaching the steps of the Great Hall, they paused to turn and look at the silent crowd. Even the music had stopped.

Then they climbed the steps. Their slow, deliberate movements reminded Jeanne of "Confucian officials of Imperial times submitting statements of moral criticism to the throne."

The students knelt before the closed central door of the Great Hall. Slowly Wuerkaixi raised the scroll above his head. When he had done so, all three, in perfect harmony, chanted for Li Peng to enter into dialogue with the students. They continued to repeat this for half an hour. Then they turned and faced the still silent crowd.

"We have tried!" Wuerkaixi called out. "We have really tried!"


SAME DAY, LATER
*Sacramento, California*

Sue Tong was on her way to her postgraduate classes at Sacramento University when she heard the report on the all-news stations of how the students had disrupted the funeral.

The thirty-one-year-old cousin of the PLA Military Academy instructor Jyan had been in America for a year. In that time she had divorced her authoritarian Chinese husband and found new love with an American artist, Rod. They planned to marry this coming June.

She pulled her car into a gas station and phoned Rod. He had also heard the radio report.

"You think this will blow over?" Rod asked.

"No. This is only the beginning. There will be no stopping them after this," Sue predicted.

"You sound like you wish you were there."

"I do," she promptly said. "I really do."

There was a pause before Rod spoke. "We've got a wedding date to keep."

"I know," she replied. "June fourth. I'll be there."

"But you just can't drop everything and go to Beijing."

This time Sue was silent.

"What would you do if you went?" Rod gently pressed.

"I don't know right now, except just be there. Sometimes it's enough to show solidarity. That's very important to us Chinese, to support each other. You Americans are so independent. We draw strength from collective response."

"If you go, when will you go?"

"I don't know. It's just I feel…this tug to be there," Sue said.

"If you go, you shouldn't go empty-handed. Those students are going to need help. Dollar help. Maybe you should start collecting from the Chinese community here."

Sue laughed. Rod's practicality was one of the things she loved about him.

"I'll start today. If everyone only gives ten dollars, it could come to a lot!"

"You really think you can go and get back for the wedding?" The date was now six weeks away.

"Just let anyone try and stop me!" Sue said.

Driving to the campus she began to plan her fund-raising strategy.

MONDAY, APRIL 24, 1989
*Foreign Legation Quarter*

Judging by what was happening in the British embassy, Brian Davidson was certain the entire legation quarter was "popping with a mixture of anticipation, excitement, and, no doubt, some apprehension that this business would really get out of hand." The demonstrations were now in their ninth day.

Throughout the weekend the press attaché had continued gathering information. After Hu's funeral, the students had paraded around Tiananmen Square. Late in the afternoon Wuerkaixi, in one of the changes of plan that would become a trademark of his leadership style and cause confusion and often resentment among other student leaders, ordered the majority of students to return to their campuses and rest. They would receive further orders by Monday morning.

Several students had been left to occupy the ground around the Monument to the People's Heroes.

On Sunday the litter-strewn square had been given over to the old men who normally flew their kites there. The graceful shapes had soared up to meet those high in the sky over Zhongnanhai. Among them was Premier Li Peng's.

Davidson had picked up hints of mounting tension inside the compound. He had reported to Ambassador Donald that his contacts were claiming the leadership was both "divided and obsessed" with how to handle the students.

Zhao Ziyang had ordered the police presence to withdraw immediately after the last official mourner had left the Great Hall on Saturday. The order had led to the students' peaceful departure.

"Zhao was clearly promoting a hands-off approach," Davidson told Ambassador Donald. "But the rumors were circulating that Zhao himself was behind the protest. The story wouldn't go away that he was using the students with an eye to actually seizing power."

"There seemed no real basis for the story, but it was a dangerous one to have your name linked to," Ambassador Donald told the press attaché. "What we are looking at here is perhaps the ultimate battle within the leadership, a power struggle between ambitious men and their competing visions of China."

The two hardliner vice-premiers, Qiao Shi and Yao Yilin, supported by Beijing Party Secretary Li Xiaming and Mayor Chen Xitong, had called an emergency meeting of the Politburo Standing Committee, a five-member "inner circle" who reported directly to Deng Xiaoping, for Monday evening. By then they wanted the police back in full strength around the square to keep the students out.

As reports came in of serious disturbances in the provincial cities of Xian and Changsha, the hardliners brought the meeting forward to Sunday morning, in Li Peng's office. Zhao was asked to attend. The hope, Davidson had learned, was to persuade the Party secretary to "see sense and support a tough line." Instead Zhao had gone off to play a round of golf and then boarded the train taking him on an official visit to North Korea. The meeting had gone ahead without him.

Furious at Zhao's casual attitude, the hardliners were about to inform Deng when Li Peng suggested a different strategy. He would arrange for Deng to receive full reports on the near-riots in Xian and Changsha, so Deng could judge for himself the seriousness of the situation. Then he could be persuaded more easily to take action. In both cities "student hooligans" and "unemployed hooligans" had attacked government offices, overturned cars, and looted shops. Police had been stoned and fires started.

Davidson had learned many of the rioters had worn Mao buttons, an indication they had scant interest in the student demands for "democracy." The Maoists had gone on the rampage demanding a return to the policies of Mao, under which there had indeed been full employment and stable prices.

On Sunday evening Li Peng had gone to see Deng. As well as the riot reports, the prime minister brought a strongly worded letter from the Beijing Municipal Party Committee, demanding the "strongest possible action to protect our city from reactionary elements."

Davidson's contacts had given him an account of Deng's reaction. China's supreme leader had read the documents. For a while he had sat in silence, smoking. Then he had told Li Peng that the students must be stopped by whatever means necessary. If there had to be deaths, so be it, Deng was reported to have said.


SAME DAY, SAME TIME
*China Daily compound*
*Beijing*

Jeanne Moore was transferring onto her computer, by far the most expensive item in her living room, the results of her Sunday spent on the Beijing University campus. It would form the basis for an article she planned to send to a Midwest newspaper. She was one of many foreign experts whose specialist knowledge had now been eagerly snapped up by the U.S. media, which sensed a major story developing. *China Daily*, however, had yet to publish anything about what was happening in Tiananmen Square or elsewhere in the country.

Jeanne had learned that the students had put up a poster listing by name and position officials who were relatives of senior Party and government personnel and demanding their removal. They had also hung posters outside the city's post offices claiming their telegrams to provincial universities seeking still more support were being intercepted.

A student in Baoding had telephoned Wang Dan to say a train had arrived from Tibet with units of the 27th Army. Baoding was fifty-

four miles west of Beijing. Wang Dan had immediately sent students
to spread the word around the factories and farming communes in
the vicinity of Beijing. The workers were to be encouraged to support
the students by allowing them to put up posters in work places and by
sending delegations to Tiananmen Square.

Jeanne had completed typing her notes when an editor called from
*China Daily*. The man's excitement and nervousness were all too plain.
He told her that Deng Xiaoping had circulated instructions on how
the Chinese media was to report the developing story.

"First, we must prepare our readers to accept Hu Yaobang made
grave mistakes in the past few years," began the editor. "We must be
ready to report that Hu was not a true Marxist and criticize those who
say he was."

Jeanne remembered Zhao Ziyang had called Hu a true Marxist in
his funeral eulogy. Now that the Party secretary was in North Korea,
the hardliners had clearly persuaded Deng to make his first serious
criticism of his fellow official.

The editor continued. Deng had ordered the attack on Hu must
emphasize he "took a very weak stand during the campaign against
spiritual pollution and wholesale Westernization."

Hu's remains were still on their way to be cremated in his
birthplace, but his reputation already "was going up in smoke,"
Jeanne realized.

When the time came, her editor told her, China's media would
blame Hu for everything that was happening. Future editorial policy
had been clearly spelled out in one last chilling paragraph from
Deng Xiaoping.

"We must mobilize the masses and use a mass campaign to stop the
demonstration. Those people, plotters, behind the students must be
reported and exposed."

To Jeanne it was obvious that Party Secretary Zhao was to be the
ultimate target. It was the first clear evidence that Deng Xiaoping
had finally decided who he wanted to be his successor. Premier Li
Peng.


SAME DAY, LATER
*Washington, D.C.*

It was still Sunday in the capital when at noon the fax machine in CIA
Director Webster's comfortably furnished home came to life with a
message from his station chief in Beijing. The report was a detailed
evaluation of the power struggle in Zhongnanhai. All the signs

pointed to Deng preparing to use his prime minister as his instrument to crush the students on this, the ninth full day of demonstrations in China.

The unspoken question in the report was: "What, if anything, should the United States do?

Webster knew what he must do. He called Secretary of State James Baker, who would tell the President. Only Bush could ultimately decide how, and at what level, the United States should respond to the decision of China's supreme leader to deal with the students.

WEDNESDAY, APRIL 26, 1989
*Deng Xiaoping's compound*
*Beijing*

At daybreak two Mercedes Benz limousines drove out of Zhongnanhai and headed north across the city, Prime Minister Li Peng in the lead car, closely followed by State President Yang Shangkun in the second. Both men preferred the custom-made German vehicles to the Red Flags used by other Politburo members.

Just south of Tiananmen Gate, the two cars pulled into a narrow alley, despite its signs warning not to enter. Fifty yards along the lane, a steel gate swung open and smartly dressed soldiers sprang to attention. The cars entered and drove down a tree-lined driveway before parking outside a dun-colored, unprepossessing building. This was Deng Xiaoping's home.

The two men were formally greeted by Deng's secretary and then escorted into the presence of the supreme ruler.

One account of what followed was subsequently pieced together by *New York Times* Beijing correspondent Nicholas D. Kristof. In this version Deng's early-morning visitors found their host in "a grim mood, outraged by the ongoing protest and deeply alarmed at the prospect of further unrest."

Deng's guests would do nothing to lighten his mood, nor, most certainly, did they wish to. Now that Deng had issued his guidelines to the media, they wanted him to go further, to put muscle into his order that the students were to be harshly treated in print.

To encourage him, both men had brought evidence of how far matters had gone. On a tenth-century table, they unfurled posters Qiao Shi's agent had removed overnight from several of the city's campuses. Each carried a vitriolic personal attack on Deng. One poster described him as "a little dwarf who has taken great power." Another attacked him as "the little bottle who approves bug corruption." (The bottle reference was a play on his given name, Xiaoping, which in spoken Chinese sounds like the words for "little bottle.") A third poster boldly stated: "Under Deng, cadres are millionaires."

Another account, from the files of a European intelligence service, portrayed Deng as sweeping the posters off the table and then walking around his office shouting that in socialist Europe, countries like Poland, whose rulers tolerated unrest, had paid a disastrous price in economic terms. Russia itself, Deng continued to fume, would go the same way unless the Kremlin showed something of the determination local commissars had in the Soviet Republic of Georgia, where thirty-one protesters had recently been summarily executed by troops.

Deng then railed against another student accusation, that he was the arch-practitioner of nepotism. One poster accused him of placing his wheelchair-bound son in charge of the China Welfare Fund for the Handicapped and then allowing him to use its charitable funds to finance a network of companies. Another poster proclaimed President Yang's cousin owed his job as chief of the army's General Political Department to family connections. Even Zhao had not escaped pillory. His son, Zhao Dajun, ran the Houhai Trading Company, which a poster claimed was "recognized for its corruption."

All this was a "threat" to China's future, Deng rasped through the smoke from his first cigarette of the day. "This is not an ordinary student movement but turmoil. We must take a clear-cut stand and implement effective measures now to stop further unrest. We cannot let them have their way. This turmoil is a planned conspiracy to transform a China with a bright future into a China with no hope. What is at stake is the very future of the leadership and the socialist system."

Deng's stenographer, the only other person present, continued to write down the diatribe as Deng's language grew more emotive. "None of us wishes to see blood spilled, but it will be spilled if it is necessary. We must be ready to use a sharp knife to cut the tangled weeds." The reference was a reminder of Deng's childhood work. Then he had cut weeds to allow rice to grow. Now he would order the students, dismissed in that phrase "tangled weeds," to be cut down by one of the most powerful armies on earth.

Abruptly Deng led the others into the situation room adjoining his office. A flag-dotted wall map showed the current disposition of the PLA. No fewer than eleven armies stood guard on China's borders. The 2d Army was on the border with Thailand; the 24th guarded against any threat from Pakistan; the 12th watched over China's flank with Burma. Nearer to hand were the 7th at Nanking and the 21st at Changshun. Even closer were the 28th and 38th armies and those first units of the 27th that had been brought back from Tibet and were now within fifty miles of Beijing.

Deng turned to his prime minister and the state president.

"We have several million loyal soldiers to do our weeding. We will allow them to start very soon."

He ordered the stenographer to transcribe his words. Like Richard Nixon, Deng liked to keep a record, but unlike the former president, China's leader did not make tapes. He feared any recording would be tampered with.

While they waited for the stenographer to return with transcripts, Li Peng and Yang Shangkun continued to play on Deng's paranoia by describing how the students had held a "congress" in the ruins of the Old Imperial Palace in the northeast corner of the city on the previous night. The outcome of the meeting was yet another student body, this one called the Provisional Beijing Students Union. Li Peng said it had only one aim: to force the government into a dialogue.

"Never!" Deng rasped. "Never, never, never! To talk to these hooligans would be a sign of weakness."

The notetaker returned with the copies of the transcript, and the three leaders sat around the table in Deng's office.

While reading, according to a Western intelligence report, Deng began to fulminate once more over the allegations of nepotism. He reminded the others his son had been crippled when, as a student at Beijing University, he had been thrown out of a window by Red Guards.

"We must never see those days again," the supreme leader continued. "That is why we must stop this now!"

To do so, he proposed publishing "a clear-cut" editorial in the *People's Daily,* which would also be broadcast on state television and radio. Theoretically it should reach every one in the land. Over a billion Chinese would know that the leadership would not tolerate any further threat to its invincibility.

While Li Peng and Yang Shangkun drafted thoughts for the editorial, Deng telephoned Xu Weichang, the most conservative of the ideologists on the Beijing Party Committee. Normally such an important policy document would have been written by Hu Qili, the Politburo member in charge of propaganda. But he was a known supporter of Zhao. Deng wanted no one to plead the Party secretary's case.

Over breakfast, Xu Weichang drafted the core of a hard-hitting attack on the student movement, in Chinese *xuechao*. Deng struck out the word and substituted *dongluan*, "turmoil," his favorite pejorative to describe the Cultural Revolution.

By midmorning the text had been completed and approved. It began by denouncing "a planned conspiracy and turmoil"; several thousand characters later, it appealed for "all comrades of the Party and people throughout the whole nation to understand clearly that if we do not resolutely check this turmoil, our State will have no calm days."

Xu Weichang left for the offices of the *People's Daily* while the others continued to plan.

Li Peng suggested that Deng should send a copy of the editorial to Zhao in North Korea and ask him to cable back his full endorsement of what was to be published. At the same time, the prime minister continued, copies of the text should be circulated to key Party and government officials.

"To wait until formal publication is too long," the prime minister insisted. "We must show them we are now ready for full action."

State President Yang gave his full support, and Deng quickly concurred.

All realized that by the time Party secretary Zhao received his copy, the text would have been widely read, and therefore he would be in no position to argue for any changes. To ensure the fait accompli, Deng ordered that the editorial should lead the main national TV and radio news bulletins that evening. Immediately afterward it must be continuously broadcast for an hour over loudspeakers at all of the city's universities.

Throughout the morning the supreme leader continued to summon officials and plan an all-out counterattack against the students. Li Xiaming was ordered to arrange a rally next day of the Party faithful in the Great Hall of the People to warn them of what Deng was repeatedly calling "dongluan." Qiao Shi was instructed to turn the full force of state security upon the students. They were to be infiltrated still further, and agent provocateurs were to be used to alienate public sympathy for the demonstrators. Yao Yilin was told to make sure that Zhao's supporters in Zhongnanhai knew that dissension would no longer be tolerated. Li Peng was given the task of briefing Foreign Ministry officials to convey to foreign diplomats that the crackdown was under way and that the world, in Deng's words, later reported by Nicholas Kristof in the *New York Times* "should clearly understand we do not fear spilling blood, and we do not fear the international consequences."

To prove the point Deng gave the order for twenty thousand

soldiers of the 38th Army stationed in the suburbs to be prepared to move "in minutes" into the city. Over a thousand more policemen were sent to defend Zhongnanhai.

Like a Mafia godfather, the supreme leader was going to war by preparing for every possibility. He had orders sent to Jiang Zemin, Party secretary of Shanghai, to stage a rally of support in that city and immediately close down the locally published *World Economic Herald,* which had become required reading in CIA Director Webster's suite and Bush's Oval Office, among other places. Other rallies were ordered to be held in cities throughout the country. Close to a billion Chinese were being once more ordered to show total obedience to the State.

Chain-smoking, Deng continued to pour out orders. Political officers at every university were to broadcast continued warnings throughout their campuses that further demonstrations would be met with "the full force of the law." Teachers were to be instructed to warn their pupils not to march; any teacher who refused was to be dismissed.

A poster campaign was to start at once attacking astrophysicist Fang Lizhi and his wife, Li Shuxian, both supporters of the students, as being two of the planners behind the unrest.

Finally, all posters, banners, and wreaths were to be removed from Tiananmen Square. At the same time there would be an official announcement that the period of mourning for Hu Yaobang was at an end.

"The students will have no further excuse to demonstrate," Deng said.

Shortly afterward Zhao called from the North Korean capital of Pyonayang to give his full approval of the editorial. The news was immediately circulated through Party and government channels. To all intents and purposes the leadership was united and the battle lines were drawn.

# 15

---

# *Power Plays*

---

WEDNESDAY, APRIL 26, 1989
*Beijing University*

Despite the dormitory windows being closed, the relentless voice of Pang Yi continued to boom over the campus loudspeakers late in the evening. The political officer was using and tried and tested combination of threats and promises that had long been the backbone of all Party means of intimidation. The demonstrations were now in their eleventh day.

Pang Yi had said he understood the concern of the students for the country. But they should make their criticisms and suggestions to the Party through "proper channels." He could assure them everything would be most carefully listened to, and there would be no punishment for "anyone voicing" demands.

A hollow laugh had greeted the words.

"Demonstrations do not help. They only add to the chaos of society. You must not forget that the Party has always done its best for you," Pang Yi wheedled.

Then, abruptly changing mood, he had warned that any student who took part in any further marches would be expelled from the campus. It would effectively end his or her stay at the university. Jeers had greeted the threat.

Pang Yi's words had grown steadily more strident. Any further disobedience would lead to arrest and imprisonment. The political officer reminded them their support within the Party leadership had been seriously eroded by Zhao's decision to endorse the *People's Daily* editorial, which had been read out on TV and radio.

"You have no support. You have humiliated your families, your university, your country," Pang Yi continued. "Your only hope of avoiding total disgrace and perhaps worse is to stop now. If you do so, the Party will be generous. It will forgive your transgressions. But if you continue, you will be destroyed. Because that is the will of the people. You cannot resist the people, or those who are there to defend them."

Turning from the window, Yang Li addressed the students in the dormitory.

"The situation is serious," he said. "Plainclothes police are everywhere. But I don't care if I am expelled or punished. I will fight on to the very end."

A chorus of agreement came from the others.

"What is happening shows the potential of our generation," Li continued. "We are all trying to do something for our country. We must be prepared to sacrifice a great deal, knowing it is worthwhile."

Like all the other student leaders, Li showed signs of lack of sleep and irregular meals. He was hollow-eyed, and stubble gave his face an almost piratical look. But his determination to continue protesting came through in his voice. Despite its hoarseness, it sounded as confident as ever.

Outside the room was the sound of a door being slammed. Moments later Li saw another angry father storming out of the dormitory block, having failed to convince his son to agree not to demonstrate any more. All day the university administration had been busing in parents to try and persuade their sons and daughters to stop protesting. In almost all cases the parents had left defeated. It was the same story on other campuses.

The youth whose father had just left came into the room to say his parent had severed all ties with him and would send him no more money. Other students had been reporting a similar response. Li told the youth what he had said to the others: "Don't worry about money. We will feed you for nothing. Once we have won our victory your parents will be proud of you."

Throughout the day students had been meeting in their dormitories to discuss tactics and give each other moral support. Many had been close to tears, partly from fear, partly from a sense of creating history. They had constantly reminded each other that Hu Yaobang had been removed from office in the first place because of his commitment to them.

Meanwhile, teachers had begged the students to give up. All the posters on the campus had been torn down by the political officers.

Students were summoned before the campus authorities and crudely threatened.

Then, just as some of the activists appeared on the point of giving up, fresh messages of support came from provincial campuses. These were swiftly circulated. Yang Li had told those in his dormitory that they had "a solemn duty" not to fail "those who are looking to us for leadership."

"Stay in the campus," roared Pang Yi over the loudspeakers. "If you leave we cannot protect you against the reactionaries who are trying to ruin you. They are out there, plotting to use you to destroy all that is good in China. We only want to protect you."

The students greeted his words with a chorus of the national anthem.

Listening from his empty classroom, Barr Seitz, the American graduate teaching English, marveled at "the courage of these students. They had nothing more than their voices, not a worthwhile weapon between them. They had simply convinced each other that if they were to succeed they must take risks."

Yet their leaders had not lost their coolness. After listening to the *People's Daily* editorial broadcast throughout the campus, Wang Dan had called a meeting of the Students Union Committee in the coffeeshop. He had said that the editorial clearly indicated the pressures within the leadership but that it was important for the students to stay aloof from any power struggle going on in Zhongnanhai.

"Everything we do must be based on the constitution," he said.

Out of the meeting had come three new demands that would form the core of further confrontation with the authorities. There must be dialogue between the government and the Students Union Committee, and it must be on an equal footing. The government must apologize for all previous violence inflicted upon the students. From now on all the country's official media must give full and unbiased coverage to the students' activities.

In return, the students were prepared to fully support the Party in its "correct" way forward to promote socialism and reform.

The decision was a shrewd move to keep the protest within the framework of Article 35, the part of China's constitution that guaranteed free speech, yet still allow the students to promote their aims.

Still more threats were being broadcast over the campus loudspeakers. Suddenly the functionary's voice was cut off. Over the loudspeakers came the voice of Wang Dan. Students at the engineering department had managed to bypass the secretary's microphone and allow him to broadcast from a makeshift studio. His message was defiant.

"Tomorrow we march! Tonight we prepare! Deng has said these are grave times. They are. So prepare yourselves. Write letters to your families. Prepare your wills. Prepare to support the correct path of leadership for the Party! Support security and reform. Long live democracy!"

A burst of cheers swept through the campus.

Standing at a classroom window of the all but deserted English Department, Cassy saw scores of Public Security agents led by Pang Yi running through the campus in search of the studio.

From dormitory windows students yelled abuse. Cassy thought it was "like a World War II movie where the Allied prisoners taunted their German guards."

Behind her she heard the door open. Daobao stood there. She was reminded of their first meeting in the building's library. Now, as then, she was surprised by his calm.

"Hi!" he said in his faintly American accent, walking into the room.

"Hi."

He came and stood beside her at the window and watched the security men rushing by.

"It won't matter if they find the studio," said Daobao. "It was only meant to be another way to show them we will not be cowed. We have prepared everything as far as we can."

She took his hand in hers as he continued to speak. "The more they threaten us, the more we want to live freely."

"But wanting and achieving are very different," Cassy said.

He took her by the shoulder, shaking her almost roughly.

"It will work this time. It has to."

He kissed her quickly on the mouth, and she felt his tears on her cheek. Then he turned and half ran from the classroom.

SAME DAY, LATER
*The White House*

The TV screens in the Oval Office were tuned to ABC, CBS, CNN, and NBC, which gave President Bush a chance to sample four presentations of the news. Only one channel had begun to carry live reports from China. Whenever the President paused in his punishing schedule to look, the CNN monitor seemed to be filled with young people on the other side of the world chanting slogans and waving banners. Bush understood enough Mandarin to grasp what they were demanding: democracy.

The President wondered how long it would be before the Beijing CNN team would be joined by the troika of U.S. network news: Dan Rather of CBS; Tom Brokaw of NBC; and Peter Jennings of ABC.

Among them the trio was watched by forty million Americans. Every night. If they went to Beijing and reported on what the students were trying to achieve, they could have a powerful effect on public opinion. The President knew it could force him to go public and offer some sort of support for the aspirations of the students. But until then he would say nothing.

It was no secret around the White House that National Security Adviser Brent Scowcroft, for one, wanted Bush to "soft-pedal and weigh the long term," the words of one of Scowcroft's aides. No one had to be reminded that Scowcroft brought to his new post the same steely determination to have his way that he had displayed when running the Washington office of Kissinger Associates.

The consultancy could now count on another former employee, Lawrence Eagleburger, an undersecretary of state, to remind the White House of just what was at stake for the United States in China, those billions of dollars invested in scores of projects. Against them the idealism of those students on the CNN monitor seemed painfully inadequate.

SAME DAY, SAME TIME
*China Daily compound*

Jeanne Moore was typing a story for the midwest newspaper. It was a reflective piece aimed at the op-ed page. Her words caught perfectly the mood of the city.

"Whatever happens next, politics in China will never be the same. The government has underestimated the silent majority," she typed on an elderly manual. "The editorial has been dismissed with anger and contempt, not only by the students, but the public. In the meantime the students are now stockpiling food in their dormitories. They are going to war—and they are ready to die. A sense of crisis is everywhere. The city is as close to martial law as it could be without it actually being declared."

Around her colleagues were collecting information they would not be allowed to publish in their own newspaper but were feeding to her.

There had been violence at a rally at the University of Politics and Law, where militiamen had attacked students. There had been running fights on the Normal University campus between students and campus security men. But there had also been clashes between students themselves over what the next move should be.

"Moderates at Qinghua University who have cautioned a wait-and-see approach have become the object of bitter anger among the more militant students," Jeanne typed. "On other campuses professors and administrators have tearfully begged their students to return to class. But here in Beijing there's an overwhelming decision to march at dawn tomorrow."

SAME DAY, SAME TIME
*Sacramento, California*

Sue, the Chinese postgraduate student, and Rod, her boyfriend, had abandoned any thought of sleep. Instead they sat in their pajamas on the couch before the TV set, switching channels in the hope of catching further news from China. On the coffee table before them were a radio tuned to an all-news channel and a jar almost filled with dollar bills, Sue's first efforts at fund-raising among her fellow Chinese. There was already over $1,000 in the jar. More was promised. Every donation had been entered in a notebook.

"There's a tremendous feeling of wanting to do something," Sue told Rod. "It's like being back home."

Sue wanted to collect $5,000 before she left for Beijing. But she had no idea how the money should be used.

There had been nothing on TV about China since the eleven o'clock news. But at midnight the radio commenced a live report from outside Beijing University, saying that several of the student leaders had fled their dormitory headquarters and gone into hiding, fearing they were about to be arrested. The radio reporter described how the campus gates were padlocked. On the railings someone had put up a poster: IN GOD WE TRUST.

Rod turned to Sue. "It's going to be very dangerous, and it could be even more dangerous when you get there."

"It's always been dangerous to protest in China," Sue replied. She tried to sound reassuring. "But don't worry. Nothing they do can be as bad as the Cultural Revolution."

Once more she took him back to that dark, turbulent time in her people's history. Then, the authorities had imposed a real reign of terror. What was happening now in China was "probably no more than an intricate game of bluff and counterbluff," she said. "Both sides will probably go on pushing hard. But if it comes to real violence, they'll also both pull back. No one in China today wants violence."

Rod said he really hoped she was right.

In the anteroom of the operating theater suite Dr. Jenny Guangzu heard the anesthetist say, "I'm going to tube him." The daughter of one of China's foremost exponents of traditional medicine watched intently.

With surprising speed, the anesthetist pushed the tube in over the patient's tongue to provide a permanent airway into his lungs, then connected the visible end to the oxygen machine. The anesthetized squeezed the rubber breathing bag a few times as the patient breathed in. If he had been properly anesthetized, the action would halt voluntary breathing. She stopped squeezing for a moment. The man did not breathe. She resumed squeezing the bag.

From the OR came the sound of the same all-news station Sue and Rod were listening to. Some surgeons preferred to listen to music while operating; Jenny's boss liked to keep abreast of the stock market reports.

Scrubbed and gowned, Jenny followed him into the OR. The radio was on a trolley on the "nonclean" side of the room, isolated from the actual operating area by sterile curtains. The anesthetist and her trolley worked there because it was impossible to sterilize her cylinder and bottles.

The patient, a road accident victim with head injuries, was being positioned on the table. The two high instrument trays were wheeled into place and draped with sterile cloths. Other tables filled with sterilized equipment stood on the clean side of the OR.

Jenny checked that the endotracheal tube had not been disturbed. Beside her one of the nurses snipped away the man's hair, exposing the damaged skull.

"Guess your traditional doctors would do things differently," the surgeon said.

"Yes, they would," Jenny replied quickly. She suddenly felt protective of the kind of medicine her father practiced.

She had tried to call him several times in the past days. Each time the hospital switchboard in Beijing had said he was not available. When she had tried to ask the operator what was happening in the city, the woman had abruptly said a few troublemakers were giving the country a bad name.

Now, as the operation got under way, the radio carried a report from Beijing saying that night-shift workers in factories throughout the city had stopped work as a gesture of support for the students.

"This thing could rock the stock market," said the surgeon as he turned to the X rays fixed to the viewing frame on one wall.

"It could also destroy a lot of lives," Jenny said grimly.

The surgeon squinted at her and said she should count herself lucky she was here.

That was the moment, Jenny later realized, when she decided she would return as soon as possible to China. She would leave Zhong and take Peter with her. They would move in with her father. The intuition she had inherited from her mother told her she was needed back home to play her part in China's destiny.

THURSDAY, APRIL 27, 1989
*National Defense University*

At dawn Kao Jyan awoke and climbed off the bedroll he had spread late at night before on the floor of his office. Like all the other instructors, Jyan had spent the night in the military academy, coordinating plans for the 38th Army to march into the city. This morning he would travel with a convoy of troops to the Great Hall of the People. Other troops would move into the network of tunnels beneath Beijing. The soldiers would be armed with assault rifles, though force was to be kept to a minimum. The intention was surprise. Intelligence supplied by Public Security indicated the students did not plan to return to Tiananmen Square before midday. They would find the military waiting for them.

Over breakfast in the staff dining hall, Jyan reviewed the tactics with colleagues. "These are kids,' he said. "They're not like the Tibetans, trained for this sort of thing. When we show up, they'll leave. They know they've had their fun and that now it's all over."

Leaving the academy to rendezvous with the convoy, Jyan was still a little surprised by one decision. During the briefing for this operation it had emerged that units from a number of armies were placing a cordon around the city. To the perceptive captain instructor it indicated someone in Zhongnanhai "was more nervous than necessary."

Jyan thought again how foolish and ungrateful the students were. They represented only a minute part of society. Yet they had so much more than other people: education and an assured place in their society. He really could not understand their behavior. This democracy they wanted was something alien and dangerous and surely had no place in the China he knew.

SAME DAY, LATER
*Beijing University*

The sound of a bolt cutter snapping through the padlock broke the silence. Yan Daobao and Yang Li swung open the main gates of the campus. Behind them, stretching as far as they could see up the broad avenue, ranks of students gave a sustained cheer. The gates had been padlocked on Pang Yi's orders to keep them on campus. A similar measure had been taken at all other universities and colleges in the city.

Wang Dan stepped forward and real aloud, through a battery-operated bullhorn, Article 35 of the constitution. His amplified voice carried clearly in the still air.

When he finished, the accordionists from the music department struck up a brisk marching tune. Members of the various campus choral groups led the singing as the students marched out, once more on their way to Tiananmen Square.

At the same time students were emerging from the dormitories of the city's other forty-one universities and colleges in the same orderly manner. Fifty thousand in all were on the march. As they tramped through the streets, factory and office workers joined the columns, falling into step and lending their voices to the singing. Soon the number of demonstrators had doubled, then doubled again. Two hundred thousand and more were on the march, gathering still more people to them by the minute.

From her bedroom window in the Friendship Hotel, Cassy and several other foreign experts watched the scene. For most of the night they had debated what to do. The university administration had warned them to take no part in any demonstrations. Doing so would be a breach of contract and could lead to their arrest. But they had been told that they would also be breaking their contracts if they attempted to leave the country to go home. Some of the teachers had wondered whether they were being held hostage to deter their own countries from offering support for the students.

Barr Seitz found that suggestion fanciful. Better than most, he had an idea how the State Department would view the student protest: "A real pain. What was happening was going to rock a lot of boats in

Washington. The trade boat in particular. American businessmen would not like what they were seeing on their TV screens. Every step the students were taking was threatening to trample on a lot of deals. The last thing the State Department would be doing was to encourage what was happening. Indeed, Washington would be doing everything possible to keep a distance from the students."

Barr, on the other hand, had every hope of getting into the thick of the action. The ABC-TV bureau in Beijing had promised him a job as a reporter, a runner for its correspondents, should the story "really catch fire."

Watching from the window of the hotel, he thought "the flames were beginning to glow nicely."

Despite the warning to stay away, Cassy knew nothing could stop her marching. She joined a group of hotel staff, which quickly became absorbed in one of the seemingly endless columns.

In one of them was Jeanne Moore. Despite the "excitement, tension, and a feeling of not knowing what was going to happen," she maintained her reporter's cool eye for detail. She noted that none of the students carried identification, in case they were arrested. Their marshals used a prearranged set of hand signals and commands to direct and control the marchers. The music and singing were coordinated so that as the columns from various campuses began to merge with each other, they all played and sang the same patriotic songs.

Half an hour into the march, the students encountered their first opposition, a cordon of police stretched across an intersection. Wuerkaixi, at the head of the first column, turned and addressed the marchers.

"Do not be violent. But remember if blood is to be shed, we are all ready to do so."

The crowds lining the streets began to chant for the police to stand aside. The cordon broke, and the police, who a moment before had looked so threatening, were smiling and waving the students on their way.

Moving slowly through a hundred side streets, the columns flowed into the city's major avenue, completely stopping traffic. Workers poured from every alley, factory, and shop. From office blocks the length of Bingani, Diamen, and Dansishitiao avenues, clerks and typists ran to join the marchers or stood on the sidewalks flashing victory signs and cheering. Diplomats Brian Davidson and Brendan Ward this time agreed that close to a million were either on the march or cheering.

"This is serious," Davidson told his Irish colleague. "The authorities have either got to do something to appease them or stop them right now."

But from their vantage point on Changan Avenue, there was no sign of either happening.

It struck Brendan Ward that "an official paralysis seemed to have set in. What police there were on duty just didn't know what to do. In the end they were simply brushed aside by this human juggernaut rolling through the city. Though they were completely unarmed there was something very intimidating about the way they marched, as if they knew they were unstoppable."

By midmorning the entire area just north of Zhongnanhai across the width of the city was a seething mass moving inexorably south toward Tiananmen Square.

Time and again police lines broke, fell back, regrouped, and crumpled again. Many policemen simply faded into the *hutongs*, cowed and defeated by the unstoppable formations.

As Jeanne's column skirted the northern wall of Zhongnanhai, passing along Jingshaw Road and then wheeling right on to Wangfujing Avenue, the entire staff of the China Art Gallery emerged to join the marchers. On Wangfujing a gang of steel erectors shinned down from the scaffolding to march. Moments later shop assistants streamed out of a department store to join them.

Scribbling as she walked, Jeanne noted: "The slogans and songs were calculated to look and sound more Communist than the Party, more patriotic than the army, more law-abiding than the police. Nothing appeared planned: Clearly everything was. The banners down to the last characters stayed within the law. They all proclaimed support for true socialism. Every demand for democracy is buttressed with citations from the constitution. Most brilliant of all, they have taken Deng Xiaoping's own words and used them to telling effect. His own criticisms are now directed at corrupt Party officials."

Swinging past the squad of police standing guard over the Beijing Hotel, the column burst into the theme from a popular Chinese television series, "The Plainclothesmen."

From a suite on the seventh floor, maverick rocket-gun scientist Dr. Gerald Bull was among the hotel guests watching. Most were businessmen whose thoughts were probably reflected in Bull's words to a colleague.

"The kids are a menace to their own country. Right now the last thing China wants is to get caught up in some fancy notions about democracy. That kind of talk will just get in the way of what China wants and is good at, making deals with the West."

Bull was back in Beijing to firm up his own deal with Norinco, the state-run arms conglomerate, to supply them with the technical know-how that would enable Norinco to secretly arm Saddam Hussein with long-range guns. Bull's only concern was that the demonstrations could escalate to the point where people like him would be told by their governments to stop trading with the Chinese "until they sort out the students." Bull had no doubt what should be done: "Kick a few butts. Put their leaders in prison for a while."

As if in answer to Bull's words, soldiers were jumping from trucks parked in front of the Great Hall of the People.

Stationed near the Great Hall, Captain Instructor Jyan knew the troops were too few and too late. There were fewer than a thousand lightly armed soldiers to stop the biggest demonstration he had ever witnessed.

There had been a clear failure of intelligence about the size of the crowd supporting the marchers. Thousands of people were scrambling out of every alley and side street to stand twenty deep along Changan Avenue. If they became violent, an entire army would be needed to hold them back. But by the time reinforcements could reach the area, it would be far too late. Jyan knew that the best thing to do would be to stage an orderly withdrawal.

Sensing the indecision of the soldiers, the crowd had occupied the stands in front of the Forbidden City and began to chant at the soldiers: "Go home! Or join the march! Remember, the People's Army should love the people!"

For a moment Jyan wondered whether the troop commander would order his soldiers to clear the area, if only to make a gesture that the army would not be so humiliated. But even as he turned to seek out his senior officer and caution him against such action, Jyan found himself swept aside by the first rank of marchers. In moments the soldiers were overwhelmed, escorted to their trucks, and ordered to climb back on board.

On a command from Wuerkaixi, the ranks then parted to form a corridor running east on Changan through which the troops could leave. As they ran the gauntlet, the visibly shaken troops were deafened by a continuous chant: "Go home! Turn your guns into posters! This is the first nonviolent revolution in our history!"

When the troops had gone and there was not a policeman in sight, Wuerkaixi led the student leaders to the pediment of the Monument to the People's Heroes. Dozens of foreign TV and radio crews and print-media reporters were using it as a vantage point to record what was happening. Through their microphones, Wuerkaixi deliberately addressed the world for the first time.

"This is China's history you are witnessing. We have come here to proclaim a simple truth. It is that we want change. We want democracy!"

He ordered the marchers to return to their campuses in the same orderly way they had come here.

To Brian Davidson it was "a masterly move. He was showing leadership skills well beyond his years. He was saying, in effect, 'We have conquered Tiananmen, the very heart of the Party's power.' He wanted the old men in Zhongnanhai to know that from now on the students would come and go as they liked."

Watching the first ranks once more moving off, Wuerkaixi turned to Wang Dan and said: "Hundreds of thousands of people have thrown cold water in the face of the leaders. Let us hope it has woken them up!"

It had, but in a way even Wuerkaixi had not anticipated.

The brief exchange between the two leading student activists was carefully noted by a CIA operative, one of several foreign intelligence agents prowling the square. By this time, the thirteenth day of the demonstration, a cautious understanding appeared to have developed among the intelligence men. They took steps not to crowd each other, and made no attempt to blow each other's cover of either being bona-fide diplomats or news reporters. Several of the KGB men claimed they were from the Soviet news agency Tass, preparing reports for the Gorbachev visit, now less than two weeks away.

The students, their gullibility no doubt compounded by tiredness, answered questions freely, enabling the operatives to have a continuously updated picture of what was being planned.

The democracy movement had already become one of the most infiltrated and compromised protest movements in living memory.

The "bunch of kids," as CIA Director Webster had once referred to them, were indeed no match for the experienced agents currently working the ninety-eight arid acres of Tiananmen Square.

# 16

# *Countermoves*

Monday, May 1, 1989
*The White House*

Webster continued to brief the President in that soft, flat, emotionless voice some members of the cabinet found hard to follow. Bush clearly found it absorbing. The President sat listening intently to the CIA director. Those present included Secretary of State James Baker and some of his aides.

This May Day marked the seventeenth day of student protest in China. Over the past few days events there had moved into the top spot in the intelligence summaries making up the President's Daily Brief.

Details had included the surprise announcement that had come hours after the students had marched back to their campuses. Radio Beijing had interrupted its programs to carry an announcement from the State Council, a body of ministers drawn from the upper echelons of government. The council pronounced it was "ready to conduct dialogue with the students at any time." In return the council asked that the students give up protesting.

Bush asked why the students kept marching in and out of Tiananmen Square, instead of just staying put and bringing matters to a head. One of Baker's aides suggested they "were testing the temperature, seeing how far they could push before it came to a real shove back."

Webster told the meeting that the latest intelligence gleaned from within Zhongnanhai indicated that disagreement among the leadership had reached a new intensity. The hardliners wanted a total crackdown now, with the student leaders arrested and sent to China's

177

Gulag. One of the CIA's intercepts included China's spymaster, Qiao Shi, insisting his snatch squads could arrest all the leaders in a citywide swoop and so break the back of the movement. But once more Deng Xiaoping had hesitated.

Yet Deng's anger with the students had not diminished, cautioned Webster. Some reports reaching the CIA suggested it had increased. But Deng was a pragmatist, Webster reminded the others.

Mikhail Gorbachev would be arriving in Beijing for his four-day visit in two weeks. For Deng to behave harshly so close to such an historic event could create far more serious problems for him.

Bush suggested the turnout for the last student march must clearly have shown Deng the extent of public support for reform. China's leaders would want to do nothing that could turn that support to violence.

Webster concurred. The steady spate of EYES ONLY encoded faxes reaching him clearly revealed Deng's concern that if any of the student leaders were arrested, Beijing, and perhaps other cities, could rise in protest. That would totally destroy the careful mood of "orderly calmness" Deng wanted during the visit of the Soviet leader.

According to one aide present, Bush said Deng "is in a real bind." But the United States, insisted the President, would do nothing to make things more difficult. Any approach by the students to the U.S. embassy in Beijing for help was to be firmly refused.

That same source would later say, "The President's view was that the reality was they [the students] were not going to achieve very much, and we don't want to be on the losing side. His view was that could set us back in all sorts of ways, politically and economically. The President saw our good relations with China as crucial to our influence in Asia and the Pacific Rim. That was the bottom line none of us was allowed to forget."

On Friday, April 28, CIA agents in Beijing had slipped out of Spook City, their building in the embassy compound, to observe student leaders from every university, college, and institute in the city attending a meeting Wuerkaixi had called at Beijing Normal University.

The student leader had been as ebullient as always, flashing that all-knowing smile, slapping his fellow student leaders on the back. He had become the consummate leader.

Wang Dan, as always, was happy to take a secondary role. The intelligence operatives noted he looked paler than usual. So did Chai Ling. Like many of the student leaders, she was only able to snatch a few hours' sleep at a time, sleeping in a new place each night in case arrest orders were issued.

Wuerkaixi proposed the formation of yet another committee, the Autonomous Union of Students. It was a further shrewd move by the volatile yet hardheaded Wuerkaixi. By abolishing all previous committees, it allowed him to remove from the leadership those students he felt were moderates. In their place came young people ready to stage hunger strikes, to the death if necessary.

Webster's agents had reported that the meeting concentrated on how to exploit the forthcoming Gorbachev visit. Wuerkaixi said their most powerful weapon would be the ability to organize further demonstrations in the two weeks remaining before the arrival of the Soviet Leader.

"Rather than risk that, the leadership will want to talk to us," Wuerkaixi predicted. "We must try and get as many concessions as possible now. After Gorbachev has left, it will be harder to deal with Zhongnanhai."

Next day, Saturday, April 29, the President's Daily Brief had contained further evidence of how far the students were ready to challenge the leadership. Forty-five students had been invited to meet members of the State Council for a "dialogue." Almost all were members of official student unions subservient to the Party. Eager to make a point that it was willing to listen to demands, the leadership had invited Chinese TV to broadcast live what was being promoted as an "important moment" in the country's recent history.

Uninvited and unannounced, Wuerkaixi and Wang Dan arrived at the meeting in the Great Hall of the People, bounding up the steps and giving boxer salutes.

Stunned, yet unable to stop the moment's going out on national TV, the State Council had no alternative but to invite both students to join the discussions.

Wuerkaixi immediately began to repeat the now familiar demands for "proper talks" with Li Peng, a full public apology for all previous violence done to the students, and unbigoted reporting by the Chinese media.

The scandalized State Council members said all this was beyond their authority. Wuerkaixi stormed out of the meeting.

"The boy's a firebrand," Webster once more told Bush at the Monday morning briefing. The President made one of his hand-chopping movements and repeated the United States should do nothing to encourage Wuerkaixi.

After Webster completed his presentation, the President honed in on the issue that concerned him: the wider question of human rights that underscored the student demands and whether those demands were likely to interfere with the Gorbachev visit.

The issue of human rights had come into dramatic focus with the news the previous day, Sunday, April 30, that there had been demonstrations in the Chinese city of Changsha over the death sentences imposed on nine people involved in the disturbances there eight days before. Bush wanted to know whether the United States should protest about the sentences.

Baker advised against doing so, given that a few hours after the penalties were imposed, the U.S. embassy in Beijing had sent a telegram describing how the authorities were making "every effort to defuse the student situation."

Beijing Party Secretary Li Xiaming had publicly revealed his income and the jobs his children held. The city's Party secretary earned $85 a month; his eldest daughter was an oculist, at $50 a month; her sister's paycheck as a medical technician was $35.

"By implication the Beijing Party Secretary was saying the students were way off base when it came to accusations that the Party's top officials were guilty of nepotism or lining their own pockets," Baker quoted from the telegram.

Bush made another hand-chopping motion and asked another question: Zhao Ziyang, the Chinese Party secretary, was now back from North Korea, and was there any indication of how he might react given the way he had been outmaneuvered over the now-notorious editorial in the *People's Daily*?

Webster said Zhao had summoned to his Zhongnanhai compound those in the leadership known to support him, including the key figure of Bao Tong, the secretary of the Politburo. The indications were that Zhao was planning to distance himself from the editorial and so gain favor among the students.

If the Party secretary achieved that goal, Bush suggested, Zhao might be able to convince the students their "kind of street protests" would ultimately get them nowhere. They never had before, they never would, Bush added. He repeated again he was not against the students trying to get a better deal, but he also didn't want anything to wreck the Gorbachev visit.

Bush reminded the others Gorbachev had recognized that Communism was in a historical retreat, and that the only way for it to survive as a force was to allow more freedom in the lives of those it controlled. But unlike in central Europe, change could not be rushed in China.

Based upon his own firsthand experience, the President believed what was needed was a long-term process of increasing economic pluralism in which change would come slowly; otherwise China would continue to face strong confrontations within its borders. The United States was ready and eager to play its role in ensuring the economic success of China and take its own legitimate profit in the process.

Implicit in the President's words was that a bunch of students led by a hothead like Wuerkaixi must not be allowed to threaten that aim.

Thursday, May 4, 1989
*Beijing*

Coming through Beijing airport, Melinda Liu, Asia editor of *Newsweek,* was already working, asking questions, absorbing the answers, forming her first judgments. She had followed the protest marches from reports coming into her bureau in Hong Kong, and at this stage she wanted to get a firsthand look at what was happening in Beijing. The demonstrations there were now in their twentieth day.

Liu was one of the best correspondents working the Asia beat. Shot up and shot at, she carried her physical scars like badges of honor; they were proof she was no barfly reporter but one who went out into the field to talk to guerrilla leaders, terrorists, and the warlords of the Golden Triangle. Quoted and admired by her peers, Melinda was the kind of reporter regimes feared.

Airport officials treated her with the respect due someone who had interviewed Deng and most of the Chinese leadership over the years. Her contacts in Beijing were the envy of most foreign intelligence operatives there.

By the time Melinda had arrived at her hotel, she knew she had once more timed her arrival perfectly. That very morning the students had actually delivered a formal ultimatum to Zhongnanhai. Either the Politburo Standing Committee met them, or there would be further demonstrations.

Her first call was to the government spokesman, Yuan Mu, a flunky she instinctively mistrusted. He stiffly said the government firmly rejected the ultimatum. He added that the students were being "naive and impulsive." He told her he was "satisfied that there were people behind the scenes giving the students ideas in an attempt to create social upheaval."

Yuan Mu would not be drawn further. But for Melinda "it was the old bogeyman, Imperialist troublemakers being dusted down ready for another outing. Things must be getting out of hand when that bogeyman was being blamed."

As she had been about to ring off Mu added, "We are not planning action against the students *yet*. If we take action now, it would be too soon."

Melinda began to call her Chinese contacts in the state media to find out what Yuan Mu meant. She discovered the journalists were all taking part in yet another march to Tiananmen Square. Carrying banners calling for a free press, hundreds of reporters had joined more than forty thousand students. There had also been new demonstrations in a number of provincial cities.

A further hour of working the phones provided clear evidence Zhao Ziyang had made a daring and, for the Party secretary, a potentially dangerous move. Appealing for calm and unity while addressing the governors of the Asian Development Bank that morning, Zhao had completely rejected the editorial in the *People's Daily* with its references to "turmoil."

He had told the bankers that "student demonstrations are still under way in our cities. But I deeply believe the situation will become calm. There will be no great turmoil in China."

The bankers she had reached to check the quote had been reassured by the words. But Melinda recognized they were not directed at Zhao's immediate audience in the Great Hall of the People. They were aimed directly at Deng Xiaoping and his claim that the student movement was "turmoil."

In the world of coded signals in which both Zhao and Deng lived, Melinda understood, this was "tantamount to a declaration of war between the two men." She could not remember anyone delivering such a public rebuke to the supreme leader.


SAME DAY, SAME TIME
*New York*

On the third floor of the ABC building at 47 West 66th Street in Manhattan, a sudden sense of urgency, unusual at this hour, 11:00 A.M., swept the newsroom that is the backdrop for "World News Tonight," anchored by Peter Jennings. Every available reporter and producer was either working a phone or typing onto a computer screen.

What Bob Murphy, the vice president of TV news coverage, was repeatedly calling "the China situation" had finally burst upon the awareness of ABC. It had taken twenty days to do so.

Murphy had ordered a special "World News This Morning Report," a bulletin that would cut into the network's morning output of game shows to give millions of Americans a picture of what was happening in Beijing.

Already Peter Jennings was at his massive desk, leafing through the news copy before him.

On the CNN monitor, one of twenty-eight in Jenning's vision,

Chinese Premier Li Peng was telling the people of his country that the time had come to restore public order.

In the newsroom journalists were trying to decide what this meant. Martial law? A military crackdown? Or just more rhetoric?

Jennings shook his head. His caution is legendary. He would rather be second with the news than mislead his audience. Nothing he had read or heard had yet convinced him that China was about to crush the students with military force.

Moments later he delivered a crisp, no-nonsense update on what was happening in Beijing. He concluded by saying the city "is rampant with rumors."

By inference, Jennings not going to add to them.

SUNDAY, MAY 7, 1989
*People's Liberation Army Barracks*
*Western Hills, near Beijing*

Bing Yang struggled to follow what the political commissar was saying about the latest developments in Beijing. The more he listened, the greater was Bing's confusion. He suspected most of the other soldiers on the barracks square felt the same.

On the long train journey from Lhasa, the commissar had portrayed the students as little short of being counterrevolutionaries who would have to be dealt with by full military force. Now he was telling them that many students had given up protesting and were returning to their classrooms. Only at Beijing University and the Normal University had students continued to demonstrate.

Yet even those students were no longer considered now to be a serious threat, the commissar said.

Tan Yaobang, Bing's commander, demanded to know when they would be returning to Tibet. There was still real soldiering to do there. The commissar could not say. His orders were that the units were to remain at full readiness until further notice.

Throughout the hills to the west of Beijing other commissars were saying the same thing. Tens of thousands of troops were at full battle readiness to deal with a threat that seemed to have all but disappeared.

SAME DAY, SAME TIME
*Foreign Office*
*London*

Her desk covered with diplomatic cablegrams from the British embassy in Beijing, Chinese newspapers, and copies of the mimeographed leaflets the students had distributed, Susan Morton continued to look beyond the immediate events to forecast developments. Her carefully judged reports over the past few weeks had helped her foreign secretary keep abreast of events. She made a note that the demonstrations were now in their twenty-third day.

It was increasingly clear to Susan that this was shaping up to be a confrontation like no other in China's history. She interpreted the decision of most of the students to return to their campuses as only "a chance to regroup"; significantly, the protests continued at two key universities, Beijing and Normal. Even more important, the capital's citizens had continued to support the demonstrations. Many had even joined the fledgling Workers Federation, one of several new organizations born out of the protests, to challenge the position of the state-approved trade unions.

The latest diplomatic bag from the embassy in Beijing had brought to Susan's desk more samples of how radical the protest had become. A poster the Workers Federation was distributing simply asked a question: "How much does Deng Pufang spend on gambling at the Hong Kong race course?" Deng Pufang was the son of China's supreme leader. Susan knew the answer, thanks to MI6. Its officers in the colony had pieced together a detailed picture of Deng Pufang's wins and losses; right now he was on a losing streak.

Another poster proclaimed LONG LIVE THE PEOPLE! Susan knew that would be regarded by the leadership as "highly subversive, tantamount to a call to insurrection." Other leaflets sent to her for analysis called upon the Party to define its meaning of *revolution* and *reaction*, sacred words in the official lexicon. To even ask such questions was heresy. A cartoon now widely displayed around Beijing showed a mandarin with an opium pipe; the caption read "Democracy on high."

But in judging the national mood and where it could be leading, Susan found most useful the poems that were being stuck up everywhere. They were a mixture of scorn, satire, and political argument. They helped bind together the strands of disparate dissent.

Yet in trying to cope with the pressure, the Party and its leaders were all too clearly seeing their options reduced. China under communism, Susan wrote for her latest position paper, had "always been a place that swings from thaw to freeze." There had been a thaw, enough to allow the students to protest corruption and nepotism. Now the struggle had clearly reached a critical phase on both sides that could decide the next freeze.

Susan wrote: "The leadership is clearly even more divided, while the students have continued to display a sharper political edge. In the division within Zhongnanhai, the role of Zhao has become crucial."

The young analyst had spent hours studying the latest snippets of information about the Party secretary. It had given her a clear picture of what Zhao had done since returning from North Korea.

Susan had underlined key phrases in the Party secretary's pronouncements. "The students have raised problems which must be resolved." "We must push forward with economic reform." "The way forward is by political restructuring." "Our students are by no means opposed to our fundamental system, rather they are asking us to correct mistakes in our work."

For the past two days, Zhao had ordered such excerpts from his speeches to be featured on national TV and radio and the front page of the *People's Daily*. He had been careful to do it all, he kept insisting, in the "name of harmony between us and the students."

Susan had learned from information supplied by, among others, MI6 and the CIA that Zhao's words had deeply angered Deng. One intelligence report described an angry confrontation in Zhongnanhai on May 6 between Li Peng and Zhao in which the prime minister accused the Party secretary of "portraying us as villains." Zhao had calmly replied, "If I made incorrect remarks I will bear the responsibility."

Their row had carried on into a Politburo meeting the following day. The clashes there between hardliners and Zhao's moderates were the most bitter since the onset of the Cultural Revolution. In the end Zhao and his loosely knit group had refused to listen, driving Li Peng to brand them as betrayers of the Party.

Susan added to her position paper: the polarization has led to virtual paralysis in the leadership in dealing with the students. "Deng is clearly fixated by the calendar. Mikhail Gorbachev will soon be in Beijing."

Intelligence sources had told her that the students were planning a spectacular welcome for the Soviet leader, a massive hunger strike on Tiananmen Square.

MONDAY, MAY 8, 1989
*China Daily compound*

On this, the twenty-fourth day of the demonstrations, Jeanne Moore had concluded that "we can't see any evidence that China has a formal government."

Phone calls to ministries went unanswered. Requests for "guidance" on what could be published were ignored. "No one seemed to know what to do or say," she had noted.

By late afternoon she had discovered, by calling her contacts at home, that the country was being effectively run by a small group, all survivors of the Long March. They had held their first meeting in Deng's compound that morning to decide what to do about the students. Each member of the group was a long-standing confidant of Deng's.

Once more Tiananmen Square had begun to fill. By noon the number was estimated at fifty thousand; hours later it had doubled, an influx of Beijing citizens joining the students. They told the police they had come to see the preparations for Gorbachev's visit. From all the buildings around Tiananmen Square hung Chinese and Soviet flags and emblems proclaiming mutual friendship. The police, "having no clear orders, have done nothing. Most significantly, there are no soldiers to be seen," Jeanne had noted.

That seemed to confirm what she had gleaned from her sources in the U.S. embassy, that there was no agreement within Zhongnanhai to use military force. She had been told that Zhao was largely instrumental in stopping troops being sent. He had even managed to persuade some hitherto hardline members of the Politburo to support him, albeit reluctantly.

Earlier in the afternoon Jeanne had been assigned to translate an article by Zhao that would be published in the *People's Daily*. It promised human rights and argued for yet more reforms. Her own editor, a fervent Zhao supporter, and a man committed to liberalizing China, was ecstatic. He called Zhao's article "a beacon that will light the way forward for the students and the Party."

Now, Jeanne knew differently. She discovered by checking constantly updated obituaries in the newspaper's library that Deng's cabal were "the hardest of the hardliners." There was Deng Zhen, eighty-six, who walked with a frame; Chen Yun, eighty-four, who needed a wheelchair; Wang Zhen, eighty-one, who could not go anywhere without a doctor and nurse at his elbow. Yet despite their physical frailty, these men and the only woman Deng had allowed into the cabinet, Deng Yingchao, the widow of Chou En-lai, were still extraordinarily powerful.

Jeanne had been told by her contacts in government that at the morning meeting Deng had demanded to know where he should draw a line. The cabal had all given the same response: There had been enough concessions. State President Yang Shangkun had added: "We must not retreat from our duty, however harsh it must be."

Jeanne's contacts had told her that afterward Deng had held lengthy telephone conversations with the commanders of the country's seven military regions. In her diary she had confided: "Time is running out. But no one wants to believe it."

SAME DAY
*New York*

In that other center of network news, the high-tech home of NBC in Manhattan, senior executives had passed on the China story. The visit of Mikhail Gorbachev to Beijing was, in their view, not a grabber for the evening news. And at ABC, executives reminded one another that Peter Jennings had been right to be cautious. Nothing was really happening in Beijing: When CNN showed another panning shot of the protesting crowds in Tiananmen Square, it was a big yawn. It certainly was not worth investing a million or more dollars in sending Jennings and his entourage just to cover that.

ABC's senior vice-president Rick Wald summed it up: "The Chinese had already told us that the Gorbachev visit was entirely ceremonial. We sent reporters to cover that sort of thing, not a program."

He could have been speaking also for NBC.

When the news reached the White House, there was a sense of relief around the Oval Office. The story really was not going to take off: No need for Bush to go public on what those students ten thousand miles away were doing.

Everyone assumed Dan Rather of CBS would also pass on the story.

SAME DAY, A LITTLE LATER
*U.S. Embassy compound*
*Beijing*

Tom and the other CIA officers at the agency's Beijing station now knew that Deng Xiaoping had persuaded all his military commanders to mobilize their forces to deal with what the supreme leader was calling "the greatest threat to the country I could remember." One of the CIA operatives joked that Deng must be suffering from amnesia to have forgotten the Cultural Revolution.

On Tiananmen Square other intelligence operatives continued to infiltrate and probe, each with a clear agenda.

The Russians were primarily concerned with the effect the demonstrations could have on the Gorbachev visit, now only a week away. "If this was happening in Moscow," one KGB man was overheard saying, "The Red Army would have moved in and cleared everyone out."

Intelligence operatives from other Soviet bloc countries—Romania, Bulgaria, Hungary, Czechoslovakia, and East Germany—were trying to establish if anyone was masterminding the demonstrations.

"They simply could not accept that this was planned and executed by the students," said Irish diplomat Brendan Ward. "In their own countries, something so well organized and determined would have received some powerful driving force. What these people could not grasp was that the students were being motivated by that most powerful force of all, a need for democracy."

European intelligence agents, especially those of Britain, France, and West Germany, were concerned to discover what external support the students had, especially from Hong Kong and Taiwan. Three weeks into the demonstration these operatives had discovered not only that sizable sums of money were being smuggled in from Hong Kong and Taiwan to purchase food for the demonstrators, but that escape networks stretching for thousands of miles had been set up to smuggle students out of China before the authorities arrested them.

The intelligence officers realized that what had begun as a funeral rite for a beloved leader, Hu Yaobang, had assumed a far more significant meaning, one increasingly disturbing to foreign business-people. They had started to come to Tiananmen Square to see for themselves what was happening. Between them they had bankrolled China in the past decade with $37 billion. Twice that figure was scheduled to be placed in the country in the next five years. For men like George Kenneth Liu, chief executive in China of the giant General Foods Corporation, the situation was "of deep concern."

The view was being echoed by executives at the Chrysler Corporation's Beijing Jeep plant, the Philips Radio plant in the capital, at C. M. Ericsson's telephone-equipment factory on the outskirts. In a score of foreign-managed corporations, there was growing unease over the possibility that the students could force the government into taking action that would lead to a global collapse of confidence in China's ability to manage its own affairs.

The reverberations from events in Tiananmen Square were not confined to Beijing's foreign business community. The unease had spread through the entire country. In Shanghai, the Volkswagen plant was producing at half capacity as workers there continued to march in support of the students. Along China's long southern coastal belt, foreign-financed clothing factories found their sewing machines increasingly idle for the same reason. It was the same in those plants producing electrical appliances, radios, and toys for the U.S. and European markets.

The situation was exacerbated, in the view of many business-people, by the increasing number of print and television reporters who had arrived to cover the Gorbachev visit and found themselves with a running story outside the hotel they had made their headquarters, the towering, monolithic Beijing, a few minutes' walk from Tiananmen Square.

Reporters from over 150 nations visiting the square all filed basically the same story. China was in the grip of something momentous. The outcome could either be another triumph for democracy, as in the Philippines, or a crushing failure, as in Burma. Was China on the verge of historic events like the Hungarian uprising of 1956 and the Prague Spring of 1968? Or was it about to plunge into some terrible abyss?

The correspondents and camera crews did not, could not, know. But there is nothing like a story that can go either way to dominate the media. Increasingly events in China did that around the world. Those reports led to deepening anxiety and concern among the global business communities, which began to exert still more pressure on their governments to either persuade the Chinese leadership to make some concessions, or make it absolutely clear to the students that they could expect no support.

"There was a lot of pressure from a number of sources," Britain's ambassador, Sir Alan Donald, acknowledged.

Tom, the CIA agent who had become almost a permanent presence in Tiananmen Square, put it more bluntly. "If the Chinese were going to act, they should do so now. To the outside world it looked as if a bunch of kids were hijacking their government. No one could support that, even if it is done in the name of democracy."

Those words reflected a policy decision taken in Washington by Webster. His agents would continue to probe the students but would provide them with no information in turn, such as that piece of news that Deng Xiaoping now had the full support of the army in crushing the demonstrations.

When measured against the wider interests of the United States and her European partners, the students were expendable. No one wanted them to die. But no one among those intelligence officers, businesspeople, and their governments would risk their own interests to ensure that the students succeeded.

SAME DAY, A LITTLE LATER
*Beijing Airport*

The long flight from California had been even more tiring than Jenny had expected. Thankfully, little Peter had slept for most of the journey. Even now she could not quite believe how swiftly events had happened.

Once Professor Guangzu's daughter had made the decision to go home, the Medical Center's administration in Los Angeles said she could have an extended leave of absence. Several colleagues had pressed sums of money on her. Zhong, her husband, had been coldly furious when she had told him she was leaving. He had refused to drive her to the airport. As she left the apartment, she had quickly shaken his hand. She knew then her marriage was effectively over.

During the flight she had wondered what she would tell her father. Now that she was there, she felt suddenly nervous. Should she phone him from the airport? Or just show up at the apartment?

Jenny turned to Sue Tung and sought her advice.

They had met on the flight, drawn to each other because they were the only two Chinese women among the passengers. In the long hours across the Pacific they had shared life stories. Sue had told her about the $10,000 she had collected and said she still had no clear idea of how it should be spent. Jenny had suggested Sue could ask her father what was needed.

"Don't just turn up. Call him," advised Sue as they lugged their cases through the customs hall. "Parents hate surprises."

Sue had decided to telephone Jyan as soon as she could. She was certain his position at the Military Academy would enable him to provide a clear report on the situation. She would also call Rod. Already she missed him. But she had promised to be back in Sacramento in time for their wedding.

Out in the airport arrivals hall, crowded as usual with hucksters trying to entice passengers to stay at certain hotels, the two women went in search of phones. Suddenly Jenny felt a tap on her shoulder. She turned to face her father.

"Papa," she gasped. "How did you know I was here?"

"Your husband called," Professor Guangzu said. He picked up

Peter in his arms. "Hello, my little American," he smiled. "Do you speak any Chinese?"

The child shook his head. Professor Guangzu sighed and turned to his daughter. Jenny introduced Sue. The professor looked at both women.

"You come at a very interesting time," he finally said. "A very interesting and troubling time."

FRIDAY, MAY 12, 1989
*Beijing University*

One by one the chosen students made their way into the campus coffeehouse at midday, fifty volunteers who were prepared to starve themselves to death. Daobao and Yang Li had been among the first to step forward. But the other student leaders had insisted they were too important to be used for such a purpose.

Instead they had spent the morning of the twenty-eighth day of their protest helping to prepare a sumptuous farewell banquet for those who had promised to die. Cassy was among the other leaders who had prepared the food. Every table in the coffeehouse was filled with bowls of rice, meat, and fish. There were bottles of beer and the strong *Maotai* sorghum spirit. Everything had been donated by the people of Beijing.

Watching them eat, Cassy was close to tears, moved by the thought that in a country where widespread starvation was still common, these volunteers were going to use hunger as their final weapon to try and convince the regime to meet their demands for democracy.

The meal over, she joined other students escorting the volunteers to Tiananmen Square. As they cycled through the campus gates, Cassy wondered how many would ever return. Yet she could not believe the authorities would deliberately let them die in the full glare of the foreign media.

Watching them arrive on Tiananmen Square two hours later, Jeanne Moore recognized that publicity was the students' most powerful weapon. In all, she counted over four hundred volunteers, drawn from campuses all over the city.

Once the reason for their presence became known there was a sustained cheer from the tens of thousands who now permanently occupied the square.

Wuerkaixi ordered the volunteers to form ranks before the Monument to the People's Heroes. Then he administered a ceremonial oath, his voice close to breaking with emotion.

"You will all agree not to eat until we have obtained substantial, concrete, and real dialogue with the Party leadership, and until we receive official recognition that our cause is patriotic and democratic."

A chorus of agreement came from the volunteers. Wang Dan then addressed them, much to the visible irritation of Wuerkaixi. The relationship between the two leaders had become openly strained. Now Wang Dan brought a touch of farce to the proceedings. He said all the hunger strikers must also give up smoking. The news was greeted with a collective groan from the volunteers.

Wuerkaixi called the other leaders to meet with him in the roped-off space below the pediment that had become their "conference corner." He said Wang Dan was wrong to demand a smoking ban, that cigarettes would sustain the volunteers in the difficult times ahead. Daobao and Li then explained that they had learned that IRA hunger strikers such as Bobby Sands had survived so long by using nicotine to dampen down their hunger pains. Wang Dan relented and told the students they could smoke.

He then led them to the exact spot on the square where in two days' time State President Yang Shangkun was to formally welcome Mikhail Gorbachev. The volunteers sat down in ranks.

Once more Wuerkaixi addressed them.

"In this sunny, brilliant month of May you are going on hunger strike. During this most beautiful moment of youth, you have chosen to put the beauty of life behind you.... You do not want to die. You would like to lead a good life because you are in the prime of your lives. None of us wants to die. Rather we would like to study hard. Our country is very poor. You will be leaving our country behind if you die."

Cassy saw that some of the onlookers were weeping openly as Wuerkaixi paused. She thought again how skilled he was at crowd manipulation.

Nearby Jeanne Moore and Melinda Liu were both writing down his words.

"Death is not our goal. But if the death of one person or a group of few would ameliorate lives of a larger group of people and succor the prosperity of our nation, we would not have the right to escape death."

Brendan Ward, one of the scores of foreign diplomats on the square, felt it was "like being back in O'Connell Street, Dublin, listening to some of the great protest figures in my society." Ward knew enough about what he called "the politics of hunger" to realize that the volunteers were deadly serious.

To Brian Davidson they had "a touch of what the kamikaze pilots must have looked like."

As Wuerkaixi spoke, the students put on white headbands bearing the words HUNGER STRIKER or DEMOCRACY WARRIOR. They stared fixedly at Wuerkaixi as he continued.

"Our country has already reached a stage where prices are soaring, official profiteering is rife, the mighty tower above, bureaucracies are corrupt, many of those with lofty ideals are lost, and social order grows worse by the day."

Raising his voice, Wuerkaixi declaimed: "At this crucial point of life and death for our race and nation, compatriots, every compatriot with a conscience, please listen to our plea."

When he stepped back there was total silence, the ultimate show of respect.

Then thousands of nonfasting students, still without speaking, formed a protective outer ring around those who were pledged to die to give meaning to what had been said. There was only the sound of weeping among the onlookers.

# 17

# *Turmoil on Tiananmen*

SATURDAY, MAY 13, 1989
*Tiananmen Square*

Dressed in a beige safari jacket, chin thrust forward, Dan Rather
once more set out to show why the CBS network thought he was
worth almost $3 million a year as their anchorman for the evening
news. It was the twenty-ninth day of the demonstrations.

Hours before, Rather had arrived from New York by what the
airlines call "the stagecoach route" to the Orient, with stopovers in
Paris and New Delhi. In Paris, Rather had heard the news that
Panama was about to boil over—and here he was, on the far side of
the world, with a major story, possibly *the* story, erupting in America's
backyard. It had helped add to Rather's anxiety, so much so that
having checked into Beijing's Shangri-La Hotel, where Chinese
musicians in tuxedos played Brahms during the Happy Hour, Rather
had gone at once to Tiananmen Square, accompanied by some of the
seventy crew people needed to support him.

Flanked by his producer and director, Rather went directly to the
Monument to the People's Heroes. For the next hour he explained to
Wuerkaixi and Wang Dan why he was there and what he intended to
do, "make your cause fully known to the American people."

The two student leaders listened politely. In the past few days
other revered names of European broadcasting had beat a path to
them, seeking interviews, offering primetime exposure, shrewdly
assuring Wuerkaixi that he was already a world-famous figure, so
every word he said would be carefully listened to in the corridors of
government. It was a heady prospect for a twenty-one-year-old who
had counted his audience in hundreds until a few weeks ago.

194

The CBS team assured Wuerkaixi that the story would now be noted in the White House, and that Dan Rather was the very man to also get the American people all fired up. Wuerkaixi and Wang Dan promised the anchorman they would do everything possible to help him do that.

Shortly afterward Rather delivered in a dramatic, emotional voice, perfect for the occasion, his opening statement from the square.

"Gorbachev comes to China seeking to heal old wounds and neutralize America's strategic position in Asia. He is upstaged by striking students seeking to change the face of Communism. Getting to the center of the square means passing through an ocean of students, bicycles, loudspeakers, slogan-chanting, singing, and applause. Determination, not rage, is on the faces and in the voices. They defied a government order to be out of the square by the time Gorbachev arrives, and no one seems afraid. Police are around in force, but instead of breaking up the crowds, they broke into patriotic song, and the students sang back."

In those words Dan Rather had stamped his authority on the demonstrations. In New York, NBC and ABC news executives realized they had badly misjudged. While Panama, where Manuel Noriega had initiated a vicious physical assault on political opponents and thousands of U.S. troops were pouring into the Canal Zone, was indeed an important story, what was happening in China was not just news. It was history.

SUNDAY, MAY 14, 1989
*Tiananmen Square*

Late in the evening on the thirtieth day of the demonstrations for democracy, Professor Guangzu and his daughter, Jenny, walked among the hunger strikers, now two thousand strong. Themselves close to exhaustion after their long day in the square, they continued to check vital signs and then order medical students to carry away those strikers closest to collapse. Scores of other doctors were doing the same.

As soon as one stretcher was carried away to the hospital, another student lay down on the ground and prepared to die. Each time, Jenny felt fresh tears prick her eyes.

All around her, other doctors and nurses tried to control their emotions in the highly charged atmosphere. There were close to a million people in the square, listening to and commenting on the claims and counterclaims coming over the loudspeakers.

Daobao and Yang Li had set up the students' own relay system to broadcast speeches repudiating those put out by the Party from a studio in the Great Hall of the People.

Away from the hunger strikers, the atmosphere struck Cassy as "part Coney Island, part state fair, part political convention."

Vendors were selling food. The air was filled with competing rock music, and over everything blared the voices from the loudspeakers. They continued to give sharply differing accounts of the first real contacts between the student leaders and the authorities the previous evening.

For an hour they had met in a building opposite the gates of Zhongnanhai. Prime Minister Li Peng had sent Politburo member Yan Mingfu, the only real moderate in the government still openly supporting the students, to plead with Wuerkaixi and Wang Dan to order the students to leave the square. Unknown to those at the meeting, intelligence chief Qiao Shi had bugged the room. Throughout this Sunday the tape had been cleverly used to create the impression that the students were not really interested in reforms but simply wanted to shame China in the eyes of the world on the eve of Gorbachev's visit. The government broadcasts explained how Yan Mingfu had offered the students a place where they could continue their hunger strike in peace and had even offered an apology for "past mistakes."

Finally, the broadcast described how Yan Mingfu had made an almost tearful appeal. Through the loudspeaker had come his secretly recorded voice. "If you insist on dividing the Party into factions, you should realize your action is going to seriously harm those of us who support reform. You will make it very difficult for Comrade Zhao Ziyang and all the other comrades working for what you all want."

Qiao Shi had helped strengthen the suspicion that Party Secretary Zhao was using the situation in a bid for ultimate power.

Sensing this, Wuerkaixi had once more broadcast that the student leadership publicly distanced itself from everyone in the government.

In the past hours the young student leader had assumed almost a new personality. He no longer walked, but half ran everywhere, issuing orders, brooking no argument. The more the world's TV cameras were trained on him, the more theatrical Wuerkaixi became. To Cassy he "was an actor who had found his stage."

Other student leaders went about their business of running the protest with less show. Wang Dan huddled with others at the foot of the monument, his eyes blinking furiously behind his glasses as they reviewed strategy. Chai Ling was everywhere, urging students not to leave the square. Liu Gang, his Western-style sports clothes badly in need of cleaning, moved around the square, judging the mood. Yang Li's muscular frame seemed to be in perpetual motion as he prowled the square, quietly giving encouragement.

Daobao made regular forays from the monument to check on the supply of posters, food supplies, and the desperate need for more toilet facilities. Slit trenches had been dug on one side of the square and tents erected over them. But the trenches were filled to overflowing, and an overpowering stench drifted from the area. More trenches were now being dug. But with a million people now in the square it would not be long before they were also filled.

But to Jeanne Moore "the situation had become a celebration of rejection and utter contempt for China's leaders, Zhao included. We are as close to revolution as we can be yet without a shot being fired."

Now, this Sunday evening, she saw the government about to become further publicly humiliated. Through the crowd came Beijing's mayor, Chen Xitong and Li Xiaming, the city's Party secretary. They were flanked by nervous aides and a phalanx of police. Reaching the Monument to the People's Heroes, and trying hard to ignore the scores of foreign TV cameras trained on them, both men appealed to the student leaders to withdraw from the square.

Wuerkaixi pointed dramatically to where the hunger strikers were.

"To leave will be for us to betray what they are doing!" he cried out. "We will not leave until we have achieved our aims. Long live democracy!"

The cry was taken up by the crowd. Visibly shaken, the delegation withdrew.

Shortly afterward the unmistakable voice of Qiao Shi came over the loudspeakers announcing the square was to be closed for the Gorbachev visit; all students must leave by three o'clock the following morning.

On the pediment, Wuerkaixi turned to Chai Ling. She grabbed one of the microphones and addressed the crowd.

"History demands we stay. And stay we will!"

She had spent hours writing and polishing what she would say. For ink she had used blood from a cut she had deliberately made in her arm, collecting the blood in a dish into which she dipped her calligraphy brush. The gesture was typical of the highly-strung young woman, whose strong sense of theater was only equaled by Wuerkaixi's.

Holding the parchment before her. Chai Ling's childlike voice carried to the furthest corners of the square. Under the impact of her words a stillness came over the crowd.

"People of China, we feel the purest patriotism! We offer the finest of our hearts and souls. Yet we have been described as 'rioting' and filled with 'ulterior motives' and being led by a 'small group of people.'"

Brian Davidson, the British press attaché, was among those who saw her pause and turn to face the portrait of Mao on Tiananmen Square.

"Honest citizens of China," she continued, "each of you put your hand on your heart and ask the goodness that is in your heart, what are we guilty of? Are we rioting? No! We mean a peaceful demonstration! Yet our emotions have been manipulated time and again. We endure hunger to seek truth. But we are met with police brutality. We go down on our knees to plead for democracy!"

Barr Seitz heaved a long sigh. He had not left the square in the past twenty-four hours, acting as a runner for the ABC camera crew roaming the area. His job was to set up interviews and carry film back to the nearby Beijing Hotel, where the network had established a base, though it had not sent its star anchorman, Peter Jennings. The sight of the tall, smiling Barr had become a familiar and welcome one to the students. Speaking their language, he had shared with them their dreams, which Chai Ling continued to articulate so eloquently.

"Democracy is life's greatest safeguard. Freedom is our heaven-given right since the beginning of man! Yet now we have to fight for them with our young lives. Can the Chinese people be proud of this?"

*Newsweek* correspondent Melinda Liu admired the way Chai Ling worked the crowd. The student knew more about public speaking than most seasoned professionals. Melinda decided she would use the student as a sidebar to the main story she would be filing.

Chai Ling continued: "We have no choice but to go on hunger strike. It is our only choice. We use language which enables us to face death, to fight for the life which is worth living."

Brendan Ward was once more reminded of some of the great speakers who had made their mark on his own country's history. The Irish diplomat had been about to return to his embassy to send another telegram to the Department of Foreign Affairs in Dublin, describing the day's events, when Chai Ling's words had stopped him. Ward stood mesmerized like those around him.

Her voice beginning to grow hoarse, Chai Ling reminded the crowd of basic truths.

"We are still children! All of us! China is our mother, for all of us! Mother, take a good look at your sons and daughters! Hunger is destroying their youth. Death is stalking ever closer to them. Can you remain unmoved?"

For the first time since she had spoken a sound came from the crowd: part moan, part groan. Then thousands of voices answered Chai Ling's question.

"No, we cannot remain unmoved."

With a quick shake of her head. Chai Ling silenced them. Then she pointed to the hunger strikers.

"I speak for them when I say we do not want to die. None of us. But when we are enduring hunger, fathers and mothers, don't be sad. When we are saying farewell to life, uncles and aunts, please don't break your hearts. We have only one wish. That is to allow all of you to lead better lives. We have only one request. Please do not forget that what we are seeking is in no way death. For we know democracy is not the affair of a few, and we realize it cannot be achieved by one generation."

Around Jenny and her father, people were sobbing. She thought, we are doctors, used to pain and suffering. Yet who cannot be moved by such eloquence? Her mind turned toward little Peter, resting at the back of the first-aid tent. This taut-faced young woman on the pediment was trying to ensure her son's future, the future of untold millions of sons and daughters of Mother China. Finally tears began to run down Jenny's own cheeks. Her father looked at her, then looked away, his own eyes misty.

Over the loudspeakers, Chai Ling was quoting a poem to the hunger strikers. "'When a man is about to die, his words would be kind; if a horse is about to expire, his cries would be sorrowful.'"

Those hunger strikers who still had the strength to do so raised their hands in salute before sinking back on the ground, too exhausted to speak. Doctors moistened their lips with water and tried to make them as comfortable as possible. It was the third day of their hunger strike.

Over the loudspeakers, the voice had risen.

"Farewell, comrades, take care! May those who die and those who live share the same loyalty. Farewell, beloved, take care! I cannot bear to take leave of you, yet there is no choice but to take leave. Farewell, our parents! Please forgive us. Your children cannot manage to be loyal and filial at the same time. Farewell, our people. Please permit us to demonstrate to you our loyalty in this desperate fashion!"

Chai Ling stepped back from the microphone. The silence remained total.

MONDAY, MAY 15, 1989
*Beijing Airport*

Soviet Ambassador Troyanovsky liked to quote Balzac on diplomacy: "a science which permits its practitioners to say nothing and shelter behind mysterious nods of the head." He watched the Aeroflot Ilyushin jet coming in to land and smiled ruefully. Balzac's words had taken on a new meaning in the enervating noonday sun.

The sun made the chunky diplomat mop his face with a large silk handkerchief which complemented his Hong Kong tailored blue silk suit and one of the several dozen pairs of custom-made shoes he regularly bought from the colony.

All around him on the airport tarmac, the Chinese delegation waited to welcome Mikhail Gorbachev. They continued to give little Balzac-like nods to each other and murmur in those quick, hissed whispers that the ambassador found hard to understand, though he spoke Mandarin fluently. But it wasn't hard for the diplomat to guess what was on the delegate's minds.

Because of the demonstration, the Party had been forced to abandon its carefully laid plans to greet Gorbachev at Tiananmen Square. Shortly after dinner, Troyanovsky had been telephoned by Qiao Shi. The security chief was calling on his mobile phone from the roof of the Great Hall of the People. He said it had been decided it would be "more appropriate" for the welcoming ceremony to take place at the airport. Qiao Shi had added that as there would be so much to discuss during the first Sino-Soviet summit in twenty years, the sooner the diplomatic greetings were over, the better. Therefore the arrival ceremony would be cut to the absolute minimum. Troyanovsky had not been fooled. He could recognize a crisis.

The ambassador had promptly ordered every possible diplomat not involved in the welcoming ceremony to Tiananmen Square to report what was happening. Troyanovsky had then used the embassy communications room to call the airport at Irtytisk, the Siberian city that was Gorbachev's departure point for China. The Ilyushin was already airborne. The ambassador was patched through to the flight deck via a satellite link. Knowing that his conversation was most certainly being monitored by United States intelligence, and probably by the Chinese, the ambassador was circumspect about the latest change of plan.

Nevertheless, Gorbachev did not bother to hide his astonishment. Andrew Higgins, the Beijing correspondent on the British national daily *The Independent*, was one of several reporters who would learn of the exchange between the plane and the ground. "The Ilyushin's radio crackled with whispers about the extraordinary scenes which lay ahead," Higgins would write. "The reports...sound barely credible. 'How *big* is the square?' asked the amazed Gorbachev."

A few minutes ago, as the Ilyushin swept over the airport perimeter fence guarded by, among other PLA forces, Bing Yang's platoon, Troyanovsky's deputy, Minister-Counselor Ivan Fedotov, who was coordinating the reports from the embassy staff on Tiananmen Square, had come through on the ambassador's car phone.

Smiling apologetically at the Chinese, Troyanovsky hurried to the car parked in the official cavalcade waiting to sweep Gorbachev and his hosts away.

"There are nearly a million people here," Fedotov reported. "They are all singing and dancing. The students have put up Comrade Gorbachev's portrait opposite Mao's on Tiananmen Square. It's an even bigger photo, and they keep calling for perestroika."

The ambassador's groan of near-despair was heard by the pool of journalists covering the airport ceremonies.

A week ago Troyanovsky had foreseen this could happen: The students would use Gorbachev to embarrass their own government. Three times in the past few days he had gone to Zhongnanhai and spoken to Li Peng's office. The ambassador, with a deserved reputation for attention to diplomatic minutia, had asked whether the state visit should be delayed. He had been told that to do so could have unpredictable consequences for Sino-Soviet relations.

As well as being a student of Balzac, the ambassador was something of a specialist in understanding Chinese face-saving. Deng Xiaoping wanted the visit, even though in Troyanovsky's graphic later description "China's leaders were like Nero, fiddling while everything was going up in metaphorical flames around them."

The ambassador hurried back to take his place with the ranks of Chinese watching the Ilyushin rolling to a stop.

State President Yang Shangkun braced his wiry frame and walked to the foot of the steps. The aircraft door opened and Gorbachev, followed by his wife, Raisa, appeared.

For a moment the Soviet leader stood, composing his face into a smile. Then he and his wife came down the steps onto the bare tarmac. In the near-panic decision to switch the welcome from Tiananmen Square, someone had overlooked laying a red carpet. However, the PLA honor guard were in place and snapped to attention as Gorbachev and the president passed in review, accompanied by the sound of a twenty-one gun salute.

Gorbachev turned and looked about him expectantly. Where was the microphone for the welcoming speeches?

"Later, later," the state president smiled quickly, turning to lead Gorbachev to one of the waiting cars.

Gorbachev's anger was plain. He pursed his lips and hunched his shoulders. Raisa looked faintly bewildered as a Chinese flunky shoved a bunch of flowers into her arms.

One of the Soviet officers rushed to the press pen and handed out copies of the speech Gorbachev had not been allowed to make. It began with suitable allegoric fervor: "We have come to China in springtime, the good season of burgeoning nature and the awakening of new life. All over the world, people associate this season with renewal and hope."

As the motorcade swept away, the journalists scrambled for telephones. Gorbachev's words were bound to be interpreted by the students as support, and by his hosts as a calculated slap in the face.


SAME DAY, SAME TIME
*Tiananmen Square*

Postgraduate student Sue Tung continued to describe to Rod in Sacramento what was happening, using a mobile phone an American television reporter had loaned her in return for allowing him to film the call. Trying to ignore the camera team, Sue spoke to Rod.

"Even in the two days I have felt a change. People are more open and determined to push this through. The songs have become more militant and more mocking of authority."

"Just like our protests over the Vietnam War," Rod said.

"But different," Sue insisted. "The people here are fighting for democracy. I'm standing now beneath the flagpole where the hammer and sickle should be flying. Instead the students have run up a huge banner carrying the words HUNGER STRIKE. All around are banners. One says 'Mother, we like food, but we like democracy even more.' Another says 'Our children are going hungry, Deng Xiaoping. What about your children?'"

"Courting couples stroll arm in arm. Fathers carry their children on their shoulders. Many of the kids have headbands with the same two words, FREEDOM and DEMOCRACY. I don't think that you can call this any more just a student movement. It's a people's movement. I've spoken to people who have cycled fifty miles just to be here. One many said he had come from a hundred miles away by train. There are teachers, factory workers, writers, intellectuals. I just don't remember anything like it."

Sue and the camera team eased their way through the cordon of students around the hunger strikers.

"The scene is quite incredible. Just hundreds and hundreds of bodies spread out everywhere. Someone has just told me they've taken away fifty so far to the first-aid posts that are now all around the square. It seems that as soon as they feel strong enough, the strikers will return. In the meantime they are refusing everything except glucose and water—and cigarettes!"

Rod's suddenly excited voice interrupted Sue.

"Honey, are you wearing a yellow dress and a sunhat?"

"Yes. How'd you know?"

"You're on CNN! They've got live pictures coming from the square. I can see you clearly!"

Sue looked around. A few yards away a CNN crew was filming. She waved at its camera.

"I wish you were here," Sue said.

"I'll come, if you like. We could get married right there!"

Sue smiled. "I don't think that would be possible. Besides, I've set myself on having a proper American wedding."

They said they loved each other and hung up.

Dan Rather and the CBS team had gotten into their stride, powered partly by the sheer excitement of being at the center of a major news story, partly by the satisfaction of knowing that they were beating their rivals, ABC and NBC. While those networks had correspondents in the square, none had the stature of Rather.

In the florid prose that so well suited the moment, he continued to paint a portrait of "roller-coaster events."

Because of the thirteen-hour time difference with New York, Rather and the crew were working around the clock from a mobile unit in the square itself. When not on air they trudged back to the Shangri-La, too exhausted even to listen to the tuxedo-clad Chinese musicians playing Brahms.

This semblance of normality encouraged some of the foreign businesspeople who had arrived in Beijing to check on their investments.

SAME DAY, SAME TIME
*San Francisco*

Shao-Yen Wang, the daughter of a senior official in Beijing, was watching Rather's newscast from Tiananmen Square while talking on the phone.

"We must keep up the pressure," she was saying. "We do that, and maybe one of the diplomats in the consulate will crack. If even one defects, it will be a huge loss of face to the old men in Zhongnanhai."

The previous day Shao-Yen had been among several thousand Chinese, students and workers from the Chinatown district, who had demonstrated outside their country's consulate in the city. From time to time, faces had appeared at the windows of the building. Some had given V-signs.

The gesture had convinced Shao-Yen that a diplomat might be considering defecting.

"I saw those faces," she said again. "Everyone in that building is trained to show nothing. But some of them looked as if they wished they were out there with us. If we keep protesting and telling them it's all part of democracy, maybe one will come and join us."

Shao-Yen was speaking to a woman who was an important member of the local Chinese community. She told Shao-Yen she did not wish to be personally identified with the protest until it was "absolutely certain the students back home will not fail."

Trying to enlist support, Shao-Yen had encountered the same hesitancy among a number of wealthy or influential local Chinese. Several had flatly refused to help, explaining they wanted nothing to jeopardize their trading links with their motherland. One or two had warned Shao-Yen of the risk she was taking.

One man had reminded her of the Chinese Secret Intelligence Service agents in the city, who by now had almost certainly reported back to Beijing on those first demonstrations outside the consulate.

Shao-Yen had replied she would do nothing to discredit China but would continue to try and help persuade its leaders to recognize that introducing democracy was the "only way to make China as great as America."

In her mind the young actress and aspiring screenwriter had a scenario in which she would one day bring the story to the screen. Perhaps she would even play Chai Ling. The excerpts of her speech broadcast on CNN had moved Shao-Yen to begin to think about a new screenplay. Somehow those Chinese secret agents she had been told were in San Francisco must also be worked into the story.

The FBI had also become involved. Its agents had cast an electronic surveillance net over the consulate. Already they had established that in the wake of the demonstration, coupled with the flow of diplomatic traffic from Beijing, the consulate staff had become polarized. Senior diplomats invariably supported the hard-liners in Beijing, while junior diplomats had begun to express support among themselves for the students.

Among them was the consulate's twenty-five-year-old cultural attaché, Zhang Milin. Handsome, carefully groomed, confident, until a few days ago he had been a total believer in his country's political system. But in the past days, the FBI eavesdroppers had picked up hints Zhang had been angered by his government's attitude toward the students. He had been overheard asking his seniors how he should explain what was happening in China to his American contacts. He had been told to say "reactionaries" and "hooligans" were trying to create trouble with the help of "imperialist spies."

About the time Shao-Yen was insisting on the phone to the woman about the need to keep up the pressure outside the consulate, Zhang had been heard on one of the many electronic bugs focused on the building, saying that the latest news from China, that Mikhail Gorbachev was supporting the students, was a further sign that the rest of the Communist world was turning against the old men of Zhongnanhai.

This made the attitude in Washington all the more curious, the cultural attaché had told a colleague. The Chinese embassy there had sent the consulate a lengthy message quoting unnamed White House and State Department officials as still hoping the students would stop confronting their government.

Zhang had "the strange feeling" that the U.S. administration had almost as much distaste for what the students were doing as his own government. In one of those moments of black humor that lightened the young diplomat's otherwise serious demeanor, Zhang had joked about whether the United States would find itself on the same side as China in trying to persuade the Soviet Union that it too should be openly discouraging the demonstrations.

SAME DAY, LATE AFTERNOON
*Beijing*

Using their separate but equally well placed contacts, Melinda Liu and Jeanne Moore were piecing together what had happened after Mikhail and Raisa Gorbachev had been driven from the airport at high speed to the State Guest House, a palace on the outskirts of the city.

While Raisa had freshened up and studied a schedule that by now bore no resemblance to what was being "feverishly replanned," Mikhail Gorbachev was holding a meeting with Ambassador Troyanovsky and other Soviet officials.

Gorbachev, according to Melinda's sources, was "close to hopping mad" at what he was being told. Because of the demonstrators in Tiananmen Square, now estimated to be in excess of 1.5 million, the

Soviet leader was going to be driven through the back streets to keep his official appointments.

Gorbachev, in his role as the new liberating force of European Communism, had planned to conquer Beijing with the kind of public relations campaign that had worked so well in other capital cities. He knew how important it was to be seen "pressing flesh" and "gladhanding with the citizens" if he was to succeed behind the scenes in what he had come to do: persuade the leadership that further reforms were essential to ease the pressure on them and allow them to remain in control.

Now he had been informed there would be no walk-abouts, no carefully stage-managed stops to shake hands, no photo-opportunities for Raisa and himself to do what they always did superbly, delivering the few words of their host's language to the local citizens.

Gorbachev's chief spokesman, Gennady Gerasimov, later remembered the Soviet leader's anger was "quite monumental." Late in the afternoon of this Monday, though, the personable Gerasimov was doing his best to prevent the press corps camped outside the State Guest House from discovering what was really happening.

In midafternoon, when the Gorbachevs were due to be formally greeted by State President Yang in the Great Hall of the People, Gerasimov issued a brief statement that the Gorbachevs were resting.

"In reality Gorbachev, encouraged by Raisa, was demanding to be treated like a world leader, not someone from a banana republic," one of Jeanne's contacts had told her.

Close to 6:00 P.M., the matter still unresolved, the Soviet leader and first lady entered their limousine to go to meet State President Yang. They were already two hours late. But instead of coming down the imposing main driveway of the Guest House compound, the motorcade went round the back of the palace, leaving the grounds through the tradesmen's gate. Entering the city, the cavalcade drove into the maze of hutongs, bouncing and bumping over the cobbles.

Professor Guangzu and Jenny had left Tiananmen Square to eat at the Oriental Restaurant, a modest establishment in one of those back streets, when they were startled to see official cars passing their window table. The Gorbachevs' limousine came to a brief stop. Jenny was convinced Raisa looked "longingly at our food, then with a little wave and smile they were gone."

The motorcade drove past warehouses, factories, and gray courtyard homes before it finally reached a gate at the back of the west side of the Great Hall of the People. The entrance was usually used by the cleaning staff.

It took a little honking before the gate was opened by two soldiers. The cars crept past piles of garbage bags before stopping on a disused basketball court.

The Gorbachevs climbed out and stared stoically back at the gate. A group of students had appeared and were unfurling a banner: "In Moscow they have Gorbachev and freedom! In China we have Deng and corruption!"

The soldiers closed the gate, and silent, crimson-faced flunkies escorted the Gorbachevs into the Great Hall.

From Tiananmen Square the constant, thunderous chant reached them.

"Give us democracy, Comrade Gorbachev!"

State President Yang smiled stiffly and remarked how glad he was to welcome his guests at such an important moment in China's history.

Gorbachev glanced around the salon where the funeral rites had been conducted for Hu Yaobang just a month ago. Perhaps remembering what Hu had tried to achieve, and what he had come to represent to the students. Gorbachev departed from the prepared phrases of his script. He told his hosts that down the generations "we have become smarter. My hope is that the next generation will be even more smarter."

The smile left the state president's lips. For the second time in a few hours Gorbachev had delivered a judgment on what was happening outside the windows of the salon.

Worse followed. Still extemporizing, Gorbachev pronounced no society could really exist without " a sensible balance between the generations."

He paused to give the eighty-seven-year-old state president a brief, thin smile. Then, deliberately looking toward the windows and raising his voice to overcome the turmoil on Tiananmen Square, Gorbachev delivered his most stinging rebuke so far.

"What is needed is for us all to recognize the energy of young people and their right to speak out against conservatism."

He paused once more, this time to look at his increasingly stunned hosts.

"But also they must recognize the wisdom of the older generation." The balm did nothing to heal the anger of the Chinese.

The message he had come to deliver was plain: There had to be changes.

For a few moments there was an embarrassed silence in the salon. Then a trickle of applause came and went. Gorbachev rocked slightly back and forth on his heels. He looked like a boxer who had delivered his first real body blows. Now he was waiting for the expected counterpunch.

It came at the end of Yang's response. Having delivered a string of banalities, the state president announced: "My colleagues and I feel the speed is too great. We must reduce it somewhat."

In a mood that Jeanne Moore likened to the one that "marks the short step from the death cell to the execution chamber," hosts and guests trooped to the welcoming banquet in the magnificent gallery of the Great Hall. One of its many features was the panoramic windows overlooking Tiananmen Square. The drapes had been drawn to help block out the chanting and that endlessly repeated cry for Gorbachev to somehow give the people of China democracy.

The meal passed in desultory small talk. Raisa barely touched her soup, noodles, and chicken. Like her husband she drank only water. Only when it came to the formal toasts did they sip wine.

Standing, glass in hand, Gorbachev said: "Today we have been able to see at close quarters something of your great city we would not have expected to see. We drove through your streets and saw your people. What most impressed us was their openness and friendliness."

At that moment another sustained roar came from the square.

"Give us democracy! We need perestroika! Give it to us, Comrade Gorbachev, initiator of glasnost!"

Some of the Chinese looked at the Soviet leader as if somehow he had personally arranged this further humiliation.

Struggling to his feet, visibly shaking, the state president was briefly at a loss how to respond. Then his scratchy voice made a remarkable admission.

"It is not easy for us to have a situation in which to hold these historic meetings."

It was the first official glimpse of what was happening behind the scenes.

The Gorbachevs and their entourage were virtually smuggled out of the building by their hosts, who were determined the students should have no glimpse of the Soviet leader. Three hours later Qiao Shi delivered over the square's loudspeakers what was no longer a threat but an abject plea.

"Please go back to school," the security chief began. "If you do, be assured that the Party and government will study most carefully all reasonable suggestions and demands and will take feasible measures and steps to resolve the questions."

Wuerkaixi responded instantly from the pediment. No one must leave. In the meantime, he added, he was joining the hunger strikers.

Cassy watched him swagger across the square to take his place beside the other starving students. Wuerkaixi's behavior troubled her. She had overheard him telling Yang to arrange for a bowl of noodles to be waiting in the back of the car he was using to snatch a few hours sleep. He had explained it was necessary for him to eat because "as leader, I need to conserve my strength, and I also have a heart condition."

When Cassy told Daobao what she had heard, he told her not to speak to anyone else about the matter, because they would not understand. But Cassy had begun to wonder whether Wuerkaixi really had the courage of his convictions or whether he was on an ego trip.

# 18

## *The Beckoning Abyss*

The demonstrations were now in their thirty-second day. Even here, five miles to the north of Tiananmen Square, and despite the immediate area around the compound being an exclusion zone patroled by Deng Xiaoping's elite guards, what was happening throughout Beijing continued to dominate the discussion going on into the night in Deng's office.

The large, airy room was richly furnished with priceless artifacts from the Forbidden City. On one wall hung a piece of calligraphy commemorating China's twenty-seven-hundred-year-old imperial system, still the longest-enduring of all political systems. Beside it hung a quotation from Mao stating that Communism would survive even longer.

With Deng Xiaoping were the handful of men he now most trusted to bring an end to a truly disastrous situation.

Li Peng was there, cold and aloof as always, his fish-eye stare showing nothing of the fury he must have felt at being a prime target of the students' anger.

With him sat Security Chief Qiao Shi, baggy-suited, another pair of chain-store socks on his cheaply shod feet. He drew on an eight-inch Cuban cigar, the aroma mingling with the acrid smell of the Panda cigarettes Deng chain-smoked.

Li Xiaming, Party secretary of Beijing and political commissar of the city's garrison, a key player in any military action against the students, sat, as always, squat and muscled, thick neck chafing against his shirt collar, face suffused with blood. It made his renowned lack of grace and humor more marked, his temper more evident.

State President Yang Shangkun sat beside Deng. If the eighty-two-year-old felt any irritation at being kept from his bed, he did not show it. Like Deng, he wore a dark gray high-buttoning jacket.

Present too was Vice-Premier Yao Yilin. He would soon be seventy-three. But the passing years had not diminished his liking for confrontation. His rough tongue concealed a formidable intellect.

They first dealt with the schedule for the remainder of Gorbachev's visit.

There would be no tour of the Forbidden City, no ceremonial drive along Changan Avenue, no opportunity for Gorbachev to pay homage at Mao's mausoleum. He and Raisa were to be kept virtually incommunicado in the State Guest House in between formal contacts with the leadership. The Soviet leader's meeting with Zhao Ziyang in Zhongnanhai later in the day could proceed, because the route to the compound would avoid the midtown area.

The only time the Gorbachevs would once more come physically close to the students would be during the formal climax to their visit the following day. They were then scheduled to meet Deng himself in the Great Hall of the People in Tiananmen Square.

State President Yang had been driven straight from there after the banquet to report Gorbachev's remarks. According to one European intelligence source, Deng had listened enigmatically, then dismissed Gorbachev's intervention as coming from someone poorly briefed.

By now every foreign intelligence service with officers in Beijing had focused its attention upon Deng Xiaoping's compound. So had many of the foreign journalists.

Nicholas Kristof of the *New York Times* learned that the cabal's anger was not so much directed against Gorbachev as some meddling outsider, but against Zhao. They reportedly warned Deng that the Party secretary was using the demonstrators "as pawns" to further his own ambition.

Melinda Liu's contacts conjured up a scene of the old men grouped around Deng, wan-faced from lack of sleep, demanding he should sack Zhao. Deng had sat impassively, smoking another of his high-tar Panda cigarettes, saying nothing.

Yao Yilin wondered whether Zhao should be asked to produce details of the speech he would deliver to Gorbachev and whether he should be permitted to go ahead with his plan to have it televised. The vice-premier growled, "We have heard enough of his words lately."

Deng said he saw no need for Zhao to clear his speech or for his remarks not to be televised. Everyone understood the unspoken portent of the decision. Zhao was being given sufficient rope to hang himself.


SAME DAY, LATER
*Tiananmen Square*

From a phone box on the square, Sue Tung had several times tried to telephone Captain Instructor Jyan at the PLA academy without success. Each time the operator said he was not available. Some instinct stopped Sue from visiting his home. Jyan's mother, she suspected, would ask difficult questions as to why she was here. And what would she say if Sue told her she had handed over an unheard-of sum for a Chinese, those $10,000 she had collected in Sacramento, to the student leaders? With her strong Party loyalty, Jyan's mother would regard such support as an act of rank subversion.

Sue still couldn't get over how casually the money had been accepted. When she had asked for a receipt, Daobao had scribbled one on a scrap of paper. She had asked how the money would be used and Yang Li had given her a half-smile, adding it would be spent on "whatever we need."

She had found the student leaders friendly but a little distant. She had a feeling that while they welcomed the constant foreign media attention, they were not that interested in having overseas Chinese share in what they were doing. Several Chinese from Hong Kong who had volunteered to join the hunger strikers had been brusquely told there was no place for them.

Sue could see two of the student leaders on the steps of the Great Hall of the People. They were arguing with several young men who did not look like students.

She hurried to see what was happening. She had been struck by the orderliness of the demonstrations. She had not heard or seen a single expression of violence. That made the arguments on the steps that much more surprising and alarming. She was close enough to hear the increasingly angry exchanges between the young men and Yang Li and Daobao.

"Stand back!" the men were shouting at the two students. "We're going to destroy this place!"

"No!" Daobao yelled. "This is a peaceful demonstration!"

"Who are you?" Yang Li demanded.

"Your supporters," yelled one of the men.

"You're not students," Daobao said. "We don't need your support."

"Stand back!" yelled the men, beginning to shove the two students aside.

Daobao shouted for help. Sue turned and repeated the cry. Passing students ran to form a line to stop the men.

When she had last walked past the building, Sue had seen several dozen policemen on duty. Now they had all disappeared. She sensed something sinister was going on.

On the steps Daobao was still shouting for help.

"We have agents provocateurs here! They are trying to destroy all we have achieved! Come and stop them!"

Suddenly hundreds of students were running to help. Leading them was Chai Ling. Beside her was a student carrying an electric bullhorn.

But now more rough-voiced men were pushing their way toward the steps. They too were shouting they were there to support the students and wanted to storm the building.

Confused and frightened by what was happening, onlookers began to mill around nervously.

Sue realized that if fighting broke out people could be trampled to death. Already the first scuffles had started between the students and the men driving them back up the steps. Some of the men had produced hammers and other weapons from under their jackets. Sue knew then this was a well-planned provocation to provide an excuse for the security forces to take over the square. Furious at what was happening, she began to shove her way to join Daobao and Yang Li on the steps.

Over the bullhorn came Chai Ling's voice.

"Citizens! These people are nothing to do with us! They have been sent by the government to cause trouble! Help us stop them! But do not harm them. Only take them from here!"

Hundreds of people began to escort the men from the square. In moments the last of the twenty or so troublemakers had been removed.

Chai Ling walked slowly back to rejoin the hunger strikers. As she passed, Sue heard her say to Daobao: "They will try again. but it means we are winning."

Dr. Jenny Guangzu watched Chai Ling take her place on the quilted coats and blankets that had been given by the public to form a gigantic bedroll. She felt "a growing love for all the hunger strikers. They were the very symbol of what was going on."

In the time she had spent on the square she had seen much that made her uneasy, especially the bickering between the student leaders Wuerkaixi and Wang Dan. The pair seemed able to agree on precious little. Wuerkaixi was clearly intent on becoming still more militant; Wang Dan was for a more cautious approach.

The young surgeon was struck by not only their markedly different physical appearances, but also their mental states. In his now-celebrated denims, Wuerkaixi was a hyperactive showman; Wang Dan's face was increasingly drawn, his clothes were stiff with dried perspiration. His eyes still burned bright, but to Jenny he looked like a man burning up his physical reserves.

A short while ago she had heard them arguing again at the foot of the Monument to the People's Heroes. Wuerkaixi had pointed to the crowds.

"Look! Now we must push even harder, because everyone's behind us," he told Wang Dan.

It seemed true. The thousands of banners already on display had been joined by those brought by workers from many of the state-run corporations: iron and steel foundries, auto manufacturers, breweries. Among them marched hotel bellboys and Mao-suited cadres from a ministry. Even the national volleyball team was there, marching between shaven-headed Buddhist monks and students from one of the country's few Christian seminaries. They had finally set up camp under the banner CHINESE CHRISTIANS FOR DEMOCRACY.

But still Wang Dan had urged caution. He said he would only be convinced that the country was indeed fully behind them if the People's Liberation Army sent even a token force of troops to march in the square.

Wuerkaixi had shrugged and walked away to rejoin the hunger strikers.

After only a few hours of lying among them, Wuerkaixi returned to his position on the monument to hold yet another of his "strategy meetings."

A short time later Jenny had seen him go to one of the cars parked behind the monument. Her father had later told her he had seen Wuerkaixi wolf down a bowl of noodles. The student had then returned to the monument to urge the hunger strikers again to continue their fast.

As they walked among the hunger strikers, her father now told her they were now reaching the critical stage.

"After four days we can expect to see the first serious signs of physical and mental collapse. It is important to keep noise around them to a minimum," Professor Guangzu explained.

Each time they stopped to check a striker's vital signs, he asked how long the student intended to continue. Each time he was given the same response: "Until our demands are met." Some of the students had swollen faces covered in perspiration, signs of the stress they were experiencing.

By now doctors from almost every hospital in the city were tending them. Professor Guangzu took several of his colleagues aside.

"Those we send to hospital must not be allowed to return," he said. "And no more must be allowed to start fasting. They have made their point."

Together with Jenny, Professor Guangzu walked over to the Monument to the People's Heroes and told Wuerkaixi of the medical decision.

"He was quite upset," Jenny was to remember. "He kept saying how important it was to continue the strike."

Her father then quietly told Wuerkaixi that if he felt so committed to striking to the death, he should set an example. For a moment they stared at each other. Then Wuerkaixi turned away. A short while later he broadcast an announcement that no more people would be allowed to go on hunger strike, and those sent to hospital would not be allowed to resume their protest.

Jeanne Moore, Melinda Liu, Dan Rather, and the hundreds of other foreign reporters in the square converged on the strikers.

"Some of the students seem to have lost their reason," Jeanne noted. "They are no longer lucid. When they try to stand up, they collapse. They lie on the ground side by side, like mummies. When the doctors try to persuade them to quit, they simply shake their heads and say they must continue."

Melinda noted that everything—the scorching sun, the noise, the polluted air—seemed to have an effect on the strikers. The weaker they became, the greater the anger of those watching them.

"People were saying, the government must stop this now by giving in to the demands. The more onlookers said this, the more determined were the strikers to continue. They were feeding off the anger their condition was generating. If one of the strikers was to die, God knows what would happen. The crowd could become sufficiently enraged to literally trample down the walls of Zhongnanhai. The hunger strike was the most potent weapon the students had. And some of them wanted to die."

Irritated at being confined to the CBS remote unit in a corner of the square, Dan Rather had insisted he should be allowed to do some reporting, though the network had several correspondents on hand to do just that. In the time he had been in the square, Rather had quickly established contacts with the students and, like any other journalist, wanted to exploit these professionally to the full. Now, standing in front of the prostrate hunger strikers, Rather delivered another live broadcast to the United States, describing the courage of young people prepared to die for their country.

A growing number were refusing water and had sealed their mouths with adhesive tape over which they wore smog-masks. Others had stuffed cloth in their mouths. Some had even tied their own hands to avoid any temptation to reach for a drink.

Melinda felt "a lump in my throat at the sight of such determination and courage."

Turning away, she glimpsed a solitary figure striding to the platform high on Tiananmen Gate. Though she could not see his face clearly, there was no mistaking that well-cut blue suit. She had seen Zhao Ziyang wear it before. The Party secretary continued to watch the scene through his binoculars. He struck Melinda as "an actor waiting in the wings ready to make his entrance."

Then, as she watched, he lowered his binoculars, turned, and left the platform.

SAME DAY, LATER
*The White House*

Dan Rather's report on the hunger strikers led the CBS evening news on the monitor in the Oval Office. President Bush paused in a meeting about Panama to watch the scene from Tiananmen Square. Then, without comment, he continued discussing how best to remove General Noriega from office.

SAME DAY, LATER
*Foreign Legation Quarter*

In British Ambassador Sir Alan Donald's view, the situation was "chaos. The government is increasingly having to rearrange its plans for the Gorbachev visit to avoid interruption by the students. The loss of face is considerable. Almost certainly there will have to be a reckoning after the Russians have left. But how far that will go is anyone's guess right now."

Ambassador Donald was not a diplomat easily surprised by a turn of events. But the televised broadcast he had watched in his office had left him "just about speechless." Zhao Ziyang had used his meeting with Gorbachev as an opportunity, in the words of Nicholas Kristof of the *New York Times,* "to lunge for power." While Donald would never have stated it so colorfully, he admitted to his staff gathered in his office that Zhao's speech was "something of a shaker."

Brian Davidson would remember the ambassador saying that Zhao was clearly blaming Deng for the student unrest. Donald's interpretation was based on his deep understanding of the subtleties of what he sometimes called "leadership-speak." In that language, Deng was often "the helmsman," the man at the tail end of China's "ship of state."

Zhao's speech had contained a number of flattering references to Deng as "the helmsman" and the reminder that "on important questions we still need him as the helmsman." Davidson would recall his ambassador explanation: In leadership-speak, Zhao was saying that while he would be quite prepared to meet the student's demands, Deng, as "the helmsman," was against further reform, let along democracy. The Party secretary had made a calculated attack on Deng's position and had added insult by choosing to do so in the presence of Gorbachev.

In Donald's view the "storm cones were being hoisted over Zhongnanhai."

Zhao's speech had produced similar responses from other diplomats. France's ambassador, Charles Malo, felt it was only a matter of time before Zhao was sacked, as did Canada's ambassador, Earl Drake. Lindsay Watt, New Zealand's ambassador, saw the speech as "a real cliff-hanger. Everyone was hungering to see what the response would be."

Diplomatic legmen like Brian Davidson and Brendan Ward were soon reporting the reaction of the students to Zhao's speech. New posters were hurriedly produced attacking "the helmsman who has lost the way."

SAME DAY, LATER
*Deng Xiaoping's compound*

At nine o'clock in the evening, a convoy of limousines entered the compound bringing Deng's cabal to meet with him again. *Newsweek's* Melinda Liu's sources would describe how Deng sat "hunched and hooded-eyed in his armchair, chain-smoking, ignoring everyone." The others sat tense and watchful.

At nine-thirty, Zhao's car arrived. The Party secretary wore another of his distinctive suits, a midnight blue two-piece.

As they had on everyone else, weeks of what Deng was repeatedly calling "chaos under Heaven" had left their marks on Zhao. His usual self-assurance had gone. In its place was a strained, haunted look. His eyes were red-rimmed behind his tinted glasses. He looked less like a man perfectly cast as a wise adviser, more like someone who knew he had fallen forever from Deng's favor. Now, at best all he could look forward to was spending his remaining years indulging his hobby of watching old war movies on his video player and reading Bismarck at bedtime.

He was shown into Deng's presence. As soon as the formal greetings were over, Deng launched a vituperative attack on Zhao for making such a speech before Gorbachev.

Deng's rage made the Party secretary blanch. It was the moment of supreme confrontation. Twice Zhao attempted to halt the tirade; he was ordered to remain silent. The dressing down continued for over an hour. Then Li Peng took over. He coldly reviewed the effect so far of "hooliganism" on a scale the nation had not seen since the Cultural Revolution.

Next Qiao Shi presented a detailed explanation of the threat to national security the students were increasingly presenting. He added there were "clear indications" of outside influences at work." The old bogeymen, "Imperialist spies," were on the rampage.

When the intelligence chief had finished, Deng barked a question to Zhao. What did he have to say?

The Party secretary argued his well-known position: Without further reforms there could be no real conciliation with the students. While Deng's economic policies had invigorated China as never before, these same policies had also produced an unprecedented inflation of 30 percent. The only way to reduce it was by still more reforms.

Zhao was in full flow, arguing that the students were not hell-bent on destroying China or the Party but only giving voice to all those caught in the vise-like squeeze between prosperity and inflation, when Deng interrupted.

He rasped he would not listen any longer to such talk. There would be a vote, here and now, on one issue. Had the time had come to end the demonstrations? In the affirmative show of hands, Zhao's was the only abstention.

For almost fifty years Deng and Zhao had been close friends and political allies. They had come through purgings and banishment. They had helped guide China through wars. They had together once set the country on a brave new course. People spoke of them in one breath, adding that Deng, deep in his heart, wanted Zhao to succeed him. Now the unthinkable had happened. The rift between them was irreversible from that moment Zhao had refused to raise his hand in silent obedience to his master's wishes.

The Party secretary stood up and faced Deng.

"I am sorry to see that my way of thinking is not in accord with your way of thinking," he told Deng.

For a moment longer the two men stared at each other. Then, according to one of the officials present, Deng turned away and looked at Li Peng. The prime minister could not quite hide the satisfaction crossing his face.

Zhao Ziyang walked from the room. Deng Xiaoping had begun to tell the others he had decided to introduce martial law and call in the army to reestablish order.


FRIDAY, MAY 19, 1989
*China Daily compound*

By the thirty-fifth day of the demonstration, Jeanne Moore's chronicle of events filled several notebooks. She carried them everywhere with her, a reminder of their importance. They contained a balanced view of not only what others were reporting, often with increasing hyperbole, but also insights that came from her unique position as one of the few non-Chinese journalists working in the state-run media.

Time and again this past week high-level Party contacts she was sure would not have spoken to Chinese journalists had briefed her on what was happening behind the scenes. She believed it was "because they felt more comfortable and able to trust a foreigner."

Much of what they had told her, she knew, was too sensitive to be published in *China Daily* or any other Party organ, despite the fact that both her own newspaper and the *People's Daily* had finally begun to report the student protests.

Jeanne herself had helped write several sympathetic editorials about the demands that had caused widespread comment and brought praise from the students. She had smilingly accepted their accolades as she continued to observe how the hunger strikers were fainting or suffering hallucinatory fits after a week of not eating. Over six-hundred had been taken away in the past twenty-four hours. In the most recent story she had described how those who remained on the square now "lie completely still, each with a rose on his neck. They look like the living dead, a pose which subdues the most cynical of foreign journalists. There is a dignity here that cannot be equated with anything elsewhere in living memory. That dignity is summed up by a huge tableau erected over the scene. It shows two naked, writhing figures. Between them are the words 'Save the people.'"

That kind of reporting had finally found its way into *China Daily* and the American newspaper she also wrote for. So had her careful listing of still more support from all sections of Chinese society, engineers, technicians, and schoolchildren by the thousands. The numbers in the square now never dropped below a million, sometimes it seemed close to two. Though it hardly seemed possible, the thousands of posters had become more provocative, mocking everything the Party and leadership stood for.

The previous day she had seen the unthinkable. A platoon of off-duty, crew-cut PLA soldiers had marched along Changan Avenue into Tiananmen Square behind a banner bearing the legend THE ARMY LOVES THE PEOPLE.

They had been welcomed by thunderous cheers. Even Wang Dan had felt compelled to seize a microphone and ask joyfully, "with the army on our side, how can we fail?"

Wuerkaixi, his pretense at being a hunger striker over, had told her that "victory is close. Look, there isn't a policeman in sight! We are controlling the crowds, the traffic, everything. We *are* the government because the other government is invisible!"

In one sense that was true. In the five weeks since they had first marched to the square, the students had remained a disciplined force.

The key was a deeply ingrained obedience to all orders of their leaders.

"They eat to order, they rest to order, they cheer and wave banners to order," Cassy noted. "It is the only way that a million people can be marshaled and controlled, by obeying orders."

Fresh food arrived twice a day and was paid for out of the huge hoard of Chinese and foreign currency kept under constant guard on the Monument to the People's Heroes. Refuse was stacked in great piles for city workers to remove. There were over thirty first-aid posts to deal with minor injuries.

The only problem was the lack of toilet facilities. No matter how many trenches were dug, they quickly filled. The perimeter around the square had become a stinking cesspool, as Dan Rather discovered. He had just completed another report when one of the CBS technicians asked to go to the toilet. "I took him to that latrine," Rather would recall. You have to imagine the scene. It was a huge tent, and inside the Chinese had dug slit trenches as far as the eye could see. Well, when he got inside, the combination of the tremendous smell and the shock of the scene, people squatting along trenches, and he just derricked, absolutely derricked."

Yet despite the terrible stench that drifted like a pall over the square, the mood was upbeat. People came and went, bringing news from other parts of the city and carrying news from the square. This bush telegraph proved surprisingly effective in drawing still more people to Tiananmen.

Jeanne Moore confided to her notebook that the mood was so contagious she would almost have believed victory was indeed possible. Some of her colleagues were reporting rumors that Deng Xiaoping had resigned, that Li Peng had been deposed, that Zhao Ziyang was about to form a new government.

It was that last rumor, swept across Tiananmen Square with Thursday's drizzle, that made Jeanne realize "how far reality was being sacrificed on the altar of blind hope." For she knew what had happened to the Party secretary after he walked out of Deng Xiaoping's office.

As the bemused Gorbachevs were packing their bags in the State Guest House after what the Soviet leader had told one of his hosts (who had passed on the words to Jeanne) was "the most extraordinary three days of my life," Zhao had been driven slowly around Tiananmen Square in his limousine, peering through the car's dark-tinted windows. Another of Jeanne's contact had told her "Zhao had wanted to see how big the crowd was, how many he could count on."

Yet the Party secretary's career was effectively over. The morning after he walked out of Deng's office, Zhao announced he was going on "sick leave" and would no longer participate in "any Party business." It had been a move to win over public support, which had not been forthcoming.

Now this Friday morning he was about to make a last desperate bid to elicit support from the people.

Shortly after 5:00 A.M., accompanied by a few trusted aides, Zhao was driven out of Zhongnanhai and brought to the square.

Jeanne Moore was astonished by Zhao's appearance when he stepped out of the car. Whenever she had seen him before, he had epitomized sartorial elegance. Now he was dressed in a baggy suit, crushed shirt, and badly knotted tie. His face was gaunt, his eyes puffed and red-rimmed. He walked "like a man who is beaten." His voice echoed the sense of defeat in his appearance.

Daobao handed him a red bullhorn and explained how to work it. After a couple of tries, Zhao managed to get the hang of using the device.

"I have come here to say a few words to you students," he began. Jeanne noted Zhao was close to tears, weak-voiced.

"We have come too late. I am sorry. No matter how you have criticized us, I think you have the right to do so. I am now here to ask for your forgiveness."

Zhao paused and stared at one of the buses the students had commandeered for a makeshift field hospital for some of the hunger strikers. With a visible effort he resumed.

"I just want to say that your bodies are now very weak. Your hunger strike is now in the seventh day. You cannot go on like this. We were once young too, and we all had such a burst of energy. We also staged demonstrations and I remember the situation then. We also did not think of the consequences."

Tears welling in his eyes, the broken Party secretary climbed into the bus and moved among the semiconscious hunger strikers, peering at them wonderingly.

Then in complete silence he left the square. Jeanne thought "any hope the students had that this was the man about to form a new government must have gone."

She watched Zhao's car head back to Zhongnanhai. It would be the last time he would be seen in public.

Walking through the square, Jeanne sensed a sudden feeling of unease. If Zhao was no longer there to support them, the students had no one.

Wang Dan was among those who suggested they should consider ordering a mass evacuation of the square. They had done more than anyone could have thought possible. To leave now would not be see as a defeat. Wuerkaixi rounded on his fellow leaders. That would destroy everything they had planned. He, for one, would stay to the very end. Wuerkaixi again carried the day.

But only hours later, the quixotic Wuerkaixi once more changed his mind, after a Party broadcast early in the afternoon spoke of the leadership "having to consider adopting strong measures such as military control."

Wuerkaixi promptly called another "strategy meeting" in the "command bus" he now used as a headquarters. Parked behind the Monument to the People's Heroes, it enabled student leaders to eat their meals out of sight of the hunger strikers.

Thirty-six days of running the protest movement had led to polarization within the student leadership.

Wuerkaixi remained certainly the most colorful figure, even if that all-knowing smile had become a little fixed from a thousand television interviews. But his physical stamina was awesome. He radiated energy. His natural ally remained Chai Ling. In her hip-hugging jeans and canvas shoes, she flitted around the square, repeatedly telling people, "Here we stay and are ready to die so that democracy will live." No one could doubt she meant it. Daobao, Yang Li, and Liu Gang remained key members of Wuerkaixi's entourage. All three bore signs of strain. Liu Gang had taken to biting his lip nervously; Yang Li had become almost morose. Daobao hid his own exhaustion by working relentlessly to keep up student morale.

Wang Dan continued to be the face of student moderation. He had gathered to him a small coterie of like-minded student leaders. While they did not openly challenge Wuerkaixi, knowing that would fatally wound the movement, they quietly urged that perhaps, after all, the time had come to leave Tiananmen.

Now Wuerkaixi agreed that the students should withdraw, because he had "just learned there is bloody suppression coming." He did not say who had told him. It would remain one of his many secrets.

Debate broke out among the group. Some wanted the hunger strike to end but for everyone to remain in the square. Others wanted the strike to continue and for a nationwide appeal to be made to support it. Daobao envisaged "several million more people" coming to Beijing to do so. That idea was knocked down by Wang Dan. He thought the most sensible thing would be to keep a "reasonable number" of protesters in the square, all from Beijing, and send everyone else back to work. Yang Li was among those who disagreed, saying, "We have come too far to turn back."

Then, as if in response to Daobao's suggestion, thousands of workers began to arrive from all over the city. They came by bus and truck, drawn like everyone else simply by a wish to show solidarity with the students. They announced they had formed the country's first Party-free trade union, the Autonomous Union. Its first act would be to organize a nationwide strike of all workers unless the students' demands were met unconditionally by midnight this coming Saturday.

Once again Wuerkaixi changed his mind. Such a strike, he enthused, was bound to tip the balance. Everyone should stay on Tiananmen.

That evening Mikhail and Raisa Gorbachev left Beijing the way they had come, by the back door, driven to the airport at high speed through the back streets. Their state visit had been a fiasco, reduced to a few column inches in the official print media and given only perfunctory treatment on TV and radio. It had achieved almost nothing.

*Tiananmen Square*

The more than one million people crowded into Tiananmen Square paused as the loudspeakers once again came alive shortly after midnight. Moments later the high-pitched voice of Prime Minister Li Peng echoed in the dank night air.

"This state of anarchy can no longer be tolerated. Law and discipline are being undermined. A handful of people are using the hunger strikers as hostages to coerce and force the Party and the government to yield to their political demands. They have not an iota of humanity."

Students crowded around the CBS monitors receiving pictures of the prime minister addressing the Politburo Standing Committee and rows of military officers. At the back of their ranks among other junior officers sat Captain Instructor Jyan.

The broadcast came from the PLA's General Logistics Department, a walled compound in the western suburbs. Jyan believed the venue had been deliberately selected by the prime minister. Li Peng wanted to show that the army totally supported the action he was now about to outline.

"The intention was plain, scare the hell out of everyone who was listening or watching," Melinda Liu recalled.

Certainly the television images appeared as intimidating as Li Peng's words. He was dressed in a funeral black Mao suit. Each time he squeaked out a sentence he would pause and raise his fist in the air, forefinger slightly extended as if he were about to pull a trigger. It was crude but compelling theater.

Its effect on the crowd was immediate. All day their tension had built, fueled by rumor: The PLA would parachute into the square. Thousands of troops had already arrived in the Great Hall of the People, brought there by the underground railway from Zhongnanhai. Thousands more were waiting in the nuclear bunkers beneath the city.

Some of the speculation was true. Units were positioned in the bunkers and had been brought underground to the Great Hall of the People. While no one had actually seen the troops, the protesters had convinced each other they must be there. Now the prime minister was suddenly giving substance to the rumors. People looked scared. Some began to leave the square even as Li Peng was speaking.

"The life and future of the People's Republic of China, built by many revolutionary martyrs with their blood, faces a serious threat."

Cassy, standing by the CBS unit, felt "it was like listening to someone saying the end of the world was coming. It was little comfort to see how calmly the TV crew received the news. They could just pack up and move on to the next story. But for Daobao and the others, it was different. I understood what they meant when they said this is their struggle, *theirs* and no one else's."

Cassy had made several appeals for Daobao to leave and go to his family in the country. She had even offered to go with him. Daobao had brushed aside the idea, quietly telling her his place was here. She had both loved him and admired his courage more than ever. Listening to Li Peng, she understood her Daobao was a true revolutionary martyr.

The prime minister was saying something that brought another great murmur of apprehension from the crowd.

"...the Communist Party of China, as the ruling party, and the government responsible to the people, are now forced to take resolute and decisive measures to put an end to turmoil."

Barr Seitz felt the ABC camera teams "stiffen in anticipation" when the words were translated.

"Some real action at last," said one.

For the past few days there had been little to film. One of the ABC producers had told Barr that "when you've shot one hunger striker about to pop off, that's pretty well it."

The attitude was a reflection of one held by executives at the headquarters of both ABC and NBC in New York. ABC Senior Vice-President Rick Wald had vetoed the idea of sending Peter Jennings to anchor the evening news out of Beijing, because Dan Rather was dominating the coverage. A similar attitude prevailed at NBC. Both networks would make do with correspondents.

On a monitor Barr watched the panning shot and called out the identities of those on the platform with Li Peng: Vice-Premiers Yao Yilin and Qiao Shi; Hu Qili, in charge of propaganda; Vice-President Wang Zhen. Beside him sat the state president himself, Yang Shungkun.

The ABC correspondent Barr was working with wrote down the names.

"Hard to believe old men like these have any real power," said the reporter.

"They don't," replied Barr. "They're just mouthpieces for Deng. That's why he doesn't have to show up. He's already written the script. They just have to follow it."

"Sounds like a good producer," the reporter said, grinning.

The previous afternoon, in a belated attempt to defuse the situation, Li Peng had finally received Wuerkaixi and Wang Dan in one of the salons of The Great Hall. The prime minister had been coldly condescending, but the students were in no mood to be patronized. Wuerkaixi had wagged his finger at Li Peng and repeatedly interrupted. Li Peng had fought down his anger, even giving a sickly smile when Wang Dan compared the Party with the regime in South Africa. The "dialogue" the students had sought had ended in ill-tempered belligerence on their part and total humiliation for Li Peng. Now the prime minister visibly enjoyed his role as the man chosen to herald Deng's decision.

Li Peng's place on screen was taken by the state president. Yang Shangkun's voice, trembling with anger, boomed around the square.

"To restore normal order and to stabilize the situation, there is no choice but to move a contingent of the People's Liberation Army to the vicinity of the city."

A great roar of protest swept the square.

Sue Tung was standing near the Great Hall. Until then she had been "a little frightened. But now I knew what was going to happen. I felt very calm. I was certain the troops would harm no one." Over the loudspeakers the state president continued.

"If this state of affairs is allowed to continue, then our capital will not be a capital."

Jenny Guangzu and her father had momentarily slipped away from tending the hunger strikers to watch a CNN monitor. On the screen the uniformed generals were clapping loudly and nodding to each other. Jenny's son slept peacefully in her arms.

"Jenny," began Professor Guangzu. "What about Peter? Perhaps you should leave?"

Jenny shook her head. "My place is here. They won't harm children. As long as we do nothing foolish the soldiers won't harm anyone."

A couple of hours earlier she had seen how tense matters had become. She had been passing the Monument to the People's Heroes, bringing fresh water to the hunger strikers, when she had been astonished to see Chai Ling and her husband fighting over a microphone. They both wanted to address the crowd; both were "almost crazed with exhaustion." Other student leaders had separated the pair, and Chai Ling had been led away, weeping bitterly. Jenny had told her father; he had shaken his head.

"The hunger strike is turning children into monsters," Professor Guangzu said. "The sooner they stop the better."

Watching the monitor, Jenny hoped that the soldiers would somehow be able to persuade the strikers to give up their protest. On the screen the state president continued to speak.

"What's happening is because we have no other choice. But I would like to say that the arrival of the troops is definitely not aimed at dealing with the students."

Sue Tung turned to the person beside her. "What does he mean?"

In one form or another the question was being asked by countless others in Tiananmen.

Irish diplomat Brendan Ward, who had been in the square for most of the day, realized that the introduction of martial law had moved "matters into an unknown but frightening phase."

A few hours earlier one student had described feelings with which the young envoy could readily identify. The student had spoken movingly about his deep love for his country, which he repeatedly called "my mother." The youth had developed the analogy, saying a mother was entitled to be strict with her children. "But our mother now just keeps misunderstanding us and then beats us when we try and explain."

Leaving the square to draft another telegram to his superiors, Ward had an overwhelming feeling that when he next returned it could be to a very different scene.

All around him, people began to sing the "Internationale" once more.

Jeanne Moore noticed "people are jeering at what they have just heard." Then from a million and more voices came the chant. It passed from group to group, from mouth to mouth. The same words, endlessly repeated: "Down with Li Peng! Down with military rule! Long live the people! Long live democracy!"

Then over the students' loudspeaker system came the voice of Wuerkaixi.

"Students of Mother China. People of our beloved homeland. I ask you now to join us all in a hunger strike! I ask all students to form a human chain around the square so that the army shall not enter!"

On the pediment of the Monument to the People's Heroes, Daobao and Yang Li were raising a new banner Meili had just written. It read: "We came on our feet! We will leave on our backs!"

Over the loudspeaker Wuerkaixi was urging everyone to be ready to die for Mother China, "for truly she must be weeping for us."

Writing down his words, *Newsweek's* Melinda Liu felt close to weeping herself.

# 19

# *Martial Law*

SATURDAY, MAY 20, 1989
*National Photographic Interpretation Center*

Throughout the night China watchers fed instructions to their computers. In return they received satellite photographs of the military movements under way throughout China.

Since they had photographed the first student march into Tiananmen Square to mark the death of Hu Yaobang, the satellites had until now reported no military activity of any consequence, apart from the return of a 27th Army troop train from Tibet. The close-up photos of some of the shoulder tabs on the disembarking soldiers confirmed they were the same units that had shipped out of Beijing the previous November. But instead of returning to their garrison in the western suburbs of Beijing, the troops had been positioned some twenty miles beyond the city limits.

After several hours, the photo technicians had produced a set of photographs indicating other troop movements across a wide area of China, together with deployment of naval forces in the Yellow Sea.

The information was transmitted to the CIA's Office of Imagery Analysis. From there it was distributed to the Pentagon, the State Department, and the White House.

President Bush was in Boston, where he and President François Mitterand of France were to receive honorary degrees at Boston University commencement ceremonies the following day.

A set of satellite photographs and Webster's latest report on developments in China were hand-carried to Bush at his summer residence in Kennebunkport. With the President was Brent Scowcroft. After studying the photos, Bush and his national security adviser discussed the situation in China. Both realized China was bound to come up at the news conference following the conferring of the President's honorary degree.

Hunched in a chair opposite Bush, Scowcroft began to advise the President on what he should say.

SAME DAY, SAME TIME
*PLA General Logistics Department compound*
*Beijing*

In the situation room adjoining the one from which the prime minister and state president had broadcast a couple of hours before, Captain Instructor Jyan watched and listened with growing astonishment to the reports that had started to arrive. Three hours into the military operation he had helped to plan, the largest internal offensive the People's Liberation Army had ever conducted was grinding to a halt. It was an ominous start to the thirty-sixth day of the demonstrations.

No longer were they confined to Beijing. In the south of the country, in Guandong Province, students at three universities were on hunger strike. In Canton, life had come to a virtual standstill. In the center of the country, in Hubai, students had occupied a bridge over the Yangtze River. At Hunnan, birthplace of Hu Yaobang, twenty thousand students had taken over the railway station. In Shaanxi, another ten thousand students in the provincial capital of Xi'an, six hundred miles to the west of Beijing, had burned army vehicles and facilities. In Shanghai, Nanjing, and a score of other cities and towns, the unrest was growing.

At one minute to midnight units from eleven PLA armies had started to move to the centers of disturbance. A group attack division of the air force had been positioned at Shaanxi. The navy had sent four of its Luda Class destroyers on patrol in the Yellow Sea to intercept anyone from Hong Kong or Taiwan coming to help the students. The sea blockade was also intended to step any students fleeing by boat.

The wall map in the situation room showed the perimeter that had been established around Beijing. Twenty miles beyond the city limits were stationed units of the 27th Army, which had been withdrawn from Tibet. Ten miles behind this force units of the 38th Army took up positions. Their function was to stop any more people coming into the capital from the provinces; Already an estimated half million had reached Beijing. Roadblocks had been set up and all trains were being checked. All told, seventy thousand soldiers were involved, and over half a million more troops were on standby throughout the country.

The wall map showed that troops had gone to full alert along China's borders with Vietnam and Laos in the south, Burma in the east, and all the way to Mongolia in the north. Any help from those directions would be blocked. Even the long border with the Soviet Union had been sealed. China, as it had so often done in the past, was closing in on itself, ready to devour those who were trying to destroy the country from within. The technique went all the way back to the first emperor of the Qin dynasty. Then, the emperor's foes had been slaughtered by flint-head weapons. Now their successors would be killed by the cutting edge of modern technology. The thrust of that assault would be on Beijing. It was an old Chinese maxim that once the capital was secure, the provinces would fall into line.

Jyan had watched as the first column of one hundred trucks had sped along the main western highway leading to Beijing. A similar number swung north, heading for the compuses near the Summer Palace. A squadron of tanks was deployed to enter the city through the eastern suburbs. With them was a force of two thousand soldiers.

The columns had advanced quickly and unopposed until they were a mile from the city limits. There they had waited for further orders, as instructed.

During the pause, intelligence chief Qiao Shi had received the latest news from Tiananmen Square. His agents reported the students were setting up roadblocks with commandeered vehicles on Changan Avenue and broadcasting constant appeals for the citizens to come and help them.

Jyan could now see the effect of those appeals. For the past two hours scores of thousands of people had taken to the streets to block the military advance into the capital. Every truck, tank, and halftrack had come to a halt, stopped by swarms of people clambering over the vehicles or forming human chains.

Over their field telephones unit commanders had reported they could neither advance nor retreat without causing serious loss of life. But the troops had no orders to open fire.

In the situation room, senior PLA commanders had gone into a closed session with, among others, State President Yang and Prime Minister Li Peng. While they deliberated their next step, from outside the compound came the sound of still more people rushing to join the throng. Their continuous chant carried clearly into the situation room. "The People's Army should love the people!"

Squatting on top of his T-69 tank, Commander Lee Gang, whose brother, Liu, was one of the student leaders, ordered a crewman to traverse the main gun. Instinctively the crowd drew back against the walls of the buildings on either side of the street.

Then from a doorway a figure in a headband pointed a bullhorn at the truck. It was Daobao.

An hour earlier, when the first report had reached Tiananmen Square that the soldiers were on the move, Wuerkaixi had sent "flying squads" of students into the suburbs to alert people. Among those who had gone was Daobao. He had borrowed a motorcycle and, with Cassy riding pillion, driven down Changan Avenue to the suburb of Muxudi. Both wore headbands bearing the word DEMOCRACY. They had stopped at street corners, and Daobao had used the bullhorn to warn those nearby. In minutes people were running into the streets and had started to form barricades; buses were driven broadside across the highway, then their engines were immobilized. The younger men had followed Daobao's motorcade to this crossroads, where they were confronting Liu's tank and a column of trucks.

"Why do you threaten us? The army is the army of the people. How can you attack your own family?" Daobao yelled.

The tank's gun lined up on the students.

"You will not shoot!" Daobao taunted. "But even if you do, for every person you kill, ten more will rise up!"

"No!" came another amplified voice. "Not ten, twenty!"

Once more the crowd, many in their pajamas, began to edge toward the tank. Further along the street, buses, trucks, and pedicabs were being used to form another barrier. Behind that obstacle, Liu Lee could see yet another being created.

He turned to look behind him. The trucks had all but disappeared under the sheer number of people on their hoods, on roofs, clinging to the sides, yelling for the soldiers to put down their AK-47 rifles and join "the people's revolution."

Seated in the back of the lead truck, Bing Yang felt the same bewilderment as the other soldiers. They had been told by their company commander, Tan Yaobang, that they could expect a warm welcome from the citizens, who had grown tired of the protest.

Yet they had to force their way yard by yard through the crowds even to reach the outer edges of the city. Now they were completely bogged down.

At the rear of every truck stood a student lecturing the soldiers inside on the democracy movement.

"Why are you here?" a student yelled into Bing's truck.

"You sound just like my brother," the exasperated soldier said.
"Who is your brother?"

Bing told him. The student spread the word. More students appeared, trying to coax Bing to give up his weapon and join them. He clutched his rifle more tightly. The students began to taunt him. Then from the back of the convoy came Tan Yaobang's order to withdraw. The trucks began to reverse through the cheering crowd.

Cassy joined those around her in singing the "Internationale." Someone grabbed Daobao's bullhorn and addressed the routed column.

"Tell your comrades the truth! That the people of Beijing, no, the people of China, are all behind the students. We all want to reform the country. We want to see an end to the handful of criminals who dare to call themselves our government. Long live democracy!"

In other suburbs, the rest of the soldiers were also pulling back on orders from their commanders. They had bluntly told Li Peng that they would only fire on the youngsters if the order came from Deng Xiaoping himself. In the compound, Captain Instructor Jyan could hear the crowd's chanting had coalesced into one repeated cry: "Victory to the people!"

SAME DAY, LATER
*Tiananmen Square*

As diplomats Brendan Ward and Brian Davidson walked into the square, the loudspeakers began to boom.

It was 10:30 A.M. on the thirty-sixth day of protest, an hour after the state radio announcement: In eight districts of the city, including Tiananmen, all processions and strikes were forbidden; the army would deal with infringements "forcefully."

As the diplomats began another long day of gathering information, the first decree of martial law was announced over the public address system. All journalists were forbidden from that moment to film or report what was happening. Foreigners were ordered not to "remain involved" in any activities by Chinese citizens that broke martial law, such as writing or delivering unacceptable speeches, or distributing leaflets or unauthorized banners or placards. The broadcast ended with the demand that everyone leave the square.

"They've really got the wind up in Zhongnanhai," Davidson told Ward. "But they're still bluffing, otherwise they'd just cut the power for all the TV feeds. They don't want to do that because it'll be another admission they've lost control. So really this is just an appeal for everyone to be good chaps and pack up and go home, because the action's over, while everyone knows it's just about to start."

As usual their instructions were to do nothing to embarrass their governments, but to get as close to what was happening as possible. Ward would remember saying to Davidson that if the military did manage to reach the square, they were both protected by diplomatic immunity. Davidson shrugged and asked how many soldiers would recognize a diplomatic passport.

Making their way toward the hunger strikers—always their first point of call of the day, to see how many had given up overnight—they saw that no one had paid any attention to the edict. Foreign journalists remained in force. So did their fellow envoys. Ward and Davidson exchanged greetings with both groups.

"The whole square had become rather like a raffish club," Ward would recall. "The place stank like a fish market. There was no real sanitation, and refuse was piled everywhere. But everybody kept saying it was 'only for one more day, then it will be over.' The area around the Monument to the People's Heroes looked like a M.A.S.H. clearing station, bodies everywhere, doctors and nurses coming and going. So many were collapsing after seven days of starvation that a special lane had been opened for the ambulances."

Overnight another seventy students had been taken to the hospital. But over a thousand still remained on hunger strike after eight days. Gray-faced and soaked in perspiration, often too weak to speak, they lay prostrate in the stifling heat. Summer had come early, and the temperature was already up in the eighties.

Music continued to blare. Even at this hour, after another sleepless night, people were moving in time to the sound of the Beatles and the Rolling Stones.

Yet Ward sensed a tension behind the camaraderie that had not been there the night before. Students were writing wills, photographing one another, and autographing each other's shirts. Some of them had begun to dip scarves and handkerchiefs in buckets of water before draping the cloth over their nose and mouth in case they were tear-gassed. They looked like cowboys.

The two diplomats separated after their check on the hunger strikers, Davidson heading toward the Great Hall of the People, Ward to the Monument to the People's Heroes. They would meet later in the day and pool information. This "pairing" arrangement was being operated by many other diplomats in the square.

Their presence had led to Deng Xiaoping's once more hesitating over using all-out force to regain control. Governments normally friendly to the regime had now begun to express grave concern to

China's ambassadors over the reports coming from their own envoys in Tiananmen.

The Australian government had balanced its substantial trade links with China against a sense of growing moral outrage after reading the telegram from Ambassador David Sadlier, who had maintained a constant presence in the square. So had the Dutch, whose dozen accredited diplomats had all taken turns visiting the square and reporting back to Ambassador Arne Dellira. His telegrams not only reflected the growing health hazard of a million people insisting on remaining in "a disease trap," but also gave an insight into the "anger and confusion still happening within the leadership. A sign of this was our information that the intention had originally been to declare Martial Law on Sunday (May 21st). Li Peng had persuaded Deng Xiaoping to bring the date forward by a full day in the hope of regaining the initiative."

Through their assiduous tapping of their government sources, whom they often arranged to meet in the square, other diplomats had also pieced together glimpses of the power struggle going on in Zhongnanhai.

Debnath Shaw, second secretary at the Indian embassy, had learned that "Zhao may be sick, but his supporters are still in good health. It was they who had first persuaded Li Peng that the troops sent into the city must not be given orders to shoot, and then when they were stymied by the crowds, Zhao's men had managed to get the order to withdraw the soldiers."

Iran's minister-counselor, Huzzan Farazandeh, who had played an important role in getting China to supply his country with Silkworm missiles to defend itself against Iraq, had learned from his contacts that Deng Xiaoping had refused Li Peng's request to tear-gas the entire square from the air.

The Italian embassy's military and defense attaché, Colonel Giulio Fraticelli, a hard-driving figure who walked like the fine horseman he was, had heard the same story and dismissed it as "impossible to be really effective. Any gas attack from the air could be carried by the wind into Zhongnanhai."

The most revealing insight of all into the mood in the leadership compound had come from a visit Poland's Marian Woznink had made to Li Peng late the previous evening. Ostensibly it had been a routine call to discuss expanding trade links between their two countries.

Suddenly, Woznink had reported to Warsaw, "the Prime Minister stood up and began to walk around his office. He grabbed me by the arm and took me over to a window. Outside there were more than the usual security men. Even from here we could hear the voices from

Tiananmen. The prime minister then asked me how we had come to the compound. I told him that we had come by a back route. Our Chinese driver had driven us here the same way the Gorbachevs had been brought. The prime minister seized upon this. 'Look what happened to Comrade Gorbachev! His visit was ruined by turmoil. Important people like him and diplomats like us should not have to drive through the back streets because of this turmoil.' The prime minister used the word several times. Then he said his government would have to 'take all necessary steps to halt this turmoil.'"

Poland's ambassador was not the only diplomat who had been exposed to such a diatribe. A few hours before, Richard Woolcott, an Australian government official who had flown to Beijing on a trade mission, had experienced a similarly surprising encounter with Li Peng.

The splendidly named Alfonso Gualia de Paadin y de Ahumada, defense attaché at the Spanish embassy, had sent a number of telegrams to Madrid stating that the students were not engaged in a violent takeover. The Spanish Foreign Ministry had conveyed its hope that the students would be allowed to continue to protest peacefully. Sweden's ambassador, Bjorn Skula, had sent several of his attachés to the square. Their reports had convinced Skula that the demonstration was "a genuine expression of widespread discontent." His government had conveyed that judgment to the Chinese ambassador in Stockholm.

Countries such as Hungary, Pakistan, and Somalia which had all experienced inner turmoil, had expressed the hope that any action against the students would be, in the words of Akran Zak, the Pakistani ambassador, "kept to the very minimum."

The only support for completely crushing the students was expressed by Angelo Miculescu, the Romanian ambassador. In a visit to Zhongnanhai a few days earlier he had reportedly told Li Peng that the Romanian government would do everything possible to help China "through this unhappy time," and that "whatever action is necessary must be taken."

Throughout the night, carefully couched diplomatic concern had continued to arrive in Zhongnanhai from other governments.

The exception was the United States. Washington had yet to express any real support for the students or any deep concern about martial law.

Barr Seitz, on a visit to the U.S. embassy compound to pick up press releases for ABC, had found "everyone was very low-key when it came to expressing attitudes."

One diplomat, who asked not to be named, later said that "no one wanted to say or do anything at this stage which could affect long-term situations. At the best of times the Chinese are very touchy about outside pressure. For the United States to go barging in would have been counterproductive. We just sat tight waiting to see how things would develop. Anyway, we weren't going to come out and urge the students on. A lot of us remembered what our own students had done over Vietnam. To us those students on Tiananmen were from the same cut, radicals trying to overthrow an established government that may well be repressive, but was still the government."

But from the United States had come an unexpected voice supporting the students: Wan Li, the chairman of China's National People's Congress, the country's rubber-stamp parliament.

The gremlin-like Wan was one of those figures all authoritarian regimes need, a smiling face to do the bidding of his masters in the outside world. In his years of service to Deng, the wily, irascible Wan had popped up in Europe, the UN, Tokyo, and now, all of the United States. Like an old-fashioned door-to-door salesman, he swore by what he was selling. "Invest in China," he would tell businessmen, "and your profits will multiply."

On Wan's American trip the message had been endlessly repeated at broiled chicken or beef dinners across the country. His style was feisty, rather like Henry Kissinger's. Indeed, Wan's trip had the full support of the former secretary of state and all his illustrious consultancy associates, including three former Presidents.

Sensing the growing mood of public concern in the country about the fate of the students as a result of reporting like Dan Rather's, Wan had publicly called the students "patriots" and was sure the Chinese leadership would "exercise proper restraint" and accept that China's problems "will only be settled through democracy."

Wan's words could have done little to reassure Kissinger Associates. The consultancy had helped establish more than six hundred U.S.–Chinese joint ventures. Already some of these companies were showing signs of concern over the situation in China. The San Francisco-based Bechtel Engineering and Construction Company had withdrawn all four of its expatriate executives from Beijing. U.S. executives at IBM and Chrysler's Jeep joint venture were also planning to leave.

The Kissinger consultancy was working literally around the clock, lobbying Congress and moving swiftly to stop further departures from China by calling top executives at every joint-venture company.

However, Kissinger Associates could not manage to head off the first signs of public anger in America at what was happening in Beijing. Ohio Governor Richard Celeste, after watching a Dan Rather telecast, had canceled China's participation in the state fair. A number of cities, including Los Angeles, were reviewing their "Sister City" links to China; in L.A.'s case, with Canton. Wan Li's words went some way toward reassuring city councilors in Los Angeles.

On Tiananmen Square, the news of Wan Li's intervention further buoyed student hopes after the success in driving the soldiers out of Beijing's suburbs.

Wuerkaixi predicted that the support of such a powerful figure would lead to a dramatic change. Wan Li was close to Deng; they played bridge together. The chairman of the National People's Congress had also been an open supporter of Zhao Ziyang's reform policies. With one of those boundless leaps of optimism for which he was becoming renowned, Wuerkaixi extrapolated that it would only a matter of time before the Party secretary would be back at the helm and it would be Premier Li Peng who would have to go on sick leave.

While Wuerkaixi was exuding such confidence, Sue Tung had come to a decision. The young postgraduate Chinese student from Sacramento who had put her country before her boyfriend had felt increasingly frustrated in her weeks in China. She had still been unable to speak to Jyan, her instructor friend at the PLA academy; its switchboard refused to put through her calls. The student leaders on the square were polite but distant. They had accepted the large donation she had brought from Chinese students in California and then left her to her own devices.

Sue pushed her way past the students standing permanent guard over the Monument to the People's Heroes. Among other duties, the guards decided which foreigners could be allowed into Wuerkaixi's presence. Sue thought it depended on whether the student leader wanted to "impress that day Europe or the United States." Sensing it was America's day, she persuaded the guards to let her pass.

On the pediment she found the mood pensive. Wuerkaixi's burst of optimism had just as quickly given way to pessimism. Mood changes had begun to characterize the behavior of several of the student leaders. Unused to such awesome responsibility, they found their moods hard to control. One moment they could feel jubilant, the next gripped with despair. Only Chai Ling maintained her steely determination, masking it behind a cheerful smile on her pixie face, whose eyes missed nothing.

They quickly appraised Sue, then turned back to Wuerkaixi, who was saying he was now sure the troops would return in even greater numbers.

Sue suddenly found herself speaking.

"You need expert advice," she said. "Broadcast a request for anyone with military experience to come forward to tell you what to do."

Chai Ling was the first to react. She grabbed a microphone.

"People of China. A severe counterrevolutionary coup has now been declared against us. It is initiated by Li Peng and Yang Shangkun. They have already sent their troops once to suppress us. They will do so again. We have no weapons. We only fight for freedom and democracy with words. Yet we know that China's fate is in our hands. That is why we must defend this square, defend the democratic movement, and defend this great country to the last drop of our blood. But we need expert help. We ask if anyone has knowledge of military tactics to come forward and advise us!"

No one had asked Sue to leave the pediment. She felt that the student leaders had accepted her. Wuerkaixi kept saying that the student leaders would be the first targets for the soldiers. He thought they would use tear gas and electric cattle prods to force their way to the pediment. Or they could drop paratroops who would simply shoot them on the spot.

Sue watched Wang Dan walk over to Wuerkaixi, firmly take him by the shoulders, and speak quietly to him. Wuerkaixi became calmer.

Chai Ling was about to make a fresh appeal for help when two stocky figures motioned for the student guards to let them through. Sue stepped down from the pediment and introduced herself. The men said they were instructors at the military academy. Impulsively Sue asked if they knew Jyan. They looked at her curiously. One of the instructors said that Jyan was a member of the strategy team planning to remove the students. Sue quickly explained Jyan was an old family friend, then led them to where Wuerkaixi and Wang Dan waited.

That was also the moment Sue decided to give up trying to contact Jyan. "We were on opposite sides. We would probably both be embarrassed to meet under such circumstances."

One of the instructors produced a copy of the strategy plan Jyan had helped to prepare. The man had stolen it from the military academy. He spread the paper on the ground. The students crouched around him. His companion explained they had come to help because like many other officers in the PLA they felt that the military threat against the students was wrong. Using the map as a reference point, they explained to the leaders what they should expect to happen and what they could do to counter the military moves.

The older man said, "Already this morning the order has been given forbidding all civilian planes flying over the city. This will allow military helicopters to operate with complete freedom. Two hundred helicopters are now within five minutes' flying time of here."

Wuerkaixi glanced apprehensively at his companions.

Chai Ling gave him a quick, reassuring smile. Wang Dan blinked behind his glasses. These past weeks had aged him. It was hard to believe he was still only twenty. He looked like a man who had come to terms with life, including coping with the mood swings of Wuerkaixi.

The younger instructor jabbed at the map. "All public transport is now closed. The underground and trains will be used to move the troops into the city. Already four thousand soldiers are in the railway station a few miles from here."

"What can we do," mumbled Wuerkaixi, "except give up?"

"Wait," the older instructor said, his voice sharp. "Before you decide, you must have all the facts."

The younger instructor placed a finger on the map, indicating the Forbidden City, the History Museum, and the Great Hall of the People.

"Over ten thousand troops have arrived in those places."

Several of the students glanced toward the buildings and the roofs of the Forbidden City. Everything looked normal.

"The troops are in the tunnels," said the older man. "In 1976 I was there with them when your predecessors demonstrated. When we came out of the tunnels then, it took us just six minutes to deal with the situation. Hundreds, you remember, were killed or wounded." He paused to look out across the square. "When they come, it will probably only take a little longer to clear this crowd."

This time Wang Dan addressed both instructors. "Okay, so what *do* we do?"

The two instructors looked at each other and sighed. The older man began to explain.

"You probably have little time. The first thing you must do is to prepare against attack from the air. You must get every kite you can and fly them over the square and the surrounds. The kite strings will wrap around the rotors and stop the helicopters being able to drop paratroopers. You must prepare for tear-gas attack by making everybody wear face masks or handkerchiefs. You must watch out for

Public Security agents. They are everywhere, listening and trying to provoke trouble. You need at least three hundred scouts out in the square, reporting back every hour on what is happening. At the first sign of the troops, you must mobilize the crowd so that the troops will dare not fire. They will know they cannot kill everyone and that the survivors will kill them."

"What about tanks?" asked Daobao.

"The same tactic," said the instructor. "If you are firm and resolute, no tank commander will dare run over your people."

Yang Li stood up, his voice troubled.

"I have no doubt that what you say is good military tactics. But we are not soldiers. We have come here in the name of nonviolence. If we do what you suggest, more people could die. I suggest that if the troops do come, we should try and reason with them. We should say 'the people love the people's army' and 'the people's army loves the people.' We must not fight the soldiers."

Around her Sue could hear murmurs of agreement and dissension. Once more the leaders were divided. While the two instructors watched, the students debated whether they should act on what they had been told.

Agreement was reached on flying kites. That seemed "appropriately nonviolent," said Yang Li. But he remained adamant there must be no violence done by the students. After another hour a compromise was reached. Students would be positioned all around the square to warn of soldiers approaching. At that point Wuerkaixi and Wang Dan would go forward and meet the military commanders and negotiate safe passage for the hunger strikers. In the meantime a general warning would be broadcast for everyone to have a mask ready to deal with any tear-gas attack.

Chai Ling had started to broadcast the terms of what had been decided when the clatter of helicopters filled the air. Swooping in over Zhongnanhai, they whirled across the square, jigging from side to side, dropping until they were only feet above the lampposts. As they veered to either side of the Monument to the People's Heroes, pamphlets rained down on the crowd. The leaflets called for them to leave the square.

A great roar of relief accompanied the helicopters as they headed west across the city. The mercurial Wuerkaixi probably spoke for many when he grinned and said, "It's going to be okay. We're going to zap them!"

The effect of long hours spent with American TV crews had begun to show in his speech.

SAME DAY, LATER
*The Foreign Office*
*London*

The moment analyst Sue Morton saw the latest telegram from British Ambassador Donald, she felt "a little surge of excitement."

Donald had picked up an extraordinary whisper coming out of Zhongnanhai. Within the compound, Zhao was trying to mobilize support to revoke martial law and move to have Prime Minister Li Peng impeached. The supposedly ill Party secretary had managed to gain support for his action from a third of the members of the National People's Congress, whose chairman, Wan Li, was in the United States.

Zhao appeared to have moved so quickly and discreetly that Li Peng had been completely outmaneuvered. Wan Li's words of support for the students—"They are patriots"—and his injunctions to the leadership not to act rashly lest it jeopardize lucrative trade deals, had almost certainly been seen by Zhao as a signal to strike.

Donald's telegram reported the prime minister had rushed to Deng's compound and from there tried to telephone Wan Li to order him to remain in the United States. Unable to contact Wan Li, the prime minister had sent him an urgent fax confirming his instructions. But Zhao had also cabled his own message instructing Wan Li to return "at once" to lend his authority to support the students' demands.

Wan Li was in a dilemma. In the next few days he had important speaking engagements, in Baltimore, Orlando, and New York. He planned to use each occasion to drum up more investments in China. He decided to continue with his tour, which would end with a meeting with George Bush in the Oval Office this coming Tuesday, the day after the President flew back to Washington from Boston. To cancel such a meeting would be unthinkable.

Wan Li decided to continue his American tour, much to the relief of Kissinger Associates. The continued presence of Wan Li in the United States was exactly what the consultancy and Prime Minister Li Peng wanted, a symbol that it was very much business as usual as far as the United States and China went.

That sanguine view was not shared by Susan Morton. Ambassador Donald's telegram provided a further glimpse of the serious power struggle still going on behind the walls of Zhongnanhai.

No doubt encouraged by the way the troops had been turned back in the suburbs, Zhao had somehow found the courage to make one last challenge against Li Peng and, ultimately, Deng Xiaoping.

"The struggle for power is a real no-holds-barred affair," the young researcher had scribbled on her note pad. "There was no real precedent for what was happening."

The struggle had spilled over even to the pages of the *People's Daily*, the official Party organ. The left-hand side of the front page supported Li Peng and carried stories praising the leadership, while the right-hand columns were devoted to describing the aims of the students. The latest issue of a Shanghai newspaper had even gone so far as to print a huge photograph of Winston Churchill giving his famous V sign; the gesture had been adopted by the students.

Ambassador Donald's cable painted a picture of the sky over Beijing constantly filled with helicopters keeping watch on the crowd as people turned whole areas of the city into fortified bastions. Roadblocks were constructed from commandeered public service vehicles and building site materials.

The mood of the crowd veered between "foreboding and good spirits," the ambassador concluded. He had quoted some of the opinions his tireless press attaché, Brian Davidson, had collected. One of the leaders of the newly formed Autonomous Workers Union had quoted Mao, who had said "the government has become a tiny handful."

Susan concluded that government, as such, no longer functioned in Beijing. The country was now being controlled from somewhere called Martial Law Enforcement Headquarters. Her intelligence sources had identified this to be the PLA compound in the west of the city, from which Prime Minister Li Peng and State President Yang had broadcast. But apart from them, no one else had been identified as running the HQ.

The situation, she wrote, is extremely dangerous. China could be on the verge of a catastrophe greater even than the Cultural Revolution.


SAME DAY, LATER
*San Francisco*

With considerable satisfaction Shao-Yen Wang, who was the daughter of a senior officer in Beijing, and whose own hope was to become a Hollywood star one day, saw that the crowd outside the People's Republic consulate had grown even greater this Saturday evening. Staff at every one of Chinatown's scores of restaurants had urged their customers to join in the demonstrations. Many had. They were chanting a succession of slogans urging President Bush to tell Deng Xiaoping to keep the PLA from harming the students.

A number of the demonstrators carried radios to listen to the live broadcasts from Tiananmen Square, where student loudspeakers were repeatedly warning that the troops were once more about to attack.

Then came the bell-like voice of Chai Ling saying the threat had passed; moments later, the protesters outside the consulate heard the loudspeakers in Beijing play Beethoven's "Ode to Joy." They began to hum to the music.

Inside the consulate Zhang Milin, the cultural attaché, watched from his bedroom window. The humming strengthened his resolve to defect. He had thought of nothing else for the past two days and nights: how he would do it, when he would leave.

His greatest fear was that one of the consulate's security staff would sense what he was plotting. If that happened, Zhang knew, he would be drugged and, on the pretext he had been suddenly taken seriously ill and was returning home for treatment, escorted on to a flight to Beijing. There he would be sentenced to a term in the Gulag.

The prison camps were in the desert heartland of the country. There, between stints of backbreaking work in the salt mines, would be lectures to "politically reeducate" him. Years could pass before his mentors decided he was once more ready to be returned to Chinese society. By then, Zhang feared, he could be both a physical and mental wreck.

The hardest part of defecting would be knowing that almost certainly he would never again see his family. To avoid any harm coming to them he could not tell them what he planned; he could tell no one. His great fear was that in his anxiety he might say something in his sleep. These past two nights he had awakened more than once, convinced he had let something slip that would have been heard by one of the patrolling security men.

So far no one had given him a second look. But he also knew it would only be a matter of time before the already strict security within the consulate would be further tightened, making it virtually impossible for any staff to leave the building. Starring out the window at the chanting crowd in the street, Zhang realized he must make his move soon, before that happened.

# 20

## *Marriage in Mayhem*

This was the thirty-eighth day of the demonstrations. Once more climbing the steps to the Monument to the People's Heroes, Cassy sensed a growing defeatism among the student leaders. It was not only because of lack of sleep, absence of proper food, or no chance to wash almost six weeks of grime from their bodies and clothes; hundreds of thousands of others in the square were enduring the same conditions. Rather she felt a "great malaise" had settled over the leadership.

It had been there when Cassy woke after a short sleep, squashed between Daobao and Yang Li at the base of the pediment. The first of the Party loudspeaker broadcasts had awakened them all, warning that the square would soon be cleared by force. In a new twist, the broadcast from inside the Great Hall of the People had ordered all doctors and nurses to return immediately to their hospitals to prepare for the expected casualties.

"It's psychological warfare," Cassy had told her companions. "It means they're not going to actually do anything yet."

Daobao had said no one could know what the authorities were planning. In a pensive mood he and Yang Li had gone to the command bus to join Wuerkaixi at the first strategy meeting of the day.

Hours earlier Cassy and Daobao had stood and watched Dan Rather addressing millions of Americans glued to the "CBS Evening News." The anchorman had shown few signs that he had been in the square for twenty-four straight hours without sleep. He seemed to be

243

operating on pure adrenalin. With Tiananmen Gate as his backdrop, Rather addressed the camera: "They are still here. The army is not. Incredible! China's Communist government hardliners are finally in control of the government and the Party, and they have called out the army in yet another desperate bid to break the back of the mass movement for freedom and democracy and reform. After weeks of government paralysis, while students took over the streets of Beijing and moved their protest into a national movement, soldiers are now massing to move against the protesters camped right here in the center of Beijing. The problem is, the army has been massing for hours and is still not here."

As Daobao and Yang Li walked to the bus, Cassy could see Rather and his film crew beside their beat-up Toyota, which was filled with equipment to transmit audio and video tapes via microwave to their "base camp" on the fifth floor of the Shangri-La Hotel. From there the sound and pictures were sent by satellite to New York.

Suddenly Cassy saw the CBS technician gesticulating. She walked over to see the trouble, and discovered the microwave link out of the square was not working. Someone had cut the hookup to the hotel. A short while later it was restored. But Rather presciently asked his colleagues, "For how long?"

With a camera crew in tow, the anchorman set off to "film what we could before they closed us down."

Overhead more camouflaged military helicopters swooped in over the Beijing Hotel and began to circle the square.

Rather, who knew what panic was from his days of reporting from the streets of Saigon, feared that the helicopters, swooping even lower, might stampede the crowd. To Cassy, raised in the midwest, the choppers "resembled cowboys trying to get a herd of cattle to move."

After a short while the helicopters rose into the air and disappeared westward across the city. Their pilots had thought better of risking their rotors becoming entangled with kite lines.

Wuerkaixi stood in the door of the command bus and watched them depart. Then he returned to the strategy meeting.

Outside the bus, Chai Ling was telling an ABC film crew that while some of the leaders now wanted to abandon the sit-in on Tiananmen, others were considering setting themselves on fire.

"I am ready to sacrifice myself," said Chai Ling in her bird-like voice. "I will do anything to stop this surrender mentality. Personally, I want the government to launch a bloodbath so that the world can see their true value. At the same time I feel the revolutionary cinders must be preserved to start a new fire."

She stared uncompromisingly into the camera, her face drained from her six weeks in the square. One of the film crew had offered her a lipstick before the interview started. She had quickly shaken her head, saying it was not what she looked like but what she had to say that was important.

To Barr Seitz her fervor had "a real touch of Joan of Arc. Every time she spoke to cameras millions of viewers all over the world were stirred by her dignity and courage. She had a dedication to her cause that was both ennobling and a little frightening. She was more than a patriot or revolutionary. There was something almost mesmeric about her. If she, and not Wuerkaixi, had been leading the students, things may have been different by now. As it was, despite her call to fight on to the death, there was a mood of defeatism. Wuerkaixi and the others had no experience of running something as big as this. They'd learned on the job. But the job was simply bigger than they had envisaged. They wanted to change China, to change the lives of one in four people on this earth. They just didn't have the know-how. No one probably had. And as the weeks had passed on Tiananmen, they had come to realize the awful truth. They had started something that was out of their control, but also out of control of the Party, the government, and the old men in Zhongnanhai. It was out of everyone's control, except the military."

After the strategy meeting, which simply agreed to continue "as before," Wuerkaixi began repeatedly to broadcast messages to students in the square to beware of agents provocateurs. He claimed that during the night "a division of plainclothes soldiers and security police" had infiltrated Tiananmen.

"Beware of strangers," Wuerkaixi was still calling out this Sunday afternoon, in what Cassy now called his "voice of paranoia."

There was much about Wuerkaixi she neither understood nor liked. The business of his eating secretly while on hunger strike still angered her. But when she had again tried to discuss the issue with Daobao, he had refused.

He too had changed. He was harder, more demanding; nothing appeared to matter except what was happening in the square. In this second full day of martial law, he had become, like Wuerkaixi, convinced the area was now filled with Qiao Shi's agents. This fear had been reinforced by a glimpse of the security chief on the roof of the Great Hall of the People.

Only Wang Dan had retained his calmness. Time and again he had left the pediment to talk to squabbling students in the square. The most common cause of bickering was the lack of space. Protesters who had been in the square for weeks felt proprietary over their particular piece of ground.

Early in the afternoon Cassy had gone with Wang Dan and Yang
Li to deal with yet another quarrel, which had started near the Great
Hall. A group of Beijing residents who had been on their own hunger
strike had wanted to join the students in their enclave and benefit
from the close medical supervision. Wuerkaixi had sent word they
could not be admitted. He had told Wang Dan they could be
"saboteurs." Wang Dan had persuaded Professor Guangzu to assign
some doctors to tend the residents.

Returning to the monument, Cassy found the mood there had
deepened further into gloom. Wuerkaixi was once more talking of
"facing complete defeat"; he kept saying there was no way the
students would be able to stop any military intervention. "When
that comes, we will face a time of great terror. There will be arrests
and killings. And we will be the first to die. So we must be
prepared to flee first. That is the only way we can carry on the
fight."

Gradually Wang Dan lifted their spirits. He said that if they were
forced to leave the square, they must go underground, as their
predecessors had done in the purge that led to the downfall of Hu
Yaobang. The network of safe houses and cells they had established
then still existed. All they would need now were new code names and
passwords.

They struck Cassy "as kids creating a children's secret society. Lots
of code words were suggested. Some of them wanted to have animal
names. Others, more historical. They all became very involved and
excited. Maybe this is what they needed to get them going again."

"It will cost a lot of money," Wuerkaixi said.

"You have the money," Sue Tung reminded him. "There's the
money I gave you. And all the other donations you have received
since."

Sue had seen scores of overseas Chinese, mostly from Hong Kong
and the United States, arrive at the pediment bringing donations.
Sue estimated over $250,000 in U.S. one-dollar bills alone had been
handed over. Sue thought there could be $1 million in hard foreign
currencies stashed on the pediment.

Wuerkaixi began to plan. Cassy was struck by the sheer scope of
what he was proposing.

"When Wang Dan spoke of something quite basic, a chain of safe
houses for people to hide in, Wuerkaixi was talking of a permanent
headquarters in the south of China, somewhere around Guangzhou.
He was talking of what sounded like a student government-in-exile.
The more he spoke, the more alive he became. It was as if he needed
the 'big picture' to get him going again. Soon he was moving around

the pediment, full of energy, and once more saying they should really stay and confront the army."

An interruption occurred in the midst of this discussion. Another of the student leaders, Li Liu, announced he wanted to get married. A slim, darkly handsome youth, he had traveled from the provincial campus of Nanjing University because "my head was full of dreams" to play his part in what was happening on Tiananmen.

Until then he had struck Sue Tang as a hardheaded young man, a great fixer, devoid of any romantic notions. Now he stood next to a round-faced young woman with a bobbed haircut and shy smile: Zhao Ming, another student from Nanjing. They had been dating before he had come to Beijing. Hearing what was happening there, Ming had traveled to the city to find him.

When they had met at the foot of the monument they had promptly squabbled. Li Liu said she shouldn't have come; Ming said she would not leave without him. He had then swept her in his arms and kissed her to the cheers of onlookers. Then he had brought her onto the pediment and announced he wanted to marry her as soon as possible.

"In my life I've experienced everything but sex and marriage," he declared. "I may die at any time. I owe myself this pleasure."

After the whoops had subsided, Chai Ling asked, "Why not get married now? We'll get you a tent for a bridal chamber. At least you'll have a few hours together."

The other students crowded around the couple, urging them to marry at once.

"The atmosphere was what it must have been like in wartime, a feeling of needing to live for the moment," Cassy recalled. "The old taboos on public affection had been loosened. All over the square people were behaving openly like lovers."

Li Liu turned to Ming. "Shall we?"

"Why not?" she said.

Sue said, "You'll need candy and wine to make it a proper wedding." She suddenly felt an ache for Rod. Perhaps, after all, she should have told him to come. They could also have been married in the square. Then she reminded herself she wanted to be married in America. The June date she and Rod had set was now less than two weeks away.

For the first time she wondered if she would be able to keep it. If the crackdown came, would she be trapped, driven into hiding, unable to leave? Suddenly Sue felt "just a little scared. I knew I could go to the airport today and fly back to Rod. But I also knew I couldn't do that. I had come so far with my people; I had to see this through."

Meili, whose calligraphy had produced many of the more evocative posters adorning the pediment, showed she had a practical side to her. She told Li Liu and Ming that they could eat bread instead of candy and use salt water in place of wine.

"Without them we would not have survived here so long," Meili said.

"We'll still need a marriage certificate," Ming said.

"No problem," Wuerkaixi said. "It's already being prepared."

A student came forward with a piece of paper. On it he had written: "Li Liu, male, 23, and Zhao Ming, female, 25, are willing to be husband and wife to the end of their lives. We hearby grant the necessary approval."

Wuerkaixi stamped the paper with the logo bearing the words *Student HQ*. He handed it to the couple.

"You are now free to marry, absolutely official," he said.

Everyone cheered. Then Chai Ling said the wedding ceremony should take place on the pediment right away. She and her husband volunteered to be bridesmaid and best man. Another student acted as the justice of the peace. Wuerkaixi motioned for the student guard to form a protective cordon around the pediment.

The news that a marriage was taking place swept the crowd. Thousands burst into renditions of the "Wedding March."

Professor Guangzu and Jenny were the first to bring bottles of salt water; in minutes scores of other bottles had been passed up to the pediment.

To Cassy everyone appeared to be toasting everybody. Then the gifts came, items of clothes, pens, sweets, even leaflets signed by the donors. It seemed as if everyone in the square wanted to provide a gift, no matter how small. Children offered buttons. One old man passed forward a bird in a cage. It was politely refused; the newlyweds had no place to keep a pet. By the time Wuerkaixi appealed for a half, hundreds of gifts had been given. The pediment looked like a flea market.

Sue understood why there had been such an overwhelming response. "The wedding was a symbol of what everyone wanted, a new start."

After a resounding chorus of what had become the square's anthem, the "Internationale," Li Liu stepped forward, microphone in one hand, the other waving for silence. For once Wuerkaixi seemed content to take a back seat.

The groom thanked everyone for coming. Then he told them a story that brought tears to many eyes.

"Many of you will remember another young couple who were

arrested a long time ago, because their beliefs offended the emperor. He ordered they must die. At the execution ground they announced to the whole world that they were married. They said they wanted to show that though they could be physically killed, what they believed in would never be taken from their souls."

He paused and struggled with his emotions. Then, holding his bride close to him, Li Liu continued.

"We are all now fighting with the courage that defies death for a life that's worth living. My slogan is 'We have to fight, but we must marry too!'"

All over the square voices took up the refrain: "We have to fight, but we must marry too."

SAME DAY, SAME TIME
*Boston*

On a pleasantly warm New England Sunday afternoon, with the temperature a couple of degrees lower than on Tiananmen Square, President George Bush had finally decided to speak out publicly about what was happening there.

Throughout the weekend Bush had been fully briefed. He had studied the satellite photographs showing the PLA ring of steel beginning to form around Beijing and other major Chinese cities where there was unrest. CIA Director Webster had constantly updated the President on the student's determination to remain in Tiananmen Square in the belief they would achieve their demands for democratic reform. Supporting the intelligence reports were Dan Rather's on CBS and the continuous coverage of CNN. The front pages of the newspapers the President read every day further confirmed the situation. The students were ready, if need be, to die for their belief. Underpinning all the reports was their very clear hope that the most powerful leader in the West would lend them his clearly stated and unequivocal support.

Buth and National Security Adviser Brent Scowcroft had also heard the views of France's president, François Mitterand. Like Bush he was in Boston to receive an honorary degree from Boston University. Mitterand had described the ramifications of the student protest in Europe.

The French government had come under increasing public pressure to make "some decisive move to show China our displeasure," perhaps by freezing credit, while executives of French companies such as Peugeot, Citroen, Thomson, Alintel, and Framatone were urging nothing should be said or done to upset the status quo.

In West Germany, the Christian Democratic Union Party demanded that the Kohn government threaten to freeze all trade with China unless there was a "proper accommodation" with the students. German Foreign Minister Hans-Dietrich Genscher was firmly opposed to any such threat. Executives of Volkswagen, Mercedes-Benz, and Siemens had echoed his view.

"What about Mrs. Thatcher?" Bush asked.

Mitterand had given a Gallic shrug. Britain's prime minister had let Europe's leaders know that she as "utterly opposed" to any economic or political move that would isolate China from the West.

Reassured by the support of such a formidable ally, Bush and Scowcroft reaffirmed United States policy. It closely mirrored the views of Kissinger Associates where, until he went to sit at the left hand of Bush, Scowcroft had been a key policymaker.

At a news conference at Boston University, Bush began by saying that the students should try to "adhere to the style of protest" of the late Rev. Dr. Martin Luther King, seemingly forgetting the often violent response of Southern police forces to such peaceful protest.

Warming to his theme, Bush continued. "I'm one who feels"—chop, chop with the hand—"the quest for democracy is very powerful." More hand chops and a pause to look around the faculty hall to see if anyone would challenge this truism. "But I'm not going to dictate or try to say from the United States how this matter should be resolved by those students....I don't want to be gratuitous in giving advice, but I would encourage restraint...."

Another pause to glance around the hall. A question from a reporter: Why was the administration being so cautious?

Bush's hands went into overdrive.

"I think this is perhaps a time for caution, for, because, because, we aspire to see the, the Chinese people have democracy, but we do not expect in a way...to stir up a military confrontation...and so we counsel restraint, as we would counsel powerful means of effecting change. That is sound advice. To go beyond that and encourage steps...bloodshed would be inappropriate."

Another question: Did the President have anything to say directly to the students?

Bush looked pained. It took him a few moments to formulate a reply. "It would not be appropriate for the President of the United States to say to the demonstrators and the students in Beijing exactly what their course of action should be."

Then Bush strode from the podium, watched by Scowcroft. The children of China would find no support from America.

Two days later, when Bush received Wan Li, the chairman of the People's National Congress, in the Oval Office, the President remained equally restrained in his criticism of China. He restricted his comments to asking Wan Li to use his good offices to stop the jamming of Voice of America broadcasts to the People's Republic. Then Bush had walked his guest through the White House rose garden to have coffee with Barbara Bush. Leaving Washington, Wan Li told reporters that relationships between the two countries were "as always very satisfactory."

SATURDAY, MAY 27, 1989
*PLA Base*
*Bao Bi Dian, west of Beijing*

At 4:30 A.M., the loudspeaker in every barracks block came alive. All over the camp thousands of soldiers struggled into fatigues and ran to the parade square for the first of the day's indoctrinations. Among them was Bing Yang.

Every day since the humiliating withdrawal from Beijing's suburbs, he had paraded here to be told what was happening in the city.

A succession of political commissars had repeatedly described how "reactionaries" and "counterrevolutionaries" had seized control of the center of the capital and declared a "rebellion" against the Party and the government.

This morning the assembled ranks listened to a new tape recording of Prime Minister Li Peng and State President Yang Shangkun once more praising the PLA for its loyalty. Then the voices of two of the army's most revered commanders, Marshal Nie Dongzha and Marshal Xu Xianquan, delivered a homily saying that the army must do its duty without flinching.

Afterward the taped voice of Hu Qili, the Politburo propaganda chief, addressed the soldiers. He told them that Zhao Ziyang had been replaced as Party secretary by Jiang Zemin, the Party boss in Shanghai.

Jiang was a hardliner who had dealt with Shanghai students firmly since they had marched through the city on the day of Hu's funeral. Initially he had allowed protests up to a point while constantly denigrating the students as only a "tiny handful" bent on trying to "poison the minds of the people."

When some four thousand Shanghai students and their teachers had begun a hunger strike in the city on May 16, Jiang had kept his nerve, as he had when hundreds of thousands of citizens marched through Shanghai two days later. The protest had been vocal but orderly, requiring little police intervention. Now Jiang's crowd-control skills would be called into play in Beijing.

A great roar of approval swept the ranks. The astute propaganda chief continued to psych up the troops.

"On all fronts your leaders are showing their patience and loyalty. Among them is Wan Li, who upon returning from overseas immediately pledged his full support for martial law."

It was less than the full story. The chairman of the National People's Congress had returned from Washington the previous Thursday. Landing at Shanghai airport, he had been met by Jiang Zemin.

Jiang had promptly upbraided Wan Li for his remarks about the students being "patriots." The congress chairman had countered by saying he had merely been trying to defuse public concern in the United States. He began to explain the success his trip had been in raising further investments, and the happy outcome of his visit to the White House, where he had left the President firmly convinced there was no cause for American concern over the students. Jiang abruptly said he wanted Wan Li's written support for martial law. Incensed now at his treatment, the congress chairman said he first wanted to fly to Beijing and confer with Zhao. Jiang Zemin promptly informed the tired-looking Wan Li that he needed "a rest." The congress leader was then escorted from the airport to a nearby State Guest House and told he would remain there until his "health" improved.

Twenty-four hours later, Wan Li had "recovered" sufficiently to sign a document giving his full support for martial law. That same Friday, the commanders of six of the seven national military regions and heads of twenty-seven of the twenty-nine provinces had also forwarded to Beijing their total support for martial law. Hours later the remaining two provinces and military regions also announced their support.

SAME DAY
*Washington, D.C.*

The evidence that a massive military crackdown was unfolding in China continued to emerge from the capital's intelligence communities in the form of satellite photos, intercepts of Chinese signals traffic, and ground intelligence from CIA agents in Beijing. The stream of material was sifted, analyzed, and forwarded by Webster to the White House.

George Bush was now one of the best informed Presidents in history facing a momentous event slowly moving to a climax. He still might have been able to avert it by clearly warning the Chinese leadership not to have the PLA attack the students. Alternatively, the President could have authorized the large number of U.S. intelligence officers and diplomats on Tiananmen Square to warn the students of the exact nature of terrible threat they faced, in the hope they would leave the square.

Whether President Bush even considered such possibilities was to remain his secret. All that can be said with certainty is that he had made no further public comment on the students since Boston.

SAME DAY, LATER
*Tiananmen Square*

This was the forty-fifth day of the demonstrations. Squatting on the ground near the Museum of Revolutionary History, Jeanne Moore realized she had become inured to the sights and smells of the square. She momentarily wondered if she was losing her reporter's skills, which had sustained her in these past weeks. Then she realized it was pure fatigue that enabled her to ignore the stench from the latrines. More slit trenches had been dug during the night.

Her notebook reflected something of the seesaw of events in these past few days.

She had learned that Party Secretary Zhao's attempt to have Prime Minister Li Peng impeached marked the end of Zhao's own career. He was now under house arrest in Zhongnanhai. There was talk that he could face trial for treason. If found guilty he would be executed by having a single bullet fired into the back of his head, which had long been the regime's favored method of dealing with traitors.

A sign that calm had returned had been the sight of Li Peng's kite swooping and soaring over the compound. It had risen higher than the few kits still flying over Tiananmen Square to stop the helicopters returning. A week ago hundreds of kites had formed a protective shield over the square. But no helicopters had been seen for almost three days, and most of the kites had now been reeled in.

After issuing a number of edicts, none of which had been obeyed, the Martial Law Enforcement Headquarters had fallen silent. Its last public statement had been two days ago when it had broadcast to the square a familiar reminder: The army would do everything needed to return the city to social order and stability. Jeers had greeted the threat.

Shortly afterward, a train filled with some two thousand soldiers appeared in the city's main station. Wuerkaixi and Wang Dan had led several hundred students on bicycles to block the station entrance. The troops had remained in their carriages. Finally the train had pulled out. Later, an armored column of seventy-two halftracks and three hundred trucks had been stoned as it entered the southwestern suburbs. Another column had been stopped as it tried to occupy the area around the Summer Palace. Since then the army had made no attempt to move further into Beijing.

"Those troops which remain in the suburbs mix freely with the citizens," Jeanne had written in a notebook. "There is a strange carnival-like mood about it all. Everyone knows why the soldiers are there, yet everyone is trying to pretend that there is no cause for alarm. A strange, unreal calm has come to Beijing."

Dan Rather's greater experience of such events warned the CBS anchorman this could be the calm before the storm. He told his crew that the soldiers "could turn at any moment. They could strafe, they could tear-gas. There are a lot of possibilities here."

But for the moment, he filmed the soldiers mixing with the citizens, sharing their rice bowls, allowing children to clamber over their trucks and tanks. This really was the people's army.

This mingling of soldiers and citizens had led to an easing of tension. Earlier fears that tens of thousands of armed soldiers were waiting in the tunnels beneath the city had proved impossible to verify. All attempts to investigate the tunnels had failed; the doors to the underground labyrinth had been secured. On the street itself, the police had relinquished all control. Traffic on Changan, the city's equivalent to Fifth Avenue, and other avenues was controlled by students.

Under Wuerkaixi, Tiananmen Square had become a model of the kind of bureaucracy he had vowed to end. The square had been divided up into various sectors, each of which required its own pass to enter. Only those with "a full security clearance" could now go to the Monument to the People's Heroes.

The strain had gone from Wuerkaixi's face. He was his old ebullient self, strutting around the pediment in his denims stiff with dirt and sweat. He was master of all he could survey.

Chai Ling smiled at his behavior. The longer she remained on the square, the greater grew her resolve not to leave. It showed in a newfound intimidating edge to her voice. She spoke sharply to other student leaders who asked how much longer they should stay.

Wang Dan too had undergone a change, finally shaking off his caution. He moved from one group to another offering support and promising "the end is close, victory will be ours."

Daobao had lost a personal battle. After three weeks of not smoking he had succumbed, taking a cigarette from Yang Li. Soon Daobao was back to almost chain-smoking.

By this Saturday afternoon, forty-five days into the demonstrations, many of the students and citizens had begun to drift away from Tiananmen Square. Barricades had come down on Changan, and buses had started to run freely for the first time in a week. Shops and factories along the avenue had reopened.

At the Beijing Hotel it was very much business as usual, tending to the demands of the hundreds of foreign media people who had made it their headquarters. In a day the hotel earned more hard currency from overseas telephone and fax charges than it normally did in a month. Its restaurants and bars stayed open around the clock to feed reporters and camera crews with almost nothing to do except pick through the overpriced souvenirs on sale in the lobby.

Qiao Shi's security men and officers of Western intelligence agencies mingled with them. A CIA agent had taken up a more or less permanent corner in the coffee shop near the telex room. There was a persistent rumor that he had bribed one of the telex clerks to let him read all the reporters' messages.

"The hotel had become a real haven for spies," Melinda Liu would remember. "The Chinese had the place bugged. Everybody was watching everybody and feeding rumors to each other. You got more disinformation walking the lobby than you would get in the whole square. It got worse as nothing was happening. The big-time stars of prime TV couldn't accept that. You'd hear Dan Rather saying to one of his producers, 'What do you mean, there's *nothing* to report. There has to be *something*!'"

The antics of the media continued to fascinate Barr Seitz. "The networks were spending hundreds of thousands of dollars a day, and it was all going suddenly flat. Reporters were now interviewing each other, or anybody else who had an opinion. If you wanted to start a stampede, all you had to say was 'I hear there's some movement up on the square.' The hotel lobby would empty as if the place were on fire."

"And Tiananmen itself," wrote Jenny Guangzu, as she squatted on the ground, "is a sad and sorry sight. A great dust storm has left many of the banners in tatters. Empty food packages, plastic wrappings, and leaflets lie everywhere. So do bits of clothing."

On the square itself a hard core of protesters remained. In number they fluctuated between an estimated half million at noon to half that number at dusk. People went home for meals and returned, often with food for the students. The hunger strikers continued to draw a crowd. Some of the Chinese gamblers in the crowd had started to bet on how long it would be before the first striker died. The strikers were now into their third week without food.

Despite the military cordon around the city, thousands of provincial students had still managed to reach the square.

Jeanne Moore thought "they lack discipline and purpose. The have often come out of curiosity, a feeling of wanting to be part of the action. But nothing much is happening. So in the frustration and sordid living conditions, it's inevitable that rows have broken out. Students are actually fighting about who should say what and when over the public address system. The newcomers are accusing Wuerkaixi and the Beijing student leaders of taking the best food and sleeping equipment."

There had also been angry questions about the large sums of money that had been donated. Wuerkaixi had furiously denied he or his companions had pocketed any for themselves, but he refused to give a detailed accounting of how much they had received and what it had exactly been used for. All Wuerkaixi would concede was that the money was being kept in "a safe place" ready for the time it would be needed to "continue our struggle far from here." Most reporters had assumed this meant the money was to be used to finance the escape of the leaders.

"It's very sad," thought Jean Moore, "that everything has come down to such basics."

The young reporter rose and once more began to walk through the debris-strewn square. How long could this go on?

The answer came minutes later. Over the loudspeakers came the voice of Wuerkaixi. He announced there would be a "final" rally this coming Tuesday, May 30, after which the students would return to their campuses to prepare "a new form of protest." By then their protests would have lasted fifty days.

No one knew what had prompted Wuerkaixi to make the announcement. He had consulted no one.

However, howls of anger greeted the news. Suddenly Chai Ling's voice rose over the turmoil.

"I will not leave! I shall stay here to fight to the end! Long live democracy!"

Anger turned to cheers.

"We want Chai Ling to lead us," rose the chant. "We stay to fight with her."

At that moment the mantle of power fell from Wuerkaixi and Wang Dan onto the narrow shoulders of Chai Ling. Only some two hundred thousand were there to witness it.

She promptly called for a "march of reaffirmation" around the square, and for all the demonstrators to prepare to stay and ready themselves for the next great day in the Party calendar: the meeting of the National People's Congress on June 20.

"We will stay forever," she promised, "if that is as long as it takes to bring democracy!"

The cheer was the loudest Jeanne Moore had heard.


TUESDAY, MAY 30, 1989
*San Francisco*

Inside the beleaguered consulate Zhang Milin watched the television screen that had become his one link "with reality." For days now all normal work in the consulate had been halted by the continuous demonstrations outside. The protest from the street echoed the tumult on the screen relaying live pictures from Tiananmen Square.

As Zhang watched, an extraordinary procession was making its way into view. It was dominated by a thirty-foot tall, white plaster statue of a caucasian-faced woman holding aloft a flaming torch in both her hands. The CNN commentator was saying she was called the "Goddess of Democracy."

Supported by scores of students, Lilliputian figures around this towering figurine, the status rose serene and proud over the square, confronting the portrait of Mao on Tiananmen Gate as Hu Yaobang's photograph had done all those weeks before.

The commentator described how the statue had arrived on flatbed pedicycles from the Central Institute of Fine Arts and how it was being likened to the Statue of Liberty.

The moment he heard the comparison, Zhang knew that the students were "trying to involve the United States in their protest. They hoped the statue would make Bush say something to support them." But the cultural attaché realized there was no way that President Bush would do that. The Chinese embassy in Washington continued to report that the administration was refusing to become embroiled "in China's internal affairs."

However, the arrival of the statue had put the demonstrators firmly back at the top of the newscasts. The figurine would become a "rallying symbol" for the demonstrators outside the consulate. In the past few days their numbers had dwindled. Now they would dramatically increase.

But Zhang also recognized that the arrival in Tiananmen of this "potent symbol of the capitalist world" would be seen as the ultimate provocation by the Chinese leadership. Already some of his fellow diplomats, watching the TV screen, were saying the time for action had finally come.

Zhang also knew the moment had come for him to defect. As a still trusted diplomat, he was allowed to leave the consulate. Each time he did, he smuggled out extra items of clothes under his suit and left them with a young American he had come to know and trust. He knew he must only take the bare minimum in case one of the consulate security guards ran a spot-check on his room and found his wardrobe visibly depleted. He would not be able to smuggle out his books or records; all he could risk taking would be letters from his family. When he felt he had removed all he could, he would make one last trip, to freedom. He had not thought beyond that point. He suspected the FBI would wish to question him. But he had vowed to himself to tell them nothing that would compromise the national security of China.

His scruples were commendable but unnecessary. The FBI's bugs had ensured it knew a great deal of what was going on inside the consulate, including those angry words from the consul to his staff for their government to deal with this latest "outrage" by the students in Beijing.

THURSDAY, JUNE 1, 1989
*Tiananmen Square*

Again British press attaché Brian Davidson and Irish envoy Brendan Ward agreed on a number: Probably fewer than ten thousand remained encamped in the square.

In the past few days, despite Chai Ling's "march of affirmation" and her promise to remain in the square, there had been a steady exodus. Many of the public complained they could no longer tolerate the stench from the latrines. Others said they could no longer stay away from their work. Many of the students felt too exhausted to camp out. Others wanted to go home for the summer vacation. Hour by hour the million-plus who had occupied the square only a week ago had drifted away. Now, on this hot, sultry morning, only a relatively small number remained.

Moving among them were scores of Public Security photographers. They would stop before each group of students and carefully photograph them before moving on.

Ward thought it "quite extraordinary the way the students made no protest. Several just smiled defiantly into the cameras. Some even posed proudly beneath the goddess's statue."

As an attraction, the figurine had not been a success. The crowds who had come to stare had quickly dwindled. Davidson felt it was "because the figurine was alien to most Chinese. The similarity with the Statue of Liberty meant nothing to people who knew nothing of the world outside their hutongs."

Nevertheless, the authorities had been quick to attack the statue as "proof that the counterrevolutionary rebellion is inspired by outside enemies of the people." A number of "outraged intellectuals" had written to the state media pointing out that the "foreign monument" actually was standing on the very spot where the portrait of Sun Yat-sen, the founder of China's Republican movement, was displayed on high days in the Party calendar. Such "heresy" must be punished.

This had been also one of the themes of several demonstrations organized by the Party in the past few days. Several thousand demonstrators had been bused to a football stadium in the suburbs to chant slogans such as "crush the People's enemies" and wave banners proclaiming OPPOSE TURMOIL.

The state media had called the occasion "a spontaneous display of anger against bad elements."

That image had been spoiled for Ward because most of the demonstrators had spent their time giggling into the TV cameras while Party cadres tried to stoke their fury. The demonstration had ended with the burning in effigy of astrophysicist Fang Lizhi, who was China's most renowned dissident, and an unnamed "conspirator."

"It has to be Zhao Ziyang," Ward had told Davidson.

"Who else?" the press attaché had agreed as they walked on through the square.

Several of the other foreign diplomats in the square had heard the story that Zhao was now under house arrest in Zhongnanhai.

Geert Andersen, a counselor at the Danish Embassy, had been told that Zhao had suffered the ultimate indignity of having his limousine taken away. Horst Lohmann, the military attaché of the German

Democratic Republic, had heard that Zhao might soon face trial for treason.

"So many reports were always a sure sign no one really knew," Ward would say.

Chai Ling remained encamped on the pediment of the Monument to the People's Heroes. With her were a tired-looking group of students. But there was no sign of Wuerkaixi and Wang Dan.

Melinda Liu had spotted both asleep in the back of a bus. It would make a line in the story she was preparing for *Newsweek*. She had decided it would probably be a wrapup. The simple truth was that the students had begun to lose the interest of her editors. It happened with any long-running story. And this one had run longer than most, since April 15, forty-nine days now.

Melinda decided she would return to Hong Kong the coming weekend.

Glancing around the square she thought, "They've achieved very little. But that's the way it often is in China."

FRIDAY, JUNE 2, 1989
*Deng Xiaoping's compound*

Shortly after midnight, the small group of Politburo members once more arrived to confer with Deng Xiaoping. With them was General Hongwen Yang, commander of the 27th Army. He had driven there with his relative, the state president.

Grouped in the obligatory semicircle of armchairs facing Deng, the cabal spoke in turn. Western intelligence sources would later agree there was little debate. In the words of one European operative monitoring the situation through his Chinese contacts "they were just rubber-stamping what Deng had decided."

Those same intelligence sources would concur that what had finally driven Deng to action was a combination of developments.

Intelligence chief Qiao Shi presented a report showing that unrest in other parts of the country had spread. In the southern city of Guandong, a thousand miles from Beijing, a crowd of thirty thousand continued to keep a permanent vigil in support of local students. In Hunan province, Hu Yaobang's birthplace, six hundred miles south of the capital, there was a continuous sit-in outside the local government headquarters. In another provincial capital, Xian, up to three hundred thousand protesters were continuously marching. In all, some twenty cities across China were now in a state of "turmoil."

Qiao Shi insisted that the widespread disruption was being master-minded by the Beijing students. His agents had intercepted their phone calls and obtained copies of their faxed messages. They all clearly showed that a small group of students were determined to create what the security chief now also called "chaos under Heaven" throughout the country, led by Wuerkaixi, Chai Ling, and Wang Dan.

When Deng finally spoke he said he was now convinced that he had little to fear from the United States, Britain, or West Germany in terms of military reprisals for acting decisively against the students.

Chinese ambassadors in all those countries had told him that the official protests likely to follow would be short-lived, coupled to short-term diplomatic and trade disruption. But no more.

There would be absolutely no question of any covert military support. Not even the CIA was going to think of arming the students.

The way was clear to deal with the students once and for all.

General Yang was the last to speak. He assured the others that his forces were ready to end the rebellion.

No one asked for operational details. Yang did not offer any.

At 2:00 A.M., the meeting broke up. While other members of the cabal returned to the Zhongnanhai compound, Prime Minister Li Peng and State President Yang Shangkun drove with General Yang to the General Logistics Department compound in the western suburbs. From here they would watch the final operational plans being activated. This time there would be no turning back.

SAME DAY, LATER
*Tiananmen Square*

Sue Tung strolled though the square in the early afternoon sunshine planning her return to Sacramento. There was a flight in the morning. Sixteen hours later she could be back with Rod, telling him how everything had fizzled out. She was still glad she had come, but the trip had ended in disappointment and, she had to admit, in downright farce.

Near the goddess's statue, a new hunger strike had started, but it was a far cry from that of the two thousand students who had vowed to starve to death until they had been ordered by Wang Dan to stop after twenty-three days. Many had been hospitalized, but they were now recovering.

This strike consisted of just four people, led by Hou Dejian, a pop singer and self-publicist, who had come from Taiwan. He had announced he could "only starve" for two days because he had to be in Hong Kong this coming Monday to cut a new record, and he could not afford to damage his voice by going hungry too long. His companions had also set a strict time limit on their fasting, no longer than three days.

Nevertheless, Chai Ling had welcomed what she called their "courageous act." She had struck Sue as prepared to endorse anyone who "could get things going again."

But already, after a couple of hours' squatting on the ground, the quartet of hunger strikers had become an object of wry comment. Some of the students were teasing Hou and his companions, offering them sweets and drinks.

Jenny Guangzu and her father had walked over to cast a professional eye on the four and then returned to the first-aid tent.

"They've got enough fat on their bodies to last a week," Professor Guangzu grunted. He left the square to return to the hospital to look at some of the student hunger strikers who were recovering there.

Jenny had curled up in the back of the tent to snatch a few hours' sleep. One of the medical students had volunteered to look after Peter. The girl had taken the child to the Beijing Hotel. A TV reporter had told her she could use his bathroom to freshen up. A number of students had established the same relationship with the media.

For the first time in weeks Cassy Jones felt she had nothing to do. Daobao had gone back to his dormitory on the campus to change his clothes. She sat near the goddess's statue to write postcards home. She had actually bought the cards on the day Hu Yaobang died. They were views of Tiananmen Square.

To a friend in Chicago Cassy wrote: "After all the weeks of tension, it's all over. No doubt you've seen the Goddess of Freedom (the first version actually went up in Shanghai a week before the one here) on TV. People just drop by from work to see if it's still here. But it's no big deal."

Behind her Hou Dejian had started to sing another number from his repertoire.

"This place is a bit like Woodstock," Cassy added.

Suddenly she longed to go home.


SAME DAY, LATER
*PLA Barracks*
*Bao Bi Dian*

Shortly before dusk, Bing Yang and several thousand other troops were paraded to be lectured by their political commissar.

They were once more told the center of Beijing was now in the hands of "armed and highly dangerous counterrevolutionaries"; that "foreign mercenaries" were helping them; that the citizens were in "mortal terror of their lives."

After the harangue, Bing and his companions were told they must be ready to move out at a moment's notice.

One of the U.S. satellites positioned over the area gathered up the order and transmitted it to Washington. The technicians at the National Photographic Interpretation Center sent the order on up the intelligence community chain of command. It would form part of the next President's Daily Brief, ensuring George Bush would be among the first to know that full-scale military action was now under way against the students. There would still be time for him to warn the Chinese leadership against such a response, if he chose to do so.

# 21

## *Massacre*

At a little after 2:00 A.M. on this fifty-fourth day of the protest, Daobao brusquely ordered a PLA officer out of the telephone booth outside the Military Museum on Fuxing Avenue in the western suburbs. The officer had tried to call his headquarters to get fresh orders for his squad of unarmed recruits. They were surrounded by a crowd, most in their nightclothes, who taunted the soldiers.

A couple of hours earlier some five thousand troops had passed into the city on foot east and west, planning to meet on Tiananmen Square. Dressed in green baggy fatigues and rubber-soled boots, they had run like marathoners through the silent streets of sleeping suburbia.

When they has reached a crossroads in the Muxudi District, four miles to the west of Tiananmen Square, where they were supposed to rendezvous with a police jeep that would lead them into the city, the vehicle had been involved in an accident, killing three people. The incident had brought residents into the street. Seeing the soldiers, they swung into action.

Barricases had once more been swiftly erected from buses, trucks, vans, handcarts, and bicycles. No one expected the barrier would hold back the troops for long, but they might buy enough time for more substantial defenses to be erected further back in the city.

A pedicab driver had cycled up Changan Avenue yelling, "They're coming, they're coming!" Along the avenue, which was three times the width of New York's Fifth Avenue, people appeared at windows, realized what was happening and took up his cry.

Alerted by the shouting, students in the square had begun to run down the avenue as Wuerkaizi and Wang Dan joined Chai Ling on the pediment of the Monument to the People's Heroes. All previous bickering was forgotten. This was a time for concerted action.

They dispatched students to report back on what was happening. Daobao was sent to the Muxudi District. Cassy had again ridden with him on a motorcycle as it sped down Changan Avenue, passing students ripping up traffic dividers and using them to reinforce barricades. Others were using tools to pry up paving stones, which were broken into handy pieces to throw at the troops.

Reaching Muxudi, Daobao and Cassy found that most of the soldiers had run into side streets to bypass the barricades rather than try to dismantle them. They were reduced to small groups that were easy to surround, like those trapped on the steps of the Military Museum.

Having evicted the officer from the phone booth, Daobao called one of the kiosks on Tiananmen Square. Another student answered, and Daobao reported what he had seen. A third student ran to the pediment with the news. Reports in this manner were coming in from all quarters, enabling those on the pediment to have a clear picture of events.

By now the first TV crews were coming from the Beijing Hotel, led by Barr Seitz. Running into Changan Avenue, he was astonished to find that "out of nowhere" a crowd of several thousand had pinned a column of soldiers against the walls of the China Ocean Shipping Corporation.

Barr shouldered his way to the front of the crowd, which was jeering at the troops. He saw that several of the soldiers were weeping. Most looked cowed or bewildered. Barr began to question them.

"They were teenagers, mostly country kids. They'd run some fifteen miles into the city without a gun between them, or seemingly any clear orders. Their officers kept saying they would be told what to do once they reached Tianamen Square," Barr recalled.

The ABC crew filmed several of the soldiers simply walking away into the crowd, repeatedly saying they didn't want to harm anyone.

"For a military operation, this is a real fiasco," Barr told his producer. "Let's go see if we can find some real action."

Half a mile further back along Changan, Jeanne Moore had been awakened by the commotion. By the time she reached the street, a crowd had surrounded another squad of soldiers.

The boldest of the onlookers prodded at the backpacks the soldiers carried and removed biscuits, rice cakes, and water bottles. They tasted the food and wrinkled their noses in disgust.

"If this is what they feed you, no wonder you look so scared," a man said, spitting out a biscuit. There was good-natured laughter. The tension was broken.

The crowd now began to coax the soldiers. "Go back to your bases. Or join us in supporting the students. You're just being used."

More soldiers drifted off with members of the crowd or began to walk back along Changan. Finally only officers remained. They glanced at the crowd, and then they too began the long walk back to base.

A half mile to the west of Tiananmen Square, *Newsweek*'s Melinda Liu once more found herself in the right place at the right moment. She had been awakened in her room on the seventeenth floor of the Beijing Hotel by an informant with news that troops were "surging in from the west."

She ignored her colleagues heading for the square and ran on down Changan, keeping to the center of the great boulevard that bisected the city. At the intersection leading to Zhongnanhai she found a couple of thousand people pressed around four buses filled with armed troops. The sight of gun muzzles sticking out of sacks had inflamed the crowd. They were rocking the buses in an effort to tip them over. The soldiers were trying to scramble through the windows.

Melinda spotted ammunition boxes hidden beneath blankets inside the buses.

The crowd's anger deepened. They began to scream at the soldiers. "Why do you want to kill us?"

Some of the troops began to tremble and weep. In her notebook Melinda jotted: "Scene very adrenalin provoking and disturbing."

As one of the soldiers tried to climb out of a window, he changed his mind. "Too late. The crowd grabbed his arms, a tug-of-war began. The trooper has his hat in his mouth, as if he's scared to lose it. The crowd take off his shoes. They know the greatest humiliation they can do to a Chinese soldier is to leave him barefoot," Melinda noted.

"In minutes they had removed the footwear of a score of soldiers. the shoes and boots piled in the form of a mock shrine, consisting of boxes of ammunition, rifles, copies of Mao Tse-tung's textbook on military themes and the Communist party manual, both of which are obligatory for all soldiers to carry."

The mood of the crowd lightened. They began to laugh and chant: "The army and the people are as close as fish and water."

The soldiers grinned sheepishly.

Melinda continued on down Changan Avenue, noting the students standing over their piles of broken paving stones and the traffic dividers strewn across the streets. Did they really think any of this could really stop a determined army? The sight of those guns and ammunition boxes continued to trouble her.

She remembered what China's most revered military philosopher, Sun Tzu, had written: "When capable, feign incapacity; when active, inactivity. When near, make it appear you are far away; when far away, that you are near. Offer the enemy a bait to lure him; feign disorder and strike him."

## The White House

It was Friday night in Washington, D.C., and Barbara Bush, like millions of Americans, had settled down to watch the latest episode of "Dallas" when a bright red "CBS News Special Report" sign filled the screen. J. R. Ewing was cut off in the middle of trying to justify another piece of skulduggery, to be replaced by Dan Rather, live from Beijing, confronting two Chinese officials over his right to broadcast.

Rather was using all his skills and authority to persuade the officials CBS still had a firm agreement with the Chinese Foreign Ministry allowing them to broadcast live. The Ministry now wanted him to end all such transmissions, clearly because of the powerful effect they were having on U.S. public opinion.

While Rather negotiated with the two officers, he continued to describe to his audience what was happening all around him.

"At almost every intersection, there are crowds," Rather said into his handheld microphone. "Though martial law has been declared, the army has engaged in tremendous restraint...."

In the Oval Office, the President had continued to receive hard intelligence of what the army was doing out of range of Rather's cameras, but all too clearly caught in the lenses of U.S. satellites and other intelligence gathering methods. Prints from the National Photographic Interpretation Center had been hand-carried all day to the White House, together with summaries of PLA radio traffic. The CIA's Beijing station had continued to send updates, while U.S. diplomats in Beijing had transmitted situation reports to the State Department.

They ensured that Bush had the clearest possible view of what was already happening in Beijing, and what was almost certainly going to happen. A massive pincerlike movement, involving over a hundred thousand troops, was encircling the city and preparing to move forward. Supporting it were battle tanks and weaponry of a kind more suitable to full-scale war: rocket launchers, heavy-caliber machine guns.

American surveillance reports also showed that the People's Liberation Army was poised to support armed police in other cities. From Canton in the far south, to Shanghai five hundred miles up the coast, all the way inland to the industrial cities of Wuhan and Chengdu, the PLA had deployed close to another fifty thousand troops.

Although he joined his wife to watch the CBS report, the President did not need Dan Rather to tell him that almost eight weeks of high drama was moving to a terrible climax.

Outside the White House events were being monitored by nongovernment analysts. One was Joseph Brewda of the Washington-based Economic Intelligence Bureau. To Brewda it seemed "incomprehensible that even now George Bush, who knew the Chinese mind-set every bit as well as did Rather, and who, in turn, was respected and probably feared a little by the old men in Zhongnanhai, made no move to warn them that America would react strongly to any military move against the students. The President could have threatened to cut all diplomatic ties, to freeze all credits, to withdraw all economic and technical assistance. He could have consigned China to the boonies. Or, at the very minimum, he could have given other Western leaders a lead by telling the students we were with them 100 percent in calling for democracy."

SAME DAY, LATER
*The Foreign Office*
*London*

Analyst Susan Morton had found that the best way to cope with the almost overwhelming flow of material arriving on her desk was to strictly segregate it. Her growing piles of accounts included those from Brian Davidson.

The press attaché had reported that well-armed units inside the Great Hall of the People and in the tunnels under the city could now number twenty thousand soldiers.

Other reports claimed that Deng Xiaoping had suffered a sudden collapse with his invasive cancer, that Li Peng had been fired. A short while ago these reports had been formally denied by a Chinese Foreign Ministry spokeswoman in Beijing.

Another item that had caught Susan's eye was an intelligence report about China's minister of defense, Qin Jiwei, and the deputy chief of the PLA general staff, Xu Xin, visiting military units to the west of Beijing. The two men had urged troops "to make martial law a success, so as to add glory to the armed forces and make new contributions to stabilizing the situation."

SAME DAY, SAME TIME
*Northeast suburbs of Beijing*

Sue Tung had been sent to Andingmen Avenue, four miles to the north of the square, to watch for any approaching troops.

Like everyone else who had spent time in Tiananmen Square, the young postgraduate student was operating on adrenalin. She had snatched food and sleep when she could and washed her underwear under a cold-water tap in one of the alleys behind Tiananmen Square. She had lost weight and at times, she had admitted to herself, faith in some of the student leadership.

Only Wang Dan and Chai Ling seemed to Sue to have retained their ability to focus. Both of them showed an iron resolve to see this through. Wuerkaizi still vacillated, one moment rousing those around him, the next bowed down with despair. Yet Sue was sympathetic and understood his feelings.

"No twenty-year-old should have such a great responsibility," Sue had told her boyfriend, Rod, in one of her telephone calls to him back in Sacramento.

Despite the threat by the martial law authorities to cut all overseas TV and radio transmissions, the Beijing telephone system was functioning normally, enabling foreign journalists to call their offices and file reports. Anxious to reassure Rod, Sue had telephoned him collect every day from a pay phone on Changan Avenue. In her last call a few hours ago, she had told him that she planned to stay on in Beijing "a day or two longer, as things have become interesting again."

Rod told her he had just seen the Chinese pull the plug on Rather's last transmission and said, "Things look really bad."

Swept along by the bullish mood on Tiananmen Square, Sue had once more tried to reassure him.

"The troops are a ploy. Like the helicopters and the Party broadcasts," she told Rod. "The army can see the entire population do not want them to harm the students. It could well be that the soldiers will now side with us. Then we would have a bloodless coup, just like in the Philippines. People power worked there. It will do so here."

In that optimistic mood she had hung up and cycled to her assigned post on the broad expanse of Andingmen Avenue.

She arrived shortly after dawn to find several trucks filled with soldiers parked inside Ditan Park, unable to leave because of the crowd.

The soldiers reminded Sue "of caged animals, pacing back and forth among the trucks, and rather frightened." Several asked for cigarettes and for water to refill their canteens. The crowd, numbering several thousand, Sue thought, said they would only provide supplies if the soldiers handed over their weapons.

They began to do so early in the afternoon. Soon AK-47 assault rifles were stacked on the road alongside piles of helmets and backpacks.

A little later several Chinese photographers arrived, equipped with video cameras. They said the worked for the Hong Knog media and had come to record "the people's victory." They were cheerful and polite and soon persuaded youths in the crowd to pose with the seized weapons. The youths donned helmets and began to mock-threaten the soldiers. The troops looked even more scared.

It struck Sue as "all a bit childish, but harmless fun." After a while the photographers left. Sue didn't think the incident was worth reporting to the student leaders on Tiananmen Square. Some four miles south of where Sue kept watch, Jenny Guangzu and her father emerged from the hospital where he worked and walked toward the square. Both wore white coats to distinguish them. In the early hours of the morning, Jenny had brought her year-old son, Peter, from the square to her father's tiny apartment at the rear of the hospital. One of Professor Guangzu's nurses had volunteered to look after the child, freeing Jenny to return to the square.

Father and daughter continued an argument that had begun in the apartment. He felt it was time for Jenny to return to Los Angeles and resume her studies.

"Things are moving to a new level of uncertainty," her father said.

"All the more reason for me to remain," Jenny said. She smiled at her father. "Besides, you know how much you like having Peter here."

It was true. The professor had spent every available free moment playing with his grandson. He had even brought Peter to his office and pointed out his precious collection of bottled tongues.

On Changan Avenue they were suddenly confronted by men wearing construction helmets and carrying clubs fashioned from chunks of wood. Several were stripped to the waist and appeared to have been drinking. With them were two men operating video cameras.

The men were cursing volubly and saying they would beat up any soldiers they encountered. Professor Guangzu moved to remonstrate. They pushed him aside. Jenny confronted them.

"The students don't need people like you," she said. "You're just troublemakers."

Passersby stopped and joined in, accusing the men of being agents provocateurs. In moments the crowd had grown to hundreds. The men were disarmed and sent on their way with a warning not to harm any of the soldiers. Jenny noticed that the cameramen had disappeared.

Further along Changan Avenue she heard the sounds of explosions and saw clouds of smoke drifting in the air.

"Tear-gas grenades," her father said. With others they ran into an alley.

SAME DAY, SAME TIME
*Washington, D.C.*

Lights continued to burn throughout the night on the top floor of the State Department, where the China Desk analysts worked furiously to prepare yet another briefing paper for Secretary of State Baker. It would form part of his breakfast reading along with other reports from the National Reconnaissance Agency, responsible for collecting satellite intelligence for the Department of Defense, and the National Security Agency. He would also receive a copy of the President's Daily Brief, containing CIA Director Webster's overnight assessment of the situation.

Like Bush, Baker would be in no doubt that China's leaders were finally ready to silence the students' call for democracy.

SAME DAY, SAME TIME
*Beijing*

On Changan Avenue the "action" Barr Seitz, the son of one of Secretary Baker's more senior aides, had waited so long to experience was suddenly erupting all around him. He had been returning with a cameraman from filming in the Muxudi District and had actually been passing Zhongnanhai when several hundred police in full riot gear with tear-gas grenade launchers emerged from the compound's western gate.

They just opened up as they ran, firing point-blank into the crowd," Barr would remember. His cameraman kept his professional discipline, filming the unprovoked attack which sent people scattering. As the students regrouped, the pair found themselves in a deadly crossfire. Retreating before the grenades and the swinging truncheons of the police, they had to duck the pieces of paving stones the demonstrators were hurling. Then, as suddenly as it had begun, the incident was over. On command, the police turned and ran back into Zhongnanhai.

Eyes streaming from the tear gas, people crowded back into Changan Avenue. They displayed their tears with pride and told each other that if this was the best the army could do, then there was nothing to fear.

SAME DAY, LATER
*Tiananmen Square*

Brendan Ward and Brian Davidson were back in the square, two of several score foreign envoys keeping watch. Some had mobile telephones to report instantly any developments to their embassies. News of the tear-gas attack was already being relayed to foreign ministries around the world.

Ward and Davidson had become inured to the stench, the refuse, the feeling, in Ward's words, "that Tiananmen had become 'one big toilet.'" They still had a job to do, to be the eyes and ears of their respected governments. In the seven weeks they had been coming to the square, they had made friends with many of the students. Yet under strict orders from their own superiors, neither Ward nor Davidson was allowed to alert those students to the pincer-movement the PLA was tightening around the city on this fifty-fifth day of the demonstrations.

The two diplomats began to carry out another of their routine checks, walking through the wide underpass that led from one side of Changan into the square. The walls of the underpass had become a vast bulletin board, a jungle of posters and notices. Some announced where people could be found. Others were political declarations. Reading them gave Davidson a clue to the mood of many of the demonstrators.

"A lot more think it's time to pack up," the press attaché told Ward as they picked their way through groups of students who were sprawled exhausted in the underpass.

Even though the light was poor, Ward could see "a lot of them looked pretty sick. They had that flushed appearance that comes from no real sleep or proper food. The air was awful, as if they were lying in their own excrement."

From the square came sudden shouts and the sound of people running.

Davidson and Ward bounded up the steps of the underpass and

emerged back on Tiananmen in time to see a thousand or more soldiers wearing steel helmets and carrying rifles at the ready, rushing out of the Great Hall of the People onto Changan Avenue.

The crowd, about two hundred thousand people, did not flee. The events of the past few hours had once more drawn them back to Tiananmen. To Ward, the great mass seemed to symbolically consume the soldiers. One moment the troops were a disciplined force, the next they had been broken up into small groups, each with its 'minders.' The soldiers were let to the center of Changan Avenue and invited to sit on the tarmac."

Once the troops squatted on the ground, students moved among them, checking their weapons. None was loaded.

The incident had also been seen by Jeanne Moore, the young American reporter on *China Daily*, the English-language Party newspaper.

"The mood changed at once," she noted. "Everybody is very relaxed and cheerful. They keep trying to get the soldiers to sing the 'Internationale.' When that fails, the students encourage them to sing army songs. But that doesn't work either. The soldiers just sit there in the baking sun. People are buying them ice cream and offering them water. It's the weirdest thing."

Seeking a possible explanation for the reaction of the troops, a number of foreign military attachés in the square echoed the conclusion of Horst Lohmann. The military attaché of the German Democratic Republic had seen the *Volkspolezei* of his own country use similar tactics.

"It's called testing the ground," he would say cryptically. "Make the people relax before attacking them."

Watching the soldiers, *Newsweek*'s Melinda Liu was once more reminded of those words of Sun Tzu. Was this indeed a bait to lure the students into a false sense of security?

As the sun lost its heat, the soldiers suddenly rose to their feet and ran back into the Great Hall.

An hour later the hundreds of reporters and TV crews in the square were joined by a tall, white-haired patriarchal figure, Harrison E. Salisbury, the veteran American journalist and author. He had visited China perhaps more times than any other correspondent. He was back to make a documentary for Japanese television. Quickly recognized by many of the students, Salisbury was soon signing autographs.

Watching him stride, still erect and proud at an age most men would "be hanging up their boots," Jeanne Moore thought Salisbury was like a character in Evelyn Waugh's novel *Scoop*.

Salisbury had left the square to return to his suite in the Beijing Hotel when the disembodied voice of Qiao Shi, the country's security chief, once more came over the loudspeakers.

He broadcast an "urgent warning that lawless acts still continue, and have infuriated the officers and men of your army and will no longer be tolerated." He listed a series of infractions: soldiers being threatened and impeded in their lawful duties; their equipment being stolen.

In a cafe on Andingmen Avenue, Sue Tung watched a TV news bulletin. She was stunned to see herself standing near some of the youths who had been persuaded to act as if they were threatening the soldiers. Now the youths were being described as "dangerous counter-revolutionaries who have seized weapons to worsen the rebellion in our city." The onlookers were called "reactionaries" who were supporting the.

Sue's first instinct was to burst out laughing. Then she realized everyone around her was leaving the cafe.

"If the Public Security find you, you will be arrested," an old woman told Sue. "You must hide."

But Sue could think of nowhere to go. She had given up her hotel room days ago to sleep in Tiananmen Square.

There, Jenny saw on the same newscast the group of men she and her father had watched being disarmed. The men were described as plainclothes policemen being stopped from keeping order by the mob. She realized then that "we were being set up."

Further items in the bulletin went on to show photographs of similar stage-managed scenes in several parts of the city.

Watching the newscast, Louise Branson had a "sinking feeling this is it." The tall, fair-haired, thirty-four-year-old correspondent for Britain's *Sunday Times* had earned high praise for her reporting. She turned to her husband, Dusko Doder of *U.S. News and World Report*. and said, "All hell is about to break loose."

"As long as the circuits remain open, we'll go on reporting it," he said cheerfully.

The sound of their small son, Thomas, gurgling happily in his playpen came from another part of their apartment-office, located four miles to the east of Tiananmen Square.

Melinda Liu had left the TV set permanently on in her room in the Beijing Hotel. She divided her time between standing on the balcony overlooking the roofs of the Forbidden City and Tiananmen Square and watching the TV screen. In between she kept up the pressure on the switchboard staff to connect her to her editors in New York. She wanted to warn them that "we all could be in for a long night." But many of the hotel telephone operators, like most of the other staff, had abandoned their posts to go to the square. From her balcony Melinda estimated there could now be "close to a million or more around Tiananmen."

As she once more pleased with the switchboard operator, the TV screen went blank. A caption card appeared bearing the words MARTIAL LAW ENFORCEMENT HEADQUARTERS. An anonymous voice began to speak.

"Citizens of Beijing. We are all facing a most serious situation. Thugs are creating turmoil. At the request of the broad masses of city residents the army will take strong and effective measures to deal with those thugs. They will be shown no softness. But to avoid the innocent being involved in our measures, we ask that all residents should leave the streets and stay away from Tiananmen Square. You must all remain in your own houses until further notice."

Once more the screen went blank.


SAME DAY, LATER
*PLA camp*
*Bao Bi Dian*

Late in the evening Bing Yang and the other soldiers were ordered out of their barracks and marched to the parade ground. The space was dotted with tables. At each one was an army doctor or medical assistant. A loudspeaker announcement explained their presence.

"The situation in Beijing has become medically dangerous. The counterrevolutionaries are spreading disease. To avoid any damage to your health, all of you will now receive an injection to protect you."

When Bing received his shot, he felt a warm sensation through his body. Climbing into a truck, he felt even more determined to deal with the enemies of the people. A magazine of live ammunition was locked in place in his gun; several spares filled the pockets of this fatigues. On the floor of the truck were more boxes of ammunition.

Tan Yaobang, their company commander, gave a final reminder: "Shoot to kill when the order comes."

Bing Yang and the others would be helped to do so by the injections they received. No one would be certain what drugs were used.

At 10:30 P.M., the trucks drove out of the base. Already their "victory" had been proclaimed by the country's state-controlled news agency. An hour before the wire service had distributed a "proclamation": "The glorious army of the people has the trust of the people.

By their great deeds the army has ardently shown its love for the capital and its people, and all law-abiding students. The officers and soldiers of the PLA have once more shown they are the people's own army."

A night of tragedy was under way.

SAME DAY, LATER
*Muxudi District*

Three miles to the west of Tiananment Square at a little after 11:30 P.M., almost twenty-two hours since he had ordered the PLA officer out of the telephone booth on Fuxing Avenue, Daobao was making another phone call to the square.

"Zhendan!" he screamed. "Zhendan—Live fire! Live fire!"

Company commander Tan Yaobang had relayed the order to open fire, which he had received moments before through the headset of his field wireless set. The commander was in the back of a small truck. The order had come from General Yang's headquarters in the PLA situation room in the city's western suburbs. The attack was being directed from there.

The company commander would later justify the order by insisting that "the counterrevolutionaries were armed and dangerous. They had been trying to raise rebellion for weeks. They had been given every opportunity to surrender. In the end we had no alternative but to take firm and decisive action."

Behind Yaobang another burst of automatic fire raked the barricade of buses, trucks, and pedicabs strewn across the street. Already bodies lay on the ground.

"Zhendan!" Daobao screamed once more. Then he dropped the phone and ran to where he had left Cassy, in the gateway of the compound of Building Number 22 and Building Number 24. The high-rises in the center of Muxudi District housed senior Party officers and their families.

When he reached the gateway, Daobao found no sign of Cassy. He assumed she must have fled back into the city when the shooting started.

When the firing began, Cassy had decided the gateway was no longer safe. Despite the rank of those who lived in the high-rises, the soldiers had raked both buildings with gunfire. Cassy, like others, could only assume "the troops were either drugged or gung-ho to the point where they'd shoot at anything."

In a momentary lull in the firing, she dashed from the compound gateway to seek shelter behind a barricade in the road. As she reached it, the shooting resumed. Cassy saw the arriving troops were throwing stun grenades to terrify the crowd crouching around her. The grenades exploded in the air with deafening effect. Then another burst of small-arms fire raked the barricade's jammed-together trucks, buses, and handcarts. The cries of the injured rose above the shooting. All around her people suddenly fell from the murderous fire. Cassy retreated to shelter in a doorway a little further up the street. Standing on a pile of refuse, she could see over the barricade. She would recall, "The troops took their time, often kneeling to fire. They would advance for a few yards, then once more kneel, load, and fire. It was pure murder."

Cassy saw Daobao. He was running diagonally across the street, crouching and weaving like a running back, sprinting toward the barricade. She saw him spin around and fall. At the same moment a huge burst of flame leaped from the barrier as the fuel tanks in the vehicle exploded under the gunfire. A fireball rose into the air. People were screaming in agony, running in blind panic, their clothes on fire. Cassy found it impossible to make herself heard, let alone understood. There was no way she could make her way back to the barrier to reach Daobao. Swept along by the near-demented crowd, she saw other bodies on the ground around him. Several appeared to be burning.

The troops continued to pour gunfire into the backs of the fleeing crowd. Scores more fell.

Among the marksmen was Bing Yang. He had remembered his company commander's order to shoot to kill.

Behind the troops came the first of the tanks, a T-69, commanded by Liu Lee, the brother of one of the student leaders. He smashed through the barrier, scattering flaming wreckage. Behind came halftracks and trucks. Company commander Tan Yaobang reported to headquarters that the advance into Beijing continued unopposed.

As a tank passed the mouth of a *hutong*, gasoline-filled bottles showered over it, enveloping it in flames. Then people swarmed back into the street to launch more gasoline bombs against the other vehicles. Battened down, the tank drove on up the avenue, its machine gun firing long bursts into the retreating crowd. Its tracks passed over more bodies.

The bravery of the people of Muxudi District, Andrew Higgins of Britain's *Independent* later noted, was "extraordinary and foolhardy, as people regrouped against the soldiers, only to face fresh fusillades."

SAME DAY, SAME TIME
*General Logistics Department*
*PLA compound*

Prime Minister Li Peng and Yang Shangkun, along with General Hongwen Yang and other officers continued to monitor the attack from the situation room.

To the west of the city, ten thousand troops were now advancing on a half-mile-wide front. In the east convoy of thirty vehicles led another ten thousand in a similar movement. In the south, a brigade of infantry and paratroopers had slept out of Nanyuan military airbase behind a screen of tanks and raced through the suburbs. In the north of the city, five thousand more troops were sweeping down Andingmen Avenue, systematically destroying the barriers there. Behind them waited an additional seventy-five thousand soldiers. Sue Tung, who had dashed into an apartment building on Andingmen Avenue, saw the soldiers running down the street and felt "suddenly terrified. There was a look about them, as if they were on drugs. A glazed-eyed look."

Troops were being ferried by underground train from Zhongnanhai to the Great Hall of the People. All entrances to the nuclear shelter tunnels in the city had been opened so troops waiting there could make their way up into the city.

Word of what was happening spread like a brush fire. Students who had left the square to go back to their campuses either to sleep or prepare to go on vacation, returned to Tiananmen Square by the fastest way they could. Some commandeered buses and trucks, other pedaled furiously through the alleys. Many just ran. With them came the citizens of Beijing. Construction workers downed tools, housewives left their kitchens. In a pell-mell dash to the square, office workers ran alongside factory hands. Thousands became tens of thousands, who became hundreds of thousands. In an hour a million and more were once more converging on Tiananmen Square. Among them they did not possess a weapon worth its name. All they could do was to scream for the soldiers not to harm the students.

In soft-soled shoes, the soldiers moved almost silently, just the thump of rubber on the asphalt of six-lane Changan Avenue, advancing along the road that slices Beijing in half from east to west. They wore white shirts and green pants and carried small backpacks and metal helmets as well as their assault rifles. They marched swiftly, urged on by platoon leaders counting cadence in the night air. The citizens of Beijing continued to assemble on the streets. Students on bicycles swept them along, windmilling their arms as they rode. Truckloads of workers in yellow hard hats, looking tough, alert, and confident, sped down the city's Second Ring Road, the six-lane highway that encircles the inner city and skirts the diplomatic compound. Behind them drove Edward A. Gargan, a former Beijing bureau chief for the *New York Times* who was back in China to write a book about economic and political changes in the country.

He would write that "the commotion in the streets was intense.... The stutter of automatic weapons cracked in the air. Someone hollered at me, 'they're firing at children!' A man, almost hysterical, said that he had seen thirty people shot, old people, young people."

Close by, Associated Press photographer Mark Avery had been dragged by a crowd to take a photo of a dead man. "Show the world what is happening!" screamed the crowd. Avery's photo ended up on the cover of *Time*.

From the PLA situation room, Prime Minister Li Peng continued to relay reports to Deng Ziaoping, whose compound was now guarded by over a thousand soldiers. They were already shooting at anyone they spotted, including women and children who were hurrying home from Tiananmen Square in obedience to the broadcast ordering them to do so.

SAME DAY, SAME TIME
*Hospital for Traditional Medicine*

The wail of ambulance sirens announced the arrival of the first casualties. Though it was years since he had worked in the emergency room, Professor Guangzu realized his presence would help. Many of the younger medical staff were visibly nervous. He walked among them, speaking softly and calmly.

"Think of this as any other disaster," he repeated.

"But I have no experience of dealing with bullet wounds," said one doctor.

"Then watch me," Jenny said. She knew the knowledge she had gained in Los Angeles treating victims of violent crime would be invaluable.

Then there was no time for reassuring conversation. The ambulance crews were wheeling in the first victims. In minutes every emergency room bed was filled. The wounded were placed on the floor, then out in the corridors. Almost all had bullet wounds in the back. Several died before they could receive medical attention. Their bodies were quickly taken away by relatives.

By midnight Professor Guzngzu estimated that over sixty victims of gunshots had been admitted. And still the ambulances were arriving. He would remember "feeling nothing, not anger, not shock, just nothing. How could any emotion cope with what was happening?"

He turned to deal with another patient, using the techniques of traditional medicine to cope with gaping wounds. Behind him Jenny used the surgical methods she had learned in Los Angeles.

Elsewhere, news correspondents such as Keith Morrison of NBC were calling the city hospitals to establish casualty figures. Morrison was to remember "talking to a student nurse in one of the hospitals. She said soldiers were pulling life-support systems from the wounded. She ran from the emergency room after she saw soldiers fighting with the staff and soldiers shooting the doctors."

As the night wore on, the reports of dead and injured grew. The Capital Hospital, a few blocks from Tiananmen Square, had received 121 injured and 46 dead by midnight. The Children's Hospital, a three-mile ambulance drive from Changan Avenue, had received 150 victims; 43 were pronounced dead on arrival, and many of the remaining 107 were in critical condition. The Xuanau Hospital, a mile south of Tiananmen Square, had accepted 38 seriously wounded and 16 bodies. The Railway Hospital, three miles to the east, had admitted 172 casualties, of whom 61 would die. At Hospital No. 2 on Youfung Avenue, to the west of Tiananmen Square, 107 victims arrived in the two hours following the shooting in the Muxudi District. Most of the victims from there had been taken to the nearby Fuxinn Hospital, 284 injured and 119 dead.

In all, Beijing's thirty-seven hospitals admitted about 4,000 dead or injured before midnight this Saturday, June 3.


SUNDAY, JUNE 4, 1989
*Andingmen Avenue*

Four miles north of Tiananmen Square, Sue Tung told herself that if she were to die, she wanted "a record left of the moment." From her purse she produced a small tape recorder her boyfriend, Rod, had given her before she left California. Sue placed it on the window of the room in the apartment in which she had found shelter for the past hour. The family who had brought her here stared in wonder. She could hear the mother whispering to her husband that Chinese who went abroad acquired some very peculiar ways.

From below in the street came the sound of tank tracks. They had been grinding down the broad avenue for the past hour, crashing over one makeshift barrier after another. Now, a little after midnight, a tank had stopped before a more substantial obstacle. Buses and trucks had been piled one on top of the other by a couple of bulldozers. To the tangle had been added tons of rubble and huge planks of wood. The great barrier blocked the way into the city.

The order of the tank commander was followed by the roar of the vehicle reversing. A little way up the avenue, there was a brief silence, broken by the shattering roar of the tank's main gun blasting a path through the barricade.

The vibration toppled Sue's recorder off the window sill into the street. From below came excited voices. Some of the soldiers following behind the tank had found the recorder and were shouting up at the windows, demanding to know who owned it.

Sue shrank back into the room A burst of gunfire flashed across the adjacent building windows. Then came the sound of the tanks grinding forward through the breached barrier. Behind them ran the soldiers. To Sue it sounded as if thousands were running past her window, firing at random and laughing as they did so.

"They sounded more than ever like crazies, as if they were drugged to the eyeballs," Sue would recall. "They laughed even louder when they heard people who had been hit, screaming. Their laughter was more frightening than the shooting."

SAME TIME, A LITTLE LATER
*Changan Avenue*

Reporter Edward Gargan could see an armored personnel carrier ablaze near the Forbidden City. People were heaving cardboard boxes and blankets onto the searing metal surface. Gargan photographed the fractured silhouette of the vehicle's .50-caliber machine gun pointing crazily into the starless sky. Nearby, buses were on fire, their window frames white with flames billowing from the vehicles' innards. Another bus rocketed through the throng on Changan Avenue, its driver wrestling with the huge steering wheel as he careered to the entrance of the Forbidden City and parked the vehicle to block any troops from emerging. Over the heads of the crowd flashed the blue lights of some of the city's 780 ambulances, all now ferrying the dead or wounded to hospitals.

Then people stopped, starring open-mouthed at the apparition calmly walking down the center of Changan Avenue. A woman with long black hair, wearing a spotless white satin dress, moved through the crowd, swinging a white patent-leather purse. Gargan "watched her for a moment, stopped by the sight of her effortless progress, her studied obliviousness to the building storm." Then, all too quickly, she was gone, turning into one of the alleys.

From the west came the thunder of engines and the churn of tank tracks. As if mesmerized, the crowd turned and saw, far down broad Changan Avenue, closely set pairs of headlights. The tanks were advancing six abreast, the barrels of their guns almost parallel to the ground. In the gap between the vehicles were troops firing up the avenue. From the east more tanks were appearing, with more troops shooting.

Edward Gargan saw "not more than a hundred people forming a thin line, not linking arms, but standing quietly. I ran up behind them. I wanted to see their faces, to look in their eyes, to see the people who stood unarmed in front of the Chinese army. The people, baby-faced students and weathered workers, gazed toward the army without fear. Suddenly there was a sharp popping sound, then a rattle, like fire-crackers going off in a neighbor's backyard. Some people in front of me fell to the ground, awkwardly, as if broken apart."

Watching the Dantean scene, Jonathan Mirsky, a distinguished China specialist, whose reporting these past weeks had been a benchmark for one of Britain's national Sunday newspapers, *The Observer*, remembered the words of a tank commander. The officer had told him a few days before that "the students were like his younger brothers and sisters, but said they were also his *duixima*, his target. Why? Because Deng Ziaoping, who was giving the orders 'is like my father.'"

The unreality of the scene was summed up for Mirsky by the voice howling out of the loudspeakers around Tiananmen Square. Now the implacable announcer was repeating two reminders: "These are disorderly times. Look out for pickpockets"; and "The People's Liberation Army loves the people. The people love the PLA. Only bad people do not love the army."

Already the first bodies were being stacked by troops on Changan Avenue, doused with gasoline, and set alight. In the early hours of Sunday morning several such pyres were ablaze. By a quirk of the wind, the stench of burning flesh carried over the walls of Zhongnanhai.

SAME TIME,
*Tiananmen Square*

The young American teacher, Barr Seitz, found himself in a new role: on-the-spot reporter, broadcasting live to the ABC radio network in the United States. A short while earlier the network's executive producer had told Barr to use his mobile phone as a microphone. "Just tell us what you see, as you see it," the producer had instructed from his improvised control room in a bedroom in Beijing Hotel. Barr's colleagues had already withdrawn from the square.

Loping through the already panicked crowds, Barr was faithfully following his orders.

"I am standing near the Great Hall of the People. As I watch, all its doors suddenly open and hundreds of troops pour out. They are all helmeted and armed. They're forming lines and coming down the steps, guns at the ready. Oh my God, people are throwing rocks and sticks at them. This is the start of a riot in the square. People are so worked up, so frightened, that they're just totally panicking. From the pediment Wuerkaizi, I think it's him, is calling out 'don't get those soldiers angry. They've got guns!' Nobody is listening. The soldiers are still coming on down the steps. It's real scary to watch them. Just advancing on in their hundreds, row after row, guns extended. People are backing away. Now there's a new situation developing. An armored personnel carrier has just come up Changan and swung into the square. People are attacking it with sticks, as if they would beat it into the ground. In the distance I can hear a new sound. It sounds like more tanks coming up Changan from the west. Somebody is saying it *is* tanks. I'm running on to Changan to see what's happening."

Behind him the armored personnel carrier had been set alight by gasoline bombs. As its two-man crew tried to scramble to safety, one was bludgeoned to death, the other rescued by, among others, Liu Gang, the brother of a T-69 tank commander. The young student kept saying to the terrified crewman that it was not students who had killed his companion, but government-sponsored "troublemakers."

As Barr reached Changan Avenue he heard a volley of shots coming from in front of the Great Hall; unable to see if the troops were firing into the air or at people, Barr reported only the sound of gunfire.

Towering over those around him, he could see some distance down the broad avenue. What he saw tested his nerve.

"Tanks. I can't see how many, but many. Each time they reach a barricade they crush it. They are rolling over everything. Buses that have been upturned, trucks, pedicabs, everything. Behind them are soldiers. They are marching in orderly lines, firing from the hip into the buildings, into the mouths of the alleys. They just load and fire, load and fire. It's like a turkey shoot for them. All around, as you can hear, people are screaming at them, 'Why are you attacking the Chinese people? Why are you killing us?' The army seems to be behaving as if it is facing another army, and not a bunch of civilians using sticks and stones."

Barr felt something whistle past his face. Behind him a woman fell, shot through the head by a bullet.

Close by, reporter Edward Gargan dived onto the pavement and began to crawl to safety.

"Two young men ran by me furiously pushing a bicycle cart. On the cart a man lay bathed in blood. More people ran by, carrying a woman whose shoulder was soaked red. There were some screams, but now I cannot remember many. Instead, there was a silent anger and a frenzy to move the wounded to the ambulances. A chant of '*ji shao shu, ji shau shu*'—'very, very few'—erupted from the mob, which regrouped in straggly lines of forty to fifty to face the troops. Again a wave of people moved to meet the army, and again the rifles cracked. More people fell.

"I ran farther east, past the edge of the square. Helmeted troops ran around the line of tanks, their engines thundering as they crept forward. Another bus sped through the retreating crowed, young men leaning from the windows waving bamboo poles fixed with crimson flags, the driver, in a snow-white headband, barreling suicidally toward the oncoming tanks.

"*Ba gong, ba gong, ba gong*,' the crowd chanted. 'Strike, strike, strike.'"

"People swarmed by me, some moving to the square. Many were weeping. Now the sound of gunfire was almost continuous. Threads of yellow light shot from the southern edge of the square, machine-gun tracer bullets, I later learned.

"I stopped a young man to talk for a moment. 'I don't believe it,' he said, his voice shaking. 'How is this possible? How could we prepare?' He stopped abruptly as another young man lying face down on a cart, blood seeping through his clothing, was pushed past us. The first young man put his hands on his face. 'You must support the Chinese people,' he said, turning to me. 'You must go to your country and support the Chinese people.'"

SAME TIME
*Washington, D.C.*

In the White House, in the State Department, out at Langley, President Bush and his key advisers continued to hear the live reports of the massacre being broadcast by the radio networks. They were also receiving reports from U.S. diplomats and CIA agents. Yet no one, not President Bush, Secretary of State Baker, or any of their aides, at once publicly deplored the carnage, or even called the Chinese embassy to formally protest what they could clearly hear was happening.

A LITTLE LATER
*Tiananmen Square*

On Tiananmen Square, Edward Gargan had become numbed by the wail of the crowd: "*Si duo le, si duo le!*" "Many are dead, many are dead." All around him the cautious and highly experienced reporter heard people say bodies were being burned with flamethrowers.

Louise Branson gathered impressions for her next report to the *Sunday Times* in London.

"They're building another barricade beneath our window. People have dragged one of the trucks filled with suddenly frightened soldiers to form a barricade."

The crowd had marshaled them to one side of the barricade and were trying to persuade them to desert.

Suddenly an armored personnel carrier raced down the street. To Louise it seemed the driver was intent on killing as many as he could. It plowed into the crowd, scattering soldiers and civilians alike, and overturned the truck. Bodies flew everywhere. The carrier continued on its way.

"A man lay dead, completely flattened, with a pool of blood oozing from where has head had been. Two soldiers and three civilians lay clearly dead, many others were wounded."

She knew that she had witnessed "just one small incident in a bloodbath."

Melinda Liu of *Newsweek* crouched low on Tiananmen Square. From further down Changan Avenue, near the intersection with Zhongnanhai, came continuous gunfire. "Heavy stuff, machine guns, mixed with the *putt-putt* of automatic rifles. The reviewing stands in front of the Forbidden City are covered in smoke, Mao's portrait looks like it could go up any moment. There are vehicles on fire. The dead and wounded are everywhere. Not enough ambulances, so pedicabs are being pressed into service. The soldiers on Changan Avenue continue to shoot. Others are in trucks, which they use as firing platforms, driving past the square and pouring down a deadly fire," noted Liu.

She ran back down Changan Avenue to the Beijing Hotel, to file her latest eyewitness account. She passed several bodies, and more than once her feet skidded in pools of blood. If anything the shooting had become more intense and was coming closer to the square.

Jeanne Moore had been at the Monument to the People's Heroes when news came of the shooting in Muxudi District. Since then she had remained close to the pediment, observing the student command structure reacting to the unfolding tragedy.

"The mood is surreal. People are dying, and here they are talking at 2:00 A.M. of holding a news conference to once more attack Li Peng. There is no sense of reality," Jeanne noted.

Now, thirty minutes later, Chai Ling had led the other visibly exhausted students to the statue of the Goddess of Democracy.

Despite the fatigue lines around Chai Ling's mouth, her eyes glowed. She was now the undisputed leader of the student movement. Even Wuerkaixi had conceded she was in command.

Wuerkaixi's bombast and ebullience had gone: in their place was a frightened young man, repeatedly saying that the soldiers would kill him.

Wang Dan remained his usual controlled self, but behind his glasses his eyes looked heavy and defeated.

The remaining half dozen student leaders were now mere ciphers for Chai Ling.

Fifty yards away from the Democracy statue, the troops were still firing into the crowd.

"People are running like wild animals," Jeanne scribbled. "Yet Chai Ling and the others seem to be touched by some magic protection. No bullets come near them. They just march on, serene and indifferent to what is happening. They seem to be living on another plane, perhaps in another world."

Reaching the statute, already pockmarked by gunfire, Chai Ling addressed her companions. She was dedicating this spot as the site of "the University of Democracy." In years to come, she trilled, people would stand here and know the meaning of freedom. Her voice rising, she pronounced an oath.

"I swear to use my young life to protect Tiananmen Square. Our heads may be cut off, our blood may flow, but the People's Square must not be lost."

One by one, the other student leaders repeated the words.

As they turned away, Cassy staggered into the square. She had run all the way from Muxudi, a distance of three miles. She started to tell them what had happened to Daobao, then she fainted. Meili and Yang Li waved down a pedicab and told the driver to take Cassy to the nearest hospital. As she was loaded onto the back of a cart, a few spent bullet casings fell from her hand.

On Changan Avenue, Barr Seitz had also picked up several casings. He wanted a souvenir of this night as a makeshift radio news reporter.

"Bullets are smashing glass and brickwork all along the avenue," he told ABC's radio audience. "There are fires everywhere. The biggest one is in front of the Forbidden City, where the blaze is casting a great fiery glow on the face of Mao's portrait. It would be interesting to know what he would think of all this. We're getting tragic reports all the time. A mother has just gone running by screaming that her husband and son have both been killed. There is a story that the soldiers have gunned down a row of schoolgirls outside Quanjude, the city's most famous roast-duck restaurant. There are so many stories. All I can tell you is that the people are fighting back with stones and bottles. Whenever they get their hands on a soldier, they beat him mercilessly. But this is really a no-contest. The soldiers are well equipped. Even as I speak, another convoy of armored troop carriers is coming up the avenue."

On the corner of Jianquomen Avenue, two miles to the east of the foreign legation quarter, Brian Davidson watched an advancing army column come to an inglorious stop. Nails and broken glass liberally sprinkled on the road had punctured the tires of their trucks. The troops disembarked and began to jog toward Tiananmen Square. Davidson estimated they numbered two thousand.

Away to his right, from just behind the main railway station, came the sound of more tanks turning on to Changan and heading toward the square.

To Davidson, "It was a grim showpiece of military power, not just designed to quell the students, but the whole country. A quarter of the world's population was being told what to expect if they ever dared again to ask for democracy, or anything else the leaders did not approve."

A couple of miles away on Wenjin Road, to the east of Tiananmen Square, the CIA officer known as Tom sat in a car with diplomatic number plates and watched another column of trucks pass. From time to time the vehicles slowed long enough to allow soldiers to jump into the road and remove all the student banners and posters from the walls. These were piled up in the street and set on fire.

From her vantage point in the Beijing Hotel, Louise Branson watched "four people fall dead under a fresh burst of gunfire. Everywhere there were burning buses, wrecked military vehicles, twisted metal barriers, and blood. A student truck drove past, three bloodied corpses displayed on the back. It stopped every few yards. A young man with a bullhorn called for people to see for themselves the horror perpetrated by the People's Army."

Other reporters, including NBC's Keith Morrison, continued to try to measure the massacre in terms of the numbers admitted to hospitals. As hospitals in the center of the city filled to overflowing, victims were being taken further and further afield. By the early hours of Sunday morning, the well-equipped Andima Hospital, fourteen miles north of Tiananmen Square, had received 196 gunshot victims; 41 had died despite the efforts of the surgeons. Three miles to the east of the square, the dozen doctors and seventy nurses on duty at Hospital Number 4 found themselves unable to cope with 177 casualties, all serious emergencies. Normally they could have transferred their overflow to one of the other four nearby hospitals. But they were also swamped, having among them 700 victims.

Professor Guangzu and his daughter, Jenny, were working "like demons. We all were," she would recall.

Matters were made worse by the number of wounded who had been taken home by families fearing troops would invade the hospitals to kill the survivors. Now, realizing that the wounded were dying from their injuries, relatives had come to the hospitals to plead for doctors to make house calls. They were told their only hope was to bring their loved ones back.

They had begun to arrive in handcarts and stretchers, or carried on mattresses. They lay on the floor, joining all the others needing urgent attention. Throughout the city's hospitals, the number of dead and injured continued to climb. No one had precise figures. There was no longer time to keep them.

Down on the northwest corner of Tiananmen Square, close to the

Great Hall of the People, Jeanne Moore watched yet another column of troops. They looked pale, as if they had spent some time underground. They carried assault rifles.

At 3:00 A.M., the metallic voice of Qiao Shi bellowed forth. "A serious counterrevolutionary rebellion was broken out. The People's Liberation Army has been restrained for some days. However, the counterrevolutionary rebellion must now be resolutely counterattacked."

Immediately Chai Ling responded. "There is no revolution! Many students, workers, and ordinary citizens have asked the student command for permission to use weapons. We share their rage at the attack on the innocent. But we remain true to the spirit of Hu Yaobang. We uphold the principle of peaceful demonstration."

Even as Chai Ling spoke, Jeanne could see people seizing whatever came to hand, ready to defend themselves against the next attack.

It came with a suddenness and ferocity that left no room for resistance. The troops at the northwest corner were joined by others coming from Zhongnanhai compound. At the same time several hundred paramilitary police, armed with long wooden stakes, swept out of the Forbidden City. Someone threw a gasoline bomb toward them. It exploded in midair, shot to pieces by a burst of gunfire.

The troops moved at a walking pace firing nonstop into the crowd on the edge of the square. Behind came tanks. Advancing up Changan Avenue from the east was another force of troops, firing into buildings and sidestreets. Passing the Beijing Hotel, they ranked its balconies, driving Melinda Liu to duck for cover.

On the square, Barr Seitz realized he was "probably the last foreign journalist still broadcasting. My producer was yelling on the mobile for me to get the hell out of there. With my height I was a good target."

But Barr continued running toward the Monument to the People's Heroes. He wanted to convey the words of Chai Ling to his audience. With his fluent Mandarin he had no difficulty translating them into English.

Her voice somehow rising above the continuous firing, Chai Ling continued to try and reason with the army.

"You are our brothers! You promised you would not use violence against the people! Please do not break that promise!"

A volley of shots answered her. On Changan Avenue, still more buses burned against the walls of the Forbidden City. A great pall of smoke drifted toward Zhongnanhai. Through it came the constant muzzle flash of guns firing.

Barr's producer was still screaming for him to pull out. But Chai Ling had chosen this moment to attempt to rally the students with a story.

She was "like a teacher addressing an unruly class," Barr would recall. "She asked the students to ignore everything and gather round. Incredibly, such was her charisma that they did."

When there were several thousand around the pediment, she bagan, one hand on the hips of her faded jeans, the other holding a microphone close to her lips. She spoke calmly.

"There was once a colony of a billion ants living on top of a hill. One day their hill caught fire. The ants formed a giant ball and rolled down the hill. Those on the outside were burned and crushed to death, but the majority inside survived. Fellow students, we in the square, we are the outer layer of people. We know deep in our hearts that only with sacrifice can we save the Republic."

Close to tears, Barr joined with them in singing the "Internationale." Then he ran from the square. Over the loudspeakers, Chai Ling was saying that those who wished to stay could do so, but those who wanted to leave could now go.

Renewed gunfire drowned out everything else. It was the signal for Wuerkaizi to board an ambulance, already filled with four people with bullet wounds. Later he would say: "I left because I knew if I did not, students who had remained just because of me would now die."

Like much else about Wuerkaixi, where he went would remain his secret. When he next emerged in public it was in Paris. He would steadfastly refuse to confirm or deny the persistent story that French intelligence smuggled him out of China.

As he ran, Barr wondered if he would be able to escape. The entire square was now surrounded by troops who were systematically firing into the crowd.

But now an unlikely negotiator had emerged to try and stay their hand. Hou Dejian, the pop singer, had abandoned any pretense of a hunger strike. With the verve and showmanship of someone used to making an entrance, Hou emerged on the pediment. Grabbing one of several microphones he shouted: "Testing, one, two, three" and then launched an appeal for the crowd to give up all their weapons.

"Show them you will obey," Hou cried.

And they did. All over the square, people dropped what weapons they had. Convinced he could stop more carnage, Hou commandeered an ambulance and ordered it to drive to the north side of the square. There he told a political commissar he had come to "negotiate an orderly withdrawal." The students would leave the square if there were no more firing. The commissar ordered a ceasefire and then disappeared into the Great Hall of the People to consult with his supervisors.

Suddenly the square was plunged into darkness as the streetlights went out. Flares from burning vehicles lit the scene. Thirty minutes later the commissar returned and announced that if the students left at once they would not be attacked. Hou hurried over to the pediment and once more pleaded with the students.

"You have made your point. You have shown you are not afraid to die. So now leave."

A wave of uncertainty swept the students. There were calls for a vote. Others said it would be a "betrayal" to leave. They called for Chai Ling. But she refused to come to the microphone. No one knows why.

The lights came back on. Again, no one knows why. The students saw that the soldiers had moved further into the square. With them was a PLA commando unit, faces blackened, wearing camouflage and combat boots. They had bayonets fixed to their rifles. They raced to the Monument to the People's Heroes and began to smash the microphones and other equipment.

The students had lost their voice and their platform. Their fifty-five days on the pediment were over. That was the moment their hope for democracy died.

On the largest square in the world lay the bone-white shards of the Goddess of Democracy, which had been faithfully modeled on the Statue of Liberty.

# 22

## A Time of Pain

SUNDAY–TUESDAY, JUNE 4–6, 1989
*Beijing*

In the hard light of a new day, the carnage on Changan Avenue became clear. Along a ten-mile length of the great avenue lay the bodies of scores of men, women, and even children. Many were heaped into funeral pyres by soldiers. No doubt the soldiers were not anxious to dispose of corpses in this way under the gaze of foreign reporters watching from the balconies of the Beijing Hotel. So they were loading the dead around Tiananmen Square aboard helicopters and carrying them to the hills to the west of the city.

From there the stench of burning flesh had begun to drift back across the city, adding to the charnel-house smell of the smaller pyres on Changan Avenue. Brian Davidson, the British Embassy press attaché, thought the air around the Nazi concentration camps must have been as sickening.

Like almost everybody else, Davidson was numbed by the ferocity of the Chinese response. Uppermost in his mind was the fate of the students, especially their leaders. Davidson feared that the sporadic gunfire still coming from the north of the city, where most of the university campuses were, boded ill for them.

The student leaders had left Tiananmen Square separately, as they had planned they would, to avoid being captured as a group.

Reaching the labyrinth of alleys on the far side of Changan Avenue, Chai Ling went to the first of a chain of safe houses set up by the student leaders for just such a contingency. There she changed her clothes and put on a wig and a pair of steel-framed glasses. She

293

was ready for the next stage of her long journey. She was taken by pedicab through the southern suburbs of the city, her driver successfully talking them past several military roadblocks, claiming they were on their way to visit a dying relative in the village of Guan just outside the city limits.

By noon Chai Ling was hidden in Guan in another safe house. When she had eaten, she insisted on preparing a tape for the country's students. That night it was hand-carried by road and rail all the way south to Canton. From there it was smuggled the short distance into Hong Kong. Two days later, Chai Ling once more addressed not only her fellow students, but the entire world over a Hong Kong radio station.

"I am Chai Ling," she began. "I am still alive. Ours was a peaceful protest. The ultimate price of a peaceful protest was to sacrifice oneself. Arm in arm, shoulder to shoulder, we sang the "Internationale" and slowly walked toward the Monument to the People's Heroes. We sat quietly at the monument awaiting with dignity the arrival of our executioners. We realized that what was happening was a conflict between love and hate and not a battle of brute forces. My compatriots, even at the darkest moment, dawn will still break."

Wang Dan did not hear her broadcast. After leaving Tiananmen Square, he returned to Beijing University to collect some of his favorite books to take with him into hiding. Waiting for him was the senior political officer on campus, Pang Yi, with a number of his staff. They arrested Wang Dan. He was taken to Public Security headquarters a few blocks from Tiananmen Square. Later that day his interrogation began. It would last many weeks.

During Sunday other student leaders were brought in. One of the first was Liu Gang. His Western-style sports clothes were in tatters. His face bore marks of the severe beating he had received when he was arrested at Beijing's main railway station. Just before he boarded a train for Shanghai, a security agent had recognized him from the days in 1986–87, when Liu Gang had also been a student activist.

Yang Li, whose brother, Bing, had taken part in the massacre, and Li's girlfriend, Meili, were also arrested at the train station. They had been trying to catch a train to Li's village on the banks of the Yangtze River. Instead they found themselves incarcerated in basement cells in the public security headquarters.

Forty-seven students were brought there in those first few hours after leaving Tiananmen Square. Almost all showed signs of having been beaten.

Bing Yang had been among the troops occupying Tiananmen Square. They had been recalled to barracks at 7:00 A.M. to have a meal of rice and pickles. They had then gone to sleep, with the praise of company commander Tan Yaobang for a job well done echoing in their ears. Not for a moment, Bing would later say, had he or the other soldiers had doubt about what they had done.

On Andingmen Avenue, twelve miles north of where the students were held prisoner at police headquarters, Sue Tung was planning her escape. At dawn the sound of gunfire had eased outside the apartment block where she was hiding. The family who had sheltered her was now as anxious as Sue was for her to be on her way out of the city, beginning her long journey back to Sacramento.

Sue had thought of telephoning Rod to reassure him she was alive, but the nearest public phone was several blocks away. Then she remembered that because of his position at the military academy Captain Instructor Jyan had a telephone in the apartment he shared with his mother. The building where they lived was only a short walk from Andingmen Avenue.

Profusely thanking the family, Sue stepped out onto the avenue. There were bodies on the street, some being hefted onto bicycle carts, others just lying on the pavement. Soldiers stared indifferently at the corpses. Once more Sue was struck by the idea that the soldiers had been drugged. "There was a strange look in their eyes, sort of glazed. I'd seen that look when I'd visited friends in hospital," she said later.

The soldiers ignored her. Trying to walk as calmly as possible, Sue cut through the alleys to reach her destination.

Jyan's mother was astonished to see Sue when she opened the door. Sue decided that despite the old woman being a member of her local street committee, she had no alternative but to trust her. Once inside the apartment, Sue told her why she had returned to China, and what she had witnessed on Tiananmen Square and during the night, ending by describing the bodies she had seen on Andingmen Avenue.

Jyan's mother listened intently and without interruption. Finally she looked at Sue.

"My son had no part of this," the old woman said firmly. "He would never allow the army to harm the people."

Sue felt a sudden tension in the room. She regretted having come; she feared Jyan's mother would call the police. Sue suspected that what she had told the old woman was sufficient to send her to prison for many years.

At that moment Jyan arrived. His appearance shocked both women. To Sue "he looked like a man who had looked into hell."

In little more than a whisper, Jyan described what he had seen when he left the situation room in the PLA compound and drove past Tiananmen Square: tanks and armored personnel carriers rolling over bodies, grinding them to pulp, soldiers mowing down the fleeing crowd, more tanks flattening the bodies.

"So many bodies," Jyan kept repeating. "It is terrible, terrible."

"He spoke for an hour, as if by doing so he could exorcise what he had seen," Sue would recall. "By then his mother had no doubt about what had happened. Her attitude changed. She was like someone who has seen a terrible truth about someone she had trusted, the leaders of China. She started to say they had betrayed the people."

Jyan cut her off, insisting this was not the time for recriminations. What they must do was help Sue leave China so she could spread the word about what had happened.

"The leadership will lie," Jyan predicted. "They will say there was no massacre."

While Jyan and his mother helped Sue plan her escape, his political commissar, Zhang Gong, was already briefing Deng Xiaoping and the other members of the Politburo on the official version of events to be broadcast on radio and published in the *People's Daily*, the official mouthpiece of the Chinese government.

The version began as it would continue to be given.

"The whole people of the capital and the country will understand the fact that the troops did not kill or hurt one single person. In fighting against the counter-revolutionary riot, the troops were forced to defend themselves, but they only fired blank rounds. Four officers, soldiers, and police were murdered brutally by those inhuman protesters. Their brutality cannot be imagined by ordinary people!"

Deng Xiaoping ordered the Big Lie to be promulgated even as the slaughter continued.

Throughout Sunday, June 4, the gray-brown haze over the city thickened and grew more obnoxious as the smoke from the funeral pyres added to the natural air pollution.

Reporters continued to revise upward the number of dead and injured. By noon all the city's thirty-seven hospitals were completely filled with casualties, the vast majority with gunshot wounds, usually in the back. There were 107 such victims in the city's main children's hospital, all under the age of fifteen.

The Friendship Hospital reported 134 admissions: Tongren Hospital, 198: Xyum Hospital, 209: Hospital Number 1, 181. Even the city's two hospitals specializing in treating infectious diseases had between them admitted close to 400 wounded.

By noon the totals were 6,500 wounded and 4,000 dead.

No one could be certain of the numbers. The only certainty was that they continued to climb.

Having cleared the square, the army set off in pursuit of the students, who were fleeing northward toward the university campuses. They carried with them the bodies of their fallen. The corpses were displayed on tables in their classrooms and adorned with white paper flowers, a reminder of the bouquets the students had borne to Tiananmen on that day they marched to mourn Hu Yaobang.

By nine o'clock on that Sunday morning, Tiananmen Square had become an armed camp. Twenty thousand troops and over a thousand armored vehicles guarded its ninety-eight bloodstained acres. Every few yards was the same sign: MARTIAL LAW AREA. ENTRANCE STRICTLY FORBIDDEN.

Hundreds of troops were stationed outside the Beijing Hotel. In the hotel compound small groups of people stood and watched. They were orderly in their behavior.

Edward Gargan was one of the correspondents running through the upper floors of the hotel, trying to find a better vantage point for observing the square. "We tried locked door after locked door. One door opened into an office full of Chinese security officers with walkie-talkies. We rushed to the balcony, but the security people forced us back. Racing back down the hall, we found a stairwell to a fire-escape that led to the roof. Shoving aside planks that had been piled on the exit to block access, we ran to the edge of the roof. Chinese security people on another corner of the roof began moving toward us. We stared for a minute, perhaps two, toward the square, the scene of the previous night's carnage."

At one minute past ten, without warning, the soldiers positioned outside the hotel opened fire on the crowd that had gathered in front of the building. Scores of people fell dead. An ambulance called to the scene was machine-gunned. It burst into flames, its crew killed by the gunfire.

All over the city similar unprovoked attacks were taking place.

At the Hospital for Traditional Medicine, Professor Guangzu was about to snatch a few hours sleep when troops arrived in the emergency room. They demanded to know if any "counterrevolutionaries" were receiving treatment.

When the professor remonstrated, one of the soldiers shoved a rifle butt in his chest and threatened to execute him on the spot. Jenny rushed forward and pulled her father away. To her experienced eye "the soldiers seemed to be doped. They were extremely high."

With two of the soldiers standing guard over the medical staff, the others entered a postoperative room. What happened there is forever etched in Jenny's memory.

"The soldiers just pulled out all the IVs from our patients." Several would not survive the abuse.

Once more Professor Guangzu urged his daughter to leave China with her small son, Peter. Jenny firmly refused, cutting short further argument by saying "we have work to do."

She had decided that she would remain in China, that in its "hour of darkness" she had an important role to play. She knew she would miss America, but life often demanded sacrifices, she reminded herself.

In their apartment Captain Instructor Jyan and his mother had completed preparations for Sue Tung's escape. His mother had given Sue the only suitcase she possessed, a large battered relic of the old woman's only trip outside the city, to see relatives in Shanghai. She had filled the case with old clothes and bedding. These would provide cover for Sue's story if she were stopped by troops at the railway station: that she was traveling to Shanghai to get married.

Jyan would accompany her to the station. Before leaving the apartment, Sue tried to call Rod. The line was dead. Jyan said the authorities had probably cut all communications with the outside world.

Jyan's mother insisted Sue should eat, and take food with her for the journey. While this was being prepared, Sue turned on the English-language waveband of the small radio in time to hear a brave attack on what had happened. Defying the Great Lie being broadcast in Mandarin on other channels, an announcer told something of the truth in a voice vibrant with emotion.

"A most tragic event has happened in our capital. Thousands of people, most of them innocent civilians, have been killed by fully armed soldiers who forced their way into our city. The soldiers arrived in armored vehicles and used machine guns against thousands of local people and students who tried to stop them. When the army succeeded in overcoming the opposition, they continued to fire indiscriminately at crowds on the street. Some armored vehicles even crushed foot soldiers who hesitated in front of the resisting civilians. We appeal to all our listeners to join our protest for the gross violation of human rights and the most barbarous suppression of the people."

The radio then played Beethoven's Fifth Symphony, the opening notes of which echo three dots and a dash, a symbol for the "V" for victory.

Suddenly the broadcast went off the air. Troops had invaded the studio and arrested the announcer. His fate, like so many others, would remain unknown.

A little while later, sitting on the back of a pedicab and clutching the suitcase, Sue was taken through the streets by Jyan. Because of his uniform, they were waved through the roadblocks. They passed piles of burning bodies. When they reached Changan Avenue, they saw the slaughter was even more widespread. By the time they arrived at the railway station they had counted over one hundred corpses. They had to stop frequently to allow helicopters to land and disgorge more troops before airlifting out some of the corpses.

The station was surrounded by a cordon of troops. Once more Jyan's rank enabled them to pass untroubled. Sue recognized several students from the square being arrested by police and bundled into waiting trucks.

Her ticket purchased, Jyan escorted her to the train. In one of the carriages Sue spotted Cassy Jones.

Cassy had made her way from the hospital to her room in the Friendship Hotel. She had packed her belongings and headed for the station. With her fluent Mandarin Cassy had convinced the soldiers she was an American diplomat traveling to Shanghai on urgent business.

"They were country boys, who had not seen many foreigners," Cassy would remember. "Especially one as ballsy as I felt then."

Sue decided that to travel with a foreigner now would be to attract attention. She wedged herself into a carriage of elderly Chinese.

Jyan formally wished her a safe journey and was gone. She sensed that she would never see him again, and she was right.

On Monday, June 5, fifty-six days after the first demonstrations, the army continued to shoot the people. That morning Melinda Liu of *Newsweek* saw several dozen cyclists outside the Beijing Hotel "simply shot out of hand for biking too close to the troops." Their bodies lay for several hours in the street before they were taken away in army trucks.

That afternoon from a balcony of the hotel, Barr Seitz witnessed an encounter that brought tears once more to his eyes. A young man strode out on "Changan Avenue and confronted a squadron of tanks driving out of Tiananmen.

"He just stood there, arms outstretched, daring the lead truck to run him over while we all watched. The first truck rocked on its tracks, with a great grinding noise. When the tank moved to the right to get around the man, he just went with it. When the tank moved to the left, the guy moved with it. Back and forth. We just held our breath. Then the man climbed on the tank and shouted at those inside. 'Go back! Turn around. Stop killing our people!' Then his friends rushed and pulled him from the tank. The man just walked away as calmly as if he did this for a living."

The footage of the incident Barr's colleagues had shot would become one of the lasting images of the rape of Beijing.

That Monday in Spook City, the building in the U.S. embassy compound that housed the CIA station chief and his staff, operatives were preparing the first analysis of what had happened.

The document was a masterpiece of CIA-speak, presenting its intelligence agents as having forecast events accurately. A part of the draft document read:

"It is widely reported that some of the soldiers were heavily drugged so that they would not be scared by their own action. The use of drugs, however, can only explain the behavior of individual soldiers. It cannot explain some actions of the military as a whole. Soldiers were reported to gun down everybody in sight; they even chased people all the way to back lanes just to kill them. Not only did they try to prevent medical workers from rescuing the wounded, but they even rushed to the hospitals to pull off life-supporting systems from the wounded. This was not trigger-happy, individual behavior, but the carefully planned and organized efforts to kill all the eyewitnesses if possible.

"The government effort to prevent any eyewitness from escaping was also achieved in Tiananmen Square. The square was completely sealed by the military vehicles and troops before the killing started. Though both the Chinese government and some eyewitness accounts mention the negotiated withdrawal of the students from the square, there were some students left in the square. While outsiders did not know what exactly happened inside the square, the potential eyewitnesses were perhaps all killed. The Chinese government have insisted that no one was killed in Tiananmen Square. This is largely because that no one actually saw the killing.

"The postmassacre roundup of student leaders and execution of those participants is a continuation of the 'no eyewitness' policy.

"Given the above analysis, which indicates a violence-maximization policy by the government, the remaining question is, who was actually in charge of all this?

"There was no doubt that Deng was the commander-in-chief. He made the decision to crack down on the student demonstrations on April 25. But in China, it is those who are able to carry out the decision that actually obtain the greatest power and benefit most. On the other hand, it was just impossible for an eighty-four-year-old man to oversee every operational detail.

"What the hardliners needed was not simply the recapture of the square. They needed a redistribution of political power at the top without any moderate elements, not only for the present situation, but also the post-Deng era.

"The hardliners have succeeded, but only for the time being. By removing the moderates from the top, the link between top leaders and the reforming forces at various levels of the society has finally been severed. By so doing, they have polarized the entire political spectrum in China. They have done so with the support from the old guard. It is doubtful if they can continue such a policy without the old guard, given a disastrous economy, a discredited image of the Party, and discontented population.

"In the next few months up to the fortieth anniversary of China's national day on October 1, Chinese leaders have to convince the population that China's economy will be better off with the political crackdown. The prospect, however, is so bad that it will be very difficult, if not impossible, to recentralize the economy, to control the inflation and investment. Failing that, what the Chinese government will face won't be another intellectual revolt, but serious and large-scale social unrest."

The CIA version of events was one of several reports on the massacre that were faxed from the U.S. embassy compound to Washington. They would be endlessly scrutinized by those composing what President Bush was saying would be "a measured response."

It took a full day before the presidential reaction emerged.

On Tuesday, June 6, in an evening news conference, Bush announced he would suspend U.S. military sales to China and end contacts between U.S. and Chinese military officials. He offered to extend the visas of Chinese students studying in the United States. He also recalled a number of U.S. diplomats from Beijing.

Bush then revealed he had tried to telephone a Chinese leader whom he refused to name, to underscore the point that America still viewed its relationship with China "as important, and yet I view the life of every single student as important."

The President admitted the Chinese leader had refused to take his call. "Nonetheless," he added, "there's a relationship over there that is fundamentally important to the United States that I want to see preserved. And so I'm trying to find a proper, prudent balance…and I think we found a proper avenue."

The President then went on to lambaste the regime in Iran for underwriting terrorism. One reporter murmured to a colleague that the United States trade links with Iran were currently zero.

In Washington analyst Joseph Brewer later say, "Bush's implicit message to U.S. corporations with a total of many billions of dollars invested in China was clear. Despite the massacre, they should regard the situation very much as business as usual. The apologists of Kissinger Associates could not have expressed their position more clearly than had the President."

In Beijing and elsewhere in China, few U.S. firms felt it necessary to withdraw their executives as a protest over the killings. And after all, nobody else was doing that. The Japanese, British, and Europeans were staying put. The prevailing mood in the foreign business community was perfectly summed up by George Kenneth Liu, chief executive in China of General Foods Corporation. "We are vigilant but we are not pulling out." George F. Truber, in charge of American Telephone and Telegraph Company operations in China said: "We are not in a panic. We still regard China as a market for the future."

That Tuesday in Beijing, in her apartment in the *China Daily* compound, Jeanne Moore wrote her wrapup story for her American newspaper.

"With so much killing, a death fatigue sets in and the stories people trade of what they've seen and what they've heard can only be endured if they contain distinctively unusual features. The young man whose beautiful face was left in the doorway, or the five provincial tourists who, according to a Chinese journalist, had just arrived in Beijing's main railway station knowing nothing of the situation and eager to see the city, they wandered too close to the soldiers and were mown down. The unthinkable becomes the norm and then even natural."

Jeanne had decided to remain in China for the foreseeable future, in the hope of "being able to report a change for the better."

That same Tuesday, Chai Ling was making her way out of China. Repeatedly changing her disguise, the young student visionary traveled from one safe house to another. Her exact route would remain a closely-guarded secret shared only by a handful. It would be many weeks before she would emerge in Hong Kong. From there she would fly to Paris to join Wuerkaixi.

While Chai Ling wended her way to safety, a young American actress, Debbie Gates, was also making her escape.

She had arrived in China two months before to star in the role of reporter Helen Shaw, an American journalist who had been caught up in the Chinese Civil War in the 1930s, in a feature film to be shot on location some six hundred miles south of Beijing. Her costar was Hollywood actor John Perry.

Filming had all but finished when news of the massacre in Tiananmen Square reached the location. Gates immediately turned on the Chinese crew and its director and accused them of "complicity in the murder of women and children."

The film's producer promptly confined the two Americans to a hotel, well away from the Chinese cast and crew. Gates and Perry were warned they would be imprisoned if they "spread any more lies."

The next day they learned their contracts had been canceled and the Chinese would not help them leave the country.

Finally they escaped from their hotel and went to the local airport. They waited six hours for a flight. Strapped to her body was Gate's diary of life on a Chinese location, along with photos she had taken of local demonstrations in support of the students. The couple flew to Canton. From there they took a boat to Hong Kong, where they stayed for three days, sleeping on the airport floor among the throngs of people waiting for a flight out.

A week later Gates and Perry were back in Hollywood. She was ready to sell her story to the highest bidder among its two thousand producers. There were no takers.

That same boat that brought Gates and Perry to Hong Kong also carried Cassy Jones and Sue Tung out of China.

Sue and Cassy flew home together, landing at San Francisco. Rod was waiting at the airport. Over a celebratory drink they watched the local evening news. The headline story was the defection of Zhang Milin. The young Chinese diplomat had finally walked out of the consulate, vowing he wanted to help China to a better future.

His words were yet another epitaph to the fifty-five days that had shocked the world.

# 23

## *For the Moment*

The world's response to the massacre was vocal but, in practical terms, limited. Public opinion may have made China a pariah, but politically its leadership was barely touched.

A week after the massacre Deng Xiaoping appeared on television, surrounded by his Mao-suited Politburo. The supreme leader looked surprisingly chirpy; there were reports that he had been given a number of blood transfusions. He praised General Yang and other military commanders for crushing the "rebellion" and described the People's Liberation Army as China's new "Great Wall of iron and steel."

In those days after the massacre, people came to the administration building of the Institute of Politics and Law in Beijing to stand before the battered body of a student. His skull crushed, he lay on a table surrounded by blocks of ice. Students filed slowly past, small swatches of black fabric pinned to their sleeves. No one knew the student's name, only that he had died when the army moved into Beijing.

One day the remains were gone. It was another signal that the past was as dead as that corpse.

Weeks after the massacre it was almost impossible to know what had happened. Flowers bloomed along Changan Avenue and the city's other thoroughfares. Shops were as busy as ever. Women, as the city's major announced proudly, "continue to have babies."

A closer look at buildings like the Beijing Hotel showed that the bullet holes had been repaired, but imperfectly. On Changan itself, spruced up and constantly bedecked with Party banners, the millions who cycled along found the smooth ride gave way to a bumpy passage as tires rode over the few remaining furrows of tank tracks. The furrows were what Melinda Liu called an "absolutely small, yet potent, reminder of what had really happened."

From time to time she and the other journalists who reported those fifty-five momentous days in China have returned not just to monitor the physical coverup of what had occurred, but also to continue gathering the recollections of those who experienced the nights of horror, those millions who took to the streets demanding change, asking for democracy. Memories are less easy to erase than tank tracks.

In the months after the massacre Amnesty International and other human rights groups estimate that ten thousand had died and perhaps twice that figure had been injured in the massacre in Beijing. The figures for the rest of China were put at twenty thousand killed and around forty thousand injured. In truth no one could be really sure how many bodies had been burned and how many of the wounded had been snatched from their hospital cots and taken away for interrogation.

The six prisons in and around Beijing were allegedly crowded with students. There were persistent reports that up to three thousand were being held for questioning. Many of those were said to have made abject confessions and been sent to that string of prison camps in the inhospitable heart of the country. Again, it was impossible for even the most diligent reporter or intelligence officer to get precise figures or exact details of the files of those being held.

To all intents and purposes, China had become a closed society, suffocating under a blanket of repression.

During a few brief weeks in 1989 areas greater than the British Isles, with populations larger than those of some European countries, had been in uproar. In the Yangtze Delta alone some sixty million people had raised their voices and taken up the nearest weapon in support of the students. Now they had all been brutally silenced under the pall that had fallen across the land.

But uncomfortable questions were being whispered from mouth to mouth in the alleys of Beijing.

Why had the superpowers, the United States, Russia, Great Britain, France, and West Germany, who had known *beforehand* that thousands were going to be butchered in Tiananmen Square, done nothing to warn or help the students?

The suspicion that the West had sold out the students added to the anguish of those who asked the question. Of course, they had no proof either way.

The first anniversary of the massacre found Dr. Jenny Guangzu still in China. The authorities had told her she was not permitted to return to Los Angeles to complete her studies. In the summer of 1989 she was sent to work in a provincial hospital. Her small son, Peter, accompanied her. They are still there at the time of writing. Her father died suddenly three months after Jenny left Beijing.

By then Barr Seitz had departed from China and returned to the United States. In May 1991, shortly before the second anniversary of Tiananmen Square, Barr's father, Raymond, was appointed United States ambassador to the Court of St. James's. Part of his brief was to help maintain a common Anglo-Saxon policy toward the Beijing regime—that the recent past was over. Barr meantime had found romance—falling in love with a pretty German girl, Brigitte, who, coincidentally, had the same surname as his. Currently they live in Munich, where Barr is learning the hotel business.

Shortly after Barr left China, Cassy Jones was granted a visa to return as a foreign expert at Beijing University. She remained there for six months, during which she tried and failed to discover what had happened to Daobao. Most likely he was cremated on one of the funeral pyres, which burned for a week in the streets of the city and even longer in the hills to the west of Beijing.

Cassy once more left China. She has no further plans to return.

Sue Tung married Rod a few days after she landed in San Francisco, where Shao-Yen Wang has begun a career as a model. Zhang Milin, one of several Chinese diplomats who defected, has found "some problems" in establishing a new life for himself in California.

In China, Captain Instructor Jyan was promoted later in 1989, much to the delight of his mother.

Yang Li, whose brother, Bing, took part in the massacre, was among several student leaders who reached Hong Kong some months after the massacre. He and his girlfriend, Meili were re-leased after two months of detention. They still do not know why they were freed. The young couple remained in Hong Kong until late 1990, when they successfully applied for immigration to Australia.

For a few months they lived together in Sydney until Li took up with another Chinese girl student he had briefly encountered on Tiananmen Square. The couple have no plans to marry. Meili remains single.

Li has written several letters to Bing but has received no reply. Bing Yang remains in the People's Liberation Army.

While those young lives were being rearranged, two former U.S. secretaries of state, Henry Kissinger and General Alexander Haig, and President Bush's brother, Prescott, were engaged in the delicate task of fully reestablishing China as America's most valued trading partner in the next decade.

Haig was currently chairman of Worldwide Associates, Inc., a consultancy with powerful connections in Washington, not least to Kissinger Associates. He was personally conducting discussions to fund new joint ventures with CITIC, the merchandise banking arm of the Chinese government. The value of the proposed joint ventures was put at $4 million.

Kissinger was also in active discussions with CITIC. In September 1989 the *Wall Street Journal* reported that Kissinger Associates "could be on the verge of earning hundreds of thousands of dollars from a limited partnership set up to engage in joint dealings with CITIC."

Prescott Bush, with the full knowledge of his brother, the President, was touring China in September, once more as a consultant to Asset Management, International Financing and Settlement Ltd. He had $60 million to invest in joint-venture agreements. In Shanghai he told U.S. businessmen that "if we don't get back into this market fully here and now, we'll lose out to the Japanese and Germans."

Other businessmen were also beating a path to China. From Baghdad had come Saddam Hussein's arms buyers, seeking Silkworm missiles and other weaponry in preparation for the attack on Kuwait that Saddam was already beginning to plan. China obligingly filled their order books with an arsenal of weapons, paid for in the U.S. dollars China so badly needed.

On August 7, 1990, Chinese weapons formed the spearhead of the attack on Kuwait.

In the months that followed, as America prepared to go to war with Iraq, the importance of China in the administration's strategic thinking became increasingly clear.

China was a permanent member of the United Nations Security Council. Its veto would throttle President Bush's plan to go to war with the full support of the UN. China also knew exactly where Iraq had positioned the arms it had supplied. That information was crucial to the Pentagon as it planned Operation Desert Storm. China, because of its close ties with Iraq's neighbors, could provide a critically important insight into Arab thinking that would not be available to U.S. diplomats.

China, then, had to be accommodated. In Washington, as the clock ticked inexorably closer to war, it became an article of faith that it was "time to put Tiananmen behind us."

From December 1990 onward it became a prime objective for Secretary of State Baker to explore with the Chinese what they wanted in return for their support. Baker was told in a New York meeting with Zhang Tuobin, China's minister of foreign economic relations and trade, that China wanted an end to all trade restrictions imposed after the Tiananmen Square massacre, as well as Washington's help to enter the world trade organization, GATT, and secure for China a full resumption of World Bank lending, suspended since the slaughter.

Baker agreed.

China then provided the United States with data on its military deals with Iraq that NSA satellite surveillance and CIA ground intelligence had not been able to discover.

By early January 1991 the Pentagon had been given the exact location of every Silkworm missile site in Iraq and details of other weapons provided by China. Included in this intelligence data were details of the amount of lithium 6 deuteride—a compound used in the manufacture of the hydrogen bomb—which the Chinese had supplied from its nuclear facility in the deserts of Inner Mongolia.

The United States now possessed all the information it needed to launch a spectacularly successful air war against Saddam's key targets.

A week before the Persian Gulf War started, Beijing informed Washington there was one other matter over which it wanted "understanding." Before the Chinese New Year started on February 15, the Beijing regime intended to try the student leaders it still held. The old men of Zhongnanhai made it clear they neither wanted, nor expected, any official U.S. protest over what would be a series of short trials. The public would be barred from attending. The only crime the accused had committed was to have demonstrated peacefully for democracy.

Despite the passionate plea of the distinguished Chinese writer Liu Binyan, then scholar-in-residence at the Woodrow Wilson International Center for Scholars, for the Bush administration "to stop stroking Beijing's butchers," neither the President nor his aides condemned what was once more unfolding in Beijing. In a passing reference, the State Department confirmed that "at least 1,000 have been sentenced since the troops moved in on Tiananmen." Spokeswoman Margaret Tutweiler, no doubt wishing to be helpful, added that the sentences appeared determined by the degree of remorse shown by the accused.

On an icy cold morning in late January 1991, Wang Dan stood before the People's Intermediate Court in midtown Beijing. He wore the sweatshirt and black baggy pants that had been his distinguishing uniform on Tiananmen Square twenty months before. He had lost weight, and his glasses kept slipping down his nose as he blinked owlishly around the courtroom. Paneled in light-colored wood, it was a stark, functional room. Wang Dan stood before his judges, three middle-aged men dressed in Mao jackets.

When he spoke his voice was little more than a whisper. He offered no defense to the charge that he had attempted to overthrow the Chinese government.

He stood, head bowed, looking shrunken and far older than his twenty-two years. The senior judge explained that one of the court's functions was to "redeem criminals" who oppose the state by re-educating them, by sending them to remote border areas, or prison, where they would be taught that the way back into Chinese society is through a "full understanding" of Marxism, together with a "proper understanding" that the sentence about to be passed was only for Wang Dan's own good.

He was sentenced to an undisclosed term in a maximum security prison in central China. As he turned to leave the court, Wang Dan addressed the judges.

"The series of concrete criminal acts listed in the indictment were objective facts. I keenly regret and feel sorry for the consequences arising from the turmoil and rebellion, and I am willing to assume full responsibility for my actions. I will conscientiously draw a lesson from the past. I will never again create chaos under Heaven."

Then he was led away.

Throughout the day, students came and went, each reciting an act of contrition that seemed so well rehearsed. Liu Gang received four years in a labor camp. Other sentences varied from three to thirteen years. By late afternoon, seventeen students had been sent to prison.

Two months later, on March 20, 1991, a remarkable poem appeared in the *People's Daily*:

East Wind urges plum to flourish its petals, soft as DOWN;
The hawk unfurls its wings, soars far away, WITH the wind.
The moon shines, sheds tears on the LI-ward sea,
And a sojourner in the PENG-hu islands thinks of home.

I'll strive to the END and realize our hopes for the motherland.
The PEOPLE'S gift to me is worth more than millions.
RAGE, impetuous rage, invigorates the good earth,
As we wait for spring to spread all over the land.

The seemingly innocuous words had been penned by a Chinese student in the United States. The words caused a furor after it was studied by Party scholars in Beijing. For the poem was what is known as "a diagonal acrostic," and its literal meaning was "Li Peng step down; mollify the people's anger."

Professor Eugene Eoyang, who teaches comparative literature and East Asian languages and cultures at Indiana University, explained in the *New York Times* the challenge in translating the poem.

"First it must be rendered in a way that demonstrates why the *People's Daily* was eager to publish it. The lines must reflect the 'patriotic devotion of a student sojourner at spring (something like Robert Browning's 'Oh to be in England, Now that April's there'). The second challenge is to hide the protest, yet let it be visible. In the transliteration of Li Peng's name, I resorted to a few devices. His family name, Li, means 'plum'; his given name, Peng, signifies a mythical bird, like a roc, that flies huge distances. But neither 'plum' nor 'roc' conjure up a person's name. To retain Li, I resorted to a phonetic pun in English, and, as there is no phonetic equivalent to 'Peng,' I introduced a reference to 'Peng-hu,' the Pescadores Islands between Taiwan and the mainland, on which a homesick sojourner might be imagined to be brooding. Inevitably, there are some distortions and deletions, but perhaps the spirit of the poem has not been lost altogether."

A month after the poem appeared, reports reached the United States that the editor responsible for publishing it had been arrested.

The reports came at the same time as Li Peng gave what Nicholas D. Kristof of the *New York Times* described as "a vigorous defense" of the Tiananmen Square massacre. China's prime minister concluded his press conference by saying that his government was ready to use similar methods to crush further protests. As he left the conference, called to mark the end of the 1991 session of the National People's Congress, China's rubber-stamp parliament, Li Peng continued to smile and attempt, in Kristof's view, "to foster a more friendly and down-to-earth image." The prime minister was still smiling when a reporter asked him about the poem.

"Not worth mentioning," said the prime minister, adding that Deng Xiaoping, now eighty-six, was "in good health." But even if the country's senior leader was to die, nothing would change, Li Peng assured the reporters. "The Party will remain totally in control."

A few days later the *People's Daily* announced that 72,000 Party members had been expelled, and a further 256,000 "punished." They were deemed to be "unreliable and corrupt." It was the biggest purge in recent years of the 49 million member party.

A week after the Gulf War ended, Qian Qichen, China's foreign minister, announced that all those involved in the "counterrevolutionary rebellion in 1989 have been dealt with." In one of those chillingly memorable phrases that will ensure Qian's footnote in history, he promised: "Those who should be freed have been freed, and those who should have been shot have been shot."

The words were a reminder of the ancient Chinese saying, "By killing one we educate one hundred."

Early in April 1991 Britain's foreign secretary, Douglas Hurd, became the first world-ranking Western diplomat to visit China since the Tiananmen Square massacre. As he was escorted past the square by Qian, the foreign minister reminded Hurd "that the standards of one country or group of countries must not be imposed on other countries." Hurd nodded politely.

Shortly after, ex-President Jimmy Carter visited Beijing. He told Deng Xiaoping that China should now have most-favored-nation trade status with the United States and it was high time to "put the Tiananmen Square tragedy behind us."

A few days later President Bush confirmed he wanted to give China those special trading privileges. Most-favored-nation status fixes tariffs on imports at the lowest prevailing rates, and is not usually granted to communist countries. But the President insisted he did not wish to "isolate Beijing" and indicated he was trying in part to reward China for not blocking actions at the United Nations during the Persian Gulf Crisis.

"I look at the big picture," Bush said. "I look at the support we got from China back in Desert Storm, the importance of China as a country. And I don't want to see us isolate them...I got back to the days when I was in China as the equivalent of an ambassador, and though there are major problems in China, things we don't like about their system, things are an awful lot better than they were back in 1975," the President said.

Meantime, the Bush administration continued to secretly draw even closer to the Beijing regime. Undaunted by the failure of a highly secret mission in December 1989 to Beijing by National

Security Adviser Brent Scowcroft and Deputy Secretary of State Lawrence S. Eagleburger, both old Kissinger Associate hands, Bush dispatched another envoy to China, Robert M. Kinsmitt, the under secretary of state for political affairs. The ostensible purpose of the visit was to hold "candid discussions on human rights, trade, and weapons sales."

Like the Scowcroft-Eagleburger venture, the Kinsmitt mission was also to explore with Beijing the Bush administration's growing fears that Japan was becoming an intolerable threat to U.S. economic interests.

In one of his last actions before leaving office in May 1991, CIA director Webster had approved plans to recruit moles in the boardrooms of Japanese corporations, such as Sony, Honda, and Mitsubishi. Webster had done so on the direct orders of Bush, who has come increasingly to fear that the United States could be embroiled within the next twenty years in an increasingly bitter economic war with Japan, one which could even eventually flare into fighting.

Bush's fears had been synthesized by a most secret CIA-sponsored report, describing the Japanese as "creatures who are amoral, manipulative and live by a controlling culture that is intent on world economic dominance." The same report also described Japan as "a racist, nondemocratic country whose population believes might is right and who feel superior to other people."

Two recent books had helped to fuel Bush's fears of the Japanese. The first, *The Coming War with Japan* by George Friedman and Meredith Lebard, respected American economists, argued that economic competition for markets between the world's two largest economies *will* almost certainly end in war as Japan tries "to force the U.S. out of the Western Pacific." The authors claim that the United States will see this move as Japanese aggression and, as in the 1930s, both sides will engage in a cold war which will eventually end in physical fighting. Some White House aides sensed the President already felt the cold war was coming to some sort of climax.

The second book, by Japanese businessman Shintaro Ishihari, titled *Japan Cannot Say No*, claims that Japan was poised to sabotage American military might by withholding the delivery of crucial microchips.

Bush had ordered his aides to study both books and use them as a reference in the administration's dealings with China. Webster had told his own analysts that nowadays the President increasingly saw China as America's ally in the Pacific against Japan, with its "win-at-any-cost society," where "the poor are downtrodden and there is a systematic discrimination against foreigners."

The President insisted that China must not only have mo
favored-nation status, but in every way possible be drawn ever clos
to his administration to help defeat what Bush saw as Tokyo
aspiration to dominate the world. In that overview there could be no
room for justice for a handful of students.

On Wednesday, April 24, 1991, a group of university students in
Beijing circulated an eleven-page document describing continued
student opposition to the regime. They appealed for "energetic" help
from, in particular, the United States to bring democracy once more
to China.

The document described failed "attempts to brainwash us. During
these sessions we pretend we cannot remember anything that happened on Tiananmen Square."

At the end of the document its authors issued a blunt warning.
"The students of China are no longer scared by blood or by
punishment. The blood that was spilled in 1989 has taken students
from fanaticism to calmness and awareness. We now recognize how
formidable is the process of pursuing human rights and democracy.
But we will pursue them and we will succeed, if not today, then
certainly soon."

The old men who still run China must surely know that the farther
they are from the events of 1989, the closer they come to the next
uprising. Next time they may not be able to crush it.

# *Explanations*

E arly in my career I had the good fortune to work for two of the great editors of modern journalism, Arthur Christiansen of the *Daily Express,* then Britain's foremost mass-circulation newspaper, and Ed Thompson of the *Reader's Digest.* Both were absolutely firm about always using two sources for an important fact, and both believed that attributed reactions such as "felt," "sensed," "thought," "understood," or "believed," must accurately reflect the particular portion of the interview being written up.

Ken Auletta, another veteran of our business—the re-creation of historical events after the dust has settled—has synthesized the whole complex question of primary and secondary sources, on- and off-the-record conversations, and describing an event through the use of unpublished documents, letters, diaries, and file notes. Auletta has written that "no reporter can with 100 percent accuracy re-create events that occurred some time before. Memories play tricks on participants, the more so when the outcome has become clearer. A reporter tries to guard against inaccuracies by checking with a variety of sources."

Luckily for me, the time frame of the story comes when the memory is still clear. That is why a few of those who were directly involved asked for guarantees that their identities would be suitably protected for professional or personal reasons; in some cases the reminder of their experiences still traumatizes them. Those persons chose the identities by which they wished to be known in the text. Cassy Jones and Sue Tung were two who did. Their decision in no way diminishes the honesty of their eyewitness accounts.

In all, some 240 hours of taped testimony were taken.

Immediately after the massacre, interviews were conducted in China, Hong Kong, the United States, and Europe between June and October 1989. Follow-up interviews by telephone and correspondence took place between December 1989 and February 1990. In all some one hundred persons, the vast majority eyewitnesses, were spoken to either directly by me or by researchers acting on my behalf.

All serving intelligence officers insisted they would only speak off-tape and without direct attribution. This is an accepted form of briefing by them, though a word of explanation will perhaps be helpful.

In 1986 I interviewed the late William Casey, then director of the Central Intelligence Agency. We met at the International Club in Washington, D.C., on Friday, March 21, and at the same venue four days later. Casey said he would "mark my card" on how to deal with him and anyone else in the U.S. intelligence community. All information they supplied must be written up as "background," a catch-all phrase that means information provided can be fully used, but not directly attributed.

It worked for the project I was researching at the time; it has continued to do so for this book. Long before Casey's guidance, when I was reporting on intelligence matters for the *Daily Express,* the *Sunday Express,* and the Press Association, Britain's major wire service, I had never subscribed to the canard that intelligence services constantly spend their time and money creating stories to deceive journalists and authors. While all agencies spread disinformation among the more gullible in any profession, they do not do so all the time.

The contribution of the diplomatic community in Beijing is generally acknowledged throughout the text; a few diplomats asked to speak off the record, fearing that direct attribution could embarrass their governments. Special thanks are due to Brian Davidson, Brendan Ward, and Susan Morton. They gave freely of their time and experiences.

A word of similar thanks is due to the martial law authorities in Beijing. They turned out to be surprisingly willing to state their side of the story, that "rebellion" had been in full cry and that the People's Liberation Army had no alternative but to intervene. To support that view, the Chinese authorities provided me with a pass allowing me to visit Tiananmen Square when it was still a proscribed area. There I interviewed Captain Instructor Jyan, company commander Tan Yaobang, and the young PLA soldier, Bing Yang. I was also given a conducted tour of the National Military Academy in the western suburbs of the city, various PLA bases in and around Beijing, and, most gratifying of all, a short visit to Zhongnanhai. At all times the PLA provided translators, and I have no reason to think they were less than accurate in putting my questions and translating the answers.

From April until June 1989, the story was front-page news on every major newspaper around the world. Some of the best reporting was in the *New York Times;* the *South China Morning Post;* and the other Hong Kong-based English-language daily, *The Standard.* However, anxious to obtain a spread of the coverage, I compiled chronologies from the *Los Angeles Times, Washington Post,* and *San Francisco Chronicle.* From Britain I collated the reporting of the *Sunday Times,* the *Independent,* the *Guardian,* the *Daily Telegraph,* the *Times,* and the *Independent on Sunday.*

I was especially drawn to the reporting of Louise Branson of the *Sunday Times,* London, and I express my gratitude for her generosity in making available to me her original stories and background notes for the period. They provided a revealing and invaluable insight.

In assessing the value of what was published, I used the guidelines of that most estimable of investigative authors, William Manchester.

He has written that the only way to successfully approach our kind of work is to accept that no one can ever root out the truth, the whole truth, and nothing but the truth. That is a game lawyers play, and as Bill says, "there is something touching about their naive assumption, that we get the full story by putting a man under oath. In practice, you get very little of it. Anxious not to prejure himself, the witness volunteers as little as possible. The author, with his tape recorder, or shorthand notebook, gets a great deal more chaff, but in the long run, he harvests more wheat too."

Once more, so it was for me.

As so often in the past, colleagues proved accommodating. The Press Association, for which I am a special news features correspondent, a post that allows me to cover stories anywhere in the world, extended my beat to include China. I owe David Staveley and Neal Williams, my editors at the PA, a great deal for their support during those months I spent in the field. Through them my reports from China received wide distribution.

In the end, however, it was colleagues in China who made the book work. First and foremost, I must thank Melinda Liu of *Newsweek.* In the late summer of 1989 she found time in her hectic schedule to sit down with me for a series of lengthy taped interviews. She also provided copies of all her original stories and the telex traffic between her and her editors. Jeanne Moore of the *China Daily* was also a prime source. She gave a lengthy interview, then made available the deeply moving diary she had kept during those fifty-five days in Beijing. Several other Chinese journalists in the city spoke long and frankly, in return for guarantees of anonymity. The book owes much to them.

I also gratefully acknowledge the invaluable help of Barr Seitz. His testimony proved to be that cliché come true, a real treasure trove. He had a born reporter's eye for detail. And his astonishing memory was reinforced by his diary.

In Hong Kong, I was repeatedly helped by Nelson K. Fung, manager of the Broadcast Department at Hill & Knowlton, the international consultancy and public relations agency. His colleague Gordon Chan, senior consultant in Corporate and Government Affairs at the agency, was another valuable source. Deborah Biker, head of the same agency's Creative Services Division, provided unlimited access to news footage and media coverage from China, Japan, Korea, and Indian sources, little of which has surfaced in the West.

Many of the interviews with students who had managed to escape to Hong Kong were conducted in the colony's Kowloon Hotel during September and October 1989. I was greatly assisted by the translations of Suzanne Chan, Tan Li, and, briefly, Gali Kronenberg.

But my greatest support was David Jensen, a former White House correspondent. David still has his tabs on Washington, and time and again he pointed me in the right direction, not only around Capitol Hill, but around the Pacific Rim. He probably has as many good contacts there as any working journalist. Quite simply, without him this book would not have been written.

# *Notes*

### 1. The Tiananmen Trump

This chapter is based upon an interview conducted by the author with Jeanne Moore and on articles in the *New York Times,* Dec. 1, 1990; *Newsweek,* Jan. 6, 1990; *The Times* (London), Jan. 6, 1990; *Independent on Sunday,* Jan. 6, 13, 21, 1990.

### 2. Seeds of Fire

For this chapter I have relied upon my interviews with Melinda Liu, Jeanne Moore, Brian Davidson, and members of the U.S. intelligence community.

### 3. Illusions

For "Illusions" I interviewed Cassy Jones, Jia Guangzu, Jenny Guangzu, and Li Yang, and relied on interview by others of Wuerkaixi, Chai Ling, and Meili Chang. Additional sources were the *China Daily* (all issues for Oct.–Dec. 1989), the letters of Jenny Guangzu and Jia Guangzu, the diaries of Jenny Guangzu and Cassy Jones, and photos by Cassy Jones and Jenny Guangzu. Also helpful was the Emergency Action Plan for the City of Beijing, published by the mayor's office, Nov. 11, 1989.

### 4. Secrets

Various members of the U.S. intelligence community in Washington, D.C., and Beijing were interviewed for this chapter, as well as Melinda Liu, Jeanne Moore, and Jenny Guangzu. James Laracco was also interviewed. Other sources were the diary of Jenny Guangzu, letters to Jenny Guangzu from her father, and a report by Laracco on the economic situation in China.

### 5. The Watch Keepers

This chapter was based on my interviews with Li Yang, Tan Yaobang, Kao Jyan, Zhang Zhen, General Bull, and Susan Morton, and interviews by others of Earl S. Drake, Gerard Chesnee, Nicholas Chapuis, and Charles Malo. Other sources were the *China Daily* (all issues for Oct.–Nov. 1988); the *South China Morning Post*, Dec. 10, 12, 1989; the *Standard*, Dec. 20, 1989; and *The Chinese Secret Service* by Richard Deacon (Grafton Books, 1989).

### 6. States of Mind

For this chapter I relied upon my interviews with Shao-Yen Wang, Kao Jyan, Cassy Jones, and Sue Tung, and various members of the U.S. intelligence community. Other sources were the diary of Cassy Jones, letter of Sue Tung, and screenplay of Shao Yen Wang; the *Washington Post*, Nov. 22, 1988; and the *South China Morning Post*, Nov. 29, 1988.

### 7. The Roof of the World

This chapter is based on my interviews with Li Yang, Tan Yaobang, Bing Yang, and Kao Hyan, and an interview by another of Liu Lee. Other sources were the *People's Daily*, Jan. 2, 1989; the *China Daily*, Jan. 7, 1989; and *The Chinese Secret Service* (Deacon).

### 8. Persuasion

For "Persuasions" I interviewed Cassy Jones, Brendan Ward, Brian Davidson, and Li Yang, and relied on interviews by others of Liu Gang, Wuerkaixi, Ian McGuinness, and Fang Lizhi. Other sources were the *World Economic Herald* (all issues from Dec. 1, 1989–Feb. 1, 1990) and a letter from Fang Lizhi to Deng Xiaoping, Dec. 31, 1989.

### 9. Camelot, Almost

I based this chapter on my interviews with Jia Guangzu, Jenny Guangzu, and Cassy Jones, and on an interview of Li Zhao Hu. Other sources were the *People's Daily*, Jan. 6, 1989, and the *China Daily*, Jan. 6–7, 1989; letters between Jia and Jenny Guangzu; and *The Yellow Emperor's Classic of Internal Medicine* (Chinese Academy of Traditional Medicine).

### 10. Presidential Pragmatism

For this chapter I relied on my interviews with Cassy Jones, Li Yang, Barr Seitz, Melinda Liu, Jeanne Moore, and Bing Yang, and interviews by others of Wuerkaixi, Chai Ling, Qian Qichen, and Fang Lizhi. Other sources were the diaries of Cassy Jones and Jeanne Moore, the *China Daily*, Feb. 1–10, 1989, and the *People's Daily*, Feb. 1–10, 1989.

### 11. Death in the Politburo

I based this chapter on my interviews with Melinda Liu, Jeanne Moore, Barr Seitz, Jia Guangzu, Li Yang, Vladimir Troyanovsky, Brian Davidson, Brendan Ward, Charles Malo, and members of the U.S. intelligence community in Washington, D.C., and Beijing, and on interviews by others of Li Zhao Hu and McKinsey Russell. Other sources were the *People's Daily*, Mar. 9, 1989; the *China Daily*, Mar. 9–14, 1989; *Time*, Mar. 8, 1989; *Newsweek*, Mar. 8, 1989; Melinda Liu's faxes to *Newsweek;* diaries of Jeanne Moore and Barr Seitz; and *The Chinese Secret Service* (Deacon).

## 12. Overtures

"Overtures" is based on my interviews with Cassy Jones, Barr Seitz, Jeanne Moore, Melinda Liu, Alan Donald, Brian Davidson, Brendan Ward, and Susan Morton, and interviews by others of Wuerkaixi, Chai Ling, Wang Dan, Liu Gang, and Li Liu. Other sources were the diaries of Jeanne Moore and Cassy Jones; faxes from Melinda Liu; the *China Daily*, Mar. 15–31, 1989; the *People's Daily*, Mar. 15–31, 1989; and the *South China Morning Post*, Mar. 15–31, 1989.

## 13. Surges

"Surges" is based on my interviews with Cassy Jones, Jenny Guangzu, Barr Seitz, Jeanne Moore, Melinda Liu, Alan Donald, Brian Davidson, Brendan Ward, Sue Tung, Jia Guangzu, Kao Jyan, Shao-Yen Wang, and Li Yang, and interviews by others of Wuerkaixi, Chai Ling, Wang Dan, Fang Lizhi, Boris Klimonko, Vladimir Kudinov, Anatole Bykov, and Raymond Burghardt. Other sources were the *China Daily*, Apr. 19–24, 1989; the *People's Daily*, Apr. 19–21, 1989; the *South China Morning Post*, Apr. 20–21, 1989; the *Standard* (Hong Kong), Apr. 20–24, 1989; the diaries of Cassy Jones, Jeanne Moore, Melinda Liu, and Sue Tung; faxes of Melinda Liu; and a letter from Jenny Guangzu to her father.

## 14. A Time of Decision

For this chapter I relied on my interviews with Cassy Jones, Jia Guangzu, Yang Li, Melinda Liu, Barr Seitz, Sue Tung, Brian Davidson, and Brendan Ward, and interviews by others of Wang Dan, Wuerkaixi, Chai Ling, Feng Conde, Liu Gang, Xiong Yan, and Yang Tao. Other sources were the diaries of Cassy Jones, Jeanne Moore, and Sue Tung; an "Open Letter to Beijing College," published Apr. 22, 1989; various transcripts of Radio Beijing broadcasts, Apr. 21–30, 1989; the *New York Times*, Apr. 21–30, 1989 (especially the reports of Nicholas D. Kristof); *Newsweek* for Apr. 1989; *Time* for Apr. 1989; the *Reader's Digest*, Apr. 21–30, 1989; and the *China Daily*, Apr. 21–30, 1989.

## 15. Power Plays

"Power Plays" is based on my interviews with Melinda Liu, Jeanne Moore, Cassy Jones, Barr Seitz, Jenny Guangzu, Jia Guangzu, Sue Tung, Kao Jyan, Li Yang, Brian Davidson, and Brendan Ward, and interviews by others of Wuerkaixi, Chai Ling, Liu Gang, Xiong Yan, Yang Tao, and Wang Dan. Other sources were the diary of Jeanne Moore and faxes of Melinda Liu.

## 16. Countermoves

For this chapter I relied on my interviews with Jenny Guangzu, Melinda Liu, Susan Morton, Barr Seitz, Bing Yang, Jeanne Moore, Cassy Jones, and various members of the U.S. intelligence community in Washington, D.C., and Beijing, and on interviews by others of Wuerkaixi, Wang Dan, Jenny Guangzu, and Cassy Jones. Other sources were the diaries of Barr Seitz and Jeanne Moore; faxes of Melinda Liu; the *People's Daily*, May 2–4, 1989; the *China Daily* (all issues for May 1989); and *Newsweek* for May 1989.

## 17. Turmoil on Tiananmen

I based this chapter on my interviews with Jia Guangzu, Jenny Guangzu, Barr Seitz, Jeanne Moore, Brian Davidson, Brendan Ward, Alan Donald, Sue Tung, Shao-Yen Wang, Zheng Milin, Melinda Liu, and Cassy Jones, and on interviews by others of Wuerkaixi, Wang Dan, Chai Ling, Feng Conde, and Vladimir Troyanovsky. Another source was the *Independent* (all issues for May and June 1989, especially the reports of Andrew Higgins).

## 18. The Beckoning Abyss

This chapter is based on my interviews with Brendan Ward, Brian Davidson, Melinda Liu, Jeanne Moore, Sue Tung, Kao Jyan, Li Yang, Jia Guangzu, Jenny Guangzu, Cassy Jones, and Alan Donald, and on interviews by others of Wuerkaixi, Wang Dan, and Chai Ling. Other sources were the diaries of Jeanne Moore, Cassy Jones, Sue Tung, and Barr Seitz; the *New York Times* (all issues from May 15–June 6, 1989, especially the reports of Nicholas Kristof); and the *China Daily*, all issues from May 1–June 6, 1989.

## 19. Martial Law

"Martial Law" is based on my interviews with Kao Jyan, Melinda Liu, Brian Davidson, Brendan Ward, Jeanne Moore, Sue Tung, Bing Yang, Debnath Shaw, Huzzan Farazanden, Susan Morton, Shao-Yen Wang, and Zheng Milin, and interviews by others of Liu Lee, Wuerkaixi, Wang Dan, Arne Dellira, Giulio Fraticelli, Marian Woznink, Alfonzo Alumada, Bjorn Skula, and Angelo Miculescu. Other sources were the "Proclamation to the People of China" by Chai Ling, mimeographed on Tiananmen Square, May 20, 1989; the diaries of Jeanne Moore and Sue Tung; and the faxes of Melinda Liu.

## 20. Marriage in Mayhem

This chapter is based on my interviews with Cassy Jones, Li Yang, Barr Seitz, Sue Tung, Jia Guangzu, Jenny Guangzu, Bing Yang, Melinda Liu, Zheng Milin, Brian Davidson, and Brendan Ward, and on interviews by others of Chai Ling, Wang Dan, Wuerkaixi, Li Liu, Zhao Ming, Geert Andersen, and Horst Lohmann. Other sources were the diaries of Jeanne Moore, Sue Tung, and Barr Seitz; and the faxes of Melinda Liu.

### 21. Massacre

"Massacre" was based on my interviews with Cassy Jones, Sue Tung, Brian Davidson, Brendan Ward, Melinda Liu, Jeanne Moore, Barr Seitz, Alan Donald, Susan Morton, Jenny Guangzu, Jia Guangzu, Louise Branson, Bing Yang, Tan Yaobang, Kao Jyan, David Blackstock, Lindsay J. Watts, Earl Drake, Patricio Martinez, Denis Biggs, Brix Andersen, and Hou Dejian, and interviews by others of Wuerkaixi, Wang Dan, Chai Ling, Charles Malo, Gerard Cheznel, Rolf Berthold, Horst Lohmann, Hans-Peter Hellbeck, Bjorn Skala, Bilal Simisar, and James W. Brown. Other sources were reports by Louise Branson in May–June, 1989, and the diaries of Jeanne Moore and Barr Seitz.

### 22. A Time of Pain

For this chapter I relied on my interviews with Jenny Guangzu, Sue Tung, Melinda Liu, and Barr Seitz.

### 23. For the Moment

This chapter is based on my interviews with Sue Tung, Jenny Guangzu, Li Yang, Shao-Yen Wang, and Zheng Milin.

# *Index*